Guardians of the Tradition

Rochester Studies in African History and the Diaspora

Toyin Falola, Series Editor
The Jacob and Frances Sanger Mossiker Chair in the Humanities and University Distinguished Teaching Professor
University of Texas at Austin

Recent Titles

Edward Wilmot Blyden and the Racial Nationalist Imagination
Teshale Tibebu

South Africa and the World Economy: Remaking Race, State, and Region
William G. Martin

Enchanted Calvinism: Labor Migration, Afflicting Spirits, and Christian Therapy in the Presbyterian Church of Ghana
Adam Mohr

Ira Aldridge: Performing Shakespeare in Europe, 1852–1855
Bernth Lindfors

Blood on the Tides: "The Ozidi Saga" and Oral Epic Narratology
Isidore Okpewho

The Politics of Chieftaincy: Authority and Property in Colonial Ghana, 1920–1950
Naaborko Sackeyfio-Lenoch

Nigerian Pentecostalism
Nimi Wariboko

Building a Peaceful Nation: Julius Nyerere and the Establishment of Sovereignty in Tanzania, 1960–1964
Paul Bjerk

Kingdoms and Chiefdoms of Southeastern Africa: Oral Traditions and History, 1400–1830
Elizabeth A. Eldredge

Manners Make a Nation: Racial Etiquette in Southern Rhodesia, 1910–1963
Allison K. Shutt

A complete list of titles in the Rochester Studies in African History and the Diaspora series may be found on our website, www.urpress.com.

Guardians of the Tradition

Historians and Historical Writing in Ethiopia and Eritrea

James De Lorenzi

University of Rochester Press

First published 2015
Reprinted in paperback and transferred to digital printing 2018

University of Rochester Press
668 Mt. Hope Avenue, Rochester, NY 14620, USA
www.urpress.com
and Boydell & Brewer Limited
PO Box 9, Woodbridge, Suffolk IP12 3DF, UK
www.boydellandbrewer.com

Hardcover ISBN-13: 978-1-58046-519-9
Paperback ISBN-13: 978-1-58046-928-9
ISSN: 1092-5228

Library of Congress Cataloging-in-Publication Data

De Lorenzi, James, author.
Guardians of the tradition : historians and historical writing in Ethiopia and Eritrea / James De Lorenzi.
pages cm. — (Rochester studies in african history and the diaspora, ISSN 1092-5228 ; v. 66)
Includes bibliographical references and index.
ISBN 978-1-58046-519-9 (hardcover : alk. paper) 1. Ethiopia—Historiography. 2. Eritrea—Historiography. 3. Ethiopia—Intellectual life. 4. Eritrea—Intellectual life. 5. Historiography. I. Title. II. Series: Rochester studies in African history and the diaspora.
DT380.5.D4 2015
963.0072—dc23 2015015825
2015015825

This publication is printed on acid-free paper.

For Ruth and Celestina

Contents

List of Illustrations ix

Preface xi

Introduction 1

1 The Inherited Tradition 13

2 Gäbrä Krestos Täklä Haymanot and the History of Progress 37

3 Gäbrä Mika'él Germu and the History of Colonialism 67

4 Ḫeruy Wäldä Śellasé and the New Queen of Sheba 94

5 The Triumph of Historicism? 114

Conclusion 127

Abbreviations 141

Notes 143

Glossary 189

Bibliography 191

Index 213

List of Illustrations

I.1	Cover of Ḫeruy Wäldä Śellasé's book catalog, 1927	3
2.1	EFS native teacher training, ca. 1911	41
2.2	Inside the Asmära EFS press, ca. 1931	42
2.3	Evangelical congregation of Addis Ababa, ca. 1931	48
3.1	San Michele trade school, Sägänäyti, ca. 1917	70
3.2	Gäbrä Egzi'abḥér Gilay	77
3.3	Frontispiece of Gäbrä Mika'él Germu's historical compendium	85
4.1	Illustration from *Addis aläm*, by Ḫeruy Wäldä Śellasé	101
4.2	Ḫeruy Wäldä Śellasé and companions visiting Nikko, Japan	103
5.1	Inside the National Library, ca. 1945	118

Preface

Amharic, Tigrinya, and Ge'ez transliteration follows the *Encylopaedia Aethiopica* standard, with simplifications for the fifth (é) and sixth (e) orders to eliminate the frequently occurring schwa (ə). The Ethiopian calendar is seven or eight years behind the Gregorian calendar. All dates are given in the Gregorian calendar, except in direct quotations and bibliographic references for which it is not possible to determine the precise date of publication. In these instances, the use of the Ethiopian calendar is indicated by the abbreviation EC.

This book has produced a considerable number of debts—far more than can be mentioned here. It is a pleasure to reflect on the many relationships, old and new, that have sustained this project for nearly a decade, and to have the opportunity to recognize in some small way those whose ideas, suggestions, criticisms, and encouragement have shaped the book that is its final result. The kindness of strangers is remarkable.

I am particularly grateful for the many colleagues who read portions or all of the manuscript, and who in several instances shared materials with me. Their assistance has been invaluable. These include Bairu Tafla, Lee Cassanelli, Peter Garretson, Getatchew Haile, Ruth Iyob, Heather Sharkey, Shiferaw Bekele, Lynn Lees, Xerxes Malki, and Irma Taddia. Matteo Salvadore has discussed this project more than any other person, and for this reason deserves special mention. In addition, I have benefited tremendously from conversations with Abbebe Kifleyesus, Donald Crummey, Elizabeth Wolde Giorgis, Kindeneh Mihretie, Janet Neigh, Richard Pankhurst, Bertie Pearson, Semeneh Ayalew, and Tekeste Negash, and from the comments of the attendees at the International Conference of Ethiopian Studies and the Addis Ababa Junior Scholars Seminar. At the University of Rochester Press, Toyin Falola, the series editor, and Sonia Kane, the editorial director, have both patiently guided me through the publication process. Two anonymous readers also offered very useful comments, and David McCarthy meticulously reviewed and edited the manuscript.

I owe a unique debt to my patient Amharic teachers, Afework Wogayehu, Telaye Gebremedhin, and Zewditu Fesseha, and equally to Ermias Zemichael and Levon Djerrahian, who checked and corrected my Amharic translations. This project would not have been possible without the many hours we have spent together, and I look forward to those still to come. Selamawit Legesse and Joseph Venosa assisted with Tigrinya translations, and Christopher Schindler and Bianca Kallai provided Swedish and German translations, respectively. All translations from Amharic, Italian, and French are my own, unless otherwise noted.

The travel that has furthered this project has been one of its greatest rewards. In Addis Ababa, I have been very fortunate to enjoy the gracious hospitality of Munir Jemal and family through the years, and the staff of the Institute of Ethiopian Studies has assisted me in innumerable ways. In Stockholm, I am indebted to the staff at the National Library and the Stockholm Stadsarkiv; and in Rome, to the staff of the Biblioteca Nazionale, the Archivio Storico at the Ministero degli Affari Esteri, and the Istituto Italiano per l'Africa e l'Oriente. At John Jay College, my institutional home in New York City, I have enjoyed many stimulating conversations with my colleagues in the History Department, especially Allison Kavey and Hyunhee Park. I am also very grateful for Karen Okamoto of the library faculty, who fulfilled my countless inter-library loan requests, and also for Marianne LaBatto, who assisted me at the Robert Hess Collection on Ethiopia and the Horn of Africa at Brooklyn College, also of the City University of New York. Finally, I thank the many John Jay students who have bravely taken my courses on historiography, and who have helped me clarify my thinking on many of the questions this book explores.

I have been lucky to receive funding for this project from the American Philosophical Society, the Hill Monastic Manuscript Library, the National Endowment for the Humanities, the Office for the Advancement of Research at John Jay, and the Professional Staff Congress of the City University of New York.

Finally, my family has sustained (and endured) me since long before this project began. My greatest debt is to my parents, Albert and Gina De Lorenzi, who nurtured my love of learning and history from a young age. Their encouragement made this book possible. I also thank my indulgent extended family for their never-ending support and hospitality: in Ontario, Bruno and Celestina De Lorenzi, Carlo De Lorenzi, Ruth and John Henry, Dawna Henry, Marta and Armando Leonetti, Judy Losier, and Alexander Rowlson; in England, John Henry and family; and in Seattle, Tom De Lorenzi and family. In New Mexico, I have had the additional good fortune to be welcomed by the Maloy, Nolan, Di Greco, and Martinez families. Finally, I am extremely fortunate to have Jennifer Maloy as my caring and perceptive partner in life.

This book is dedicated to my grandmothers, both lovers of history.

Introduction

After nearly two decades, *blatta* Ḫeruy Wäldä Śellasé (1878–1938) decided to return to an old endeavor. Years before, in 1911, he had attempted to produce a catalog of Ge'ez and Amharic literature, going so far as to visit the University of Oxford as part of his research, and now, in the late 1920s, he was ready to amend his youthful effort at panoptic bibliography. He had good reason. Since the publication of his pioneering 1911 work, the region had witnessed a veritable explosion of local language printing, and as a result, there was a host of new publications that needed to be included in a comprehensive catalog. There were also several older texts that had been omitted from the first project, and these too could be added to a new work. And finally, he now enjoyed a greatly improved perspective on his subject. A budding but still obscure young scholar at the time of his original study, Ḫeruy had become one of the preeminent intellectuals of his day. He was the author of more than twenty books on a variety of learned and popular topics; he had achieved the rank of Director General in the Ministry of Foreign Affairs, and advised Crown Price Täfäri Mäkonnen, the future Emperor Ḫaylä Śellasé; and he was easily among the most well-traveled Ethiopians of his generation, having visited Europe, the Middle East, and the United States. He was thus at the peak of his intellectual powers, and with his extensive network of personal and political connections, he was ideally situated to survey Ethiopia's changing textual landscape. To this end, he prepared a list of every Ge'ez and Amharic text he could locate, drawing upon his colleagues' collective learning and resources, and he catalogued his findings by genre, author, and subject. When his research was finished, he completed the project with a concise introduction to Ethiopian intellectual history, thereby setting his texts in their proper context. In 1927, the Täfäri Mäkonnen Press of Addis Ababa published his work as *Bä'ityopya yämmigäñu bäge'ezenna bamariña* q^{w}*anq*^{w}*a yätäṣafu yämäṣaḥeft katalog*, or *Catalog of Books Written in the Ge'ez and Amharic Languages Found in Ethiopia.*[1]

A careful reader might compare *blatta* Ḫeruy's 1911 and 1927 works. Both feature meticulous outlines of Ethiopia's Orthodox Christian canon, with many pages devoted to the categories of scripture (*qeddusan mäṣaḥeft*), homiletics (*dersan*), hagiography (*gädl*), and exegesis (*tergʷamê*). Both are implicitly sectarian in that they largely ignore Islamic scholarship.[2] Curiously, both catalogs also ignore the distinction between manuscripts and printed books: for Ḫeruy, the significance of a text clearly arose from its content, not its material form. But these similarities aside, Ḫeruy's two studies strike the reader with their differences. To begin, there is the simple matter of quantity and scale: the first catalog lists 180 works, while the second features nearly 450. Equally significant are Ḫeruy's subtle innovations in methodology. While he organized the entries in the 1911 catalog by discipline or genre, he identified many works in the 1927 catalog by author, breaking with the tendency toward anonymity that generally prevailed among Ethiopian and Eritrean writers. He also included many works by Westerners, or *färänǧ*, like the missionaries Karl Wilhelm Isenberg (1806–64) and Olle Eriksson (1878–1962), as well as the orientalists Jacques Faitlovitch (1881–1955) and Ignazio Guidi (1844–1935).[3] To these foreign books he added an array of eclectic, nontraditional texts by Ethiopians and Eritreans: grammars and bilingual dictionaries, poetry and folktale collections, health and childcare guidebooks, geography and mathematics textbooks, and even an Amharic translation of John Bunyan's *Pilgrim's Progress*.

The pages of Ḫeruy's two catalogs also document a remarkable profusion of historical writing. In his original survey, he had identified only five histories of note, whereas in 1927 he counted more than forty works of history addressing a wide range of topics. Among the many entries under the heading "Books of History," he included three biographies of Emperor Menilek II (1844–1913), a history of Ethiopia by Feśśeḥa Giyorgis (n.d.–1931), and several eclectic works, including a study of the Oromo by *abba* Aṣmä Giyorgis (1853–1915), a world history by Gäbrä Krestos Täklä Haymanot (1890–1932), and a short history of the Ethiopian Orthodox Church by an unnamed author. Elsewhere in his catalog are more histories: three works on Ethiopia's history by the illustrious *aläqa* Tayyä Gäbrä Maryam (1860–1924), a historical novel on Cleopatra and Mark Antony by "Professor" Afäwärq Gäbrä Iyäsus (1868–1947), two world histories by the Swedish missionaries Isenberg and Eriksson, and even several of his own efforts—a biography of his patron Crown Prince Täfäri Mäkonnen, a study of Emperor Yoḥannes IV (1837–89), a historical dictionary of Ethiopian notables, and a prosopography, or group history, of Ethiopia's rulers and church leaders. Although it is true that Ḫeruy added many examples of traditional historiography to his 1927 catalog, his other additions have a markedly innovative and heterogeneous quality, and this is a significant point. If Ḫeruy's two surveys are viewed as maps of the region's changing intellectual terrain—as two snapshots of a world of learning in transformation—they suggest that in the early decades of the twentieth century, history was booming on the southern shore of the Red Sea.

Figure I.1. Cover of Ḫeruy Wäldä Śellasé's book catalog, 1927.

The historian's craft was a topic of particular interest for Ḫeruy, and he addressed it in the introductions to both catalogs. Comparing Ethiopia's long-established tradition of historical writing with those of other parts of the world, he observed that the scholars of his country overlooked the fundamental distinction between the sacred and the profane, as Voltaire had once put it.[4] Specifically, Ḫeruy felt his colleagues too often ignored the boundary between theology (*téwologiya*), or the study of "religion and spiritual matters," and philosophy (*fälasfa*), or the study of human endeavor—"work and carnal matters," as he put it.[5] This disregard for the distinction between faith and flesh led historians to inappropriately mix these two subjects in their works. As he explained by way of example, many writers of dynastic history (*tarikä nägäśt*) improperly strayed from their worldly subjects to consider hagiography, homiletics, martyrology (*semä'etat tarik*), and scripture (*qeddusan tarik*)—topics that properly belonged not to the secular realm of history but to the domain of faith, as they were so considered in the rest of the world.[6]

Though this charge of intellectual carelessness might seem a pedantic quibble, it was in fact a provocative critique, since it addressed the methodological rigor of a very long historical tradition. Ethiopian scholars had been writing biographies, compiling king lists, studying church history, documenting genealogies, and outlining universal histories since late antiquity, and their free mixture of the sacred and profane had long served them and their learned readers well. Ḫeruy was suggesting that in recent years, something fundamental had changed, that the concerns and methods of his intellectual forebears were no longer suited to current circumstances. In his pithy reflections on the historian's craft, Ḫeruy was thus respectfully but boldly calling for a new kind of history—for a way of being modern through the past.

This book explores the rich and dynamic historical universe that produced Ḫeruy's modest scholarly call to arms. Ethiopia and Eritrea are home to Africa's oldest written historical tradition, one whose origins lie with the monumental epigraphy and Byzantine-inflected manuscripts of Aksum, the ancient Red Sea empire of Northeast Africa and South Arabia. This venerable tradition flourished in the medieval and early modern periods, and it has endured through Ḫeruy's day into our own. Yet as Ḫeruy's two catalogs suggest, the early twentieth century was a pivotal moment in the development of this tradition, for it was then that many Ethiopian and Eritrean intellectuals reconceived the nature and significance of historical inquiry. Living in a moment of dramatic imperial competition and tumultuous social and cultural change, and inhabiting an increasingly cosmopolitan intellectual environment infused with new languages, texts, and ideas, many of Ḫeruy's contemporaries explored new questions, genres, methods, and sources in order to grapple with the modern world. They wrote histories for local readers that made provocative political claims, explored the nature of their communal ties, assessed their inherited institutions and ideas, and evaluated foreign ideas and technologies. In many cases, they did so by deliberately fusing the tools and insights of Western scholarship with the concerns, conventions, and analytic categories of their indigenous historical tradition. For this reason, their collective project of creative inquiry and critical adaptation has a dual significance. On the one hand, it represents a key turning point in the trajectory of this venerable non-Western tradition of historical writing; on the other, it documents how the forces of turn-of-the-century globalization fostered tremendous intellectual change through new interactions between the local and the global. This fertile and multifaceted historical dialogue is the subject of this book.

History in the Vernacular

Ḫeruy made his reformist plea at a moment when many Africans and Asians were struggling with history. From the quarrels among Egyptian journalists over the contemporary significance of the pharaohs to the debates about the Indian past that raged between Bengali and British intellectuals, and from the Persian histories of Iran's pre-Islamic golden age to the South African "war of books" waged over the question of Zulu origins, the late nineteenth and early twentieth centuries witnessed an efflorescence of creative historical argumentation in Africa and Asia. The motives behind these projects varied. For some, historiography was a powerful instrument for cultivating and defending national identity. Thus the Bengali intellectual Bankimchandra Chattopadhyay (1838–94) proclaimed, "India must have her own history. Otherwise there is no hope for Bengal. Who is to write it? You have to write it. I have to write it. All of us have to write it."[7] Similarly, the Egyptian Muṣṭafa Kāmil (1874–1908) asserted, "History, History! This is the common school for all classes of the nation. This is the instructor that will acculturate the glorious prince, the celebrated minister, the erudite scholar, the student, and the ordinary poor man."[8] Although such patriotic sentiments were widespread, other intellectuals used historical writing to foster less grandiose visions of community and shared heritage. The Nigerian Samuel Johnson (1846–1901) wrote an ethno-history that described the enduring distinctiveness and cultural unity of the Yoruba, while his countryman Isaac Babalola Akinyẹle (1882–1964) wrote a history of Ibadan's urban notables.[9] For these individuals and others like them, historiography promised to help readers appreciate the affinities that bound them together in a complex and heterogeneous world.

But this was not the only reason to write history. Some African and Asian intellectuals documented the achievements of respected elites, fusing research and political activism. In Egypt, Muḥammad ʿAbduh (1849–1905) and Jurji Zaydan (1861–1914) publicly debated the significance of the modernizing ruler Muḥammad ʿAlī (1769–1849), while in the Gold Coast, Osei Agyeman Prempeh II (1892–1970) described the genealogy of his august Asante ancestors.[10] Still others wrote history to provide moral and spiritual instruction: the Sudanese Muḥammad ʿAbd al-Raḥīm (1878–1966) and the Luo Paul Mboya set down the traditions of their predecessors for the edification of future generations.[11] Apolo Kagwa (1864–1927) of Buganda fused both goals, advancing his own political fortunes by marshaling historiography to the project of inventing tradition.[12]

In the past two decades, this explosion of historiography in Africa and Asia at the turn of the twentieth century has provoked a raucous debate about the origins of historical consciousness. For some, the coincidence of these struggles over history and the onset of colonial rule is highly significant. According to this view, history is a uniquely Western mode of understanding the past that modern-minded Africans and Asians embraced under European tutelage, much like the railroad, the novel, and the ideal of the liberal nation state. Thus Ashis Nandy argues that Indians were fundamentally ahistorical before the advent of British rule: they remembered the past in mythic terms, recalling people and events with a moralistic, present-minded, and highly selective "principled forgetfulness" that is fundamentally at odds with the historian's concern for linearity and factuality.[13] Vinay Lal agrees, and attributes Indians' precolonial ahistoricism to the potent interaction of Hindu cosmology and the traumas of foreign domination, which impelled them toward "willful amnesia" and devalued the memory of a painful past.[14] These arguments call to mind the colonial-era assessments of Mohandas Gandhi (1869–1948), who observed that history "is a record of the wars of the world," and as a result, "a nation which has no history, that is, no wars, is a happy nation."[15] Numerous contemporary scholars, novelists, and literary critics have made complementary arguments about the absence of history in Africa, East Asia, and the Middle East.[16] Collectively, these writers make a bold claim: the urge to understand the past historically is not universal, and history's lineage outside the West begins with colonial institutions and the specific mindsets they engendered. As one V. S. Naipaul character puts it, "Without Europeans, I feel, all our past would have been washed away."[17] History was a Western export.

Others find these arguments disturbingly similar to colonial-era European denials of history among colonized peoples.[18] Velcheru Narayana Rao, David Shulman, and Sanjay Subrahmanyam offer an especially spirited critique in this vein in their *Textures of Time*, a work that challenges Eurocentric genealogies of history by considering the indigenous historical texts of early modern India.[19] Examining sixteenth- and seventeenth-century vernacular writings of South Indian civil servants, they conclude that this literature contains properly historical claims that (1) distinguish fact from fiction and (2) flag historicity for readers through the use of subtle linguistic and literary markers, or textures. The authors suggest that while these writers made their claims about the past in a range of literary genres (often outside the realm of clearly defined historiography), and although they often employed an epic style, their works are nonetheless properly historical because they represent the past factually, empirically, and in the style of a report. Thus in India, history was not "a poisoned gift of colonial rule" but instead a dynamic indigenous tradition.[20] By extension, their argument suggests that history is a mode of understanding the past that can emerge anywhere, even if it varies in its external appearance.[21] It can be entirely homegrown and vernacular.

This critique suggests a series of related questions. If history can indeed be written in multiple styles, then how do we explain the contemporary global dominance of its Western disciplinary variant? Does one form of history rule the others, and if so, then what is the precise nature of the interactions between the world's various historical traditions? Here too there is much debate. Peter Burke suggests that all societies possess forms of history, but that the historical tradition of post-Renaissance Europe uniquely combined preoccupations with causation, specificity, linear development, and the avoidance of anachronism and bias. As the norms of this tradition spread in the nineteenth century, its uniqueness waned through its interaction with non-Western traditions, which ultimately fostered the emergence of a new, properly global historical paradigm. Thus the contemporary historical discipline is a European-brokered synthesis of the world's many ways of representing the past.[22] Against this rather rosy view, Hayden White and Dipesh Chakrabarty instead see antagonism between the world's historical traditions. In their assessment, the norms and institutions of Western academic history dominated and displaced non-Western forms of history, relegating these rivals to the realm of the popular and amateur.[23] Ranajit Guha agrees and goes further, suggesting that the agents and institutions of colonial rule ultimately assimilated Africa's and Asia's highly complex and culturally specific forms of historicality, the autochthonous and heterogeneous "prose of the world," into the reductive analytic categories of the Western historical discipline, the state-centric "prose of history."[24] As a result, "a particular manner of thinking about the past has . . . been inflated into a genre."[25] Though the particulars of these assessments differ, they all acknowledge the eventual dominion of the Western historical model over the world's diverse historical traditions.

So is there one history, or many? It is true that the Rankean paradigm of positivist academic history[26] extended its domain during the colonial era, and that European-educated African and Asian intellectuals applied its tools to the study of their own societies in various struggles over history.[27] In many cases, these new historians—figures like Egypt's Muḥammad Shafīq Ghurbāl (1894–1961), India's Jadunath Sarkar (1870–1958), and Nigeria's Kenneth Onwuka Dike (1917–83)—used indigenous chronicles and oral traditions as source material for what they considered "real" historical research. Because their works were pioneering scholarly achievements that conformed to Western disciplinary standards, they are remembered today as historian founding fathers who adapted an imported intellectual apparatus to nationalist and indigenous subjects.[28] Their efforts complemented early postcolonial state projects that aimed to institutionalize heritage and memory in national museums, libraries, and archives.[29] This new historical language aided the struggle for freedom and national emancipation, but it sometimes silenced other forms of history.

However, many of the world's vernacular historical traditions adapted to the challenges of the modern era, in some cases even flourishing as parallel or counter-traditions to nationalist, academic, and institutionalized history. In recent years, research has highlighted the vibrancy of some of these little-noticed varieties of local historical writing. Bengali historians of the early twentieth century engaged in public debates about the historicity of indigenous genealogical texts, dividing between academic positivists, who embraced rational source criticism and the tools of Rankean analysis, and a "folk-oriented" or nativist school, who critiqued the impoverished historiography of their westernized colleagues and who understood history as the essence of the past as preserved by the community.[30] Elsewhere in South Asia, Marathi intellectuals used the chronicles of western India to attack the claims of colonial administrators,[31] while Sikh historians carefully framed their studies to suit the intellectual sensibilities of different audiences, drawing upon multiple historical voices and generic conventions to strengthen their claims about Punjabi rulers.[32] In North Africa, numerous Tunisian, Algerian, and Egyptian scholars drew on Ibn Khaldūn (1332–1406) and the Arabic historical tradition to critique the structure of European scholarship and articulate new pan-Arab forms of identity.[33] Clearly, not everyone adopted the Western prose of history, as Guha terms it, and some actively contested its monopoly on representing the past.

What are we to make of these seemingly liminal historical projects—curious chronicles lurking in the interstices of colonial culture, nationalist politics, and the dominant narratives of African and Asian history and the historical profession more generally?[34] What do they tell us about the era that produced them? And what do they reveal about the genealogy of history itself? In a collection devoted to African historians of the colonial and early postcolonial periods, Giacomo Macola and Derek Peterson suggest that the authors of such vernacular histories are best understood as "homespun historians": public intellectuals who wove together multiple traditions of knowledge.[35] This analysis can reframe the debate about the genealogy of history by highlighting the paradox at the heart of many of Africa's and Asia's vernacular historians and their histories. On the one hand, these writers produced eminently local texts, for they are rooted in local languages, institutions, and historical subjects.[36] Indeed, they are very often historical representations of home—and occasionally the wider world as viewed from home—and they were in most cases intended for local readers. Yet at the same time, their hybrid composition attests to the pervasive influence of ideas, politics, and historical forces originating in the wider world, and this influence makes this new generation of chroniclers fundamentally different from their forebears. Africa's and Asia's homespun vernacular historians were cosmopolitan, entrepreneurial, and intensely modern rather than traditional, amateur, or anachronistic, and they often wrote in both the prose of the world and the prose of history. Their efforts thus represent an alternative variety of modern historiography, one that occasionally spoke a Rankean language with a thick local accent.

These questions are a point of departure for the present study, which examines the creative activity of Ethiopian and Eritrean historians at a pivotal moment in Northeast African history.[37] Like their counterparts elsewhere in Africa and Asia, Ḫeruy and his contemporaries began experimenting with new forms of historical writing in the late nineteenth and early twentieth centuries, often by engaging and adapting the questions, methods, and sources of Western academic disciplines. Their efforts are the result of a wide-ranging cross-cultural dialogue that is distinct in the long-term intellectual history of the region. Several decades earlier, the productive interaction between indigenous and foreign scholarship—between the prose of the world and the prose of history—did not exist. Decades later, in the tense years of the Cold War, the study of the past became increasingly dominated by the imported historical paradigms of institutionalized area studies, and, leading up to and after the 1974 revolution, Marxism. It is in the years between the Scramble for Africa and the cataclysmic Italian invasion of 1935 that the Ethiopian and Eritrean historical imagination most openly and creatively asserted its vernacular origins. Viewed from the perspective of our present day, all too often characterized by the Scylla of xenophobic ignorance and the Charybdis of vapid multiculturalism, the era's collective project of open inquiry and informed critical synthesis is striking. This was the meridian of Africa's oldest historical tradition.

History from Aksum to the Därg

This book consists of a series of interlinked case studies. My principal claim is that Ethiopia and Eritrea possessed a highly developed vernacular historical tradition that flourished in the early twentieth century through its complex interaction with Western scholarship. This interaction did not entail the export, diffusion, or hegemony of an abstract complex of ideas related to intellectual "modernity" or a culturally alien prose of history, but rather a process of selective, critical appropriation by Ethiopian and Eritrean intellectuals. Vernacular historical writing was not westernized; instead, Western historiography was indigenized. This process took place in a diverse range of institutional and social contexts, both at home and abroad, and these settings further shaped the aims and scope of Ethiopian and Eritrean historical writing. In addition to being eminently dialogic and creative, then, the era's historians and histories were also homespun and private, politicized and public, academic, contested, and shared.

The protagonists in this story are a small but prolific cohort of relatively obscure Ethiopian and Eritrean intellectuals. While their lives, careers, and scholarship are worthy and rich subjects in their own right, they are of additional interest because of what they reveal about local intellectual life as well as a number of larger historical questions. This is not because of their representativeness—indeed, the subjects of this book were in many ways unconventional and even iconoclastic—but because the exceptional features of their lives and ideas illuminate subtle but far-reaching changes in the possibilities for thought and action.[38]

This is especially true in terms of the impact of large-scale historical dynamics on everyday life. By the late nineteenth century, the Red Sea region had become a critical artery between the Mediterranean and Indian Ocean arenas, and was for this reason a zone of heated imperial and economic contest. These developments fostered the growth of new and distinctly modern patterns of globalization in the Horn of Africa.[39] In Ethiopia and Eritrea, the most notable manifestations of this development were the growth of modern state institutions, a deepening integration into the world economy, the related expansion of transportation and communication networks, new patterns of migration and travel, and the emergence of broad and sometimes public struggles between reform and traditionalism. Cutting across the Muslim-Christian divide, these dynamics created new trajectories of economic and sociocultural integration and schism that profoundly shaped the era's historical writing. For the principal subjects of this book, these developments became objects of historical inquiry in their own right: the new historical dynamics generated their own chroniclers. For this reason, this book can be read as a microhistorical study of the literary manifestations of translocality, or inter-regional dynamics that are more than local but less than global.[40]

Six chapters follow. Chapter 1 sets the stage by introducing Ethiopia's and Eritrea's vernacular historical tradition. It explores the origins and development of traditional historiography, and broadly surveys the genres, methods, and aims of local historians up to the nineteenth century. The chapter contends that this inherited tradition had two aspects: one official and focused on documenting the observed present, and the other traditionalist, compilatory, and concerned with preserving the memory of the distant past.

The next three chapters explore the evolution of this tradition in the late nineteenth and early twentieth centuries. Chapter 2 examines the life and times of Gäbrä Krestos Täklä Haymanot, the founding editor of Ethiopia's *Berhanenna sälam* newspaper and Ethiopia's first public historian. After sketching his educational background and rise to prominence in the reformist milieu of the 1920s, it argues that his 1924 world history exemplifies several new directions that were then emerging in Ethiopian historiography. The chapter concludes by evaluating his historicized study of progress as a manifestation of the new dialogic turn in local historical writing.

Chapter 3 builds on this discussion by considering the parallel life of Gäbrä Mika'él Germu (1900–1969), one of the first historians of Eritrea. It outlines his career as a colonial civil servant and postcolonial journalist, surveys the evolution of local historiography during the colonial period, and examines his 1930s study of Italian colonialism in the Horn of Africa, one of the region's first problem-oriented histories. The chapter argues that Gäbrä Mika'él's works exemplify a new, distinctly Eritrean variety of colonial-inflected vernacular historical writing.

Chapter 4 shifts the discussion from historiography proper to instructive travel writing, a new literary genre that fused biography, cultural geography, and world history. Ethiopian travel writing emerged from the institutional and intellectual milieu of urban reformist culture, and its proponents often made a range of historical and pseudo-historical claims. These are illustrated through a study of one of the first printed Amharic travel narratives, Ḫeruy's account of *wäyzäro*—later *etégé*—Mänän Asfaw's (1883–1962) journey through the Red Sea, Egypt, and Mandatory Palestine. While travel writing is not conventionally understood as history per se, this chapter contends that its Ethiopian variant was in fact a highly creative elaboration of the vernacular tradition and a historicized, literary manifestation of local interactions with the wider world.

Chapter 5 considers the fate of Ethiopia's and Eritrea's vernacular historical tradition in the postcolonial period. It focuses on the emergence of historicist currents, the institutionalization of area studies, and the impressive achievements of the first generation of postwar historians, both academic and vernacular. While earlier historians had attempted to enrich their inherited tradition, this later generation increasingly sought to overcome its perceived limitations. This shift to a dualistic historical culture began after the restoration of Emperor Ḫaylä Śellasé and reached its apex during the post-1974 revolutionary period, when Marxist historical materialism became the dominant framework for understanding the Northeast African past.

The conclusion briefly reflects upon Jomo Kenyatta's observation that European orientalists and anthropologists systematically ignored the intellectual achievements of their African colleagues. It does so through two brief case studies of scholarly collaboration and discord.

1

The Inherited Tradition

"Speech is God's gift to man," a historian once declared, "[but] the ability to know things that are hidden and to discover that which is secret is also inspired by God."[1] So begins an anonymous biography of the Emperor Gälawdéwos (r. 1540–59), the defender of sixteenth-century Christian Ethiopia. This preface illuminates its author's underlying conception of the historical enterprise. Historiography, in his view, was doubly revelatory: the historian should endeavor to narrate—to "speak"—the story of his chosen subject, while simultaneously attempting to excavate—to "discover"—its elusive deeper meaning. In point of fact, Gälawdéwos's biographer adeptly pursued these two goals. His long and nuanced study relates the events of his subject's tumultuous life, but it also seeks to reveal and explain the emperor's greater moral and historical significance. It is thus a history with two overlapping dimensions, one related to a man, and the other to his meaning. As a field of intellectual endeavor, historiography allowed the chronicler to proceed from the visible to the hidden, and from speech to discovery.[2]

This interplay between the seen and unseen suggests a duality at the heart of the Ethiopian historical tradition. Like our anonymous chronicle, vernacular history has two sides. One relates to the articulation and organization of power. It has been argued that Ethiopian historiography is an official tradition, a branch of learning expressly predicated on celebrating the agents, values, and institutions of the Solomonid imperial order.[3] This is certainly an apt description of many Ethiopian historians and the works they produced: royal biographies and dynastic histories, for example, document and generally laud the achievements of Ethiopia's Christian rulers, who routinely commissioned them. The elegiac chronicle of Emperor Gälawdéwos is in this respect an exemplary royal biography, since its author openly venerates his subject. This variety of history is closely linked to the observed personification of power in the present, and to the representation and collective remembrance of the past through the prism of Solomonid authority.[4]

Yet it is equally true that Ethiopian historiography emerged from an intellectual culture profoundly shaped by traditionalism. The memory of a distant and sacred past exerted a tremendous influence on our chronicler and his contemporaries, all the more as this past became increasingly remote. For this reason, many Ethiopian scholars wrote to preserve and transmit their historical inheritance, a large and heterogeneous repository of oral and written knowledge that described this past and encompassed related fields like patristics, hagiography, computus, and folklore.[5] History's deep entanglement with these "nonhistorical" branches of learning is precisely what led *blatta* Ḫeruy to lament his ancestors' insufficient appreciation of the distinction between the sacred and profane. However, in their elision of this border, Ḫeruy's forebears sought to protect the hidden and obscure from oblivion. These preservative efforts represent a traditionalist variety of historiography that is distinct from and occasionally antagonistic toward official, state-sponsored historical writing. It is thus helpful to imagine vernacular historiography as a spectrum with two extremes: one politicized and contemporary, and the other traditionalist and occasionally present-averse. Over the long term, Ethiopian historians produced works that represented both these tendencies, in some cases at the same time.

This heterogeneity of purpose highlights an additional key issue. Ethiopian historiography is history, but it endeavors to reconstruct the past in ways that are quite different from the contemporary, discipline-based understanding of historical inquiry. Vernacular historians did not always place a high premium on verisimilitude, explanation, or the comprehensive representation of all that happened. They understood causation in terms of providence and supernatural agency, and they rarely gestured toward objectivity, often remaining silent on matters of controversy. Yet unique methods—like blurred conceptual boundaries—are hallmarks of history in the vernacular, and they do not diminish the fundamental point that Ethiopian historians aimed to describe the past accurately through chronological narratives predicated on factuality. They sought to do so truthfully, and they sometimes did so brilliantly. This chapter briefly surveys their efforts with two questions in mind: How did Ethiopian scholars write history? And why did they do it?

The Lineage of History

Ethiopian historiography was deeply shaped by the vicissitudes of imperial and regional politics. These dynamics underpinned much of the impetus to represent the past in factual narrative form, and as a historical subject unto itself, the drama of the Solomonid dynasty pervades the written historical record. Put simply, politics defined the context of historical writing and provided much of its content. To make sense of Christian Ethiopia's disparate corpus of historical materials, this section will introduce a basic typology and periodization. If the presentation is overly schematic, it is in the interest of bestowing order upon a complex literary tradition that spans one and a half millennia.[6]

The earliest attempts to represent the past historically emerged from the written culture of Aksum and its antecedents. For roughly six centuries, from the beginning of the Common Era to the turn of the seventh century, Aksum was a major regional empire and flourishing commercial emporium. At its greatest extent, it encompassed both shores of the Red Sea, stretching from the northern highlands of present-day Ethiopia to the coast and hinterlands of southern Arabia. Aksum thrived because of its triply-strategic location: it benefited from the temperate climate and rich agricultural potential of the highland plateau, from its close proximity to the inter-regional trade networks of the ancient Near East, and from its access to commerce from the African interior. It was the peer of the late antique empires of the Mediterranean, which it engaged through military ventures, diplomatic contacts, and regular cultural and material exchange.[7] In the fourth century, these wider connections led the Aksumite emperor Ézana (325–n.d.) to learn of and convert to Christianity, and thereafter the empire was officially Christian under the jurisdiction of the Patriarch of Alexandria.

Although Aksumite culture is still poorly understood, there are some fascinating if ambiguous traces of its incipient historical culture. One manifestation of this is the numerous Greek and Ge'ez epigraphic texts that celebrate the achievements of its rulers and elites, and which represent a public record of events. Inscribed on stone tablets, commemorative thrones, and monumental obelisks in present-day northern Ethiopia, Eritrea, and Yemen, these short works describe victorious military campaigns, royal edicts, diplomatic conferences, and philanthropic activities in a terse style of first-person, pseudo-autobiographical attestation, often with scriptural embellishments. The more detailed of these include the fourth-century trilingual royal inscriptions of Emperor Ézana, which celebrate his military campaigns and imperial dominions, and the sixth-century Greek inscriptions of Emperor Kaléb (ca. 520) on the Adulis votive throne, which similarly describe Aksumite conquests on either side of the Red Sea.[8] Though fragmentary, these epigraphic texts are examples of inchoate official historiography. Ḫeruy considered them to be the genesis of the vernacular tradition.[9]

There are two other works that further suggest the place of history in the Aksumite world. The first are the so-called Gärima Gospels, a set of fourth- through seventh-century Ge'ez manuscripts illuminated in a Byzantine style. The second is the recently discovered Aksum Collection, a fifth- to seventh-century Ge'ez codex that includes a text called "the Alexandrine History," consisting of three chronologies of Egyptian Episcopal sees and bishoprics, apparently derived from Greek materials in the Alexandrian Patriarchal archives.[10] It would appear to be an early example of traditionalist or preservative historiography, as distinct from commemorative political pronouncement. In light of its title and rigidly chronological nature, it has been described as the first properly historical Ge'ez text.[11]

The fragmentary nature of these epigraphic and manuscript works makes it difficult to generalize about Aksum's historical culture. They are clearly manifestations of a larger world of thought and learning of which there are now few traces.[12] At a minimum, we can infer that the Aksumites esteemed the memory of the past. Their eschatology rested on a universalistic chronology: they practiced a monotheistic faith rooted in a notion of sacred time that linked earlier acts of creation and salvation to the present and a future apocalyptic end-time. Thus the founders of the church described in "the Alexandrine History" represented an intermediate chapter in a larger and still-unfolding history, one that began with the antecedent scriptural accounts of Jesus of Nazareth and the earlier trials of the Israelites, and continued with the deeds of Aksum's emperors. Beyond these scriptural influences, the memory of past imperial glories also shaped some Aksumite royal epigraphy: most conspicuously, later Aksumite rulers clung to the idea of their predecessors' overseas conquests in Arabia long after the latter ceased to be a political reality.[13]

More concretely, the physical landscape of the Red Sea region was suffused with traces of past complex societies. Close to Aksum, in present-day Tegray, there was Yeḥa, the monumental relic of the pre-Aksumites, and in Adulis, on the coast, there was a Greek stela that celebrated the achievements of Ptolemy III of Egypt (r. 246–221 BCE).[14] Further afield, there were the ruins of Kush and Egypt, both apparently known to the Aksumites.[15] Their living neighbors were also historically minded, both through the wide orbit of monotheism and Greco-Roman culture in the Red Sea area and the influence of comparatively local traditions, like those of the Bedouin Arabs and the Ḥimyarite Jews. The Aksumites thus practiced a faith and inhabited a region saturated with ideas about the past, and these facts surely informed their efforts to represent their own past in writing.[16]

These Aksumite expressions of historicality have a tenuous connection to the vernacular historical tradition of later centuries. They are formally and stylistically similar to medieval and early modern Ethiopian historiography, but it seems that little of the original Aksumite historical material was directly transmitted to later scholars.[17] The latter often referred to people and events of the Aksumite era, but they did not necessarily do so through direct reference to the Aksumite historical record itself, though there are some fascinating exceptions to this tendency.[18] This disregard is likely because the record itself was partially Greek, by then a relatively obscure language.[19] However, the issue of textual transmission is further complicated by the fact that the earliest Ge'ez literature, translated directly from Greek, was later mixed with and replaced by subsequent translations from Coptic and Arabic.[20] For these reasons, we can say that Ethiopia's medieval historians largely built their tradition anew and not upon a received antique foundation. The influence of Aksum was more symbolic than direct, and in this respect, historiography was no different from the larger imperial culture of which it was a part.[21]

Susbequent developments gave new meaning to these memories. As Aksum began a slow decline after the sixth century, new regional polities emerged in the Horn of Africa. The polytheistic and later Christian Zagwe dynasty dominated the northern highlands, while Muslim sultanates reigned in the coastal lowlands. In the thirteenth century, this situation changed when a Christian dynasty seized power in the highlands: the Solomonids, so named because the dynastic founder, Emperor Yekunno Amlak (r. 1270–85), claimed lineal descent from an ancient liaison between Solomon and Makedda, the biblical Queen of Sheba. The political fortunes of this new dynasty were subsequently secured by the military victories of Emperor Amdä Ṣeyon (r. 1314–44), who triumphed over his rivals, conquered lost dominions, and quelled restive tributary states in present-day Somalia and eastern Ethiopia.

The Solomonid regime change emphasized a symbolic connection to the Aksumite past. This link was directly asserted by coronation rituals held in the town of Aksum, and indirectly manifest in the *Kebrä nägäśt*, or "Glory of Kings," the dynasty's foundational Ge'ez epic.[22] The *Kebrä nägäśt* legitimized the Solomonid claim to power by purporting to document the dynasty's lineal ties to ancient monotheistic forebears. Ostensibly derived from an older Copto-Arabic text by a thirteenth-century Ethiopian ecclesiastic named Yeseḥaq, the Ge'ez version of the work relates the epic tale of Makedda, termed "the Queen of the South," and her liaison with Solomon; the birth of their son Dawit, later known as Menilek, the founder of the Solomonid line; and the consequences of these events, including an account of the sixth-century Aksumite defeat of the South Arabian Ḥimyarites. There has been considerable debate about the date of composition of the now-lost Arabic original: it is likely a tenth-century work with links to various Ethiopian, Coptic, Arab, and Jewish traditions.[23] Whatever the date of its creation, the language, nomenclature, and concerns of the Ge'ez version are very much a product of medieval Christian politics and culture, though it curiously says little about the putative restoration of the Solomonids and the heightened Muslim-Christian rivalry that defined the era.[24] Its chief role as a textual link with earlier times lies not in its preservation or factual representation of ancient history but in its stylized evocation of a tremendous Aksumite inheritance—in its depiction of a foundational mythic past carefully dressed in pseudo-historical trappings. It was thus somewhat epigenetic. Its influence upon the Ethiopian historical imagination was profound, rather like the impact on the English of the near-contemporaneous pseudo-history of King Arthur by Geoffrey of Monmouth.[25] Ḫeruy described the *Kebrä nägäśt* as history, and it was certainly perceived as such by many of its readers.[26]

The early era of the Solomonid restoration saw the reemergence of historiography proper, which clearly drew inspiration from the *Kebrä nägäśt*. The first known manifestation of this development is the biography of Emperor Amdä Ṣeyon, who presided over a blossoming of Ge'ez literature and Arabic translation, and who commissioned a narrative account of his military campaigns against the Ifat and Adal sultanates of the eastern borderlands. This work can be seen as the foundational text of royal biography, the prestige genre of vernacular historiography.[27] The lavish narrative is driven by the drama of its Christian protagonist's struggle with his Muslim rivals: we read of their bellicose diplomatic correspondence, their epic military conflicts, the humiliating submission of the sultans, and ultimately the redemption of Amdä Ṣeyon as a pseudo-messianic savior of Christian Ethiopia.[28] Although the authorship and precise date of composition of the text are unclear,[29] it has been called one of the greatest works of Ge'ez literature.[30]

In the following century, Amdä Ṣeyon's successors followed his example by commissioning chronicles of their own. The result was a small but significant historical literature of both complete and fragmentary texts. These include two anonymous biographies of the scholar-Emperor Zär'a Ya'eqob (r. 1434–68), one a rather critical annalistic account written by a contemporary member of the court, the other a more sympathetic thematic study.[31] The emperor himself also wrote homilies addressing historical episodes as moral and spiritual object lessons, thereby acting as an autochronicler of sorts.[32] His successor Emperor Bä'edä Maryam I (r. 1468–78) was the subject of two chronicles,[33] and the latter's sons and grandson, emperors Eskender (r. 1478–94), Amdä Ṣeyon II (1494), and Na'od (1494–1508), were themselves the subject of fragmentary histories.[34] Several of these works appear to have been written by the preceptor of the royal family, and for this reason, the multipart saga of Bä'edä Maryam and his descendants is a concise early example of what would later be termed dynastic history, or *tarikä nägäśt*.[35]

Related and contemporary to these works are the hagiographies of the Zagwe rulers, the Solomonids' immediate dynastic predecessors.[36] The most notable of these is the pseudo-chronicle of the saint-emperor Lalibäla (ca. 1200), which appears to have been written during the reign of Zär'a Ya'eqob.[37] It is clearly addressed to a Solomonid audience, termed "the new children of Israel," and it invests Lalibäla with proto-Solomonid qualities, synthesizing what appear to be posthumous traditions about his miraculous deeds.[38] The text itself describes the circumstances of the emperor's birth, the trials of his life, his reign and the construction of his famed monolithic churches, and finally his desire that his descendants would not inherit his throne. It is widely attested in manuscripts, and also exists in an abbreviated version.[39]

This budding historical and pseudo-historical literature continued to grow in the sixteenth century, a watershed era in the Horn of Africa. The ongoing regional struggle between the Ethiopian Christians and their Muslim rivals was at that time engulfed in the larger imperial conflict between the Ottomans and the Portuguese. The contest for the Red Sea region began in 1507, when the Portuguese established a brief foothold at Soqotra; intensified in the 1520s, when the Ottomans first sent musketeers to aid their local co-religionists; and reached its apex in the 1540s, when the Ethiopian Christians allied with Christóvão da Gama (1516–42), the son of the Portuguese explorer, against the Ottomans and the Adal Sultanate, then based in Harär. These developments required local Christians and Muslims to assume roles in a much larger geopolitical drama, and the next century witnessed recurring Muslim-Christian and Orthodox-Catholic conflicts against the backdrop of mass Oromo immigration into the highlands.

These heightened regional and inter-regional tensions pushed Ethiopian historiography in new directions.[40] Most notably, the royal biographies of the era became increasingly elaborate, aggregative, intertextual, and attuned to translocal historical forces. The first histories of this period are the short accounts of the reign of Emperor Lebnä Dengel (1508–40), highly annalistic descriptions of the emperor's struggles with the famed Adali *imam* Aḥmad Ibrāhīm al-Ġāzī (1506–43), known to Christians as Grañ, "the left-handed."[41] Their close focus on the emperor's campaigns make them episodic histories rather like the earlier chronicle of Emperor Amdä Ṣeyon. More comprehensive and expansive is the biography of Emperor Gälawdéwos, written by a brilliant historian whose exact identity is unclear: the chief candidates would appear to be Sennä Krestos, an otherwise unknown scholar who is cited as author of the chronicle by a near contemporary, and *eč̣č̣äge* Enbaqom (1470–1560), a prolific and learned Yemeni-Ethiopian abbot.[42] Like the chronicles of Amdä Ṣeyon and Lebnä Dengel, this work is principally a narrative account of the emperor's heroic struggle against non-Christian antagonists. It is, however, considerably more detailed than any of its antecedents. It describes Gälawdéwos's family history, his coming of age in an era of intense religious warfare, his accession to the throne, and his campaigns against a series of dastardly and occasionally intrepid Muslim foes: Aḥmad Ibrāhīm al-Ġāzī, his nephew and successor Abbās b. Ibrāhīm (n.d.–1544), and finally Özdemir Pasha (n.d.–1560), the Ottoman general and one-time governor of Yemen.[43] The chronicle also describes the emperor's alliance with da Gama and the Ethiopian church's growing concern with the Iberian Catholic missionaries, which intensified after the arrival of the Jesuits in 1555.[44] The narrative concludes with an elegy for Gälawdéwos modeled upon the lamentations of Jeremiah.

The histories of Lebnä Dengel and Gälawdéwos in turn informed the official biography of Emperor Minas (1559–63), Gälawdéwos's brother and successor. The account of his reign is divided into two parts: the first deals with his life prior to his accession to the throne, which apparently included a brief conversion to Islam and a planned marriage to Grañ's daughter, and the second describes his troubled years as emperor, including his campaigns against internal rebels allied with the Portuguese.[45] This work was continued and completed by the biographer(s) of Emperor Śärṣä Dengel (1563–97), likely the remarkable ecclesiastic *abba* Baḥrey (b. 1535).[46] His chronicle, which included introductory chapters on Lebnä Dengel and his son-successors, describes, among other things, the emperor's campaigns against a series of insurgent nobles, their Ottoman allies, and the Bétä Esra'él, or Ethiopian Jews. It is dense in historical detail and rich in literary flourish as well as biblical allusions, and since it includes prefatory chapters based upon earlier works, it has been described as an epic cycle.[47]

In addition to expanding the scope of royal biography, the period's considerable sectarian tumult also encouraged some historians to examine the empire's non-Christian enemies. These were not seen as historical subjects in their own right; instead, Ethiopian Christian scholars discussed the Oromo, Muslims, and other stranger groups—including co-religionists such as Armenians, Greeks, Copts, and Portuguese—in terms of their impact upon local history.[48] The best-known example of this tendency is the detailed ethnohistory of the Oromo by *abba* Baḥrey, who endeavored to describe and explain the military successes of the empire's principal non-Christian rivals.[49] His study is without precedent in its sophisticated analysis of the institutions, social categories, and religion of non-Christians. Similar in focus are the era's Grañ histories, which are essentially episodic studies of a watershed moment in the Solomonid saga.[50] Translated works added to this small literature: these include biographies of Muhammad and histories of the Jews, Safavids, and Byzantines.[51] Muslims and Westerners also appear in the hagiographic literature of the day.[52]

These literary developments had their institutional complement in the redefinition of the station of the court historian, or *ṣäḥafé te'ezaz*.[53] This official was tasked with maintaining and presenting the royal seal, promulgating the orders of the emperor, and chronicling the deeds of the ruler and dynasty. Prior to the sixteenth century, these duties fell to the royal confessor, the *yäneguś näfs abbat*, and it would appear that the *ṣäḥafé te'ezaz* was not a defined title per se. Indeed, very few of these early historian-confessors are known by name. In the Grañ era, however, the work of the court historian became so onerous that the position began to be reserved for the most qualified senior church scholar, who received the official title of *ṣäḥafé te'ezaz* in addition to whichever church title he already possessed. In many cases, there were two appointed court historians, and they occupied a distinguished place at the court in relative proximity to the emperor. This arrangement remained in place until the Gondärine era (see table 1.1).

Table 1.1. List of court historians since the reign of Emperor Susenyos, by *blattén géta* Marse'é Ḫazan Wäldä Qirqos

In the reign of *aṣé* Susenyos (1597–1623EC) *azzaž* Ṭino *ṣäḥafé te'ezaz* Täklä Śellasé	In the reign of *aṣé* Täklä Haymanot (1763–70[EC]) *ṣäḥafé te'ezaz* Nahuda
In the reign of Ṣädequ Yoḥannes (1660–74EC) *azzaž* Ḥäwarya Krestos *ṣäḥafé te'ezaz* *azzaž* Wäldä Haymanot *ṣäḥafé te'ezaz*	In the final reign of Täklä Haymanot (1772–77[EC]) *ṣäḥafé te'ezaz* Gäbru
In the reign of Adyam Säggäd (1674–98EC) *azzaž* Ḥäwarya Krestos *ṣäḥafé te'ezaz* *azzaž* Wäldä Haymanot *ṣäḥafé te'ezaz* *azzaž* Zäwäld *ṣäḥafé te'ezaz* Akalä Krestos Zäwäldä Maryam *ṣäḥafé te'ezaz*	In the time of *aṣé* Téwodros (1845–60[EC]) *aläqa* Zännäb *ṣäḥafé te'ezaz*
In the reign of *aṣé* Téwoflos (1700–1703EC) *azzaž* Aksé *ṣäḥafé te'ezaz*	In the time of *aṣé* Yoḥannes (1863–81[EC]) *ṣäḥafé te'ezaz* Wärqenäh
In the reign of *aṣé* Bäkaffa (1713–23EC) *ṣäḥafé te'ezaz* Sinoda *abba* Arsé *ṣäḥafé te'ezaz*	In the time of *aṣé* Menilek (1881–1906[EC]) *ṣäḥafé te'ezaz* Gäbrä Śellasé *ṣäḥafé te'ezaz* Afä Wärq
In the reign of Iyyasu of Qwarä *abéto* Ṗawlos *ṣäḥafé te'ezaz* *abba* Téwodros *ṣäḥafé te'ezaz* *liqä mä'emerän* Neway *ṣäḥafé te'ezaz* *azzaž* Gälasyos *ṣäḥafé te'ezaz* *azzaž* Téwodosyos *ṣäḥafé te'ezaz*	In the time of *negeśt* Zäwditu (1909–22[EC]) *ṣäḥafé te'ezaz* Afä Wärq *ṣäḥafé te'ezaz* Wäldä Mäsqäl
	In the time of Ḫayle Śellasé I (1922–66[EC]) *ṣäḥafé te'ezaz* Wäldä Mäsqäl *ṣäḥafé te'ezaz* Ḫaylé Wäldä Rufé *ṣäḥafé te'ezaz* Wäldä Giyorgis Wäldä Yoḥannes *ṣäḥafé te'ezaz* Täfära Wärq Engeda Wärq *ṣäḥafé te'ezaz* Aklilu Häbtä Wäl

Source: Translated from Marse'é Ḫazan, unpublished manuscript, 398–99.

The intervening centuries witnessed further elaborations of this literature. Royal biography remained the most significant pursuit until the end of the Gondärine period. While not every sovereign was the subject of a study, some were accorded more than one. The era's chronicles include the very long accounts of the reign of Emperor Susenyos (r. 1607–32), jointly written by Meherkä Dengel (ca. 1540–?), the emperor's confessor, and *azzaž* Täklä Śellasé (d. 1638), nicknamed "Ṭino," his secretary and counselor.[54] The emperors Yoḥannes I (r. 1667–82), Iyyasu I (r. 1682–1706), and Bakkäffa (r. 1721–30) were all subjects of biographies.[55] Some of these were written jointly. Emperor Bakkäffa, for example, employed at least four court historians over his short reign: Sinoda, who was assisted by Demetros, and *abba* Arsé, who was replaced by a scholar named Hawaryat Krestos.[56] Bakkäffa's successors, Iyyasu II (r. 1730–55) and Iyyo'as (r. 1755), were the subject of a detailed dynastic history of sorts, a single history of two reigns.[57] The last royal chronicle of the Gondärine era is that of the first reign of Emperor Täklä Giyorgis (r. 1779–84), a detailed account of his accession to the throne and military campaigns that ends abruptly four months before his deposition. It was written by *aläqa* Gäbru, a church scholar who was a close companion of the emperor and the court historian of his predecessor.[58]

As centralized political authority disintegrated during the Gondärine period and the subsequent *zämänä mäsafent*, the chaotic "era of the princes" during which power devolved away from the figure of the emperor, Ethiopian historians increasingly looked beyond the genre of royal biography. The early contours of this politically induced shift are evident in the chronicle of Iyyasu II and Iyyo'as, which focuses on *etégé* Mentewwab—the queen regent—and her powerful coterie of kinsmen.[59] This shift away from the royal subject per se was more prominently manifest in the emergence of a new historical genre: the general dynastic history, or *tarikä nägäśt*, commonly described in the specialist literature as "the Short Chronicle."[60] The original example was created when an ecclesiastic named *azzaž* Täklä Haymanot assembled a general history of Ethiopia that explicitly fused universal and Solomonid history.[61] This work appears to have been originally based on either a Grañ history or a universal chronography, and it includes genealogical, annalistic, and narrative chapters.[62] These begin with the origins of mankind and the lineage and chronology of Adam through Aksum, the Zagwe, and the Solomonids, and continue through the medieval era to conclude at various points in the early modern period. This compiled universal-dynastic history provided the basis and inspiration for a large number of variant elaborations, which added new material to deal with subsequent reigns, up to and including the twentieth century. It became a genre of historiography unto itself, as André Caquot observed.[63]

In addition to royal biography and dynastic history, other comparatively minor historical genres emerged in this period. Perhaps the most common of these was universal chronography, or *yä'aläm tarik*. This genre is annalistic rather than narrative-based, relying upon sparse chronologies of dates associated with individuals and events. It is thus considerably less literary in form than royal biography or dynastic history. A second notable feature is that it is not confined to the reign of an individual ruler or dynasty, but instead attempts to present the complete history of humanity and the saga of God's covenantal people,[64] thereby linking individual stories in a comprehensive framework that spans the pre-Christian era—the *amätä feda* (lit. "era of hardship")—and the Christian one that succeded it—the *amätä meḥrät* (lit. "era of grace"). It can thus be described as an annalistic analog of *tarikä nägäśt*.

The canonical examples of universal chronography are the translated works of Abu Šaker, John of Nikiu, and Giyorgis Wäldä Amid, which collectively introduced historical material from Arabic and Copto-Arabic literature to the Ethiopian tradition.[65] However, these prestige texts complemented and inspired a great many short, anonymous examples of the genre that appear as interpolated texts in manuscripts dealing with a wide variety of topics. Whether original or derivative, nearly all of these minor works employ the same tripartite periodization: they typically begin with the biblical account of human origins and antiquity, continue with events of early church history, and conclude with the arrival of Christianity in Ethiopia and the emergence of the Solomonid dynasty, at which point they sometimes provide greater detail.[66] They are prone to characterizing complex topics through brief references to people and events that are assumed to be known to the reader, and for this reason, we may speculate that they were used as reference works. The oldest examples appear to be derived from early seventeenth-century materials.[67]

Related to world chronography is the more general extra-generic practice of historical listing. This could take the form of genealogical lists, such as those that begin the Short Chronicle or the biography of Iyyasu II. Similar kinds of genealogies can be found as interpolated texts in many manuscripts. Also common was the practice of listing the Aksumite rulers, the church fathers, and the church patriarchs.[68] Some of these lists are overtly chronological, associating their subjects with particular years, while others simply present an undated sequence of succession. Though extremely sparse, it can be argued that they possess skeletal narrative elements.[69]

Throughout this long period, historiography was firmly and fruitfully planted in a broader and richly variegated historical culture. The most significant manifestation of this contextual link was the oral tradition, which in tandem with written history informed a host of social practices with historical dimensions.[70] These varied considerably. The royal chronicles were sometimes read aloud, possibly as part of public ceremonies, and so for this reason were texts whose words, themes, and arguments reverberated beyond the court and the rarefied world of literacy and learning.[71] Beyond historiography proper, land inheritance and tributary rights were critical components of social relations that involved recourse to precedent and proof, and their particulars were documented orally and through genealogical notes, administrative documents, and marginalia in church manuscripts.[72] Courtly protocol likewise required regular recourse to precedent, and on some occasions, the assertion of royal authority involved public rituals of lineal attestation.[73] Poetry and songs often addressed historical themes.[74] All these performances of history paralleled other ostensibly "nonhistorical" invocations of the past. In scholarship, these could be close relatives of history, such as hagiography and patristics, which looked to the past and approached devotional biography and prosopography, or more distant kin, as with computus and etymology. Narrative painting visually related historical and mythic episodes,[75] and even the physical landscape and its monuments were conceived through historical prisms, either through their association with events of the recent past or the sacred geography mapped by the scriptures.[76] All these practices invoked history outside the realm of prose chronology. Beyond them lay the even more capacious realm of social memory, through which past aspects of individual and collective experience were jointly understood.

The nineteenth century was a transitional moment that witnessed several critical new developments in local historical practice. Among the most significant of these was the growth of historiography in Amharic. The various royal biographies of emperors Téwodros II (r. 1855–68), Yoḥannes IV (r. 1871–89), and Menilek II (r. 1889–1913) exemplify this turn.[77] A second trend was the proliferation of new genres. These include noble biography, exemplified by the works devoted to *ras* Alula Engeda (1827–97), Emperor Yoḥannes's lieutenant, and *ras* Gobäna Dači (ca. 1820s–1888), one of Emperor Menilek's governors.[78] They also include regional historiography, typified by the chronicle of Goǧǧam written by *aläqa* Täklä Iyäsus Wäqǧira (1868–1936); the history of the kings of Šäwa by *ṣäḥafé te'ezaz* Gäbrä Śellasé, who used this work as the basis for his biography of Emperor Menilek; and the histories of Aksum and Ḥamasén by various local scholars.[79]

These developments received their professional corollary in 1908, when Emperor Menilek incorporated the position of *ṣäḥafé te'ezaz* into his ministerial cabinet as the Minister of the Pen, or *yäṣeḥefät minister.* The duties of this new minister were redefined as follows: to act as head of the court secretaries, working in the palace as a kind of historian-in-chief; to preserve a copy of every written document produced by the palace; to maintain an archive of documents and books in the palace; to bestow decorations on recipients; and finally, to serve as head of the government presses.[80]

Ultimately, though, these linguistic, generic, and institutional developments are manifestations of broader historical changes that were then reshaping the region. For this reason, they are best understood in relation to the increasingly complex historical culture that emerged in the last decades of the nineteenth century, the focus of the remainder of this book.

Uses of the Past

Alexis de Tocqueville once observed that books make history.[81] What did this entail in Christian Ethiopia before the twentieth century? The answer to this question encompasses several additional and interrelated questions: How did Ethiopian scholars represent the past? And how did they conceptualize this act? What were the purposes of their books of history—the *yätarik mäṣaḥeft* of Ḫeruy's study? And how were these woven into the region's social and political fabric?

We can begin with the ontological imagination of the historians themselves, an understanding that lurks in the margins of their works. Ethiopian scholars cast historical actors in moral roles: men—and a few women—were mostly either good or evil, with some occasional interlopers and lost souls. These roles and their significance derived from the all-encompassing religio-historical process that began with the events of the scriptures, continued through the early Church, culminated in the flourishing of the true faith in Ethiopia, and would continue to unfold as foretold in prophecy and described in eschatological literature. Individual agents—whether good or evil—were through their moral roles major and minor players in this universal history, much as they were in the Hebrew and Christian scriptures.[82] The different genres of Ethiopian historiography—royal biography, dynastic history, and universal chronography—simply described this grand saga from different vistas and with varying levels of complexity. The hand of God could be overtly visible in the course of events, in the form of triumphs, miracles, and premonitions, or it could be subtle and hidden, requiring careful excavation and illumination. It fell to the historian to empirically document and elucidate this personified morality, thereby making the unseen and divine visible.[83]

This conception of the historical enterprise is evident in the prefatory and concluding statements historians periodically offered to the reader, the antecedents of the introduction, or *mäqdem*, that became common in nineteenth- and twentieth-century historical writing. In some cases, these statements take the form of a kind of "historian's prayer" which beseeched God to guide the writer toward sound historical truth.[84] Thus *abba* Baḥrey, the royal biographer and ethno-historian, asked "that the Lord gives us a learned language to make known that which we will say, and that he gives to our thought the science of prudent men, in which intelligence is alive and knowledge heard, that we will think internally and say externally the great things and portents that the Lord makes by the hands of this king, powerful and victorious over his adversaries."[85] In other cases, historians addressed the reader as a fraternal steward, inviting the reader to join them in the task of comprehending and preserving the past. For example, Emperor Gälawdéwos's unknown chronicler wrote: "My brothers, you who are intelligent, accept this book that your pressing solicitations pushed me to write. Compensate, I request of you, for the gaps due to my ignorance. Straighten that which is torturous and flatten that which is bumpy, for the intelligence of one man alone is not able to give to a writing a perfect beauty, just as the light of one star and the beauty of one flower are not sufficient to adorn the sky and the earth."[86] Other writers urged their readers to the attentiveness required of history. Thus one of Emperor Iyyasu II's four chroniclers admonished his audience: "Listen, all you, O Christian people, and lend your ear, you who reside in the royal house, judges and governors, and you all, O soldiers and young valiant men . . . Listen to this, all you people, prick up your ears, you who inhabit the world, each in his space, sons of man, rich and poor, for we say to you that which we have . . . heard from our ears and which our fathers have told."[87]

The historical inheritance invoked by these passages was, however, by definition incomplete. One of Emperor Iyyasu II's biographers made this very point in a frank reflection on the daunting scope of the historical enterprise: "This has been the enumeration of genealogy. That which is known has been written, and that which is not known has been omitted. Of the rest, if each and every particular is written, the world will not contain it. Amen. Amen."[88] *Abba* Baḥrey offered a similar admission of the difficulty of writing a truly comprehensive history, noting that God "knows all that is hidden and all that is manifest. We do not seek to discover it because it would be useless."[89] If historiography—the effort to discern and document the contours of a beautiful and divine history—was a task inspired by God, it was also constrained by individual failings, the limits of collective efforts, and the vastness of its subject. It was in these respects imperfect and human.

These issues of imagination, conceptualization, and purpose are distinct from the more practical questions of the historian's craft. In many cases, our basic methodological model is that of an observational historian: an individual who writes about and seeks to understand events that they personally witnessed or of which they themselves heard reports. Outside of their introductory and concluding addresses, observational historians are generally self-effacing in terms of their authorial identity, though they sometimes describe their own actions when these relate to their larger narrative in some way.[90] Observation and reportage were especially significant for court historians, who sometimes explicitly mention what they themselves saw, what rumors they heard, and which testimonies they found credible and incredible.[91] As one chronicler explained, "all of this history of the virtues of the victorious king Mäläk Säggäd, we have heard it, we have seen it, and we have learned of it through questioning."[92] In many cases, court historians travelled with their subjects in their capacity as the official chroniclers of witnessed power, though they occasionally introduced veiled and not-so-veiled criticisms of their patrons or their ancestors.[93]

Some less prominent scholars documented their personal observations and experiences in private and comparatively obscure texts. One example of this is the annalistic autobiography written by a sixteenth-century monk named *abba* Ṗawlos (1510–78), one of the earliest examples of this genre.[94] It outlines the religio-political conflicts of the era and their impact upon the life of the author: the destruction of the author's monastery by Muslim invaders from Adal, the author's failed attempt to make a pilgrimage to Jerusalem, the arrival of the Ottomans and Portuguese, the campaigns of Grañ and his successors, the slave raids of the Oromo, and the drama of Solomonid dynastic succession. It also mentions miscellaneous and comparatively mundane aspects of his personal life, such as astronomical phenomena, his acquisition of a slave, and the theft of his cows. Like the writings of observational court historians, his political betters, his autobiography was rooted in the description of lived experience, not the results of scholarly inquiry.

Not all historians were so rigorously observational in method; there are also many examples of compilatory historiography. One is the case of the late eighteenth-century *tarikä nägäśt* jointly produced by the ecclesiastic *abéto* Abägaz (n.d.–ca. 1800) and his patron and friend *däğğazmač* Ḥaylä Mika'él Ešäté (1753–ca. 1809), both from Šäwa.[95] The two lamented the late Gondärine decline of imperial power and the deterioration and destruction of Christian Ethiopia's manuscript patrimony, and these concerns inspired them to produce a historical compendium. After Ḥaylä Mika'él collected a very large number of manuscripts from "many regions and many islands," *abéto* Abägaz produced a massive synthetic history that spanned the ancient Israelites through Aksum and the era of the Solomonid dynasty, a work that he hoped would "revive . . . the memory of the kings and the great ones."[96] The history fused disparate elements, drawing upon the universal history of Wäldä Giyorgis Wäldä Amid, the Short Chronicle, and the royal biographies.[97] It was an attempted *summa* of Ethiopia's endangered historical inheritance.

Abéto Abägaz was not the only historian to pursue this kind of compilatory undertaking. Another was Täklä Haymanot, whose original Short Chronicle brought together a number of texts and oral knowledge, and was in turn used in later aggregative historical works. He was apparently a widely read historian: his original compilation was derived from several other works, and on occasion, he rhetorically presents his work as a survey of all extant knowledge.[98] In some cases, his use of other texts is unacknowledged: for example, his account of Emperor Śärṣä Dengel's reign includes an illustrative but ultimately minor episode that is clearly taken from the emperor's chronicle, but with no mention of the source.[99] At other times, Täklä Haymanot mentions his sources explicitly: he discusses, for example, the synaxary, a hagiographical compilation, and he refers by name to Hawarya Krestos, the author of Emperor Iyyasu's chronicle.[100] To these various borrowed materials Täklä Haymanot added his personal observations and considerable knowledge of court drama and doctrinal controversies, both within the Ethiopian church and between the Ethiopians and the Iberian missionaries, who feature prominently in the text and whose ideas are discussed in considerable detail.[101] The result can be described as a universalistic *tarikä nägäśt* with a special focus on the nuances of early modern church and intellectual history.

There were other less prominent historian-compilers. One was *liq* Aṣqu (ca. 1770–1840s), a Gondärine scholar and judge who collected manuscripts and assembled two general histories of Ethiopia.[102] Another was *däbtära* Assäggakäñ, a mid-nineteenth-century copyist and epistolographic archivist of sorts.[103] Some court historians compiled histories at the request of their sovereign: this was the case with Sinoda, who reported that he was ordered to do so by Emperor Bakkäffa, his patron.[104] The writers of world chronography generally produced annals with an intensely accumulative quality: they brought together facts and dates, likely for their own reference or for use in computus. All these examples of aggregative—rather than observational—historiography demonstrate the deep influence of traditionalism upon historical practice. These collections, elaborations, copies, and syntheses were intended to preserve, refine, and transmit received knowledge—the historical truths that "our fathers have told."

This kind of accumulative historiography need not be unoriginal, though.[105] In some cases, the act of compilation had generative and even polemical dimensions. This is well-illustrated by the so-called Liber Aksumae, a historical collection produced under the direction of *ras* Mika'él Seḥul (ca. 1691–1777) of Tegray, at the request of the Scottish adventurer and bibliophile James Bruce (1730–94). The manuscript consists of a variant of the *Kebrä nägäśt* and a series of short texts related to both the ancient and the later history of the city of Aksum. The texts relating to more recent history included administrative documents, church records, and a group of chronologies related to antiquity, the Solomonids, and various Near Eastern caliphates. As Anaïs Wion has argued, these heterogenous texts can be read collectively as an argument for the sovereignty of Aksum, and by extension, the continued significance of Tegray in an era of Gondärine dominance.[106] Put simply, the texts in the collection offer a historicized defense of regionalism. Similar kinds of polemical aims are evident in the chronicle of emperors Iyyasu II and Iyyo'as, which contains interpolated elements related to *ras* Mika'él and Tegray more generally, and the so-called interpolated Short Chronicles, which sometimes introduce political asides to recensions of Täklä Haymanot's text.[107] As all these cases suggest, acts of collection, assembly, juxtaposition, and interpolation could produce innovative results.[108]

Observation and preservation—what purposes did these methods serve? What were the larger goals of historical inquiry? If we survey the corpus of vernacular historiography, several distinct goals can be discerned. The most basic aims of the historian were instruction and description, while the more sophisticated were epic celebration and analytic explication. These four aims are sometimes hinted at in metatextual introductory statements and asides, but they are more clearly seen in the use of different historiographic modes, or suprageneric styles of historical writing. The interplay between these modes is a hallmark of Ethiopian historiography in the years before the twentieth century. We will consider them in turn, proceeding in order of complexity.

Some scholars clearly wrote to edify the reader. This was the stated intention of the anonymous author of Emperor Lalibäla's hagio-chronicle, who evocatively described the morally nourishing "sweetness" of history: "The history of the just satisfies much more so than a well-laid table, than drinking wine and mead; it has more sweetness than oil and fat, as it is said by the prophets: 'His words are more sweet than butter.'"[109] Intriguingly, this writer's notion of "sweet history" resurfaces literally and metaphorically through several episodes in the text, from his account of the Lalibäla's birth, when the future emperor was surrounded by bees looking for honey, to his years as ruler, when tribute pots of honey were lost in a river crossing only to be miraculously redelivered, and finally to the poetic coda that reflects on the work's purpose.[110] A few other writers explicitly referred to this satisfying quality of historical narration: thus Wäldä Giyorgis, the chronicler of Emperor Yohannes I, observed that history's sweetness "invites the mouth to tell and the ear to listen."[111] In some cases, historians tried to edify through open didacticism—by imparting lessons to the reader. Thus Hawarya Krestos and Zäwäld, the chroniclers of Emperor Iyyasu, concluded their account with an illustrative episode that explicitly asserted the instructive potential of the past.[112] All these writers aimed to inform and thereby sustain their audiences.

Historians also endeavored to accurately describe. This intention is most clearly evident in the long lists of names, dates, and places that can be found in histories of all sorts. Genealogical listing and dynastic chronology were among the basic tasks of the scholar—the facts of descent and succession mattered, and the historian had to get them right. But historical description also encompassed a host of other particulars. Rather than asserting that an army was fearsome or vast, for example, a descriptive historian might outline its composition in terms of leadership or place of origin. This could also involve a pronounced sense of numeracy: for example, the author of the Amdä Ṣeyon chronicle lists the governors in the Adalite coalition and determined that their combined forces numbered exactly 12,048, while the Gälawdéwos chronicle quantitatively compares the size of the Christian army with the Adali forces of Naṣraddīn b. Aḥmad (n.d.–1542), the son of Grañ.[113] Naming was another common form of historical description, from lists of rebels executed in the plaza to the names of the vanquished and the spoils of war.[114] On occasion, the descriptive urge led historians to venture beyond precise reportage to the realm of literary art. Some offer rich, almost immersive and experiential accounts of events. Thus Emperor Bakkäffa's biographer evokes the splendor and sumptuousness of a Gondärine royal banquet scene with an effusiveness that suggests the *teǧ*, or mead, spilling from the chalices of the king and his guests.[115] The pursuit of historical truth led these historians to the details, the factual particulars of past reality. These were, after all, manifestations of a mysterious divine plan.

The informative and descriptive modes just discussed often complement the more general aim of epic celebration. Historians writing in this mode bestowed grandeur on contemporary events and people by associating them with a heroic and sacred past.[116] They could establish this link in several ways. Most basically, scriptural quotations and references might suggest ancient or holy precedents for later events. Chronology could forge this same connection: world chronography, for example, implicitly temporalizes the Solomonic lineage of Ethiopia's rulers by tracing the history of their covenantal inheritance, as the leaders of a chosen people. Beyond these associative methodological tools, more overt and literary forms of symbolic celebration are evident in many of the royal biographies, especially those depicting conflicts between the glorious Solomonids and their villainous Muslim adversaries. The Amdä Ṣeyon chronicle, for example, is replete with factual and metaphorical elements presenting its protagonist as a messianic, Christ-like figure and his Muslim opponents as sinful infidels led by an "impious son of a viper and dragon, the son of a barbarian of the race of Satan."[117] This Christian symbolism is especially pronounced in the final chapters of this work, when the emperor recovers from a near-fatal illness to offer himself in sacrifice through battle with the vast forces of the Adalite *qadi* Ṣāliḥ, thereby saving Christian Ethiopia and securing the territories of the newly expanded empire.[118] *Abba* Baḥrey achieves a similar end through more elegant literary means. His biography of Emperor Śärṣä Dengel is divided into two parts to evoke the structure of the Gospel narratives: his account of the emperor's oppression was followed by a description of his victories, just as "the Evangelists began with the history of the crucifixion of our Lord Jesus Christ, and placed after it the history of his resurrection and ascension to heaven."[119] As these examples suggest, it is in epic historiography that the moral judgment of the historian is most openly displayed. Facts might matter, but historical truth also involved the larger question of the righteousness of one's subject.

This point is especially evident in how epic historiography deals with subaltern voices. It is highly monoglossic: this mode assimilates all historical discourse into the worldview of the author or his protagonist, reserving little room for alternative voices.[120] The Bakkäffa chronicle demonstrates this tendency nicely. Much of it relates the emperor's punitive campaigns among the Oromo of Lake Tana and the Blue Nile. In many cases, the Oromo, whose words appear in the narrative, offer stylized collective confessions (e.g., "Sin is our nature"), requesting clemency from the good and noble emperor.[121] When the latter obliges, their fears are assuaged; when he does not, his just retributory carnage "spreads abundant tears, like the water of the rainy season."[122] Though the historian presents the Oromo as independent—if monovocal—actors, their words and deeds are entirely incorporated into the politico-religious historical framework of the Christian imperial order. They can play the role of either wayward sinning children who can be forgiven by a just ruler, or recalcitrant disruptors of the peace who deserve only death. They are foils for the emperor's specific historical role, burnishing its brilliancy.

This kind of writing stands apart from historiography that seeks to argue, analyze, and explain—to uncover "that which is secret," as Emperor Gälawdéwos's chronicler put it. This explicatory mode employs the same literary flourishes, scriptural analogies, detailed lists, and extended quotations as instructive, descriptive, and epic historiography, but it also uses metadiscourse and evidence-based argumentation to mine more lustrous riches from this same bedrock. It is easily the most subtle variety of traditional historical writing, principally because Ethiopian historians rarely advance their claims openly. In many cases, they instead reveal their arguments and analysis through the device of supernatural premonition.

This approach organizes the short biography of Emperor Na'od, for example. Its author begins his account by reporting that prior to Na'od's accession to the throne, a monk named Yoḥannes heard a heavenly voice deliver a prophetic couplet, which, through cryptic wordplay, asserted that Na'od's reign would be esteemed and distinctive. The historian went on to explain that this prophecy initially perplexed him, but that its meaning was subsequently revealed by the course of events. As the monk predicted, Na'od proved to be an especially capable emperor, and as a result, "all of the people of Ethiopia were strengthened by his faith and the greatness of his kingdom. The good lowered their heads, the wicked were removed, and the good were glorified by him."[123] To illustrate the prophecy's veracity, the historian relates several episodes that demonstrate the emperor's just and capable reign: his deft handling of an insurrectionary notable; his wise response to the tumult caused by allegations of wrongs committed in years past; his dutiful reburial of Zär'a Ya'eqob, his grandfather, in Dägä Estifanos, a Lake Tana monastery; and his "unmasking" of Jews among his people.[124] In the historian's estimation, these were all appropriate responses to good and evil. His biography of the emperor is carefully structured to make a historical argument: if the introductory prophecy represents the claim, the narrative offers the factual evidence that sustains it, proving the truth of the puzzling words from the heavens.[125]

Rather more ingenious is the role of supernatural premonition in the biography of Emperor Bakkäffa. Its author reported that prophecies about the good nature of his future reign were "on the lips of the *liqawent* and the hermits," from his birth until his accession to the throne. But possibly recognizing the reader's understandable suspicions of Christian magic and doubts about the significance of retrospectively reported prophecies, the historian proceeds to relate an episode demonstrating that "the pagans also knew [of] his future reign." He explains:

> Listen to me, you who are the guardians of the kingdom, listen to what I say to you, I, the author of this history. For I was following his father the king to the country of Gibé. While the king marched through a land that is called Tulu Quba Luba, a Galla [Oromo] found me and spoke at length with me, saying "Show me . . . the son of the king called Bakkäffa." And I showed him to him. After three days, this Galla found me again and said to me: "Know therefore, o man, that this child who is called Bakkäffa will rule powerfully and . . . [bring into submission] the Mečča and the Tulama together." I said to him, "How do you know this, you who are a pagan?" And he responded to me, "I know it through my father's divinatory signs." Returning to the city of the king, Gondär, I related this event to the king and informed many individuals so that they could be my witnesses, because I attest to what I have seen and heard.[126]

As with the Na'od chronicle, the evidence of Emperor Bakkäffa's greatness is subsequently outlined in the remainder of the history, confirming all the premonitive claims, Christian and pagan alike. This was a subtly historicized argument, one that documented a reality that was of mysterious design.

Other historians made their arguments without recourse to prophetic claims, endeavoring to let the facts speak for themselves. This kind of implicit argumentation is evident in works that describe rulers with unusual, suspect, or contested claims to power, such as the histories of Emperor Bä'edä Maryam, *etégé* Mentewwab, and *ras* Mika'él.[127] The author of the first of these exemplifies this approach: he subtly but forcefully advances a case for the legitimacy of his subject's claim to dynastic succession, a question that apparently generated some dispute during his reign. The earliest sections of the account outline in tremendous detail the tributes Bä'edä Maryam obtained and the pious endowments he made, showing his close connection to the church. After the author's description of the challenges to the emperor's fitness to rule, the final sections document the emperor's work as a defender of the faith and its institutions by describing his campaigns against some of the empire's non-Christian neighbors. After his conquest of the latter, he continued to act as an agent of the development of Christianity by building lavish churches and encouraging conversions. Throughout, the historian's account mixes chronological narrative with asynchronous topical discussions, and there is an absence of metaphorical language. At many points, the historian attempts to aid his purpose by strictly adhering to factual reportage, offering ostensible transcriptions of royal speeches, messengers, and epistles. Ultimately, the combination of these various elements was meant to show that the slanders against Emperor Bä'edä Maryam were false. The emperor was a good Solomonid, when examined closely.

Historical arguments occasionally strayed beyond matters of lineage and reputation to address more general historical questions. This is the case with the short biography of Emperor Lebnä Dengel, the anonymous author of which offers a fact-based argument about the potential historical agency of subaltern actors. After describing the conquests of one of the emperor's Muslim rivals, the Adali governor Gärad Emar, the historian explains that a poor person "whose name is unknown" sneaked into Emar's bedchamber while he was with his concubine, and killed him. This daring act then led the historian to reflect on the nature of providence and historical agency:

> I admire the greatness of the power of God that did so in order to circumcise the arrogance of the heart of Christians and Muslims. If a Christian noble had done such a thing, he would have said: "It is by my own strength that I have done and not by the power of God"; the entirety of Ethiopia would not be able to contain him or elevate him high enough, especially if he was one of the chiefs of Tegray. But God, who knows the hidden things, wanted to shame the powerful, making use of a poor person of which nobody thought, and the strength hit neither by lance nor sword, but by a little dagger of two edges that we call *šotal*.[128]

In this instance, the weak accomplished with a modest instrument what the strong and haughty could not, and if historians typically focused their attention on great men and their deeds, this did not mean that the small had no role to play.[129] The chronicler's point would seem to be that while Emperor Lebnä Dengel was the preeminent agent of sacred history at that time, he had help.[130]

Analytic historical writing occasionally went further by seeking to explain change over time and historical dynamics more generally. The Gälawdéwos biography offers glimpses of this approach, since its author occasionally looks beyond the level of event to the large-scale historical conjuncture. In his later chapters, for example, he frames the discussion of the renewed Muslim-Christian rivalry of the sixteenth century in terms of the changing geopolitical context, noting the two "great worries" of the Solomonids: the Adali-Ottoman alliance and the Catholic missionary enterprise.[131] His poetic conclusion to the chronicle returned to this theme, calling the emperor to action "lest the Muslims usurp our heritage and lest the people of Rome take our land."[132] In pointing to this dual tension, he acknowledged a break with the past and the inauguration of a new era defined by heightened interregional antagonism. The sixteenth century was, in fact, an epochal "turning point" noted by several of his contemporaries, and certainly by historians today.[133]

Similar are the occasional attempts at secular comparative analysis. One such case appears in a seventeenth-century universal chronography that conceptualized variations in the human community through the lens of political authority. Beginning with the events of scriptural antiquity, such as the Great Flood, and continuing through the eras of the Israelites, the Romans, the early church, and the Solomonids, the author of this work ranges rather widely in space and time. In a revealing passage, he writes, "The kings of Greece and Rome were called the Metropolitan of Metropolitans and Caesar of Caesars. And in addition, the kings of Egypt and Jerusalem were [likewise] called the Pharaoh of Pharaohs and the Herod of Herods . . . And so it was that [Ethiopia's rulers] were called *aṣé*," that is, *negusä nägäśt*, lit. "King of Kings."[134] His underlying assumption was clear: just as Ethiopia was defined by the institution of Solomonic monarchy, so too could foreign societies be understood through the synecdoche of imperial power. Everywhere, rulers were chief agents of history.

Abba Baḥrey made similar kinds of historical comparisons in his writings. In his ethnohistory of the Oromo, he introduces his work by explaining that the Oromo, Safavids, and Muslims in general share the quality of being unfairly maligned as "bad people" by Christian historians, coming close to suggesting that the task of historical reconstruction was more complex than most of his colleagues would openly admit.[135] In his biography of Emperor Śärṣä Dengel, he offered similarly measured comparative observations of the Ottomans, the allies of the emperor's antagonist Yesehaq, and he carefully contrasted the "swaggering" of the Adalite sultan Muhammad with the noble comportment of Asma'adin, the Christian emperor's loyal and clever Muslim liege.[136] These nuanced assessments are quite different from the comparisons made in epic history, such as the passages in the Amdä Ṣeyon chronicle describing Muslim scholars, who were "neither sages nor men of learning," but "foolish imposters" who "predict the future by consulting the sand and who interrogate the sun, moon, and stars."[137] This historian sought to disparage through moral condemnation; *abba* Baḥrey sought to understand through fact.

In some texts, all four historical modes—instructive, descriptive, epic, and explicatory—co-exist. This is true of the biography of Emperor Lalibäla, which is both a hagiography of the man, and a historical discussion and description of the monolithic churches he built, with the latter kept somewhat distinct from the rest of the text. Although the writer attributes the churches to divine inspiration, they and their creation are described with specificity. He discusses the tools their construction required and noted that the common people of that time possessed considerable knowledge of the craft of rock-hewing, "a certain science." He then offers a detailed description of the physical features of the churches and their configuration, and concludes by noting the incompleteness of his account given the great difficulty of describing such tremendous achievements in words. This section of the text recalls a similar discussion of church building in the Amdä Ṣeyon chronicle, and more generally, the prophetic descriptions of the Third Temple in Ezekiel.[138]

Similar is *abba* Baḥrey's magisterial and nuanced biography of Emperor Śärṣä Dengel, certainly one of the richest contributions to the vernacular tradition. The chapters dealing with the emperor's reign are the work of a masterful historian and a skilled literary stylist.[139] The first three describe the emperor's stormy ascent to the throne and the succession struggle that ensued. In this, the emperor and his allies were opposed by *ras* Hamälmal, *azzaž* Rom Sägäd, *azmač* Täklä Haymanot (Taklo), and their coteries. While the historian relates the conflict from the perspective of the emperor's camp, he devotes considerable attention to the words, deeds, and personalities of his rivals, who each receive somewhat exonerative biographies. He then deals with the troubles of the emperor and the ensuing "time of victories and power."[140] There is an examination of the renewed conflict between the emperor and Yesehaq, and the former's rivalry with Sultan Muhammad of Adal. The climax of the narrative relates the epic battle in 1578 between the forces of the emperor and those of Yesehaq and the Ottomans (the latter's allies), described in rich detail with a host of humorous, inspiring, and graphic anecdotes. It is followed by appended chapters dealing with subsequent events.

This complex and sophisticated work unfolds on several levels: it relates the saga of the emperor and his antagonists, which is factually embedded in a series of revealed true and false prophecies, and morally situated in the ongoing struggle between justice and injustice and the oppressed and their oppressors.[141] The work is densely packed with prophecies fulfilled, "prophets of lies," and a carefully enumerated series of premonitive claims by the emperor himself. These serve to introduce analytic elements, much like the prophecies discussed above.[142] The struggle for justice, for example, is embodied in the heroic triumph of the oppressed, who are naturally (if somewhat confusingly) the emperor and his supporters—and not the numerous common folk, who are subjected to the predations of the emperor and his rivals, or the Oromo and Muslims, who continually face the emperor's sword. On the wings of this stage are the memories of emperors past, most notably Gälawdéwos, whose actions haunt many of Śärṣä Dengel's contemporaries, and who serves as an interpretive device for the historian himself.[143] This history drew stylistically and scholastically upon what was by then a large corpus of received and highly intertextual historical writings. In it, the historical urges to narrate and reveal are intertwined, just like the two divinely bestowed gifts described in the beginning of this chapter.

This was the inherited historical tradition. Its enduring features were defined by the general interplay between the influence of political power and traditionalism. This interplay was manifest in the tradition's overlapping observational and reproductive tendencies, its genres of royal biography, dynastic history, and universal chronography, and its instructive, descriptive, epic, and explicatory modes. Some of its exponents were leading scholars of the day, writing new accounts from the vistas of their lofty imperial stations. Others were modest stewards and preservers, copying, transmitting, modifying, and preserving the learning of their intellectual forebears. In some cases, historians were highly accomplished literary stylists and shrewd observers of change over time. Their efforts have become essential sources for later scholars who wish to reconstruct the Ethiopian past. Eventually, the established features of their vernacular discipline began to evolve in the last decades of the nineteenth century, making way for new forms of historical inquiry and imagination. It is to these that we will now turn.

2

Gäbrä Krestos Täklä Haymanot and the History of Progress

In 1924, Gäbrä Krestos Täklä Haymanot (1892–1932) wrote a history that looked far beyond his home in Addis Ababa. His *Aččer yä'aläm tarik bamareña*, or *Short History of the World in Amharic*, concisely surveyed two millennia of human history for the Ethiopian reader, all in a single panoptic narrative.[1] He began with a chapter on ancient history entitled "The People of India" and concluded with the contemporary "Ethiopia of Empress Zäwditu's Time," attending along the way to such diverse subjects as "The History of Japan," "The Roman State in the Time of Christ," "The United States," "How the French Became a Mob," "The Vast Wisdom of the Last One Hundred Years," and "The War of Emperor Menilek and Italy." As these topics suggest, Gäbrä Krestos made a radical break with the conventions of vernacular historiography. His innovations were threefold. He transgressed the received generic boundaries of royal biography, dynastic history, and universal chronography, disregarding centuries of scholarly precedent. He also reconceptualized the historical subject, moving beyond the Solomonid dynastic drama to consider foreign actors and global processes of change. And perhaps most significantly, he envisioned a new kind of accessible history to instruct Ethiopia's emerging reading public. This was in some respects his boldest innovation: he wrote popular history, not traditionalist scholarship, and he believed it would contribute to Ethiopia's intellectual and national emancipation. The *Short History* befit the new era.

So did its author. As a historian, Gäbrä Krestos was quite unlike the court historians and church scholars who preceded him. His professional station was entirely new: he was a civil servant, a public intellectual, the manager of a state press, and the editor of Ethiopia's most popular Amharic newspaper. The nature of his literary output was equally novel. His historical writings were neither observational testaments nor elaborations of an inherited tradition, but were instead synthetic attempts to grapple with foreign ideas and the problems of the era's burgeoning culture of reform and modernization. He also embraced a new text medium: unlike most of his predecessors and some of his peers, Gäbrä Krestos was committed to the educational power of print, a technology then transforming intellectual culture throughout the Red Sea region. Like many of his contemporaries in early twentieth-century Africa and Asia, he was a cosmopolitan intellectual who inhabited the boundary between local and translocal worlds, and his life and career was marked by the tensions between the two. Ultimately, he sought to reconcile modernity and cultural authenticity by rewriting history.

This chapter examines Gäbrä Krestos and his *Short History* with two goals in mind. It considers his life and work, and it uses these to illuminate the changing nature of historical thinking in early twentieth-century Ethiopia. It does so by examining in turn Gäbrä Krestos, the historical culture he inhabited, and his contribution to this milieu: the domestication of the idea of progress through historiography.

The Icarus of Print

In the last decades of the nineteenth century, Northeast Africa entered a period of intense and prolonged crisis. Against a backdrop of chronic drought, famine, and epidemic, the region's Muslim and Christian polities faced new and formidable European challenges to their sovereignty after the opening of the Suez Canal in 1869. That year, the Italian Rubattino Shipping Company purchased the Red Sea port of Assäb from two local sultans, and three years later, a French firm obtained a commercial concession in present-day Djibouti. The Italians then expanded to Massawa in 1885, claimed the coastal regions between their two ports, and annexed Asmära and the northern edge of the highlands in 1889. These territories were then consolidated in 1890 to form Italy's first African colony, Eritrea. Emperor Menilek II managed to check Italian expansion with a dramatic military victory at Adwa in 1896, but other large-scale challenges to European power ultimately failed. In Sudan, the millenarian Mahdist state collapsed following military defeat by the British in 1898, and in Somalia, the anticolonial jihad led by Sheikh Muhammad Abdulle Hasan—better known to European journalists as "the Mad Mullah of Somaliland"—abruptly ended with its leader's death in 1920. By that time, the region had been forcibly partitioned into Italian, French, and British colonies and protectorates, while urbanization, settler immigration, and increased market integration began reshaping everyday life. It was a tumultuous period in which local and global processes of change collided, in a region astride the intersecting frontiers of Africa, the Middle East, and the Indian Ocean arena.

Gäbrä Krestos was born amidst this turmoil in 1892, in the Eritrean highlands of rural Ḥamasén.[2] His father *aläqa* Täklä Haymanot Meherka (n.d.–1937) was a church scholar and music teacher originally from Aksum, and as a young boy Gäbrä Krestos spent his early years in the village of Wäki, where his father worked.[3] He almost certainly began his studies with a traditional church education, which would have included calligraphy, scripture, and prayer. In 1908, he left his family to "improve [himself] at the Swedish missionary school" in Asmära, the nearby colonial capital.[4] It was a decision that altered the course of his life.

Asmära was then a booming and cosmopolitan town of roughly five thousand inhabitants. It was composed of an indigenous old quarter with a mosque, Orthodox church, and traditional thatched-roof homes, as well as a growing European quarter, which included the new governor's palace, the courthouse, colonial offices, and services catering to European settlers, such as a pharmacy, theater, synagogue, and Catholic as well as Greek Orthodox churches.[5] Like the city's wide avenues and bustling markets, the Swedish missionary compound was a multicultural enclave in the northeast of the city adjacent to the train station and the so-called native quarter.[6] It was a link between indigenous and European Asmära.

The Swedish Evangelical Mission, or Evangeliska Fosterlands-Stiftelsen (EFS), was Eritrea's most active Protestant missionary organization. By the first decades of the twentieth century, its distinctive mission stations, schools, orphanages, and hospitals could be found throughout the colony, both along the coast and in the highlands. In the 1890s, the Swedes came to Asmära with the Italians, and by the time Gäbrä Krestos arrived, the EFS served a sizeable congregation and managed elementary schools, a boarding school, an industrial trade school, and a prolific mission press.[7] In 1913, the EFS made Asmära the headquarters of its mission in the colony, and by the 1920s, the missionaries served at least two hundred indigenous students in the city's schools.[8]

The growth of the Asmära mission reflected the collective efforts of a diverse group of individuals. In the early twentieth century, Jonas Iwarson (1867–1947) was the most prominent Swedish missionary in Asmära and indeed the colony. He arrived in the capital in 1897, and labored there for three decades as a pastor, teacher, and eventually the director of the EFS mission in Eritrea. He was joined by his second wife, Louise Lindfors (1874–1942), who also worked for years in Asmära and its environs.[9] They were a remarkable pair: in addition to their pastoral work, they were prolific authors and occasional missiologists, or scholars of intercultural evangelism.[10] Gäbrä Krestos later praised Iwarson as his respected and "honorable" teacher.[11]

Several Italian Protestants also worked at the Asmära school during Gäbrä Krestos's time there. One of these was Benedetto Giudici

(1862–1926). Born into a Catholic family, he had entered the Jesuit order and obtained a doctorate from the Pontifical Gregorian University in Rome before joining the Waldensian Reformed Church.[12] He worked in domestic missions until 1902, when he and his wife came to Eritrea to work with the EFS at Iwarson's request. By 1909, when Gäbrä Krestos arrived, Giudici was the head of the Asmära school for boys. Iwarson later recalled that he was "a gifted and profound" educator who was remembered with respect and fondness by his former students and colleagues.[13]

Alessandro Tron (1887–1966) was another important Waldensian at the Asmära school. He arrived in the colony in 1909, and replaced Giudici as the head of the school after the latter's departure in 1913.[14] He led this institution for the next thirteen years, save for a year-long sabbatical at a Waldensian theological school in Florence,[15] and became an increasingly prominent leader of the EFS mission, especially as colonial administrators grew suspicious of the Swedes as subversive foreigners and adherents to a "cold white faith."[16] Tron became a particularly close colleague of Gäbrä Krestos.[17]

Finally, the Asmära mission depended upon the contributions of many indigenous teachers, lay preachers, seminarians, printers, and colporteurs. These were both evangelical converts, or *keniša*, and sympathetic Orthodox reformers who supported the missionaries' vision of a scripture-based spiritual revival in the highlands. In 1909 and 1910, Iwarson ordained the first indigenous pastors, *qäši* Täwälde Medhin Gäbru (n.d.–1930) and *qäši* Täklä Täsfä Krestos, and a considerable number followed.[18] By 1917, an EFS gazette estimated that Eritrean mission workers outnumbered the Europeans by a large margin: its authors reported that seventy male and twelve female indigenous teachers assisted thirty Europeans in the colony.[19] By the 1930s, there were eighteen indigenous pastors.[20] These were the pioneers of the Eritrean evangelical church.

Gäbrä Krestos thrived in this cosmopolitan evangelical milieu. After completing his elementary studies at the Asmära school, he married and began a teacher-training program at the age of twenty, and was teaching in the mission school by 1914.[21] Its curriculum at that time reflected a hybrid of evangelical ambitions and Italian colonial prerogatives: the course of study included Italian, Amharic, and Tigrinya, as well as "arithmetic, history, geography, and various other subjects."[22] Gäbrä Krestos mastered these and was apparently a talented teacher: his son, Keflä Egzi'e Yeḫdägu, later wrote that his father was "much praised for his help" at the school, and a Swedish colleague recalled that Gäbrä Krestos "profited greatly by the education he got in the mission school, and was one of the mission's best native-born teachers."[23]

In addition to his teaching, Gäbrä Krestos contributed to the pioneering activities of the Asmära mission press. Like other Protestant missionaries,

Figure 2.1. EFS native teacher training, ca. 1911. *Missions-Tidning*, December 1, 1911. Reproduced by permission from the Swedish Evangelical Mission.

the EFS devoted considerable energy to promoting vernacular literacy and producing affordable print editions of the scriptures, which they understood as complementary modes of evangelization. As one EFS missionary observed, "one cannot be a good evangelical Christian unless one can read one's own Bible."[24] To this end, the EFS imported a press, and commenced publication at Monkullu in 1886 with an Amharic *Commentary on the Gospel of St. Matthew*, one of the first texts to be printed in the Horn of Africa.[25] After a few decades, the mission relocated the press to Asmära, where the production of printed books in local languages became torrential.[26] By 1916, the missionaries reported that they had distributed 1,053 copies of the scriptures, and printed 2,620 books on both religious and secular topics.[27]

Gäbrä Krestos witnessed and contributed to this particularly productive and creative period at the EFS press. In 1909, the missionaries began publishing a Tigrinya periodical, *Mäl'eketi sälam*, and in 1912, they produced an eclectic Tigrinya compilation called *Berhan yeḥun*, which included sermons, biographies of Italian royalty by Giudici, a mission history of Ḥamasén by pastors *qäši* Sälomon Aṣqu (n.d.–1926) and *qäši* Zär'a Ṣeyon Musé (n.d.–ca. 1940), and a critical study of Emperor Menilek by Gäbrä Ḥeywät Baykädañ (1886–1919), discussed below.[28] Gäbrä Krestos likely read these works in school, and he later applied himself to similar print endeavors with great success. In 1917, he assisted Tron with the preparation of a Tigrinya guide for the mission's native teachers, perhaps the first vernacular pedagogical manual of its kind.[29] The two then collaborated again on a Tigrinya mathematics textbook, which was published in 1923.[30]

Figure 2.2. Inside the Asmära EFS press, ca. 1931. *Missions-Tidning*, December 6, 1931. Reproduced by permission from the Swedish Evangelical Mission.

By that time, though, Gäbrä Krestos had left Asmära. Amid escalating tensions between the Italian colonial authorities and the "foreign" EFS, Iwarson began to consider the possibility of a new base of operations in Addis Ababa, the political and commercial capital of independent Ethiopia. It was then a booming city of approximately one hundred thousand inhabitants, principally Amhara and Oromo but with substantial Armenian, Greek, Indian, and European populations. The city's broad avenues hosted encounters between the peoples of the north and south, and its stately noble residences, government offices, and public spaces exemplified the imperial order and its culture of power. The new flower—Addis Ababa—was blooming.[31]

The city was also home to a sizeable community of Eritrean evangelical émigrés, and since Crown Prince Täfäri Mäkonnen seemed amenable to European missionary activity, the EFS established a mission station there.[32] It was this mission that Iwarson visited in February of 1920, when he met with local missionaries and a number of his former students from the EFS schools in Eritrea. Three months later, in May, the EFS dispatched the talented linguist and Asmära press veteran Olle Eriksson (1878–1962) to lead the evangelical enterprise in the Ethiopian capital.[33]

Gäbrä Krestos arrived one month later. According to his son, he admired the patriotism of the crown prince and the self-sacrificing spirit of the Ethiopian people, and he resolved to emigrate to Ethiopia with his wife and children.[34] The suddenness of his departure suggests that this may have been a political act. The plan was approved by the Ethiopian consul in Asmära, and Gäbrä Krestos left the Italian colony for Addis Ababa, with his family following shortly afterward.[35] In the Ethiopian capital, Eriksson was pleased to see his talented acquaintance from Asmära, whom he enlisted as a teacher for the local mission school.[36] However, before this work could begin, the crown prince selected Gäbrä Krestos to direct a venture that exemplified the modernizing currents of the era: the new state-owned Täfäri Mäkonnen Press, later known as Berhanenna Sälam, or "Light and Peace."[37] It was another turning point in Gäbrä Krestos's career. His Asmära education, mission connections, translation work, and print experience qualified him for the job of a lifetime.

In many ways, the new press was the institutional embodiment of Täfäri Mäkonnen's program of state-led educational and administrative reform. The 1920s were a pivotal period for the crown prince and the educated, urban elites who depended upon his largesse and political patronage: it was an era of intense collective focus on national emancipation and revitalization. Historian Bahru Zewde notes that Täfäri Mäkonnen and the reformist intellectuals around him shared "a conviction that the political independence that the country had achieved by a remarkable feat of arms was meaningless unless it was accompanied by the modernization of society."[38] To achieve this transformative end, the crown prince reorganized the civil administration, improved customs and tax collection, and expanded the public education system, and many Ethiopian intellectuals and civil servants began to publicly discuss economic, educational, and social reforms that would encourage what they described as *śelleṭṭané*, or "civilization." National modernization, they believed, was the key to preserving Ethiopia's political sovereignty.

These currents of change were buttressed and sustained by a state-sponsored print revolution. The first publishing house was conceived by Emperor Menilek, who in 1905 imported and installed a printing press in the palace under the direction of *qäññazmač* Däḫané Wäldä Maryam.[39] This official press—known variously as the Imprimerie Éthiopienne and Märḥa Ṭebäb, or "Guide of Wisdom"—produced official publications and two Amharic newspapers: *A'emro* (Knowledge), which appeared irregularly for the next few decades, and *Yäṭor wäré* (News of War), which described the First World War for local readers.[40] The same period also witnessed the private publication of the French newspaper *Courrier d'Éthiopie*, which focused on commercial news related to the Red Sea arena.[41]

Crown Prince Täfäri Mäkonnen decided to build upon these efforts after becoming the de facto head of state. In 1917 he created a translation bureau to prepare Amharic versions of the Ge'ez scriptures, and in 1921 he established the Täfäri Mäkonnen/Berhanenna Sälam press to bring these and other Amharic books to a large audience.[42] The state press was an extremely successful endeavor: it published nearly fifty Amharic books before 1935, produced several Amharic and foreign-language newspapers, and sponsored Amharic translations of many Ge'ez, Tigrinya, and European-language works.[43] Its output fostered the spread of vernacular literacy by providing low-cost, printed texts to Ethiopian readers, and in the process, its publications transformed the Amharic language by introducing neologisms and foreign loan-words into common usage.[44] Cheap printed books and informal learning took their place alongside the specialized manuscripts and exclusive scholarly culture of earlier times.[45]

Gäbrä Krestos thrived in this reformist milieu. After his appointment as director of the state press in 1921, he wrote an Amharic math textbook that was among its first publications.[46] The press reprinted this work twice in the coming decade.[47] That same year, he collaborated with Eriksson on an Amharic language textbook, a geography textbook, and a volume of saints' lives, all published by the EFS press.[48] By 1922, he had acquired sufficient prestige to be included in Ḫeruy's biographical dictionary of notables, which discussed his achievements alongside those of Ethiopia's and Eritrea's most respected nobles, church scholars, military leaders, and ancient heroes.[49] In 1924, Gäbrä Krestos published the *Short History*, and later that year, the crown prince selected him to be the editor of a new Amharic newspaper, also called *Berhanenna sälam*, which Gäbrä Krestos had envisioned.[50] In 1927, the press had become so successful that it relocated from the palace to a larger office in the capital, opened regional offices in Ǧemma and Harär, and began producing several additional newspapers.[51] Throughout this period, Gäbrä Krestos served as *Berhanenna sälam*'s contributing editor and the director of the growing press, effectively managing the two institutions that were the sinews of reformist intellectual life.

This was a major achievement. For many Ethiopian intellectuals, print held tremendous significance as an instrument of national emancipation. Indeed, it is difficult to overstate the meaning it had for some of its supporters. One of Gäbrä Krestos's longtime colleagues at the press, Dämessé Wäldä Gäbr'él, described the newspaper in particularly grandiose terms: "By revealing that which had been hidden, by reporting that which was distant, by illuminating that which had become dark, by making clear that which was profound, [and] by reconciling [that is, restoring] that which had been abandoned, this newspaper called *Berhanenna sälam* made a foundation for the wisdom of the ages."[52] With similar esteem, *qäññazmač* Däḫané, the director of Märḥa Ṭebäb, and *ṣäḥafé te'ezaz* Wäldä Masqal, one of Täfäri Makonnen's many appointed historians, observed that printing created an intellectual foundation for the nation,[53] while Ḫeruy lauded the affordability of printed books, which enabled "all people [to] begin to grow in knowledge and wisdom."[54] Even the crown prince, who personally financed the press and who reviewed its operations each day, recalled that "all the people . . . derived much benefit from reading what they could buy at a low price."[55] Some junior press employees shared these sentiments. Andargé Damṭé, a thirty-seven-year veteran of Berhanenna Sälam, recalled that in its early days, "all of us had the impression that there was nothing in the whole world like working in a printing press. It was something beyond description, a miracle."[56] Even the metaphor-laden names of the various newspapers and presses reflect the era's optimistic confidence in print.[57]

Yet some believed the power of print was dangerous. *Aläqa* Gäbrä Egzi'abḥér Elyas (1892–1969), who worked as an assistant treasurer in the customs office before becoming a translator, copyist, and illuminator for the Ministry of the Pen, described some of the apprehensions that emerged in conservative circles:

> The church scholars became worried saying, "We alone used to be praised, being expert on books, and we were rewarded for this. But now, after all the books have been printed in Amharic, who will come to ask us [questions]?" And true enough, as the scholars feared, all the noblemen and noble ladies bought the [new] books and were bothering the priests with questions arising from their daily reading [of these books].[58]

More worrying concerns were advanced by *aläqa* Kidanä Wäldä Keflé (1870–1944), a brilliant church scholar who argued that the influence of printing was pernicious. In his view, it undermined Ethiopia's linguistic heritage by popularizing simplified and therefore impoverished varieties of Amharic, which he termed *yämisyon* q^{w}*anq*^{w}*a*, or "mission language," and *yäšumoč* q^{w}*anq*^{w}*a*, or "appointees' language" (i.e., bureaucratese).[59] The scribe Täklä Giyorgis Naqé described more oblique fears, recalling that he had initially refused an invitation to work at a press because "I considered it a job for the devil. I was not the only one, all my colleagues thought the same."[60] Still other scholars simply ignored printing in their writings. Thus the Addis Ababa-based *aläqa* Kenfé barely acknowledged the new print culture in his detailed annals of the era, despite the fact that he closely observed Täfäri Mäkonnen and the urban elite who were its key supporters.[61] While it is difficult to gauge the relative strength of these suspicions, it is clear that some of Ethiopia's conservative scholars believed that presses and printed books were poised to undermine the traditional order they were working to protect. The fact that many advocates of print were also Protestant and Catholic converts surely added to these fears.[62]

Given these diverging perceptions of printing, Gäbrä Krestos was forced into a precarious mediating role as the director of the state press and editor of its newspaper. On the one hand, he was committed to marshalling print to the reformist program of intellectual emancipation. On the other, he had to balance this disruptive aim with his duty to preserve Ethiopia's traditions and intellectual inheritance—an especially delicate concern given his ties to the EFS and evangelical Christianity. He was thus required to be both a harbinger of change and a steward of Ethiopia's heritage.

By nearly all accounts, Gäbrä Krestos was tremendously successful in these roles. The work at the press was slow and arduous: the typesetting and printing took place in several stages, and a production rate of ten to twenty pages per hour was considered efficient.[63] Dämessé Wäldä Gabr'él, a colleague, recalled that he had "an honest and patient character," and that he disdained official rank and managerial pretensions, instead preferring to work unceasingly alongside his employees, sometimes spending months away from his home.[64] Many years later, former press employees wrote that he was "a hardworking and dedicated man, [who] never spared time even to go home for lunch. Instead he had his lunch brought to him in his office and as soon as he had finished it, he continued with his work."[65] Even the deaths of his parents did not interrupt his service to the press and his commitment to its workers.[66] *Blattén géta* Marse'é Ḫazan Wäldä Qirqos (1899–1978), who was employed at the press as a young man, recalled that "it was very tiring to train and introduce the people to the newspaper, and the perseverance of the director above all was to be admired."[67] Gäbrä Krestos's diligence evidently pleased his patron Täfäri Mäkonnen, who recognized his service with many medals and honors.[68]

Eventually, though, Gäbrä Krestos's work placed him at the center of political controversy, when his newspaper published an incendiary critique of European imperialism. It came at a particularly tense period in Ethiopian foreign relations. After Ethiopia joined the League of Nations in 1923, Täfäri Mäkonnen entered into tense and delicate negotiations with Italians over Ethiopia's maritime access, culminating in a formal declaration of Italo-Ethiopian friendship.[69] Not all Ethiopians shared the crown prince's confidence in the implications of the new diplomatic agreements. Empress Zäwditu herself was particularly uncomfortable, endorsing a more conservative approach to diplomacy that saw isolationism as the key to Ethiopia's sovereignty. At the same time, Täfäri Mäkonnen's negotiations also generated criticism among more strident nationalists, who saw it as a foolhardy negotiation with the enemy.[70]

This discontent spilled over into the March 17, 1927, issue of *Berhanenna sälam*, which replaced the usually benign contents of the "News from Abroad" column with an anonymous article entitled "Fascists and Ethiopia."[71] After an introduction by Gäbrä Krestos that explained how fascism "has changed the face of the country [of Italy]," the column continued with translated excerpts from a recent article in the French syndicalist monthly *La révolution prolétarienne*.[72] The piece repeated themes common in European antifascist politics of the interwar period, focusing in particular on the topic of Italy's imperial ambitions in the Horn of Africa. Its anonymous author suggested that war and emigration had brought Italy to a political and economic crisis that might be resolved through conquest, and pointedly observed that "if Mussolini's eye is upon attacking other countries, then Ethiopia is the one." The author also noted that while he knew the Italian people "appreciated and respected" liberty, he was "stupefied" to see a "dictator" ruling them so easily.[73]

The article was explosive. The reference to Mussolini as a dictator infuriated the Italian Legation in Addis Ababa, which immediately made a formal protest to the crown prince.[74] Täfäri Mäkonnen was displeased, and with Ḫeruy's assistance, he attempted to identify the parties responsible for the article. There were several suspects: the Austrian journalist Erich Weinzinger, the anarchist-connected Ethiopian Jewish intellectual Tä'ammrat Amanu'el (1888–1963), and the latter's Polish orientalist colleague Jacques Faitlovitch (1881–1955). But it was Gäbrä Krestos who ultimately took responsibility for the piece. As punishment, Täfäri Mäkonnen fined him one hundred Maria Theresa thalers and sentenced him to a month of imprisonment.[75] In addition, Tä'ammrat was fined, his Jewish school closed, and the issue of the newspaper containing the article was removed from circulation.[76] The affair was covered by at least two foreign newspapers, *The Times* of London and *La Tribuna* of Rome.[77] This was a local event of international significance.

Gäbrä Krestos's confession appears to have been a selfless act of managerial self-immolation. In a letter to Faitlovitch, Tä'ammrat admitted to translating the French article and "adding a few words on Mussolini." However, he claimed to have warned Gäbrä Krestos not to publish the article without first "studying the political situation." He also reported that Täfäri Mäkonnen had told the Italian Legation that Gäbrä Krestos was being punished not for publishing the article, but instead for disobeying the crown prince's request to be shown drafts of all prospective articles on foreign affairs.[78] The director was thus guilty of editorial dereliction rather than anticolonial exuberance.

Yet these details were insignificant. By the next issue of *Berhanenna sälam*, Gäbrä Krestos's name was conspicuously absent from the masthead on the front page, and later that year, Täfäri Mäkonnen appointed *qäññazmač* Däḇané's son Gäbrä Śellasé as the director of the state press.[79] The latter was replaced the following year by Maḥtämä Wärq Ešetu, with the future *ṣähafé te'ezaz* Wäldä Giyorgis Wäldä Yoḥannes serving as the deputy editor.[80] Undeterred by these developments, Gäbrä Krestos

Figure 2.3. Evangelical congregation of Addis Ababa, ca. 1931. Gäbrä Krestos can be seen at center left. *Missions-Tidning*, April 19, 1931. Reproduced by permission from the Swedish Evangelical Mission.

undertook several new print-related projects. He assisted "Hakim" Wärqenäh Ešäté (1865–1952), Marse'é Ḫazan, and Ḫeruy with the production of an Amharic geography textbook, and he collaborated with Eriksson on a new translation of Bible stories.[81] He also continued to serve the EFS congregation of Addis Ababa.[82]

Gäbrä Krestos died suddenly in 1932, succumbing to typhus fever at the relatively young age of forty-two. His death was a public event of some significance. His *Berhanenna sälam* obituary, written by his son, noted the considerable number of mourners at his funeral at Ṗéṭros and Ṗawlos Church in Addis Ababa, and it described Gäbrä Krestos as "a true son of the land." This obituary in the newspaper to which he had devoted his life included both a portrait and a mournful *qené* poem in Ge'ez by Wäldä Giyorgis Wäldä Yoḥannes, his colleague from the press.[83] In it, Wäldä Giyorgis rhetorically asked whether *Berhanenna sälam* would be able to continue its important work without him, given his personal role in its tremendous growth in the previous decade.[84] Dämessé Wäldä Gäbr'él, his long-time colleague and the author of another long remembrance in *Berhanenna sälam*, said that Gäbrä Krestos was an exemplary "friend of progress," and "a guardian [lit. *maḫedär*] of knowledge" who "sowed much in Ethiopia," and he concluded his piece with a song of lamentation for his former employer.[85] *A'emro*, the other major Amharic newspaper, featured another long article about

Gäbrä Krestos,[86] and accolades even came from the Swedish missionaries: Nils Nilsson penned an obituary for the EFS newspaper in which he noted that Gäbrä Krestos's "outward success did not draw him away from us, but with his influence he benefitted the evangelical enterprise."[87] The same paper published a photo that featured Gäbrä Krestos, characteristically, seated at his desk, surrounded by neatly stacked books.[88]

These glowing public eulogies suggest that, despite the scandal of the late 1920s, he had become one of the most prominent and public intellectuals of his day. It is telling that the *qené* poem that publicly mourned his passing metaphorically described him as the seal of Jerusalem, playing on the two meanings of the Amharic word "maḫetäm" to liken his devotion to mechanical printing to an authentic mark of piety.[89]

New Varieties of History

Though Gäbrä Krestos was celebrated as an educator, printer, and newspaper editor, he was also a historian, and he fused his many roles together in his *Short History*. Like his print career, his historical writing drew upon his varied background and dual cultural orientation. As he candidly noted in the introduction to his *Short History*, the work "did not simply emerge from my head . . . I listened to what my teachers at school told me, and wrote what I collected."[90] In this respect, his study exemplifies one of the key intellectual trends of the day: as a historian, Gäbrä Krestos was neither an observer nor a transmitter, but a creative synthesizer.

By the early twentieth century, Ethiopia's vernacular historical tradition was evolving into a more heterogenous historical culture, and local historians were boldly experimenting with new methods, sources, and analytical tools.[91] The most renowned of these innovators was Gäbrä Ḥeywät Baykädañ, one of the era's more controversial intellectuals. Born in 1886 near Adwa, he attended an EFS mission school in Monkullu, Eritrea, from whence he stowed away on a ship bound for Europe. He lived in Austria for several years, and after attending university in Germany, he returned to Ethiopia and was employed first by *leǧ* Iyyasu and then Crown Prince Täfäri Mäkonnen as a customs officer. He was a perspicacious social analyst as well as an able civil servant, and although he died at a relatively young age in 1919, his writings quickly earned him some notoriety. Even in 1922 Ḫeruy observed that "[Gäbrä Ḥeywät] was careful in his work and daring in his manner of speaking, and he really did not get along with the men of his time."[92]

This careful daring is evident in Gäbrä Ḥeywät's earliest work, *Aṭé Menilekenna ityopya*, or *Emperor Menilek and Ethiopia*, which appeared in *Berhan yeḥun*, an eclectic 1912 publication of the Asmära EFS press.[93] It is a critical study of then Emperor Menilek that begins with a discussion of the role of the historian and the nature of historical knowledge. Gäbrä Ḥeywät argues that Ethiopia was mired in an ignorance and darkness that made it vulnerable to external threats, and in his view, this situation was partially attributable to the manner in which his countrymen remembered their past. After defining the criteria of "true history," he asserted that "the historians of our country are in this respect incorrect: instead of observing the great things, they observe but the small; instead of judging equitably, they confine themselves to partiality; as their writing is disorderly, it is incomprehensible to the reader."[94] In his view, Ethiopian historians were ultimately doing a disservice to the nation by overly celebrating Ethiopia's rulers, blindly transmitting the received tradition, and avoiding rigorous and systematic analysis. The situation was so dire, in his view, that even "all the moderns [reformers] preferred elegy to criticism" in their historical writing.[95] To address these distortions, Gäbrä Ḥeywät presented what he believed was a more truthful history of Emperor Menilek, one that would possibly aid his successor *leǧ* Iyyasu. He considered the emperor's achievements and shortcomings, and he unfavorably contrasted Ethiopia's imperial system, highly dependent on the emperor himself, with the alternative of institutionalized, de-personalized political power.[96] He concluded with a series of reform proposals aiming to remedy the country's social and political ills. Overall, *Emperor Menilek and Ethiopia* is a provocative and evenhanded study, one which established a number of interpretations of Ethiopian history that have endured to the present day.[97]

Gäbrä Ḥeywät believed that modern Ethiopia required a suitably modern historiography. He apparently aimed to supply this with his second work, *Mängeśtenna yäḥezb astädadär*, or *Government and Public Administration*, a misleadingly titled study of Ethiopian history and political economy that was posthumously published by Berhanenna Sälam in 1923.[98] In it, Gäbrä Ḥeywät examines the human struggle to extract wealth from the environment, beginning with prehistory and antiquity and continuing through to early twentieth-century Ethiopia. He argues that the Ethiopian state and foreigners preyed upon Ethiopian cultivators and hindered economic development, and that widespread education and increased agricultural productivity were the keys to national progress. To make this argument, Gäbrä Ḥeywät employed a materialist analysis and a number of Marxian concepts, including modes of production, a stage theory of history, and the labor theory of value.[99] In his view, the principal struggle in Ethiopian society was not between social classes but between producers, consumers, and the state, and between Ethiopians and foreigners more generally.[100] These bold arguments about economic development and dependency resemble the contemporaneous positions of Mohandas Gandhi and Romesh Chunder Dutt, who similarly sought to understand the impoverishing impact of unequal exchange on colonial South Asia. In making them, Gäbrä Ḥeywät produced the first study of Ethiopian social and economic history—the first "truthful history," as he saw it.[101]

If Gäbrä Ḥeywät's historiographical achievements were conceptual, Tä'ammrat Amanu'el's were methodological. Tä'ammrat was an Ethiopian Jew, or Bétä Esra'él/Falasha; a descendent of the historian-compiler *däğğazmač* Ḥaylä Mika'él Ešäté, discussed in the previous chapter; and the protégé of Jacques Faitlovitch, a Polish orientalist and pro-Bétä Esra'él activist. Faitlovitch took him from an EFS school in Asmära to France and Italy, where Tä'ammrat studied rabbinic theology, Semitic languages, philosophy, and history, moved in antifascist circles, and had a romantic relationship with the famous Italian anarchist Leda Rafanelli (1880–1971).[102] Tä'ammrat returned to Ethiopia in the 1920s, where he ran a school for Ethiopian Jews in Addis Ababa and moved in reformist political circles. It was then that he became involved in the *Berhanenna sälam* controversy that cost Gäbrä Krestos his job.

Tä'ammrat's most prominent early foray into historiography came in 1936, when he published an innovative study of Ethiopian Jewish history in the Italian Zionist journal *La rassegna mensile di Israel*.[103] Writing for Italian Jews as an authentic representative of their newly conquered Ethiopian brethren, Tä'ammrat introduced and translated excerpts from *ṣäḥafé te'ezaz* Ṭino's chronicle of Emperor Susenyos that described the rise and fall of Gédéwon, a seventeenth-century Jewish warlord who aided a series of royal pretenders in campaigns against the emperor.[104] The first section of the article describes Gédéwon's alliance with a Christian rebel, which ended with Gédéwon turning on his erstwhile ally, submitting to the emperor, and delivering the rebel in chains. The latter was then crucified in the center of the imperial camp. Subsequent sections of the article describe the persecution, enslavement, and forced conversion of Ethiopia's Jews; marriage alliances between Christian and Jewish rebels; the subsequent Jewish rebellions against the emperor; and finally the defeat and execution of Gédéwon and his allies. To tell this tale, Tä'ammrat carefully selected, juxtaposed, and annotated fragmentary passages from Emperor Susenyos's chronicle, effectively reading against the grain of an unsympathetic and even hostile Solomonid source to describe the history of the Ethiopian Jews through the writings of their Christian enemies.[105] This was a bold attempt to recover the effaced history of a subaltern ethno-religious group—and it was certainly a creative departure from the established methods of vernacular historiography.[106]

Why did Tä'ammrat write this kind of historical study? And why did he publish it in a European Jewish journal? His effort certainly reflects the growing international interest in the Ethiopian Jews and their perceived plight. Tä'ammrat noted this trend in his introduction, and as a

European-educated Ethiopian Jew, he was ideally qualified to evaluate the indigenous historical record as it pertained to his co-religionists. Ṭino's chronicle was an especially rich text in this regard, since it describes a period of particularly dramatic antagonism between Ethiopian Christians and Jews. In bringing this work to a new audience, Tä'ammrat made a significant scholarly contribution to the Ethiopianist branch of Semitic studies, and to Jewish studies generally.[107]

There may have been an additional motivation behind his historical recuperation. The themes of persecution and resistance in the chronicle occasionally led Tä'ammrat to suggest its implications for the predicament of the Bétä Esra'él, and Jews more generally, in the 1930s.[108] This was an especially pressing question for Italian readers of *La rassegna mensile di Israel*: in 1938, two years after the publication of Tä'ammrat's article, the Fascist Grand Council of Italy enacted the first of the anti-Jewish race laws, and fascist party members exuberantly destroyed the office of the journal's publisher.[109] It is thus significant that Tä'ammrat occasionally hints at larger questions related to the status of Jews in Christian societies. For example, in a footnote following Gédéwon's apparent betrayal of his first pretender ally, Tä'ammrat explained that his protagonist's actions should be understood not as a gambit for power, but instead as a pragmatic strategy of communal- and self-preservation.[110] In a later footnote, Tä'ammrat argues that Gédéwon's support for the Christian rebels was a similarly pragmatic attempt to "counterbalance the arrogance" of a hostile emperor. These strategies were vindicated by Tä'ammrat's reconstructed narrative: after the death of Gédéwon, the chronicler notes that the now-unchallenged emperor was free to proceed with "the destruction of the lands of the Falasha," a development that had been delayed by Gédéwon's shrewd defensive actions.[111] By describing the persecution of the Ethiopian Jewish community and the difficult decisions of its leaders, Tä'ammrat perhaps hoped to write his subjects into the larger narratives of Jewish history.[112] At the very least, it was an Ethiopian story that would resonate with Italian Jewish readers.[113]

While Tä'ammrat focused on the history of an understudied ethnic group, Tedla Haylé examined the history of ethnic relations writ large. Originally from Šäwa, Tedla lived in Belgium and completed a thesis at the Colonial University of Antwerp in the late 1920s, after which he returned to the Horn and served as the Ethiopian Consul in Asmära.[114] His study, published in 1930 as *Pourquoi et comment pratiquer une politique d'assimilation en Éthiopie*, examined ethnic relations in Ethiopia, fusing historical analysis with policy recommendations that he believed would modernize the empire and unify its subjects.[115] Its first and second chapters offer a highly Amhara-centric history of ethnic relations and politics in Ethiopia. In them, Tedla begins by charting the origins and ancient history of what he deems Ethiopia's four main ethnic groups: the Amhara, the Oromo, the Cushites, and the Šanqella, offering descriptions of the physiognomy and psychology of each. In his view, the Amhara were "the dominant race, that is to say, the governing race," and the "fundamental base" of their "character" was the Makedda-Solomon union, which in his view underpinned Ethiopia's predestined historical greatness and enduring independence.[116] As he put it, "we are an elected people."[117] In contrast, the Oromo were but the savage antagonists of the Amhara, while the Cushites and Šanqella merited little historical attention at all. With this schema in place, Tedla proceeds through a historical study of inter-ethnic and sectarian relations from the Aksumite to the modern eras, viewing the imperial dynastic saga through an ethnic filter. Thus in the nineteenth century, "the veritable despot" Emperor Téwodros was a "proud Amhara . . . offended by the silence of England," while Emperor Yoḥannes "usurped" the dynasty that was restored and expanded by Menilek, his "supposed vassal" who forced the Oromo into submission and through Adwa "delivered a well-deserved lesson to European imperialism."[118] His conclusions were optimistic: "The reader now knows Ethiopia; he can judge it. A nation that braved the Egyptians, the Romans, the Arabo-Homerites, the Persians, Islam, the Italians, and the English can have confidence in its future, for its history shows the energy, the vitality of its race." He then noted, "Today, we are at a turning point in our history.[119]

Tedla considers this historical turning point in the four chapters that follow, which contrast Ethiopia's assimilative imperial repertoire with European methods of colonial administration. He suggests that the relationship between the Amhara and the Oromo lacked the antagonism that defined relations between Europeans and their colonial subjects, and contrasts Ethiopia with the Austro-Hungarian Empire, concluding that the dominated Oromo differed from dominated Slavs because of the former's stateless society. In his conclusion, he argues that Ethiopia was a bridge between West and East: it was tied to Europe through its Christian faith, and to the East through racial orgins. Though the study is marred by its ethnocentric analysis and arguments, it is nonetheless a pioneering attempt at both ethnic history and comparative historical analysis. It is moreover notable in its scholarly breadth: Tedla critiques European arguments and quotes extensively from European and Ethiopian sources.[120]

These were all innovative studies. Similar kinds of historical writing also appeared in local newspapers. Not surprisingly, *Berhanenna sälam* featured articles on a range of historical topics, from medieval Europe and Napoleon to the patriotism of Emperor Téwodros, Italian colonialism in the Horn of Africa, and "Ethiopia's New Era."[121] Gäbrä Ḥeywät's second work was serialized in its pages, and it also printed countless biographical obituaries of prominent Ethiopian men and women. Though *A'emro* was principally devoted to domestic politics and foreign affairs, it also occasionally featured short historical articles.[122] *Courrier d'Éthiopie* featured much historical writing, including the personal recollections of readers, reports on local archaeological and ethnographic expeditions, and articles on such assorted topics as the history of European perceptions of Ethiopia, the evolution of Ethiopia, and the origins of the university.[123] The newspapers also regularly featured book reviews dealing with both Ethiopian and non-Ethiopian history.[124]

These historical works were complemented by the Amharic writings of European missionaries, which further attuned Ethiopian readers to varieties of history beyond the vernacular tradition. A pioneering but obscure example of this is the 1841 Amharic geography and world history by the Church Missionary Society missionary Karl Wilhelm Isenberg (1806–64), which was known to Ḫeruy, but not cited by many other historians of the era.[125] Rather more influential were the works of the EFS missionary Olle Eriksson. Eriksson was a gifted linguist, the publisher of Gäbrä Ḥeywät's first work in Asmära, and a teacher-turned-colleague of Gäbrä Krestos in Addis Ababa. Like the latter, he became a prolific author of Amharic textbooks, many of which addressed historical topics. In 1924, the EFS press published *Alämen eney, Voyons le monde,* a kind of cultural geography and history textbook that included chapters on Ethiopia, India, China, the cities of Europe, and even the Sami of northern Scandinavia.[126] Two years later, in 1926, Eriksson completed *Ahunenna ṭent, Présent et passé,* a religiohistorical textbook for mission school students.[127] He also translated a missiological work that examined Africa, India, China, Japan, and Persia, with discussions of the history of each and reports on the progress of local missionary efforts.[128] It was printed by Ḫeruy's Goh Ṣebah press in 1935. In addition to these three published works, Eriksson also left unpublished a number of manuscripts on various topics. These include a short church history, a translation of Boethius, and *Dagmawi Menilek, Yä'ityopya tarik* (Menilek II, History of Ethiopia), a detailed study of more than three hundred pages.[129]

The writings of Gäbrä Ḥeywät, Tä'ammrat, Tedla, and Eriksson introduced new methods and models to vernacular historiography. However, many Ethiopian intellectuals continued to prefer the venerable genres of royal biography, dynastic history, and universal chronography.[130] These traditionalist historians—the objects of Gäbrä Ḥeywät's epistemic and methodological ire—simply preferred to examine familiar subjects in time-tested ways. Royal biographies are the most salient examples of this predilection: these include the chronicle of Gäbrä Śellasé (1844–1912), Emperor Menilek's talented *ṣäḥafé te'ezaz,* and the autobiography of Täfäri Mäkonnen/Ḫaylä Śellasé, who despite his modernizing pretensions wrote in the laconic observational style of a chronicle. Similarly, Gäbrä Egzi'abhér wrote a traditionalist joint biography of Empress Zäwditu and *leğ* Iyyasu, "following the path of past chronicles," as he put it.[131] *Aläqa* Kenfé maintained an annalistic diary of Addis Ababa in the 1920s that focused on protocol, appointments, and the activities of the nobility, very much in the descriptive chronographic style of a court historian.[132]

Dynastic history also remained popular. Gäbrä Masqal, a teacher from Gännätä Maryam, wrote a traditional *tarikä nägäśt* that concluded with Emperor Susenyos.[133] Some of his contemporaries adapted this genre to regional history. *Aläqa* Täklä Iyäsus Waqğira (1868–1936) wrote a history of Goğğam in the style of a general dynastic history, while Afäwärq Gäbrä Śellasé produced a history of the southern kingdom of Wällayta that converted the local oral tradition into Solomonid terms.[134] And many scholars continued to produce universal histories in the traditional style, despite the changing nature of Ethiopia's interaction with the wider world. Some of these are quite short, but *aläqa* Azezza, a church scholar of Addis Ababa, wrote a lengthy and detailed history in this vein.[135] All continued to use the traditional periodization linking biblical antiquity, the narrative of the *Kebrä nägäśt*, early Christianity, and the Solomonid saga.

Curiously, this tendency toward traditionalist historiography is especially pronounced in the writing of the Italian-educated literatus Afäwärq Gäbrä Iyäsus (1868–1947). A diplomat and the author of the first Amharic novel, multiple dialogues, and several other creative works, Afäwärq made several excursions into historiography, most notably *Dagmawi aṭé Menilek* (Emperor Menilek the Second), a florid 1901 biography of the then-emperor.[136] In its introduction, Afäwärq explained that his subject was sufficiently great to require a hagiography instead of a more conventional royal biography. Accordingly, his study would not recount in endless detail the facts of the emperor's life; instead, it was to be an adulation of a man whose only shortcoming was his mortality. It epitomized the epic tendencies of vernacular royal biography, and it was perhaps for this reason that Afäwärq begged the reader to forgive occasional errors of fact, since these were insignificant given the larger truth he hoped to reveal. The work itself surveyed the emperor's life in a fairly conventional fashion, concluding with his confrontation with the Italians and the resultant Battle of Adwa. Although highly stylized and clearly dependent upon Afäwärq's familiarity with the Italian literature on Ethiopia, this study recalled the adulatory style of the biographies of emperors Amdä Ṣeyon and Gälawdéwos. Tä'ammrat later said that Afäwärq wrote of Emperor Menilek "with loving esteem and great exaggeration," and of his rivals "with contempt and derision."[137] This contrasts with Afäwärq's earlier claim that he would refrain from judging the living, leaving that task to future generations.[138]

Between revolutionaries like Gäbrä Ḥeywät and Tä'ammrat and traditionalists like Gäbrä Śellasé and Afäwärq Gäbrä Iyäsus was a third group of historians who cautiously and selectively introduced Western ideas and sources into the vernacular tradition. The most famous exemplar of this tendency is *aläqa* Tayyä Gäbrä Maryam (1860–1924), a graduate of the Swedish mission schools. Born in Gondär, he travelled to Monkullu on the coast in 1880, where he met the local EFS representatives. He worked in the EFS schools and began to acquire distinction as a scholar with wide-ranging talents in poetry, languages, and history. He returned to Ethiopia in 1898, where he was eventually brought to the attention of Emperor Menilek. The latter sent *aläqa* Tayyä to Germany from 1905 to 1907, where he taught and studied at the University of Berlin. Upon his return to Ethiopia, he began working on a biography of the emperor until he became embroiled in doctrinal disputes with Orthodox church scholars. He was imprisoned in 1910, and upon his release, he spent much of his time writing. He died in 1924, a well-respected man of letters: Ḫeruy held him in considerable esteem, and Gäbrä Ḥeywät described him as a true patriot.[139]

Aläqa Tayyä spent decades working on his magnum opus, *Yä'ityopya mängeśt tarik* (History of the Kingdom of Ethiopia), which had been commissioned by Emperor Menilek in 1898. A now partially lost work of several hundred pages, this history fused its author's deep knowledge of traditional scholarship with his research into the work of European orientalists. As he explained in the only published excerpt, "we have studied, culled, and synthesized from the bible and the histories of the ancients and of scholars of later and recent times."[140] He then writes that these included, among others, Herodotus, al-Maqrizi, Abu-Farağ, Giyorgis Wäldä Amid, James Bruce, Jean-François Champollion, Hiob Ludolf, Enno Littmann, and Ignazio Guidi. Upon this broad but firm foundation, *aläqa* Tayyä aimed to systematically reconstruct Ethiopian history over the long term, from creation, antiquity, and the first migrations into Ethiopia, through the saga of Makedda, Solomon, and their son Menilek, the emergence of Aksum, the Zagwe dynasty, and finally the era of the Solomonids, concluding with succession dispute of "the *leğ* Iyyasu affair" and the subsequent reign of Empress Zäwditu. Although this work was never finished, portions of it were published by the EFS in 1922 as *Yä'ityopya ḥezb tarik* (History of the People of Ethiopia).

Aläqa Tayyä's achievement lies in his innovative approach to historical evidence. His scripturalist evangelicalism perhaps disposed him to privilege textual documentation over received precedent and authority, and he made a particular effort to explain his sources and their limitations.[141] He distinguished between different categories of sources: oral traditions (*tärät*, "stories" or "tales"), which are less reliable than their written counterparts; authoritative texts, like the Bible and the *Kebrä nägäśt*; and scholarly research, or secondary sources. The explicit interplay between these sources is his major methodological achievement: he called it "the axe of true history," suggesting that scrupulous comparison was an instrument for combating error,[142] and he elsewhere wrote that the results would be "history more beautiful and more sweet than honey."[143] Consider his discussion of the arguments about the origins of the Amhara and Amharic. After outlining orientalist arguments that associated the Amhara with Emperor Lalibäla's expedition to Egypt, he presents traditional claims of their ancient presence in Ethiopia. He supports this autocthonous position with linguistic evidence, showing the greater antiquity of Amharic toponyms and regnal names in relation to their Ge'ez and Tigrinya counterparts. Elsewhere, he uses a similar critical methodology to examine historical arguments about the Yemeni origins of the Queen of Sheba, the descent of the Ethiopian Jews from Kam, and the origins of the Oromo.[144] He has been criticized for his careless use of oral materials.[145] But in his systematic approach to source material—both oral and written, foreign and indigenous—and in his effort toward explicit source comparison and criticism, he was almost without peer in the era. The international scope of his archival research was indisputably pioneering.

Ḫeruy similarly attempted to weave old and new together. He was the author of several histories, and an even larger number of hybrid works with historical chapters and themes. Some of these display a striking willingness to blend the inherited tradition with new sources and methods. An example of Ḫeruy's creative tendency is *Ityoṗyanna mätämma* (Ethiopia and Mätämma), published in 1917–18, in which his major innovation is his choice of subject. By evaluating the campaigns of Emperor Yoḥannes against the Sudanese Mahdists, he produced an episodic study that was neither based on personally observed events nor a celebration of a ruler's life. It was instead the history of a watershed moment, rather like the earlier studies of the campaigns of Emperor Amdä Ṣeyon or the invasions of Grañ.[146] However, Ḫeruy departed from these precedents by framing his study within the existing arguments about Emperor Yoḥannes's failures, in effect situating his work within its historiographical context. In the introduction to the book, Ḫeruy outlines the most common criticisms of the emperor: that he foolishly hoped the Muslims would convert to Christianity, that he was a tyrannical puritan, and that he preyed upon the peasantry.[147] He then explained that he did not wish to dispute whether the emperor did these things, but to instead consider them in their proper historical context.[148] The four chapters that follow describe the rise of the Mahdists and *ras* Täklä Haymanot's campaign against them; the arguments for and against Emperor Yoḥannes's decision to march to Mätämma instead of Šäwa, where his rival Menilek awaited him; the siege of the city; and the emperor's death. In the final chapter, Ḫeruy subtly vindicates Yoḥannes's campaign by outlining the Mahdists' subsequent punitive expeditions to Gondär and the carnage that ensued, using oral testimony as evidence.[149] He also draws on English language scholarship, and attempts to present the Mahdist perspective through diplomatic correspondence.[150] His essayistic study thus attempts to holistically explore the dynamics of a pivotal historical moment, with an attention to argumentation that it is almost without precedent in the vernacular tradition.

Some of Ḫeruy's other historical projects were equally innovative, such as his detailed historical dictionary, published in 1922, which aimed to offer a systematic prosopography of Ethiopian historical figures and early twentieth-century notables.[151] He wrote short studies of a number of specialized historical topics, such as Ethiopian foreign relations and intellectual history,[152] and his travel writing was a unique variety of historiography, as we shall see in chapter 4. He balanced these comparatively experimental efforts with two more conventional works. The first is *Wazéma* (Eve), an eclectic historical treatise in four parts: the first section presents chronologies and narratives related to Makedda and Solomon, the Zagwe dynasty, and the Solomonids; the second considers church history; the third offers biographies of the heads of the Ethiopian Orthodox Church (*eç̣ç̣ägés*); and the fourth features portraits of its patriarchs (*liqä pappasat*).[153] It is essentially a narrative and prosopographic compendium of vernacular historical knowledge, much like the earlier accumulative *summae* of historians like *abéto* Abägaz. Ḫeruy's second traditionalist work is *Yä'ityopya tarik* (History of Ethiopia), a dynastic history focused on Emperor Menilek II, the imperial contest of the nineteenth century, and "the great victory of Adwa."[154] With such a wide-ranging oeuvre of published and unpublished works, *blatta*—and ultimately *blattén géta*—Ḫeruy was easily the most eminent and perhaps the most prolific historian of the day.

Aläqa Tayyä and Ḫeruy were by no means the only Ethiopian scholars who attempted to mine this rich middle ground between Western-inflected and traditionalist historiography. Other examples from the period include *abba* Aṣmä Giyorgis (n.d.–1915), who produced a detailed manuscript study of the Oromo and their relations with the Amhara, using oral traditions, the chronicles, and orientalist scholarship,[155] and *blattén géta* Marse'é Ḫazan, who wrote a semiautobiographical general history of the era that widened the historical subject from the emperor and the nobility to include everyday life.[156] The latter began his study with a *qené* poem on the subject of historical progress, a key theme of his work. A more obscure example of homespun history is Märägéta Berhanu of Goğğam, who wrote a *tarikä nägäśt* that partially relied upon foreign scholarship.[157]

What is the significance of this efflorescence of vernacular historiography in a modern age? It is tempting to see this moment as the genesis of modern historical writing in Ethiopia, especially given the objective rhetoric of a critical historian like Gäbrä Ḥeywät, who sought to break away from what he saw as a defective vernacular tradition. However, there are two problems with this interpretation. First, Gäbrä Ḥeywät was relatively unique in his systematic and near-exclusive use of Western theoretical tools: indeed, this singularity has contributed to his stature today.[158] Most of his contemporaries were comparatively restrained in their use of new methods and sources, but their efforts were no less pioneering in their exploration of novel topics. An undue focus on westernization obscures this fact. A second problem is that traditionalist historians like Ḫeruy sometimes employed putatively modern methods, while innovative historians like Tä'ammrat often drew extensively on their inherited tradition. Still others seem to defy categorization altogether, like the pseudo-traditionalist Italophile Afäwärq Gäbrä Iyäsus. The key point is that the interplay *between* these different varieties of history was the most novel and definitive feature of Ethiopian historiography in the first half of the twentieth century. The era's historians did not seek to westernize history, but instead to indigenize new methods and ideas through a process of creative assimilation and incorporation. This tendency is especially evident in Gäbrä Krestos's *Short History*, an Ethiopianized history of progress.

The Prose of the World

The *Short History* is both typical and atypical for its era. It is an un-illustrated printed book of just over one hundred pages, including footnotes and an index. In its brief introduction, Gäbrä Krestos explains that several individuals helped him write it. He notes that he drew upon the work of Ḫeruy and the teachings of Iwarson, his Asmära mentor, and that his Amharic had been corrected by *aläqa* Dañé and "his honorable brother" Éfrém Täwäldä Mädḥän (1905–n.d.), another Eritrean emigrant to Addis Ababa.[159] The result of all this was a work written in simple Amharic with short sentences and many neologisms and foreign loan words, precisely the style of "mission language" that *aläqa* Kidanä Wäldä Keflé critiqued. This was a history that aimed to instruct a large community of readers.

Curiously, Gäbrä Krestos's book has three different titles. The first and most prominent is "Short History of the World in Amharic" (aç̣ç̣er yä'aläm tarik bamareña), the Amharic phrase that graces its cover. In its employ of "yä'aläm tarik" (history of the world), this title invokes the established generic conventions of vernacular historiography, with which some of Gäbrä Krestos's readers were likely acquainted. One might expect a traditional world chronography. The second and equally suggestive French title is "Histoire universelle en abrégé," which appears on the frontispiece. This phrase asserts Gäbrä Krestos's cosmopolitan outlook, and it is moreover doubly intertextual: it can be seen as a further associative reference to the Ethiopian tradition of universal chronography, complementing the

Amharic title of the front cover, and—much less certainly—as a referential nod to the Western variety of comparative civilizational historiography of Arnold Toynbee and Oswald Spengler. Curiously, the latter genre is in fact rather close to the species of world history that Gäbrä Krestos produced, possibly because of his acquaintance with similar works by his missionary colleague Eriksson.[160] The third, and most vexing, of the book's three titles is a second Amharic prefatory title that follows the introduction: "yäḥezbenna yä'aḥezab tarik." The precise meaning of this phrase is thorny: "ḥezb" can be translated as "people" or "nation," while "aḥezab" can be translated as "peoples," or alternatively, as "heathens" or "infidels." Thus this second title is "Nations and Peoples," or more loosely, "Believers and Unbelievers." Both are meanings that would have been acceptable to Gäbrä Krestos, as we shall see.

These revealing titles suggest their author's grand ambitions. Gäbrä Krestos used his popular history to introduce his reader to people, places, ideas, and trends far beyond the scope of traditional historiography. His work discusses the following topics: the people of India, China, and Japan; the Arabs, Ethiopians, Syrians, and Babylonians; the Persians, the Greeks, and their relations; the Romans and their empire; the grand trends of medieval and modern history; the United States; the French Revolution; the events of the nineteenth century; and recent Ethiopian history, which he explored through chapters on "Ethiopia's New Era," emperors Téwodros, Yoḥannes, and Menilek, *leğ* Iyyasu, and finally the then-reigning Empress Zäwditu. Many of these non-Ethiopian topics had never before been presented in an Amharic text, printed or otherwise.

Gäbrä Krestos organized and linked these eclectic topics with a novel periodization. In his introduction, he referred interested parties to the scriptures for the history of the "Hebrews or the House of Israel," thereby leaving aside the details of the ancient epoch of vernacular historians. He was not interested in closely examining that aspect of antiquity. As an alternative, he explained that his work would employ a tripartite chronology:

> The history of the world is divided into three epochs: the first epoch, from the beginning until 400 years after Christ's birth; the second epoch, from 400 until 1500 years after Christ's birth; and the third epoch, from 1500 years after Christ's birth until today. The beginning of the middle epoch is when the Roman state was won by Christianity and the German people entered into Europe. The beginning of the new epoch is when the Church was renewed, America was discovered, and printing and much wisdom can be found.[161]

This periodization serves to organize his twenty-six topical chapters: thirteen chapters consider the first epoch, one brief chapter covers the middle epoch, and the final twelve chapters examine the new epoch. With this structure, Gäbrä Krestos decisively broke with the dualistic schema of traditionalist historians, who tended to partition the unified course of sacred history into the ancient era of the Abrahamic peoples and the subsequent era of Christianity, in which the church fathers and the Solomonids were seamlessly linked, and which was occasionally punctuated by local dramas like Grañ's invasions or the *zämänä mäsafent.* Further emphasizing his break with chronological convention, Gäbrä Krestos employed both the Gregorian and Ethiopian calendars, and discarded the Ethiopian calendar computational system of *baḥrä hassab* altogether.[162] Through these changes he renovated the architecture of universal history.

The narrative of the *Short History* turns upon the notion that the world is divided into distinct human communities whose history can be considered according to a hierarchy of progress. These are the "peoples" of the book's third title. Gäbrä Krestos did not begin by relating Ethiopian traditions about human origins, the scriptural account of creation, or the Makedda-Solomon tale, but instead presented his reader with a Western framework for understanding human difference.[163] He began with taxonomy of early humanity, describing the "Hamitics," "Semitics," "Indo-Europeans," "Mongols," and "Blacks," and he added that the peoples of the world are further "divided between two bundles": the "people of the East . . . Indians, Chinese, and Japanese," and the "people of the West."[164] He further defined the parameters of historical subjecthood by observing that "when we speak of the history of the world, we speak only of civilized people," using the term "šanqella" to describe uncivilized and therefore ahistorical peoples.[165] In making these distinctions, Gäbrä Krestos employed the terminology of late-nineteenth-century Western ethnology, which he noted that he derived from the work *Ancient History* by the American historian Philip Van Ness Meyers (1846–1937), a prolific textbook author and monogenist.[166] Races and nations drove world history, and for this reason, the chapters of Gäbrä Krestos's book examined not epochs or individuals but the most significant human communities.[167] In this respect, his work resembled Tedla Haylé's ethnohistory on a global scale.

History cut through these human differences. Though culturally diverse and varied in origin, the world's peoples were collectively involved in a discernable process of development—a point Gäbrä Krestos makes clear through his terminology and analysis. He frequently employs the Amharic verb *bäläṭä,* or "surpass," to describe the relative progress of different groups, often in reference to the cumulative nature of knowledge and technical achievement. He thus begins his narrative with the first state system, which belonged to "the people of India," before turning to the ancient Egyptians, who "went beyond their home through the work that they gave to others, and thus acquired the wisdom of those people who came before."[168] This was in essence a variation of Meyers' notion of "the Great Bequest" to humanity from the antique civilizations.[169] In contrast to these dynamic and progressive groups, the Chinese eventually "fell behind" because they failed to accept "wisdom from without," though they did acquire "much learning from translations of the Europeans."[170] He noted that Japan, a fascination of many of his contemporaries, had developed the printing press long before Europe, but also that "wisdom and knowledge" eventually made the Japanese "arrogant."[171] As a whole, the *Short History* thus describes not only the variety of the world's many peoples but also their contributions to and relative states of civilization, or *śelleṭṭané*.

This universal story of development is localized in the book's final chapters, which consider nineteenth- and twentieth-century Ethiopia and Northeast Africa. In these discussions, Gäbrä Krestos suggests that the principal agent of civilization in Ethiopia was Emperor Menilek, who made two major contributions: concluding the military struggle that had preoccupied his immediate predecessors, and introducing Western technology and reforms to the country. The first of these related to his defense of Ethiopian sovereignty through the "the Adwa War," which the *Short History* succinctly describes. As Gäbrä Krestos relates, Emperor Téwodros, a "good" emperor who "unified Ethiopia and the divided *ras*es," was nonetheless brought down by the intervention of Queen Victoria and the army of India.[172] His successor Emperor Yoḥannes had in turn "fought and obtained victory against the hated Italians and Turks on every coast," only to be defeated by the Mahdists, who indiscriminately "slaughtered Christian people . . . the teachers, the *liqawent*, the church, the monks, the women, and the babies."[173] This epic contest was largely as it was described in the works of Ḫeruy, Afäwärq, and *ṣäḥafé te'ezaz* Gäbrä Śellasé.

In Gäbrä Krestos's estimation, Emperor Menilek consummated his predecessors' noble but ultimately inconclusive struggles. His treatment of Menilek's reign is divided into three chapters: the first considers his life during the reigns of emperors Téwodros and Yoḥannes; the second, titled "The War of Emperor Menilek and Italy," describes the 1895 assault on Amba Alagé and the 1896 battle of Mäqällé; and the third, titled "the Adwa or Abba Gärima War," discusses the climactic battle itself, the Ethiopian victory obtained "through the blood of many brothers," and its annual commemoration on Yekatit 23 at Addis Ababa's Qeddus Giyorgis Church.[174] Adwa was Emperor Menilek's historic triumph—one founded upon the efforts of his forebears—and for this reason, all Ethiopians should endeavor to remember it and its heroes.

The emperor's second major contribution to the progress of Ethiopia was his sponsorship of technological advancement and institutional reform, by which he aimed "to make all Ethiopia like Europe."[175] As Gäbrä Krestos tells it, Menilek imported new inventions, such as telephones, cars, and trains; encouraged manufacturing, from woodchoppers to sewing machines, mechanized reapers, and a soap factory; and established new institutions, like banks, schools, hospitals, and the post office. These were significant achievements, and in biblically evocative language, Gäbrä Krestos wrote that they "made Ethiopia known to all the world."[176] The implication is that Menilek's struggle for sovereignty made these developments possible. Gäbrä Krestos effectively situates the subjects of these concluding Ethiopian chapters within their worldwide historical context, thereby locating Ethiopia in the family of modern peoples.

What is the genealogy of this Ethiopian history of the world and its peoples? Despite appearances, Gäbrä Krestos's model of civilizational attainment and historical progress diverges from the Western conceptions of modernity that it superficially resembles. In its inner workings, his *Short History* domesticates the idea of progress and avoids Eurocentrism. As many have observed, Eurocentrism—or more precisely, European universalism—can be manifest in a wide range of political assumptions, cultural beliefs, and social practices that are themselves the product of Western dominance, its structures of power, and its universalized values.[177] One of its encompassing claims is in the domain of understanding and describing the relationship between past and present. Eurocentism is manifest here in the pursuit of historicism, the notion that historical truth requires the historian to understand historical processes within unfolding chronological development. Put simply, an event is always part of something greater. Adwa, for example, was more than just a battle.

Though this view need not imply a Western-bound vision of change over time, Dipesh Chakrabarty argues that historicism tends to cultivate Eurocentrism by treating Western modernity as a universal hermeneutic. The West is the contrastive device—the foil—that gives meaning to the non-Western event, through the analytic prism of Western history and the heuristic categories that are derived from it, such as modernization, industrialization, capitalism, liberalism, or socialism.[178] Since many non-Western societies have acquired the institutions, technologies, and ideas associated with these categories, which are assumed to have first emerged in the West, the writing of historicist world history focuses on their development in those societies. A Eurocentric history of Ethiopian progress, then, would narrate this modernizing process of diffusion and derivation. However, it is precisely this orientation that Gäbrä Krestos avoids. Despite his points about Emperor Menilek's achievements, his universal history is historicist but not Eurocentric.

Consider the *Short History*'s underlying plot. Unlike other forms of writing about the past, like annals, histories attempt to make the world "speak itself as a story," as Hayden White puts it, employing a narrative with implicit meaning for the present.[179] For this reason, they can be said to have a plot. In the case of the *Short History*, the historical plot is rooted in the growth of true faith, not the development of science, the spread of material prosperity, the growth of freedom, or the triumph of a particular political creed or economic system—all key themes in Western historiography of the day. Instead, Gäbrä Krestos's periodization and narrative turn upon a fundamentally Christian model of history: the prehistory of the Hebrew Bible, the conversion of the Roman Empire, the schism between Catholicism and Orthodoxy, the Reformation, and finally the renewal of the Church in the new epoch.[180] The themes of the so-called dual revolutions—the French and the industrial—are unrelated to this unfolding macrohistorical process.

This plot is additionally manifest in the Christian morality that informs his historical discussions, and especially in his frequent claims about history's winners and losers. Gäbrä Krestos notes that faith is what gives the otherwise barbarous Germans their character, not their great military accomplishments, and he follows with approval the spread of Orthodox Christianity to Russia.[181] And when dealing with subjects that fit uneasily with this Christian historical model, Gäbrä Krestos the narrator makes explicit intercessions. He notes that while Indians produced the first complex society, they follow a pantheistic faith that "[makes] my eyes widen and fall out . . . [for through it] man kneels his head before his other creations, before idolatrous images."[182] Similarly, the Chinese, who had become weak in the new epoch, were presently being redeemed by "the work of the Gospel"—that is, by Western missionaries.[183] And the struggle to defend Ethiopia's sovereignty had a profoundly religious dimension: reflecting on Emperor Yoḥannes's death at Mätämma, for example, Gäbrä Krestos observed "*aṭé* Yoḥannes spilled his blood for his country and his religion . . . [and] it is said that God counts him among the martyrs."[184] Thus the spread and endurance of the one true faith in all its historical permutations defines world historical development. Though other Ethiopian historians had considered this topic through the saga of the covenantal peoples, none had considered it in global and aggregative terms. This was the story of the Solomonid inheritance on an ecumenical scale.

The non-Eurocentric nature of Gäbrä Krestos's understanding of progress is also evident in his deeply vernacular social imaginary. Ethiopian historians of earlier generations envisioned power and social relations through a conceptual vocabulary derived from their own lived reality. Their historical writings describe a highland imperial world in which noble and peasant (*ç̣äwa* and *balagär*) were linked in a system of land tenure and tribute (*gäbbar*) marked by violent expropriation and legitimated by the church (*kehnät*) and state (*mängeśt*).[185] Though these concepts superficially resemble the terminology used to describe European feudalism, they are nonetheless rooted in forms of power, property, inheritance, and production specific to Ethiopia.[186] By deploying this socially derived vocabulary in their histories, the chroniclers of past centuries employed Ranajit Guha's "prose of the world": they depicted change over time using their own culturally specific toolkit.

Unlike his forebears, Gäbrä Krestos treats this vocabulary and social imaginary as a set of universal categories, using it to anatomize and populate world history. He characterizes the American Revolution as a revolt of *gäbbar* farmers resentful of their British masters, and he misleadingly presents the Indian caste system as a hierarchy of *ç̣äwa*, *kehnät*, *gäbbar*, and *sudras* (*shudra*), the last a category with no apparent Ethiopian equivalent.[187] Most striking is his account of the French Revolution, which began when the French *kehnät* and court (*neguś bét*) became "drunken and debauched" and "passed their time in laziness and alcoholism."[188] Tax increases and austerity led to the resentment of the *ç̣äwa*, whose army took Paris and turned the French into a *gerreger*, or a mob, riot, or disturbance. This was the total collapse of a recognizable social system—an ultimately familiar hierarchy of status and obligation became inverted when peasants acted like soldiers. The *gerreger* was finally subdued by Napoleon, a great hero whose "powerful state made its hand into a fist."[189] These discussions suggest that Gäbrä Krestos imagined key events in the story of progress without resorting to historicist assumptions about the universal relevance of Western categories. In the *Short History*, the French Revolution neither inaugurates his "new epoch" nor suggests a future historical stage in Ethiopia's development. Instead, French actors are cast in the familiar Solomonid drama.[190] This refusal to translate historical terms and experiences points to a fundamental hostility to the universal pretensions of Eurocentric historicism.[191]

Ultimately, this was public history that gestured simultaneously toward the patrimony and the future. Though his text was bound, printed, and offered for sale, Gäbrä Krestos wrote in a conceptual language that historians like Ḫeruy and *aläqa* Tayyä—or even *abba* Baḥrey, or *ṣäḥafé te'ezazs* Ṭino and Sinoda—would have understood, but which would have seemed objectionable to Ranke, Spengler, and possibly even Gäbrä Ḥeywät. Yet despite this fundamental continuity with his predecessors, Gäbrä Krestos's historical vista also reflects a radically new orientation toward time that was then developing in local historical culture.

This shift is suggested by François Hartog's distinction between "regimes of historicity."[192] These are broad frameworks of thought that shape a society's orientation toward the past, present, and future in a given moment, informing historiography as well as a host of other fields of learning, thought, and social practice. In his view, two of these regimes are particularly significant. The first is the ancient regime, which fuses the classical notion of exemplary *historia magistra* with the Christian notion of salvation-oriented history, and which generally prevailed in the West until the eighteenth century. This is an orientation toward the past in which the past itself is the principal interest—its story should be told, its heroes remembered, and its lessons learned. The second of Hartog's frameworks is the modern regime of history, which looks to the present and future through various conceptual lenses, most notably that of progress.[193] In this regime, the past is something to be overcome or transcended. These regimes of historicity profoundly shape the contours of intellectual inquiry, and the points at which they are challenged, questioned, and undermined represent turning points in historical practice.

This notion of historical regimes illuminates a key distinction between Gäbrä Krestos and most of his predecessors and colleagues. Earlier generations of church scholars and court historians—and many of Gäbrä Krestos's contemporaries—focused on the ancient regime of history, in Hartog's sense. Traditionalism led some scholars to preserve their collectively received knowledge about the recent and not-so-recent past, which was exemplary, epic, and sacred. The more present-minded observational historians described the actions of present rulers against the backdrop of this past, understanding their subjects' lives through it, and their achievements as new contributions to it. Gäbrä Krestos, in contrast, linked the past and present to an approaching future, seeing the past as part of a story that was unfolding but not yet complete. He did not illuminate or document a previously unknown dimension of Ethiopia's past, nor did he describe observed reality or a received historical patrimony. Instead, he offered his readers a narrative of the globalization of religious truth, one that contained an implicit argument about Ethiopia's place in the world. Gäbrä Krestos embraced a new and modern order of time, and he endeavored to share it with the nation.

3

Gäbrä Mika'él Germu and the History of Colonialism

Living in the Italian colony of Eritrea during the first decades of the twentieth century, a young scholar named Gäbrä Mika'él Germu (1900–1969) decided to create a compendium of local history. He consulted numerous learned elders, church manuscripts, and European publications, recorded his findings in a small notebook, and added his own textual annotations, interpolations, and commentary. When this work was complete, Gäbrä Mika'él finished his compilation with a striking fifty-three page Amharic history of his own colonial world entitled *Tarik ịtalyanna ityopya*, or *History of Italy and Ethiopia*. In it, he used his research to survey the history of imperialism over the long term. He began with a chronology that proceeded from the Spanish conquest of the Americas to the Italian invasion of Ethiopia in 1935, and then turned to a close study of the inaugural phase of colonialism in the Horn of Africa—from the Assäb-to-Adwa drama of the Italian conquest to the dynamics of domination, collaboration, and resistance in the highlands. To present this complex story, Gäbrä Mika'él employed two intertwined conceptual frames. On the one hand, he narrated the course of events related to the establishment of colonial rule, and on the other, he offered a pseudo-prosopography of Eritrea's first generation of Italian conquerors and their often-rebellious native subjects. By fusing the study of an unfolding historical process with accounts of the individual lives it shaped, Gäbrä Mika'él reconceptualized local history through the analytic category of empire. In so doing, he produced one of the first problem-oriented histories in the vernacular tradition. Braudel would have approved.

This chapter contends that Gäbrä Mika'él's efforts exemplify a new variety of vernacular historiography that emerged in Italian Eritrea. In the years between 1890 and 1941, the northernmost branch of the Ethiopian historical tradition began to develop distinct colonial inflections, and this subtle shift in outlook began to distinguish some Eritrean historians from their Ethiopian counterparts, who were then grappling with different historical questions. The cause of this shift is relatively straightforward. As Italian subjects, Eritreans experienced a host of disruptive developments related to the colonial situation north of the Märäb River. These included the arrival of Italian settlers, the growth of a market economy and attendant forms of wage labor, the emergence of new educational and governance institutions, and the development of a distinctive colonial culture and *italianità*, or "Italian-ness." While these changes fueled the demographic and economic disruptions typical of settler colonial societies, they also shaped local historiography.[1] Gäbrä Mika'él exemplifies this transitional period: he was a multilingual graduate of the Italian school system, a decorated civil servant employed by the colonial administration, a longtime journalist, a voracious bibliophile and prolific scholar, and the region's first systematic analyst of Italian rule and its consequences. This chapter surveys his life, the distinctive historical culture of the colony, and the nature of Gäbrä Mika'él's creative contribution to it.

The Man from Bäraqit

Gäbrä Mika'él was born in 1900 in Bäraqit Abbay, a highland town in Akkälä Guzay near the Ethiopian border.[2] His parents were Germu Märḥun and Sänbätu Keflay, and he had at least one brother, Zäré Germu.[3] As a boy, Gäbrä Mika'él received a church education and learned Tigrinya, Amharic, and Ge'ez from a local teacher named *abba* Täwäldäberhan Andu.[4] He was apparently an especially precocious student: at the young age of eight, he received a manuscript from a local priest, and at the age of nine, he copied a historical manuscript found in an Adwa church, just across the Ethiopian border.[5] He was clearly reared in a milieu that esteemed traditional scholarship.

Gäbrä Mika'él continued his education at a colonial school, a decision that almost certainly brought him into contact with Italian missionaries. By the second decade of the century, government-run native education in the colony was largely overseen by the Capuchin Friars Minor, the Franciscan order that administered the newly established Apostolic Vicariate of Eritrea.[6] The Capuchins then worked under the direction of the energetic bishop Camillo Carrara (1871–1924), an ardent believer in the spiritual and pragmatic benefits of educating native Muslims, Catholics, and Orthodox Christians. Under his leadership, the order greatly enlarged its mission in the colony, opening numerous schools, orphanages, libraries, clubs, medical stations, and a prolific mission press, the Tipografia Francescana.[7] These efforts complemented the educational policy of colonial governor Giuseppe Salvago Raggi (1866–1946), who supported the development of compulsory schooling for the children of Italian settlers and a limited tiered system of education for native subjects. Over the course of his governorship (1907–14), native education was increasingly delegated to the Capuchins, and by the time of Bishop Carrara's death in 1924, the friars had de facto control of native education in the colony. This was a colonial partnership of church and state.[8]

Bäraqit Abbay was a predominantly Catholic town, and it was therefore relatively well-connected to these Capuchin endeavors.[9] Gäbrä Mika'él likely attended the order's San Michele trade school in Sägänäyti or one of the numerous Catholic mission schools in Asmära, a few days' journey to the north.[10] Both were booming during his student years. In 1914, the Sägänäyti school boasted nearly one hundred Orthodox and Catholic native students, while the Asmära native schools—which included an elementary school, a trade school, a music school, a seminary, and schools for orphans and mixed-race children—also served one hundred students.[11] In the estimation of one mission historian, these institutions attracted "the best and better" native pupils.[12] The Sägänäyti school in particular was considered a model of its kind, and hosted official visitors from Asmära and Italian Somalia.[13]

Mission education introduced Gäbrä Mika'él to a motley group of Italian friars. In Asmära, the Capuchin schools were led by Carrara's close colleague Ezechia da Iseo (1880–1947), a veteran missionary who had come to Eritrea from Brazil. In addition to his work as a teacher, he was the superior of several mission stations, a prolific author of bilingual textbooks, and the director of *Parole buone*, a monthly mission gazette. He was later recalled as "sensitive to the needs of the population" and possessed of "polished eloquence."[14] Da Iseo worked closely with Carrara's secretary, Giandomenico da Milano (1875–1936), a teacher in Sägänäyti with a "strong scholarly temperament" who contributed to *Parole buone* and wrote numerous mission histories and bilingual textbooks.[15] Other friars then involved in the educational enterprise included Apollonio da Desenzano (1885–n.d.), who taught at San Michele and the Asmära trade school, ran the mission press, and held a sincere if patronizing affection for his native charges,[16] and the aesthete Aquilino da Bergamo (1889–n.d.), a teacher who directed the Asmära mission theater and library, and who reportedly had a gift for photography and painting.[17] A considerable number of native clergy and laity also supported the Capuchin educational enterprise.[18]

Life among these men introduced Gäbrä Mika'él to a host of new ideas and experiences. According to one observer, a typical day at an Asmära native school began with morning Mass at five, after which the students studied Tigrinya and Ge'ez until mid-day, and then Italian and typing in the afternoon. Classes continued into the evening, with night courses for aspiring civil servants that attracted more than a hundred students.[19] At San Michele in Sägänäyti, native pupils studied Italian, Tigrinya, Amharic,

Figure 3.1. San Michele trade school, Sägänäyti, ca. 1917. *Pagine d'Apostolato nell' Eritrea*, 47.

geography, and arithmetic, with external workshops devoted to trades like tailoring and leatherworking.[20] The most advanced students trained to be typists, printers, and telegraph operators.[21] Everywhere, the friars' charges learned catechism, and many participated in civic events that extolled the Italian nation and the glory of its civilizing mission in Africa.[22]

As these points suggest, the Capuchin schools artfully fused faith and service. Though the missionaries were devoted to saving souls, they also aimed to develop suitably trained and loyal native subjects. By design, their schools prepared students to work in the colonial administration as clerks, typists, interpreters, telegraph operators, and *askari*, or native conscripts, and the provision of these vital intermediaries helped to facilitate the Capuchins' rapprochement with the colonial state. The friars viewed their dual role in different ways. Da Iseo saw a close connection between the goals of the mission and the needs of the colony. He thus began one of his numerous Italian-Tigrinya textbooks by proclaiming that "work is a necessity," for "our young colony feels the need to form, from the native population, good and laborious workers . . . who cooperate to the increase of industry and local commerce."[23] Galdino da Mezzana, another Capuchin writer, held similar views: in his estimation, the schools delivered "not only souls for Christ and his church" but also "competent and useful citizens."[24] Other friars believed their native pupils were simply well-suited for menial vocations. One anonymous writer observed that "If the native students were inferior to Europeans in terms of their hygiene, rational observation, and logical memory, they had a great facility for learning languages, remembering facts, names, and figures, and doing calligraphy exercises, gifts certainly not negligible for those destined to be interpreters or secretaries.[25] He added that the native pupils were "obsessed with warfare, which they saw as a true vocation."[26] He thus believed that the missionaries were simply developing their pupils' natural endowments to create productive and faithful subjects.

We can imagine that the Capuchins would have been pleased by Gäbrä Mika'él. Like many mission school alumni, he used his education to obtain a clerical position in the colonial administration.[27] His linguistic abilities made him a particularly strong candidate for this field: in addition to Tigrinya, he spoke both Italian and Amharic, and knowledge of the latter was not especially common among Tegrayans at that time, though it was an important bureaucratic and diplomatic lingua franca.[28] Gäbrä Mika'él was quite successful in his career: by the early 1930s, he had achieved the administrative rank of Coadiutore III at the colonial Office of Economic and Financial Affairs in Asmära, where he was senior to at least three other African employees.[29] This was a relatively prominent post: the Office was then managed by Narciso Mosconi Bronzi, who reported directly to the governor, and it was an institution with considerable authority in the life of the colony. It formulated economic policy, oversaw imports and exports, and assessed commodity prices, and its decisions were publicly announced in the *Bollettino ufficiale del governo dell'eritrea*, an official gazette of laws and notices produced by the Italian administration, and additionally in *Il Quotidiano Eritreo*, the principal newspaper of the colony.[30] Gäbrä Mika'él was likely the highest-ranking African civil servant in one of the capital's most important government entities.

It was during this same period that Gäbrä Mika'él made an early foray into the field of journalism, which would become a life-long pursuit. In July of 1934, he penned a somewhat lengthy article for the Tigrinya section of *Il Quotidiano Eritreo*, which accepted submissions from its Italian and African subscribers.[31] His article was a reply to an earlier piece by Yoḥannes Täklay, and it addressed the question of why people kill and steal. He somewhat unusually signed this piece "Gä. Gurmu of Bäraqit," providing his patronymic and place of birth but not his personal name, thus partially emulating the style used by the newspaper's Italian contributors. In publishing this article, he joined the very small handful of Eritrean intellectuals who actively contributed to the Italian-dominated and racially-circumscribed colonial public sphere.

We can obtain a more precise estimation of Gäbrä Mika'él's social position during this period by examining his role in the capital's annual celebration of Mäsqäl, the Orthodox Christian Feast of the True Cross—a public event involving colonizer and colonized alike. As a complement to the religious aspects of the occasion, the Italian governor hosted various native dignitaries at a breakfast, where Italian speeches on fascist imperial grandeur and Eritrean expressions of fealty were exchanged.[32] He then followed Ethiopian imperial precedent by conferring an array of honorific distinctions upon select native Christians—Orthodox, Catholic, and Protestant—who worked for the colonial administration and who had displayed impeccable professionalism and moral character, in the Italians' estimation. The most prestigious of these honorifics were neo-traditionalist political titles that corresponded to the sub-*ras* ranks of the Ethiopian imperial system. These were granted to Eritrean *capi*, or native chiefs. Subordinate to these ennobled colonial powerbrokers were *askari*, or native conscripts, who were awarded military ranks. Finally came a considerable number of nonmilitary native professionals and servants, who were granted personal firearm permits. Like the political titles and military ranks, these permits were carefully ordered in terms of the degree of honor they conferred, indicated by the type of firearm allowed.[33] The names of the native subjects who were granted the most prestigious of these honorifics were then published in *Il Quotidiano Eritreo*, celebrating the feast day through a public acknowledgment of African contributions to the colonial system.[34] Through these acts, the Italians endeavored to remake Mäsqäl into a ritual assertion of the politics of indirect rule, using the religious celebration to co-opt the potent symbolic categories and carefully graded hierarchy of native authority. This was a politico-religious invention of tradition.[35]

The archival records of the Mäsqäl feast reveal Gäbrä Mika'él's official stature in the colony. On the occasion of the 1934 celebration, the governor's office awarded him the highest of the firearm permits for native professionals, granting him the right to carry a M91 military rifle.[36] As a salaried professional, he was quite junior to the many Eritrean *capi* who obtained titles and power from the Italian administration, and who had their names publicly listed by rank in *Il Quotidiano Eritreo.* Unlike them, his name did not appear in print. Yet Gäbrä Mika'él was also senior to many of the Africans who worked directly with the Italians, including his colleagues at the Office of Economic and Financial Affairs, and more generally, a considerable number of telegraphists, interpreters, orderlies, drivers, and medical aides. With his education, profession, public identity, and outward signs of respectability, Gäbrä Mika'él was clearly a new kind of colonial species: a native intermediary—a critical player in the day-to-day operation of the colonial state.[37]

It was during this period that he began to work on his private historical notebooks. These share a number of features. Their material form reflects Gäbrä Mika'él's dual cultural orientation: though he was conversant with both traditional learning and the Italian educational system, he preferred

European-style exercise books to the vellum manuscripts of his more traditional peers. The notebooks also display his considerable linguistic abilities: he wrote in Amharic, Tigrinya, Ge'ez, Italian, and English, and he employed both Ethiopian and European dating systems. All the notebooks are written in Gäbrä Mika'él's occasionally hurried script, sometimes in both red and black ink. Most were completed over an extended period of time, and their contents are generally extremely heterogenous. A single notebook might contain copies of manuscript texts, accounts of oral traditions, excerpts from printed European and Ethiopian/Eritrean histories, and original compositions. In many cases, Gäbrä Mika'él annotated his copied texts with his own footnotes.[38] In form and content, then, the books rehearse their author's distinctive intellectual profile.

Although it is difficult to date these works with precision, we can sketch a provisional chronology. His earliest effort is likely *Zemäṣḥaf zägäbrä mika'él germu*, or *The Book of Gäbrä Mika'él Germu*, which he apparently began in 1911 and completed in the late 1930s.[39] It is a lined notebook of approximately two hundred pages that contains short genealogical notes and several eclectic original and copied historical works. These include a *tarikä nägäśt* from the Solomonid restoration to Emperor Iyyasu I; an annotated Ge'ez history of the Oromo copied from a German edition of the history of Emperor Śärṣä Dengel; a *tarikä nägäśt* copied from a manuscript by Täwäldä Medhin, originally from Wäldebbä; and finally Gäbrä Mika'él's original study of Ethiopia and Italy, discussed in detail below.[40]

His second work appears to be Institute of Ethiopian Studies Manuscript 325, a small notebook of forty-four pages that the author began in 1917.[41] It contains numerous historical works related to the ancient and modern history of Tegray. The first is a twenty-page biography of Emperor Yoḥannes IV, copied from a manuscript text by *aläqa* Märšä of Endä Ṣeyon and annotated by Gäbrä Mika'él.[42] This is followed by a similarly annotated nine-page biography of Menilek I, which includes references to the 1905–6 Princeton Archaeological Expedition to Aksum led by Enno Littmann; two shorter historical works; and a transcription of inscriptions from Yeḥa and Aksum.[43] The last includes Gäbrä Mika'él's comparison of the epigraphic South Arabian script (labeled *yäqäddemo fidäl*) and its modern Ethiopic counterpart (labeled *yahun fidäl*).[44]

The colonial era was clearly a pivotal and fertile period in Gäbrä Mika'él's professional and intellectual development. Though still a relatively young man, he had obtained a prestigious position as a civil servant and was already a highly educated and accomplished historian who read widely in local and European languages. These qualifications and achievements served Gäbrä Mika'él well during the postwar period, when he began a new chapter of his career as a prominent journalist and occasional public historian.

The collapse of Italian East Africa in 1941 triggered a period of tremendous change in Eritrea. The latter's postcolonial future became the subject of considerable local and international debate throughout the period of the British Military Administration, which lasted from 1941 to 1952. In the early 1940s, the broad-based, Muslim-Christian anticolonial organization Maḥbär Feqri Hagär served as a forum for articulating Eritrean political demands, but after this coalition dissolved in 1946, the anticolonial opposition splintered into two principal camps. Unionists favored federation or reunification with Ethiopia, thereby ending Eritrea's period of forced estrangement from its historic motherland, while the Muslim League and other separatist parties demanded outright independence. By the late 1940s, newspaper debates and public rallies had given way to political assassinations and popular unrest, both within and between the two sides. After a formal inquiry and General Assembly debate, the United Nations attempted to resolve the question through a resolution that established a federation between Eritrea and Ethiopia in 1952. This federation was in turn dissolved in 1962, when Ethiopia formally annexed Eritrea as a province.

Gäbrä Mika'él threw himself into this heady political atmosphere. Building upon his professional experience during the colonial era, he began a new chapter in his journalistic career by writing for the most prominent Tigrinya newspaper of the era, *Nay értra sämunawi gazéṭa*, or *The Eritrean Weekly News*. Founded by the British Military Administration in 1942 with the aim of establishing its liberal and democratic credentials, the paper's first director, the young orientalist Edward Ullendorff (1920–2011) recalled that "it was not so much a newspaper, rather the repository of Tigrinya intellectual life and the springboard for the creation of a literary tradition in that language."[45] Gäbrä Mika'él's colleagues at the paper included numerous prominent figures of Eritrea's postcolonial political and intellectual scene. Among them were Wäldä'ab Wäldä Maryam (1905–95), the future nationalist leader who served as the paper's editor from 1941, and Gäbrä Mäsqäl Wäldu (1907–63), the president of Maḥbär Feqri Hagär, a regular contributor to the paper, and in earlier years an occasional contributor to *Il Quotidiano Eritreo.*[46] Gäbrä Mäsqäl became a close friend of Gäbrä Mika'él.[47] Other notable employees included Gäbrä Mika'él Besrat (1925–n.d.), the assistant to the editor from 1947, and the editor after 1949,[48] and Yoḥannes Ṣeggai (1924–n.d.), the founder of the Association of Eritrean Intellectuals.[49]

In the mid-1940s, Gäbrä Mika'él contributed articles to *The Eritrean Weekly News* on a range of historical and other topics. These included a biography of Bäyen Bäraki (1887–n.d.), a former colonial civil servant, the president of the Unionist Party, and the future chief executive of federated Eritrea[50]; a critical discussion of customary law[51]; a study of ancient history as it related to Menilek and Solomon[52]; and a dialogue between a wise man and a simpleton.[53] These works represented some of the earliest historical pieces in the paper, which also featured articles on historical topics by other contributors.[54] Gäbrä Mika'él continued contributing to the paper's editorial direction for several years.[55]

After 1947, he also became the director of the Amharic and Tigrinya newspaper *Ityopya*, the official organ of the Unionist Party. This was a major achievement that only deepened his prominence in Eritrea's burgeoning public culture: by this time, he was publicly described as an "influential member" of the Unionist Party, no doubt because of his impressive scholarly and journalistic credentials.[56] He remained the director of *Ityopya* until 1951, when he was replaced by Gäbrä Yoḥannes Täsfämaryam (1911–n.d.),[57] but he continued to write articles for the paper into the 1960s.[58] Though by then a longtime Asmära resident, he remained proud of his rural origins: he continued to sign his articles in this newspaper as "Gä. Germu of Bäraqit," just as he had in *The Eritrean Weekly News* and *Il Quotidiano Eritreo.*

Politics and journalism did not distract Gäbrä Mika'él from his scholarly pursuits. In the 1950s, he began working on another compilation, a lined notebook of 130 pages that contains a number of historical works in Amharic and Tigrinya.[59] The first is a copy of *däbtära* Zännäb's biography of Emperor Téwodros, which Gäbrä Mika'él obtained from the print edition. He noted in perhaps recently acquired English that "I have given that tax [*sic*] exactly, as it was written by its author."[60] The remainder of the notebook consists of various related historical works: a dynastic history that deals with Sheba, Aksum, and the medieval Solomonids; a history of Tegray; a study of historical etymologies; and finally a short history of Emperor Téwodros.

He also completed a major original work during this period, which he titled *Mäṣḥafä meker*, or *Book of Counsel.*[61] Written in an accounting ledger, it is a 230-page blend of history and theology in thirty-one chapters. Yet its design and thematic foci are entirely novel: it is part *tarikä nägäśt*, part Catholic apologia, and part history of inter-Christian relations, with particular emphasis on the early modern period. The first chapters are written in a largely traditional annalistic style, with detailed digressions on somewhat unusual topics like Muslims and the Bétä Esra'él, while his later chapters examine in detail the vicissitudes of Orthodox, Catholic, and Protestant relations.

His other historical writings from this period varied considerably. He produced a number of biographical studies of colonial-era figures. These include a detailed Tigrinya biography of *değğazmač* Bahta Ḥagos (n.d.–1894), one of the featured subjects of his earlier *Italy and Ethiopia*, and a seven page Tigrinya manuscript study of the life of *blatta* Gäbrä Egzi'abḥér

Gilay (1860–1914), the infamous interpreter-spy, discussed later in this chapter.[62] In addition to these works, he also wrote a manuscript history of the Märäb Mellaš.[63]

By the time of his death in 1969, Gäbrä Mika'él had produced at least five major historical works and a considerable number of published and unpublished shorter studies, and according to one source, he had additionally obtained the learned title *blatta*.[64] He had also amassed a substantial collection of manuscripts and Ethiopian, Eritrean, and European publications related to Northeast African history. Many of these were acquired upon his death by the Institute of Ethiopian Studies at Addis Ababa University, whose director Stanislauw Chojnacki (1915–2010) purchased them from Gäbrä Mika'él's family. Richard Pankhurst, then employed at the Institute, recalls that he had the impression that Gäbrä Mika'él had become a rather isolated scholar by the end of his life.[65] Today, this situation is completely reversed. Gäbrä Mika'él's own works can be found in the Institute's manuscripts collection, while his substantial personal library of autographed printed books has been incorporated in the Ethiopian and European language book divisions. His life's work has become part of Ethiopia's national patrimony.

Vernacular History and Colonial Subjects

Gäbrä Mika'él's career raises a fundamental issue: to what extent was there a distinctly Eritrean variety of historiography before decolonization and the heady political atmosphere of the 1940s and 1950s? This is a thorny question, principally because of what the answer implies for later claims and counter-claims about the role of colonial rule in forging Eritrean national identity.[66] The matter is further complicated by two conceptual ambiguities. During the colonial period, most Eritrean intellectuals did not explicitly refer to "Eritrea" and "Eritreans" in their writings, instead preferring ethnemes, local toponyms, or the larger geo-historical concept of "Ethiopia," all terms that defy easy national categorization.[67] In addition, Christian Eritrean historians typically emerged from the same vernacular tradition as their Ethiopian counterparts, which means the two groups cannot readily be distinguished through their methods and intellectual lineage. Yet despite these issues of conceptualization, this chapter contends that in the years between 1890 and 1941, some Eritrean scholars began to write history that was distinct from that of their contemporaries in Ethiopia, described in the previous chapter. Put simply, the colonial situation led Eritrean historians to colonial topics.

The most renowned Eritrean historian of the era was surely the provocative *blatta* Gäbrä Egzi'abḥér Gilay.[68] Born near Asmära, he received a

Figure 3.2. Gäbrä Egzi'abḥér Gilay (A), as depicted in undated colonial surveillance photo. Archivio Eritrea, 1888–1917, busta 78.

traditional church education and studied Amharic, Arabic, Ge'ez, and Italian.[69] In 1889, he began working for the Italians, first as a clerk and subsequently as an interpreter and diplomat, and over the course of the next decade, he became one of the most important native civil servants in the colonial administration.[70] In the estimation of the Italians, he was "a perfect example" of a loyal Tegrayan subject.[71] His true allegiances, however, lay with Emperor Menilek and Ethiopia, for he led a covert network of native interpreters who used their privileged positions in the colonial bureaucracy to pass coded intelligence to allies in Ethiopia.[72] Gäbrä Egzi'abḥér's duplicity was discovered in 1899, and he was imprisoned in Naples and then Nokra, the Italian penal colony in the Dahlak archipelago. He quickly escaped, fled to Ethiopia, and spent the remainder of his life in Harär and Addis Ababa. In his later years, he wrote political poetry and reportedly produced an Amharic gazette.[73]

Despite Gäbrä Egzi'abḥér's many official and clandestine duties, he was also inclined toward historiography. His historical writings include a dynastic history, a series of letters, and several poems on politico-historical questions. The earliest and most extensive of these is his unpublished *tarikä nägäśt*, a lined notebook confiscated by the Italian authorities and now preserved in the vast colonial Archivio Eritrea.[74] In it, Gäbr'ä Egzi'abḥér begins by addressing conventional topics such as the origins of Ethiopians, the Aksumite era, the rise of Islam, and the invasions of Aḥmad Ibrāhīm al-Ġāzī, and proceeds to discuss church history, the arrival of European missionaries, and the poor state of religious belief in Ethiopia.[75] Yet these relatively conventional trappings conceal a provocative historical theme: the glory of Ethiopia in antiquity and its subsequent spiritual and material decline. Gäbrä Egzi'abḥér attributed this alarming diminution to the failures of Ethiopia's rulers and the arrival of the "rapacious" Italians, whose rule he compared to the jaws of a serpent.[76] His history is thus an indirect attempt to explain the underlying political causes of colonialism in Eritrea, which he described as "the lost nation."[77]

Gäbrä Egzi'abḥér continued to explore this problem in historically inflected correspondence and poetry. In 1899, he wrote a strident letter to Emperor Menilek castigating him for abandoning Eritrea to the Italians, apparently hoping that this would encourage the emperor to rectify past mistakes.[78] The thrust of Gäbrä Egzi'abḥér's case was historical. In his view, while emperors Téwodros and Yoḥannes had preserved and protected their ancestral homeland, Menilek was instead shredding "Mother Ethiopia's womb" through his treaties with the Italians, by which he was "disposing of Ethiopia as a person disposes of his urine."[79] The letter was apparently unpersuasive. He subsequently wrote a series of poems on anticolonial subjects and historical events, including one that explained the Ottoman defeat in the Turko-Italian War of 1911–12.[80] The boldness of Gäbrä Egzi'abḥér's writings secured his reputation as a proto-nationalist and unwavering critic of colonial rule.[81] Gäbrä Mika'él clearly held him in high esteem: he wrote at least two biographies of Gäbrä Egzi'abḥér.[82]

Less polemical but more prolific was Feśśeḥa Giyorgis Abiyä Egzi'e (1868–1931). Born near Adwa, Feśśeḥa received a traditional education before moving to Massawa, where his horizons broadened considerably.[83] In 1889, he met the Italian diplomat Pietro Antonelli, escorted *ras* Mäkonnen Wäldä Mika'él (1852–1906)—the father of Täfäri Mäkonnen—through war-torn Tegray, and helped draft the Treaty of Weččale. The following year, he departed to Italy, where he studied Latin, Italian, and Arabic, and taught Ethiopian languages at the Royal Oriental Institute of Naples.[84] It was during this time that he wrote several histories, some of which were published in Rome. These include a detailed study of northern Ethiopia in Tigrinya,[85] a similar shorter work in Amharic,[86] an autobiographical travel account in Tigrinya,[87] and a history of the Arabs and Egyptians, partially translated from Arabic into Tigrinya.[88] Feśśeḥa eventually returned to Eritrea, where he lived until his death in 1931.

Feśśeḥa's magnum opus is his manuscript history of northern Ethiopia, *Tarik iityopya.* Apparently completed before the 1890s, it is a lengthy dynastic history with a pronounced Tegrayan focus and a substantial number of ethnographic and etymological digressions.[89] In writing it, Feśśeḥa drew upon vernacular histories, oral traditions, linguistic evidence, and

European scholarship, and the result is a nuanced study of the travails of his beleaguered homeland, emphasizing above all the imperial drama of the late nineteenth century. He discusses the following subjects: the question of Ethiopian origins, the pre-Aksumite era, and the Makedda-Solomon liaison; Aksum, early Ethiopian Christianity, and the Zagwe dynasty; the incursions of Aḥmad Ibrāhīm al-Ġāzī and the arrival of the Portuguese; the subsequent conflicts between the Tegrayans, Agaw, and Amhara; and finally the neo-Solomonid saga of emperors Téwodros and Yoḥannes, the Mahdist wars, and the rise of Emperor Menilek. He concludes his study by describing marriages, funereal rites, and the various descent groups of northern Ethiopia.

This rich work reveals its author's many talents. Feśśeḥa was a shrewd observer of historical developments, an accomplished literary stylist, and an informed but caustic interloper in the scholarly debates of European orientalists.[90] But above all, he was a vast repository of Tegrayan historical traditions: his *tarikä nägäśt* offers a rare peripheral/Northern perspective on what are essentially conventional historical subjects. Thus his discussion of Ethiopia's ancient history rather unusually includes Tigrinya etymologies for regnal names, his account of Grañ's invasion explores its impact on Tegray and its inhabitants, and his analysis of the *zämänä mäsafent* focuses on the ethnic tensions between the Tegrayans and their Amhara, Agaw, and Oromo neighbors.[91] This view from the edge is equally evident in his discussion of the nineteenth century.[92] Some of his most striking historical observations relate to the Tegrayans' willingness to adopt the customs and languages of their conquerors, such as the Amhara practices of oath-taking and "shameless" concubinage.[93] Though by no means unique to the Amhara and Tegrayans, his implications are clear: oaths were often part of colonial rituals of native submission, and the Italians widely practiced interracial concubinage.[94]

Similar in focus but shorter in length is his Amharic history of Ethiopia, published as *Fitäñaytunna ḫʷalañaytu ityopya* with the subtitle *L'Etiopia antica e moderna.* In its introduction, Feśśeḥa explains his curious choice of language by noting that he hoped his work would help instruct students in Amharic, though as he noted, Tigrinya would be more appropriate for "the people of the territory of Eritrea."[95] Two chapters then follow. The first, titled "Things Told of Earlier Ethiopia," attends to ancient and medieval history,"[96] while the second and much shorter chapter, titled "Later Ethiopia," considers the migrations of the Tegrayans, their descendants, the etymologies of the place names they inhabited, and the relationship between their languages.[97] As in his *Tarik ityopya*, the distinctiveness of Feśśeḥa's analysis emerges from his combination of oral traditions and Ethiopian and Arabic sources, and from his considerable attention to linguistic questions.[98] Taken together, *Tarik ityopya* and *Fitäñaytunna ḥʷalañaytu ityopya* represent a tremendous achievement in regional history. It was likely for this reason that Feśśeha had achieved some renown by the end of his life—Ḫeruy included his *Tarik ityopya* in his second bibliography, and Gäbrä Mika'él knew of his work.[99] He is today remembered as a pioneer of Tigrinya literature.[100]

If Feśśeḥa refocused and elaborated the vernacular tradition, his contemporary *abba* Täklä Maryam Sämḥaray Sälim (1871–1942) transcended it altogether. Born near Kärän, Täklä Maryam studied at the Lazarist seminary until his ordination in 1893, after which he spent nearly two decades supporting the Catholic mission in Eritrea. In 1910, he was transferred to Dér Śelṭan, the Ethiopian residence in Jerusalem, and in 1927, he arrived in Rome, where he taught at the University of Rome and the Pontifical Ethiopian College. Throughout his travels, he conducted research into Ethiopian Christian worship, and while in Europe, he published some of his findings in academic journals and monographs, including one book produced by the same press that published Feśśeha's short history of Ethiopia. Täklä Maryam died in Italy in 1942.[101]

Much of his scholarship examined the history of the liturgy, or *qeddasé,* a subject wholly apart from the comparatively worldly concerns of royal biography, dynastic history, and universal chronography. His interest in this area related to the then-ongoing Capuchin-led Latinization of the Ethiopian Catholic liturgy, a development Täklä Maryam forcefully attacked. His first anti-Latin salvo came in 1913, when he wrote to Propaganda Fide (the department of the Church charged with spreading the faith) criticizing flaws in the existing liturgical texts and the tremendous variation in practice that obtained in the Apostolic Vicariate. His letter provoked two official responses: one from Bishop Carrara himself, who dismissed Täklä Maryam's "superficial" understanding of the issue and disputed his description of sacramental chaos in Eritrea; and another from Jean-Baptiste Coulbeaux (1843–1921), a scholar and veteran Lazarist missionary who more even-handedly considered Täklä Maryam's charges.[102] Undeterred by these reactions, Täklä Maryam continued his defense of the indigenous rite by systematically reconstructing the original "pure" form of the Ethiopian Orthodox liturgy, which he believed had been corrupted through centuries of accretions and distortions attributable to scholars' general inclination "to repudiate the old and adhere to the new."[103] This reconstruction required a critical examination of the liturgy's evolution, and for Täklä Maryam, the instrument of this recovery was a systematic comparative historical analysis bridging philology and Rankean source-criticism. This scholarly endeavor became a life-long pursuit.

The breadth of his efforts is breath-taking. In one discussion of his comparative method, Täklä Maryam claimed to have examined a vast number of sources on three continents. Many of these were missals, or guides to the celebration of the liturgy. These included the missals of Täsfä Ṣeyon (n.d.–1550), *abunä* Kidänä Maryam Käśśä (1886–1951), and *däbtära* Keflä Giyorgis (1825–1900); four Ethiopian missals from Dér Śelṭan; three Coptic missals published in translated editions; and nine missals from the Vatican library, fourteen from the Bibliothèque Nationale, and four from the British Museum.[104] He also considered a range of additional sources, old and new—hagiographies, the liturgies of Saint Mark and Saint James, the seventeenth-century works of Hiob Ludolf (1624–1704), and twentieth-century scholarship on Ethiopia and Eastern Christianity more generally.[105] This research led him to conclude that the original Ethiopian liturgy was derived from the ancient Greek liturgy of Mark, and not the Coptic liturgy of Basil, as was commonly supposed.[106] Thus, in his view, "the Ethiopian Catholic liturgy is neutral: it is neither Ethiopian nor Latin."[107] He catalogued the various additions that had obscured this distinctive origin, and published his findings in the journal *Revue de l'Orient Chrétien* and two subsequent monographs, thereby making a significant contribution to the study of Eastern Christianity.[108] Upon his death, his orientalist colleagues lauded his scholarly achievements: Enrico Cerulli (1898–1988) said his work was defined by "a rigorous scientific method," while Sylvain Grébaut (1881–1955) described him as "relentless in research and gifted with a subtle penetration."[109] Täklä Maryam was one of the most erudite and prominent intellectuals of the era, and since he pursued a philological and textualist variety of historical inquiry, he was additionally a religious historian of the first rank.

Though the nature of their achievements varied, Täklä Maryam, Feśśeha, and Gäbrä Ezi'abḥér were all recognized as scholars, activists, and stewards of their cultural patrimony. They are, however, only the most prominent Eritrean historians of the era, and the caliber of their scholarship should not obscure the fact that many of their lesser-known contemporaries also experimented with the historian's craft. *Käntiba* Gila Mika'él (1870–n.d.), an acquaintance of Gäbrä Egzi'abḥér and fellow conspirator in his clandestine network of interpreters, wrote a detailed autobiography that describes his career in the Italian colonial service and his subsequent exile in Ethiopia.[110] His contemporary *qäši* Tedlä, a local historian of Hazzäga, wrote an annalistic history of Ḥamasén that described the Italian occupation of Massawa, *ras* Alula's conflicts with the Turks and Italians, the extension of Italian rule in the region, and finally the battle of Adwa, where Emperor Menilek defeated the Italians "killing one part, capturing one part, and cutting off the hands and feet of one part."[111] The Eritrean evangelicals Solomon Aṣqu (n.d.–1926), Zär'a Ṣeyon Musé (n.d.–1940s?), and Gobezé Gošu (1883–1951) wrote autobiographies and mission histories of the EFS efforts in the Eritrean highlands, some of which were published by the Asmära mission press that employed Gäbrä Krestos.[112] Still other historians wrote biographies that touched upon colonial themes, such as an anonymous account of Emperor Yoḥannes's reign that concludes with the Italian defeat at Ṣäḥati.[113] A few even acted as amateur archivists: Täsfaṣeyon Derres (1914–n.d.), a colonial civil servant and later Eritrean separatist, was a historical enthusiast who collected poetry related to the history of Ḥamasén.[114]

The works of these intellectuals are distinct from the variety of historical writing that occasionally surfaced in Eritrea's principal newspaper, *Il Quotidiano Eritreo.* Published daily after 1929 by the longtime Asmära entrepreneur Maria Fioretti (1871–1945),[115] the paper featured Italian, Tigrinya, and Arabic sections with colonial, metropolitan, and international news, along with a considerable amount of fascist editorial commentary. The Italian section included a daily Eritrean subsection, "Life and Events in the Colony," that was largely devoted to ordinances, transportation schedules, notices of arrivals and departures, and announcements related to commerce, arrests, sporting events, and the weather. It occasionally featured articles about local events of a quasi-official nature, mostly connected to the Federazione dei Fasci di Combattimento dell'Eritrea. The Tigrinya section of the newspaper offered translations of some of this Italian material, with additional original items of interest to the paper's African readers. These included obituaries, notices on official appointments and educational opportunities, remarks on Ethiopian affairs, and on occasion, original articles by Eritrean writers. The most prolific of these Tigrinya-speaking contributors to the newspaper included *qäññazmač* Tädla Täklay,[116] *abba* Gäbrä Iyasus Haylu,[117] *abba* Yoḥannes Gäbrä Egazi'abḥér,[118] *aläqa* Equba Enderyas,[119] and Gäbrä Mäsqäl Wäldu, the last the friend and colleague of Gäbrä Mika'él at *Eritrean Weekly News.*[120]

Although the chief focus of *Il Quotidiano Eritreo* was international politics and economic affairs, it occasionally included articles on historical topics. The Italian section periodically featured reprints from the Italian press on questions such the economic depression, the nature of the bourgeoisie, the underlying causes of war, the civilizing mission in its Italian and British variants, and the role of "The Leader and the People in History." It also offered short pieces on matters of general historical significance, such as Emperor Augustus, Cleopatra and her Roman admirers, and the pre-Columbian Scandinavian voyages to North America.[121]

On rare occasions, the newspaper delved into Eritrean and Northeast African history. The Italian section sometimes featured original pieces by eminent Italian writers, such as the anthropologist Alberto Pollera (1873–1939), who wrote a biography of General Giuseppe Ettore Viganò (1843–1933) that discussed the conquest of Eritrea in considerable detail, and ministerial undersecretary Alessandro Lessona (1891–1991), who wrote an article on Italo-Ethiopian relations since the nineteenth century.[122]

The Tigrinya section also offered occasional glimpses of local history. Most commonly, these appeared in the guise of obituaries, which though often too brief to be considered biography proper, were nonetheless of historical significance for attentive readers.[123]

It is clear that the vision of the past offered by the pages of *Il Quotidiano Eritreo* was colonial and Italophilic, both in the historical voices it featured and the topics and arguments these voices took up. In this respect, its historical imagination was quite different from that of vernacular historians like Gäbrä Egzi'abḥér, Feśśeha, and even Gäbrä Mika'él. It was, moreover, a world apart from the variety of history publicized by *Berhanenna sälam*, its Ethiopian contemporary and counterpart as a local newspaper of record.[124] This was official history in a colonial language, with occasional footnotes and appendices in the vernacular.

To what extent did these different Eritrean historians—notable and obscure; Orthodox, Catholic, and evangelical; well-traveled, exiled, and anchored to home—consider the problem of colonialism? If colonial rule was indeed a formative experience for Eritrean intellectuals, then one would expect a robust discussion of its agents, institutions, and dynamics in their historical writings. The record on this point is however somewhat mixed. Some Eritrean historians declined to comment on colonial matters at all. Täklä Märyam said nothing about it in his writings, though colonial politics and institutions profoundly shaped his career and intellectual interests. *Qäši* Tedla ended his local history with the Battle of Adwa and the deaths of *ras*es Alula, Mengeša, and Wäldä Mika'él, leaving aside the issue of the new Italian regime. He explained his decision cryptically, observing "We will not [continue] to write the history of the exploits of our princes, because we do not have [sufficient] information. As our Lord said in the gospels, 'One nation [*ḥezb*] rises against [another] nation and kings against [other] kings.'"[125] In his eminently traditionalist view, Ethiopia's Solomonid rulers were the engines of historical change, and in an era in which their role had been usurped by foreigners, it was difficult to write proper history.

Other Eritrean historians focused on colonial actors and episodes with local or personal significance. Thus the Ḥamasén scholar Täwäldä Medhin described the arrival of Italian troops in Kärän and Asmära, and subsequently recounted the tale of the tyrannical chief of an Italian *banda*, one *däğğazmač* Ḥädgä Anbäsa (ca. 1854–ca. 1891) of Ḥamasén. The latter raided the villages of Ṣä'azzäga and Hazzäga, and terrorized their inhabitants until his Italian ally, a Major Di Maggio, turned upon him and imprisoned him in Assäb, at which point his followers became *askari*s.[126] Merid and Kelete, two Ḥamasén contemporaries of Täwäldä Medhin, offered similarly brief accounts of the revolt of *däğğazmač* Bahta Ḥagos.[127] Gila Mika'él discussed Italian rule in terms of the impact of his colonial employment on his own life, but ultimately, his primary historical object was his own family and the question of their inheritance.[128] These individuals used vernacular history to describe aspects of the colonial situation, not its entirety. Their efforts were not systemic.

A few writers commented on colonialism very generally. Gäbrä Egzi'abḥér obviously devoted considerable attention to the dangers of Italian rule, though he had little to say about the features of the colonial order itself. As we have seen, Feśśeḥa shied away from the topic of colonialism per se, though he describes the Napier expedition, the early stages of the subsequent Ethiopian-Italian struggle, and occasional episodes of European arrogance and racism.[129] It is in comparison to these episodic, personal, and indirect perspectives that the significance of Gäbrä Mika'él's work becomes apparent. Of all his Eritrean and Ethiopian contemporaries, he most explicitly and creatively grappled with colonialism as a novel historical phenomenon.

"Their Spirit Burned Like Fire"

This unique orientation is most evident in Gäbrä Mika'él's *Italy and Ethiopia*, a detailed study of approximately fifty-three pages. It consists of a very brief introduction and two principal sections: a chronology of imperialism from the Spanish conquest of the Americas to the Italian invasion of Ethiopia in 1935, primarily focused on the late nineteenth century; and a detailed narrative that includes extracts from relevant primary source documents.[130] The narrative is the longest part of the study. It is interrupted by three interpolated texts: a chronology of the Roman Caesars, a short history of the Grañ invasion, and a copy of and response to the *Fekkaré iyasus*, a Ge'ez eschatological text. These interpolations are distinguished by paratextual markers and skipped pages.[131]

In the narrative itself, Gäbrä Mika'él addresses the following topics: the acquisition of Assäb and its significance for Italian claims on the rest of Ethiopia; the Treaty of Weččale, the instrument of these claims, which is presented in full; the Italian occupation of Massawa; the struggle between Emperor Yoḥannes and *neguś* Menilek, then allied with Italy; the Italians' arrival in the highlands; *ras* Alula's victory at Ṣäḥati; the agreement between Menilek and Antonelli; the Ethiopian victory at Sägänäyti; *ras* Mäkonnen's visit to Italy; Menilek's realization of the duplicity of Weččale; the precise details of the Ethiopian-Eritrean boundary, as agreed upon by Menilek and Antonelli; the alliance between *ras* Mengeša and the Italians; the underlying reasons for Menilek's turn against the Italians; the revolt of Bahta Ḥagos, his demise, and the Italian reprisals against his supporters; *ras* Mengeša's turn against the Italians and battles with the Mahdists; and

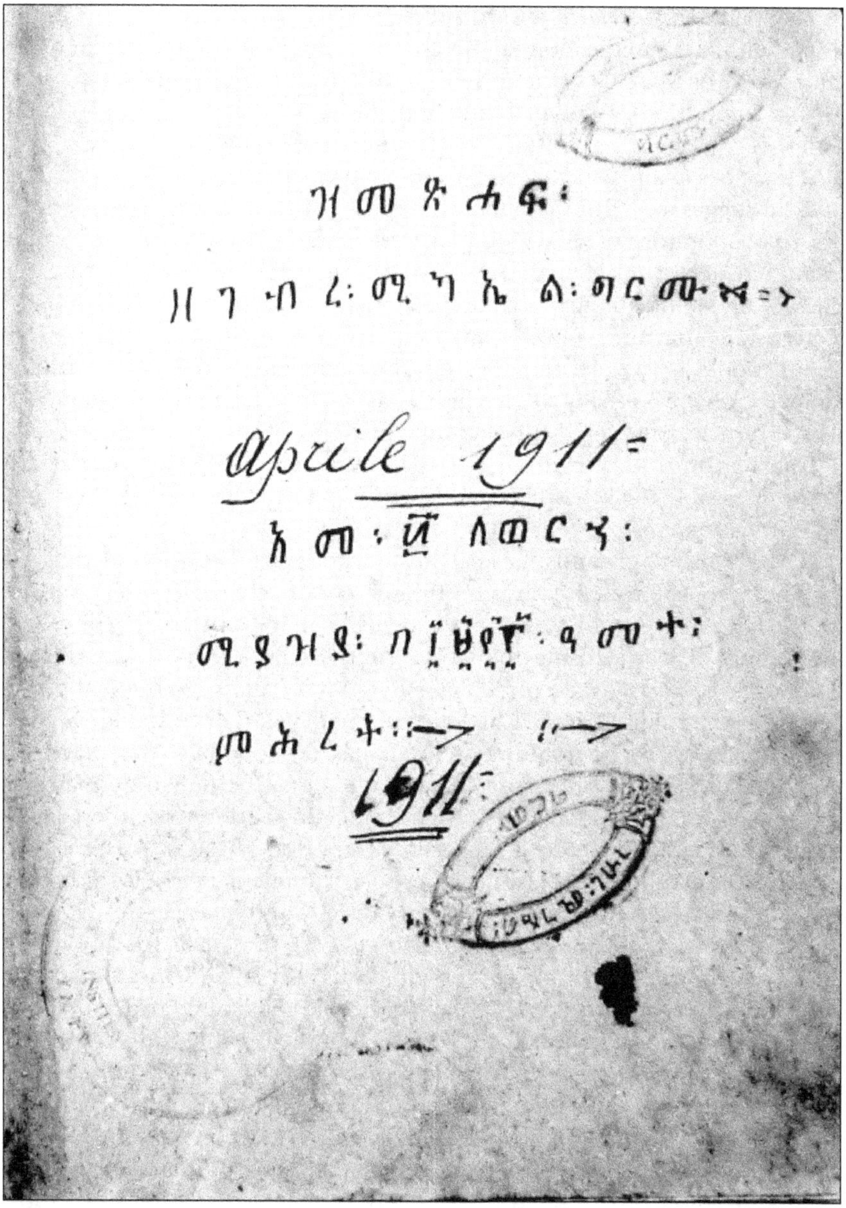

Figure 3.3. Frontispiece of Gäbrä Mika'él Germu's historical compendium, IES Ms. 324.

finally Baratieri's advance toward Adwa. The narrative ends abruptly at this point, on the eve of the momentous confrontation between the Italian forces and Emperor Menilek's vast army. The work is thus a sharply focused study of the imposition of colonial rule and the early struggles it engendered. Effectively, it describes the Italian conquest of the Ethiopian frontier.

How does Gäbrä Mikä'él explain these developments? In *Italy and Ethiopia,* he suggests that the Italian colonization of Eritrea was dependent on local collaborators, of which Menilek was—paradoxically—the most prominent and decisive. Throughout the narrative, Gäbrä Mika'él sketches the history of Menilek's surrender of Ethiopian sovereignty to foreigners by contrasting him unfavorably with Emperor Yoḥannes, who in his assessment "would never give an inch from the Ethiopian land to a foreign king and . . . [who] was ready to give his life as sacrifice for his motherland."[132] His criticisms parallel the bold indictment of Menilek made by Gäbrä Egzi'abḥér and other Eritreans of the era.[133] Though Emperor Menilek was responsible for Ethiopia's military triumph over Italy, his victory came at Eritrea's expense.

Gäbrä Mika'él grounds these claims in diplomatic correspondence. He begins by considering the various Ethiopian responses to the Italian seizure of the Ottoman port of Massawa. He explains that Emperor Yoḥannes had his deputy deliver a strong rebuke to the Ottoman consul demanding to know why he had allowed the Italians to enter a region "guarded and protected by the caliph for us." The letter ultimately declared "in the name of *neguś* Yoḥannes, we do not tolerate the Italian occupation of that place."[134] In contrast, Menilek optimistically sent a letter to the Italian government expressing his "longing to have a friendly meeting" with their closest representative. Gäbrä Mika'él next reports the two rulers' diverging responses to the Italian territorial expansions in 1886–87, immediately before the battle at Ṣäḥati escalated tensions between Ethiopia and Italy. He first presents the letter sent by Yoḥannes to an Italian general: "Last year you sojourned in Wi'a without seeking any consent, and this year, to add another slaughter to the already existing one, I have been told that you have advanced to Ṣäḥati. This country is actually my country, but you are intending to swallow it up like a piece of bread. According to your message, you claim to be vanguards of peace, but what does your persistent slaughter imply?"[135] In contrast to this confrontational position, Gäbrä Mika'él reports that Menilek wrote the following to his "dear friend Umberto I": "Because of the happenings in the Eritrean sea this year, there is much trouble in our country. When the soldiers entered Massawa and settled in the surrounding areas, it looked as if they were to enter Ethiopia . . . [However] we came to realize that the whole intention behind your majesty's move was not to harm but to seek friendship and create love and peace between Ethiopia and Italy."[136] For Gäbrä Mika'él, the denouement of the latter approach was a historical turning point. Menilek entered into treaties with Italy "to defeat *neguś* Yoḥannes jointly and reach an agreement on the future common welfare of the two countries," and after the death of his rival at the hands of the Sudanese Mahdists, the newly crowned Emperor Menilek signed the Wečč̌ale agreement, which surreptitiously attempted to establish Ethiopia as an Italian protectorate.[137]

How then does Gäbrä Mika'él explain Menilek's reversal of course and the road to Adwa? He suggests that Menilek only came to "understand the wickedness of the Italians" through the counsel of others. He explains how "the authorities of Šäwa took a firm united stand and said, in one voice, 'it is easier to shed our blood on our [own] soil rather than hand over Akkälä Guzay and Ṣäraye to the Italians' [as stipulated by the Wečč̌ale Agreement]."[138] Menilek then received letters from British and German diplomats confirming Italy's claims on Ethiopia, whereupon he finally rejected the controversial articles of the agreement and "instructed all his authorities to expel the Italians out of the country completely."[139] At a time when Ethiopian historians like Ḫeruy, Afäwärq Gäbrä Iyäsus, and *ṣäḥafé te'ezaz* Gäbrä Śellasé lauded Menilek as the hero of Adwa and the savior of the nation, Gäbrä Mika'él instead casts him as a naïve and opportunistic rival to Yoḥannes who only reluctantly recognized the colonial danger his advisors and rivals could plainly see, and as a calculating ruler who accepted the creation of Eritrea by enlisting the Italians in his local power struggles. It is one of the earliest articulations of a historical narrative that would later become common among Eritrean nationalists.[140]

Gäbrä Mika'él suggests that patriotic Ethiopians and Eritreans struggled to preserve their sovereignty even when their ruler did not. He devotes considerable attention to nobles who led campaigns and revolts against the Italians. One example was *ras* Alula, "the traditional enemy of the Italians," who in 1886 led an army to the Italian garrison at Ṣäḥati, where "within twelve hours time the five hundred soldiers of Colonel da Cristofero were mown down by the merciless hand of the brave Abyssinians."[141] In the estimation of Gäbrä Mika'él, "it was a battle that left the Italians with much fear, deep sorrow, and great terror."[142] Another resister was *däğğazmač* Däbäb Araya (n.d.–1891), a relative of Emperor Yoḥannes and rival of *ras* Alula. After supporting the Italians, he refused an order to bring his soldiers to Asmära and Sägänäyti. Agreeing with his soldiers "to shed their blood for their country rather than betraying it," he then intercepted Italian communications and planned an ambush of some colonial troops. The attack was successful, and Gäbrä Mika'él tells us that in consequence "this day became another Tedsali [Ṣäḥati] day for the Italians," likening Däbäb's victory to the humiliation that came from the earlier success of *ras* Alula at Ṣäḥati.[143] Faced with the same choice as Yoḥannes and Menilek, these two nobles sided with the former.

Gäbrä Mika'él's most dramatic example of resistance to colonial rule is the 1894 mass revolt led by *däğğazmač* Bahta Ḥagos—a figure vilified by Italians, generally overlooked by Ethiopians, and celebrated by later Eritrean nationalists.[144] *Italy and Ethiopia* offers one of the earliest and most detailed accounts of his rebellion.[145] Gäbrä Mika'él explains that after the death of Emperor Yoḥannes, the Catholic convert *däğğazmač* Bahta joined the Italians and briefly ruled Akkälä Guzay, before realizing their "cunning and wickedness" and deciding "to drive the Italians out of Ḥamasén as a whole."[146] Describing the Italian reaction to this betrayal, Gäbrä Mika'él first makes clear the perceived connections between Bahta's act of resistance and its heroic antecedents: "[The Italians said] 'Woe betide us! Däbäb the son of Araya pledged loyalty to the Italian state and at last he inflicted severe harm on us, with a weapon of our own gift [i.e., with arms supplied by the Italians]. And now again Bahta is planning to mobilize the whole Akkälä Guzay against us with our own arms.'"[147] After describing how *däğğazmač* Bahta then obtained intelligence from sympathetic French Lazarist missionaries, Gäbrä Mika'él then offers a dramatic account of the events that triggered the rebellion itself:

> *Dağğač* Bahta, his brother *azmač* Sengel, and one officer visited Lieutenant Sanguinetti at his home. Sanguinetti and another Italian officer, with a glass of alcohol in his hand, joined the guests for coffee at the table. While they were deep in friendly, casual conversation, *dağğač* Bahta and *azmač* Sengel exchanged messages through a signal. Then, the brave patriots shouted a war cry and suddenly attacked the two *färänğ*s while they were still with their cups in their hands. They threw them down and began kicking and hitting them with their sticks.[148]

While being beaten, the Italian officers ridiculed *däğğazmač* Bahta for not appreciating the superior "power and greatness of the Italian state."[149] In his scathing reply, made "with his foot on the Italian's stomach," Gäbrä Mika'él presents the *däğğazmač*'s rebuke of Italian colonial ambitions: "You with a cat's eye and baboon's hair, you white-assed sea donkey from across seven rivers! Don't you know that the Ethiopian state is better than the Italian state, and that the children of Ethiopia are greater than the Italians? You have not yet realized that all the Ethiopians will come to my side, you donkey!"[150] Gäbrä Mika'él relates the remaining events of the failed revolt as a tragedy, describing *däğğazmač* Bahta's capture of the Italian officers, the support he received from Eritreans and the Lazarists, his ambush and eventual death at Sägänäyti after a battle with Italian troops, and the subsequent imprisonment and execution of his supporters. These acts of resistance made Bahta and his fellow nobles *ras* Alula and *däğğazmač* Däbäb worthy historical subjects.

Gäbrä Mika'él supplements these dramatic examples of resistance with additional references to everyday contestations of colonial rule. By expanding the historical subject to include subaltern actors, he implicitly suggests that widespread anti-Italian sentiment underpinned the more dramatic moments of open conflict in Eritrea.[151] His examples are varied. On several occasions, he includes popular voices when leaders are reluctant to defend Ethiopian sovereignty through military confrontation. One example comes before the rout at Ginda'e (1888), in which he suggests that the fervor of the troops exceeded that of their leader:

> In the meantime, the officers and soldiers of Emperor Yoḥannes began shouting at him, saying, "Majesty, why all the delay? Let us move to Massawa, attack the Italians, and expel them out of our motherland Ethiopia." Sometimes they expressed their haste with war cries and war songs. Emperor Yoḥannes was very pleased by the eagerness his soldiers demonstrated, so he replied "My sons, I myself am willing to sacrifice myself for my motherland, so I am also coming with you."[152]

He describes a similar sentiment prevailing around the time of Emperor Menilek's acceptance of the Wečč̌ale Agreement: "The Ethiopian officers, however, were shouting in every square, complaining, 'unless Akkälä Guzay and Ṣäray remain administrative territories of Ethiopia we cannot accept Emperor Menilek's agreement as our own.'"[153] In this instance, the fervent patriotism of the masses went beyond the officers to include both "the old and the young." Ultimately, it would emerge again at Adwa, when Gäbrä Mika'él notes that the Ethiopian soldiers' "spirit burned like fire" as they bravely faced their Italian adversaries.[154] Here, Gäbrä Mika'él suggests the depth of the soldiers' sentiments through synecdochal literary embellishment:

> When Menilek II announced the proclamation of the campaign to Adwa, the campaigners began to move. A frightful glory could be read on the face of each of them. The children of Ethiopia, whose heart did not fear cannons and machine guns, had a spirit that burned like fire. They carried their swords, the task of which was to realize . . . their bearers' love of his country by the blood of the enemy. Their bearers were prompted by their habit of cutting the human body, and the swords were given a duty similar to that of a razor on hair: to hasten to cut the human body into pieces.[155]

For Gäbrä Mika'él, the lowly soldier and his simple saber were thus united by the nobility of their shared purpose.

At other times, Gäbrä Mika'él features subaltern voices that comment more generally on colonial rule. One dramatic example comes in his discussion of the events prior to the battle of Ko'atit. At that time, "The population in all the towns went out, singing "God will not deliver us into the hands of those who hate our state and our people. Ethiopia is a country blessed by God, therefore God will not deliver this country into the hands of those *färängs* who want to subjugate it."[156] Gäbrä Mika'él elsewhere suggests that pessimistic views sometimes prevailed, however. For example, after the failure of *däǧǧazmač* Bahta's revolt, he reported that "the popular song among girls at the time was, 'There is medicine for the bite of the black snake, but there is none for the bite of the white snake.'"[157] Immediately after the suppression of the largest popular challenge to colonial rule, *däǧǧazmač* Bahta's brief collaboration with the Italians perhaps seemed the only explanation as to why an Ethiopian could have lost to a foreigner.

It is possible that Gäbrä Mika'él treated subaltern actors as historical agents because he understood colonialism as a transformative historical phenomenon. It affected all Ethiopians and Eritreans, whether great or small, and its reverberations were manifest in everyday life as well as in events like revolts and large-scale battles. He takes a similarly heterogenous view of the agents of imperialism. He notes how it relied upon an array of local groups, such as the nobles and merchants of Italy, the missionaries, and the Eritrean conscript troops, as well as their supporters in the Italian metropole, such as the parliament, "the people of Italy," the press, and the Rubattino Shipping Company. And most importantly, its individual representatives play key roles in Gäbrä Mika'él's narrative: rulers like Umberto I and Vittorio Emmanuele II; ministers and diplomats such as Robilato, Geroba, Nerrazini, and Antonelli; military men like Baratieri, Toselli, and Cornacchia; Capuchins, Lazarists, and indigenous clergy; European journalists; and comparatively minor figures, such as Italian regular troops and the anonymous postman from Naples who "wrote to the Italian state saying that Emperor Menilek had violated the Weččale agreement and sent messages to the German and French states and to the Sultan of Zanzibar."[158] In effect, Gäbrä Mika'él's work is a taxonomy of the colonial situation and its actors.

In part, this sophisticated perspective reflects the heterogeneity of Gäbrä Mika'él's underlying source material. On the one hand, he valued oral testimony alongside a wide variety of texts: as he candidly noted in his introduction, "I have proceeded from written records of Ethiopian kings and from [the testimony of] elders that I have found."[159] But on the other hand, some of his "written records" were Italian books—an unsurprising fact, given his linguistic abilities and position in the colonial administration. He presents the full text of diplomatic treaties, includes the names of Italian soldiers who died in relatively minor military conflicts, describes the reception of *ras* Mäkonnen in Italy and the actions of the "postman from Naples," and in general considers the Italian perspective on colonial developments, such as the influence of a French journalist named Debat on European opinion.[160] Such details could only have come from Italian sources.[161]

These likely included the work of Carlo Conti Rossini (1872–1949), the eminent Italian orientalist and *etiopianista*. Gäbrä Mika'él owned copies of several of Conti Rossini's works,[162] and he was almost certainly familiar with his *Italia ed Etiopia dal trattato d'Uccialli alla battaglia di Adua*, a detailed 1935 study with numerous parallels to Gäbrä Mika'él's similarly titled *Italy and Ethiopia*.[163] The two works are nearly identical in periodization and scope. They each focus almost exclusively on the initial phase of Italian rule, prior to the appointment of Ferdinando Martini (1841–1928) as the first colonial governor in 1897. Both open with a discussion of Assäb and the Treaty of Weččale, and both conclude with Adwa, which Conti Rossini treats as the denouement of a series of Italian mis-steps.[164] For two scholars writing in the 1930s, this focus on earlier events was a deliberate choice: both Conti Rossini and Gäbrä Mika'él ignored three decades of subsequent developments, suggesting that the founding of the colonial order in Eritrea was the key to understanding the subsequent relationship between Italy and Ethiopia.[165]

But if Gäbrä Mika'él took some conceptual inspiration from Conti Rossini, his work was by no means derivative. Though the periodization and topical coverage of the two studies are very similar, their conclusions could not be more different. Consider their treatments of the first event of the colonial era, the Rubattino Shipping Company's acquisition of Assäb. For Conti Rossini, the purchase was intended to begin a period of amicable Italo-Ethiopian relations, one in which Italy aspired only to "open new fields of activity to its economy."[166] For Gäbrä Mika'él, in contrast, the event was both a stratagem and a harbinger: as he rhetorically asked, "Do you think that the occupation and the gain of the Italians would be confined to that small place?" He offered as an answer the following words: "But because the Italian government was given the right of colonization, [and] because it came to the land, we always spill the blood of the young and make much mourning."[167] For Conti Rossini, Italy's intentions were benign and transparent, while for Gäbrä Mika'él they were predatory and clandestine.

Diverging perspectives also inform the two authors' assessments of Adwa: for Conti Rossini, post-Assäb developments in the colony led inexorably to the "tragic outcome" of Adwa, while for Gäbrä Mika'él, the era's popular patriotic struggles had their glorious consummation in Italy's defeat. The two historians offer similarly opposing assessments of Emperor Menilek: Conti Rossini treats his initial rapprochement with the Italians as Janus-faced, while Gäbrä Mika'él sees it as naïve. Their perspectives on *däğğazmač* Bahta are even more starkly opposite: Gäbrä Mika'él offers an extensive discussion of the failed rebellion, while Conti Rossini describes it with comparative brevity, noting of the revolt only that its leader simply "cast off the mask" of duplicity and died several days later.[168] Though Gäbrä Mika'él likely drew upon the work of Conti Rossini, he clearly read against the grain of his source.[169] As subsequent scholarship has shown, this is an eminently suitable methodology for reconstructing colonial history.

When seen from the perspective of the present day, Gäbrä Mika'él is clearly a transitional figure in Eritrean—and Ethiopian—intellectual history, and this intermediary position accounts for his relative obscurity today. The issue is political. The nature and significance of Eritrea's colonial past is now a contentious question, with commentators generally divided between two positions. Some hold that colonial rule was but a brief interruption of a much longer history of "Greater Ethiopian" cultural and political unity throughout the highlands, one in which Eritrea was the northernmost province of Solomonid Ethiopia. According this view, the impact of colonial rule was insubstantial and evanescent. Others argue that colonialism was the crucible of Eritrean nationhood, a transformative development that forged or sharpened a collective sense of national distinctiveness from Ethiopia. Both of these historical assessments are taken to bear on the legitimacy of Eritrea's current political sovereignty.

Gäbrä Mika'él's conception of Eritrea and its colonial past stands apart from these two contemporary positions, just as his *Italy and Ethiopia* diverges from the contemporaneous works of Conti Rossini and Ḫeruy. His harsh assessment of Emperor Menilek even differs from that of Gäbrä Krestos Täklä Haymanot, his countryman-in-exile. This distinctiveness reveals the paradox at the heart of Gäbrä Mika'él's scholarship. Though he produced one of the first distinctly Eritrean histories by examining colonialism as a pivotal local historical development with its own pantheon of heroes (Emperor Yoḥannes, *ras* Alula, Gäbrä Egzi'abnér Gilay, and *däǧǧazmač* Bahta) and villains (Emperor Menilek and the Italians), thereby anticipating the arguments of later Eritrean nationalists, he nonetheless continued to view his own cultural heritage as essentially Ethiopian, as the title of his work and as his Unionist political allegiances suggest.[170] Indeed, some of his most heroic Eritrean protagonists explicitly affirm their Ethiopian identity. These multilayered affinities explain why one later Eritrean commentator hailed Gäbrä Mika'él's scholarship but noted that "it contained many points that could be scorned," since "his way of thinking was developed differently than ours."[171] The reason for this retrospective "scorn" is simple: Gäbrä Mika'él prefigured Eritrean nationalism, rather than embodying it.[172]

Gäbrä Mika'él can be more fruitfully understood as a producer of locality.[173] He represented a new variety of local historian who was neither a traditionalist nor a nationalist, and in this respect he resembles his Eritrean contemporaries more than his Ethiopian counterparts.[174] His approach was novel in two ways. First, he explored a smaller unit of time rooted in the historical distinctiveness of the colonial Märäb Mellaš. He wrote neither a history of Ethiopia's kings nor a regional *tarikä nägäśt*, but a history of *la colonia Eritrea*, and he treats this subject as a coherent historical space and set of actors that are largely devoid of primordialism and mythos. Indeed, his work suggests that the colony was defined by its evolving connection to larger translocal forces. This new locality overlaps and even coincides with other geo-spatial categories like Tegray and Eritrea, which eventually replaced it and appropriated much of its historical imaginary. But the three spaces are not identical. Gäbrä Mika'él endeavored to use new and old tools to understand a fleeting historical phenomenon.

Second, Gäbrä Mika'él was a product of the very historical forces he described. He was a member of Eritrea's educated and salaried urban elite, and not a church scholar or court historian. Though he emerged from and was a steward of the vernacular historical tradition, he was not a traditional intellectual in the Gramscian sense—though he was certainly respectful of the achievements of his traditionalist forebears and contemporaries. Indeed, he spent much of his life attempting to preserve, summarize, transmit, and elaborate upon their efforts, recording their oral testimonies and copying and annotating their writings. In this respect, he was very much like past generations of historical compilers. Yet as a colonial notable, he was also attuned to a new social reality, a variety of educated colonial *italianità*, and a corpus of Italian texts that was largely absent in Ethiopia. This distinctive orientation allowed him to pursue a dialogic approach to the varieties of history with which he was acquainted, harnessing all to his own ends.

4

Ḫeruy Wäldä Śellasé and the New Queen of Sheba

In 1923, *wäyzäro* Mänän Asfaw—the wife of Crown Prince Täfäri Mäkonnen—made a momentous journey from Ethiopia to the Middle East. Joined by a small group of companions, she set out from Addis Ababa to the French port of Djibouti, boarded a steamship to Suez and Port Said, and then traveled by train to British Mandate Palestine, where she visited many of the colony's dignitaries, religious leaders, and historic sites. On her return, she stopped in newly independent Egypt for tours of Cairo and Luxor before continuing home. *Wäyzäro* Mänän was accompanied on this adventure by then-*blatta* Ḫeruy, whose account of their journey offers occasional hints of the tremendous significance he believed it possessed. In one episode, Ḫeruy wrote that as *wäyzäro* Mänän and her entourage passed from the familiar landscape of the Ethiopian highlands and the Red Sea littoral to the comparatively foreign world of the Levant, the travelers took comfort in the fact that they were retracing the itinerary of an august predecessor. As they arrived in the Holy Land, Ḫeruy noted that they had reached the very "Gaza of Solomon" once visited by Makedda, or Queen Azéb—the ancient Ethiopian interlocutor of the wise Israelite king. The pilgrims were thus in the hallowed setting of the *Kebrä nägäśt*.[1] Through this allusion to the sacred past, Ḫeruy carefully positioned the journey as history in the remaking: a modern would-be empress was following in the footsteps of Ethiopia's ancient founding mother.

Some years later, in the early 1930s, Ḫeruy—by now *blattén géta* and Emperor Ḫaylä Śellasé's Minister of Foreign Affairs—again turned to the ancient tale of Makedda as he reflected upon his travels abroad. This time, it was in connection to his 1931 diplomatic mission to Japan, which he saw as the beginning of Ethiopia's historic rapprochement with East Asia after centuries of fraught relations with Europe. In the introduction to his account of the voyage, Ḫeruy characteristically offered his readers—for context—a survey of Ethiopia's interactions with the wider world, and this account naturally began with the familiar story of that first intrepid Ethiopian seeker of knowledge, the Queen of Sheba, and the son she conceived with Solomon.[2] In Ḫeruy's telling, it was Makedda and Menilek I who began Ethiopia's complex and often stormy relations with the Holy Land, the Arab world, India, Europe, and now—at long last—the distant East. With this journey to Japan, it was Ḫeruy who followed Makedda's pioneering example.

Ḫeruy was not the only intellectual of the era to describe cross-cultural travel with this potent mytho-historical metaphor. In the 1890s, Feśśeḥa Giyorgis wrote that upon arriving at the Italian port of Naples, his first impression was "just like when Queen Makedda, [upon] seeing Jerusalem, said that what she was seeing [surpassed] . . . what she had heard [about it]."[3] These two travelers' references to the Queen of Sheba reveal their shared commitment to historical didacticism. On the one hand, the analogies suggested that Ethiopia's past set a precedent for new encounters with the unfamiliar and exotic, affirming the continued relevance of their cultural patrimony. On the other, they reminded readers of the antiquity of their society's supra-regional significance. Travel writing taught lessons, and these lessons were historical.

Although Ḫeruy and Feśśeḥa were among the earliest Ethiopian and Eritrean intellectuals to recount their international exploits, they were not the only ones to explore the rich literary and instructive potential of cross-cultural travel writing. Between 1898, when Feśśeḥa produced an account of his travels in Italy, and 1934, when Ḫeruy published the last of his four travel narratives, the region witnessed an explosion of travel and travel-related writing in Amharic, Tigrinya, and various European languages. Thanks to local presses, curious readers could read about distant locales, would-be travelers could obtain guides detailing practical matters and warning of possible pitfalls, and more imaginative types could be entertained by fictionalized accounts of exotic voyages and encounters. Local newspapers like *Berhanenna sälam*, *A'emro*, *Courrier d'Éthiopie*, and *Il Quotidiano Eritreo* published descriptions of royal tours, diplomatic missions, religious pilgrimages, and even the exploration of the deep sea, and they regularly featured columns on comparatively mundane topics like the particulars of studying abroad. Many of these publications featured lavish photographs of the world's wonders and the intrepid individuals who visited them.

This chapter contends that Ḫeruy's travel writing was in fact a variety of highly stylized, instructive historiography. The most prominent—and prolific—contributor to the era's new travel literature and a stalwart defender of Ethiopia's historical tradition, Ḫeruy was a civil servant as well as an accomplished man of letters, and over the course of his long career, he made numerous diplomatic visits to Europe, the Middle East, the United States, and Asia. These were highly formative intellectual experiences, and with his characteristic verve, Ḫeruy sought to share them with his countrymen by publishing accessible Amharic accounts of his adventures. These narratives address historical subjects on multiple levels. Given their focus on individual actors, they can be seen as examples of episodic biography. But Ḫeruy fused this essentially traditional approach with wide-ranging, historically informed cultural geography, going beyond the actions of his protagonists to introduce readers to the exotic people of distant lands. These armchair tours of the world, in turn, have their own macrohistorical overtones, since they situate people and social groups within larger arguments about the stages of progress, the interplay between tradition and modernity, the problems of the modern world, and the nature of Ethiopia's place therein. Ḫeruy's travel writing engages each of these levels of analysis—individual, societal, and global—in order to explore key questions about the past, present, and future. Like *wäyzäro* Mänän and Queen Makedda, his journeys were historic.

Reversing the Gaze

The past three decades have witnessed tremendous academic interest in travel writing, especially in its modern Western varieties. Countless scholars have examined how the travelogues of European adventurers, explorers, geographers, and ethnographers mapped the wider world and articulated hierarchies of cultural and racial difference,[4] and some go so far as to argue that these discursive representations of the other and the exotic were fundamental to nineteenth- and twentieth-century European imperial dominance and self-fashioning.[5] Yet less attention has been devoted to African and Asian travel writing. Though it is risky to generalize about literatures as diverse as the *rihla* of the Muslim world, the Swahili *safari* texts of East Africa, or the memoirs of Indian visitors to Britain, the existing research highlights two elementary but occasionally overlooked points. First, non-Western travelography reveals the extent to which imperial metropoles were themselves contact zones for emigrants from the colonial periphery. London, Paris, Brussels, and Naples were observed by visitors from New Delhi, Algiers, Leopoldville, and Asmära, though this fact has been somewhat obscured by the intense focus on the outward-looking literature of European exploration.[6] Second, although non-Western travel writing depended upon the literary genres, migratory circuits, institutional networks, and transportation infrastructure of the turn-of-the-century imperial world, it was also rooted in the fertile soil of indigenous literary traditions.[7] It often mapped the new through the familiar.

These points are certainly true of Ethiopian and Eritrean travel writing. Though a fundamentally modern pursuit, it had several inchoate antecedents. Generically, its closest precedents are occasional episodes in the royal biographies that describe the arduous challenges of military campaigns and the itineraries of the imperial entourage as it camped and feasted.[8] On occasion, the chronicles also describe personal journeys as trials with religious overtones.[9] Though these episodic accounts focus on their royal subjects, their authors sometimes devote considerable attention to toponyms and geographic details. More esoteric precedents for modern travelography are the medieval and early modern biographies and testimonies of Ethiopian pilgrims and foreign emissaries, which sometimes describe travel in the Red Sea region, the Holy Land, and Mediterranean Europe. Of these, perhaps most evocative are the words of *abba* Ṗetros, who attended the ecumenical Council of Florence in 1441. In his address to Pope Eugene IV (1431–47), he contextualized his journey to the Italian peninsula by recalling "the ancient glory of the Queen of Sheba who came to Jerusalem because of the fame of Solomon, as we do to you," and diplomatically added that while the fame of his host exceeded that of Solomon, his own stature was considerably less than that of Sheba.[10] In the two centuries that followed this episode, the Ethiopian residents of the Santo Stefano degli Abissini hospice in Rome produced several brief autobiographies that mention their travels in the Red Sea and Levant, while Ethiopian visitors to Venice described their journeys in ways that blur the line between autobiographical narrative and nonvisual geography.[11] Unlike the comparatively descriptive and observational royal biographies, these diasporic texts mention travel perfunctorily. It is unlikely that they were well known in Ethiopia.[12]

All these works were overshadowed by the *Kebrä nägäśt*, the medieval pseudo-historical epic that underpinned Solomonid political authority. As discussed in chapter 1, the *Kebrä nägäśt* purports to be an adaptation of a Copto-Arabic work that describes, among other things, the Queen of Sheba's journey to Jerusalem, her conversations and liaison with Solomon, her return to Ethiopia, and finally the birth of her son Dawit/Menilek and his eventual journey to Israel, from whence he absconded with the Ark of the Covenant. Although its descriptions of the actual voyages of Makedda and Menilek are cursory and geographically inexact, the *Kebrä nägäśt* nonetheless relies on travel as its organizing principle.[13] Travel connects the main themes of the work: the exotic foreign origins of the Ethiopian people, their related status as a chosen people, and the divine nature of Solomonid power derived from this connection. Travel is thus symbolically associated with prestige, revelation, and power, fusing it with the Solomonid socio-genealogical mythos. This epic was surely one of the best-known tales in Ethiopia and Eritrea, especially in the nineteenth and twentieth centuries.[14] Indeed, a reader of Ḫeruy and Feśśeha's travel accounts would have instinctively understood their references to the Queen of Sheba's momentous journey—these were in fact nods to the *Kebrä nägäśt*. Other Ethiopian travelers made similar kinds of associations in their private writings.[15]

Various other works dealt with travel more indirectly. Hagiographies sometimes described the lives of holy immigrants, like *abba* Sälama, the fourth-century saint credited with the introduction of Christianity to Ethiopia, or pilgrims, such as Lalibäla, Éwosṭatéwos, and Feqertä Krestos, who all visited Jerusalem.[16] The Ethiopian tales of Alexander the Great offered a somewhat more fantastic treatment of foreign adventure. Based on a fourth-century Eastern Christian epic, they cast the Macedonian king as a noble and even holy figure who visits Greece, China, India, Jerusalem, and the Amazons.[17] A variety of catechistic writing even described the transmigration of the human soul from earth to heaven, through a series of trials and judgments.[18] Though these works are highly eclectic in comparison to the biographical travel episodes and the *Kebrä nägäśt*, we can speculate that they collectively tightened the link between travel, piety, and prestige.

The limited scope of this medieval and early modern travel literature reflected the patterns of literacy and migration of its era. Before the nineteenth century, Ethiopians typically ventured abroad for one of two reasons. A few traveled as pilgrims, students, or diplomatic emissaries, eventually forming a small but influential Mediterranean diaspora centered in cities like Jerusalem, Cairo, Rome, and Venice. A considerably larger number of enslaved Ethiopians involuntarily emigrated to South Asia and the Middle East, for the most part never to return. Whether free or enslaved, these diasporic Ethiopians seem to have exerted little influence at home.

During the nineteenth century, things changed as the forces of globalization altered the patterns and motives of immigration. Ethiopians and Eritreans began pursuing education at Western universities in Europe, the Middle East, and North America. In most cases, they returned home ready to deploy their new skills. Mission school graduates sometimes pursued theological and linguistic training at institutions like the Swedish Evangelical Institute or the Pontifical Ethiopian College in Rome. Other Ethiopians and Eritreans worked in foreign embassies, served as *askari* troops in Libya, and taught in the oriental studies departments of European universities.

This new diaspora was described in Ethiopian newspapers. This is especially true of *Berhanenna sälam*, whose editorials, articles, and advice columns regularly brought descriptions of the wider world home to local readers. It featured contributions from diasporic subscribers in columns such as "News from Abroad," "Telegrams from Rome," and "Letters from Abroad," which described world politics and current events, much like similar articles in *A'emro* and the earlier *Yäṭor wäré*. Other *Berhanenna sälam* pieces celebrated the emancipatory and transformative effects of education abroad, such as a 1925 article advising readers on "Learning European Languages" and a 1932 report entitled "On Studying in Italy."[19] In addition to news and practical information, *Berhanenna sälam* and *A'emro* both offered detailed accounts of the travels of Ethiopian notables, often accompanied by vivid photographs.[20] *Courrier d'Éthiopie* featured similar articles as well as pieces on the adventures of European émigrés,[21] as did the Italian section of the Asmära-based *Il Quotidiano Eritreo.*[22] For readers of these newspapers, the world had never been more readily accessible.

These old precedents and new developments underpinned the emergence of printed travel writing. The earliest example of printed travel writing is Feśśeḥa's Tigrinya narrative, published in 1895 with the title *About the Author's Journey from Ethiopia to Italy and the Impressions Made on Him by His Stay in That Country.*[23] It was apparently written at the request of the Italian orientalist Francesco Gallina (1861–1942), a professor of Amharic literature at the Royal Oriental Institute of Naples.[24] This work was followed several decades later by Afäwärq Gäbrä Iyäsus's account of Crown Prince Täfäri Mäkonnen's diplomatic mission to Djibouti and Aden, published in late 1922 or early 1923 by the Täfäri Mäkonnen Press.[25] Months later, the same press produced Ḫeruy's *The Journey of le'ult wäyzäro Mänän to Jerusalem and Egypt,* and in 1924, his *Happiness and Honor: An Account of When le'ul Crown Prince Täfäri Mäkonnen Went and Returned on a Journey to Europe,* a detailed chronicle of Täfäri Mäkonnen's historic diplomatic tour of that year.[26] In the early 1930s, Ḫeruy published two more travel narratives: his 1932 account *The Citadel of Light: the Land of Japan,* which described his sojourn in that country as well as visits to Colombo, Singapore, Shanghai, and Saigon; and his 1934 work *To Live Long and Witness Everything,* which described his further peregrinations in Palestine, Syria, Egypt, and Greece.[27] Emperor Ḫaylä Śellasé included travel narrative chapters in his autobiography, which he begun with Ḫeruy's assistance during their wartime exile in England, though it was not published until considerably later.[28] A travelographic coda to the era appeared immediately after the liberation of Ethiopia: Marse'é Ḫazan's account of Ḫaylä Śellasé's triumphal visit to Gondär, published by Berhanenna Sälam in 1947.[29] Throughout this period, many other writers produced unpublished or private accounts of their time abroad.[30]

More eclectic travel-related publications complemented these biographies and autobiographies. Ḫeruy wrote a guide for would-be travelers, offering "words of advice" on practical matters such as passports, train and boat travel, personal hygiene, and table manners.[31] Ṗawlos Män Amäno, who collaborated with Gäbrä Krestos Täklä Haymanot and served as a diplomat in Jerusalem, produced a historical guide to the Holy Land that included details on Jerusalem, Jericho, Bethlehem, and Golgotha, supplemented by a map of "Palestine and the land of Canaan."[32] These practical works were complemented by fictionalized travel writing. An early example of this genre is Afäwärq's dual-language *Ityopya: Guide du Voyageur en Éthiopie*, which presents an imagined French and Amharic dialogue between a European visitor and his Ethiopian companion.[33] Though ostensibly a text for language learners, Afäwärq creatively uses the conversation between the two travelers to critique Ethiopian backwardness and belittle European visitors to the country.[34] Ḫeruy offered a similarly creative depiction of travel with his 1932 novel *New World*.[35] Its protagonist, the young Awwäqä, hears of Europe and decides to leave Ethiopia via Djibouti to study in Paris. He returns after seven years, whereupon his new outlook leads him to challenge many church customs and face the criticisms of a tradition-minded priest.[36] A similarly fictionalized travel account was produced by the Eritrean Gäbrä Yäsus Ḥaylu (1906–93), whose 1927 historical novel relates the experiences of an *askari* whose military service in Libya awakens him to the injustices of colonialism. This work creatively blends fictional and literary elements with relatively factual descriptions of the Arabs and Maghreb.[37] Poems also occasionally dealt with travel.[38]

It is striking that travel writing figures so prominently in the earliest publications of the Ethiopian presses, particularly given its novelty as a literary genre. The book catalogs in the back pages of *Berhanenna sälam* invariably included travel and travel-related publications, which often accounted for a significant share of the total number of items listed for sale.[39] Travel writing was one of only five subjects selected for the print medium by the state press, the others being scripture, religious commentary, technical manuals, and educational textbooks (on history, mathematics, calligraphy, and grammar). Some venerable, if esoteric, traditional fields of knowledge, such as computus (*baḥrä ḥassab*), were not. How do we account for the close connection between travel writing and the emergence of print? Why was such a comparatively new pursuit worthy of sustained state sponsorship?

Comparison is instructive. In their classic study of early modern print history, Lucien Febvre and Henri-Jean Martin suggest that the transition from manuscript to print culture offered scholars and printers an opportunity to revise the received canon. Their decisions determined which existing texts would reach a wider audience as printed books, and which would risk fading into obscurity by remaining in manuscript only. The publication choices of printers and their patrons effectively document their intellectual and commercial priorities. Febvre and Martin argue that since the high costs of Europe's first printed books prevented an immediate increase in reading, this reorganization of the canon was an important immediate consequence of printing in early modern Europe.[40] In the nineteenth century, the export of the printing press outside Europe placed many African and Asian printers in similar roles as intellectual activists, reformers, and arbitrators.[41]

Figure 4.1. Illustration from Ḫeruy Wäldä Śellasé, *Addis aläm* (New World), 32.

These precedents help to contextualize the publications of Berhanenna Sälam. The development of printing gave the crown prince and his intellectual protégés the opportunity to review the inherited canon and fill any gaps, and their inclusion of travel writing suggests that knowledge of modern world constituted one such lacuna. Simply put, travel writing addressed novel questions that awaited answers. Some of these were historical. Several distant regions were involved in important sacred histories, and warranted the greater scrutiny that was now possible. Other regions were home to peoples with achievements that reformers aspired to emulate, and the careful description of these places might aid the course of progress in Ethiopia. An array of forces in the world posed challenges to Ethiopian sovereignty, from foreign commercial and financial institutions to bellicose colonial lobbies and westernizing missionary enterprises. Who were the people causing these problems? How did Ethiopia fit into the world they sought to dominate? And what kind of leaders could guide Ethiopia through this modern labyrinth? The inherited canon had little to say about these questions, but printing ensured that writers would be able to address them for a large audience. Travelography was the instrument of their inquiry, and Ḫeruy was its most accomplished master.

It's Not Easy Being Modern

Ḫeruy's four travelogues offer an armchair tour of the modern world and a survey of the course of progress within it. By describing the world's peoples, their heritage and culture, and the nature of their achievements, his works effectively outline the qualities and stages of historical development. Not surprisingly, these topics are especially evident in Ḫeruy's account of his own trip to Japan, then widely considered an exemplar of successful non-Western modernization.[42] His narrative contains a very long illustrated chapter on the achievements and customs of the Japanese (*śeranna nuro*), in which Ḫeruy abandons autobiography to address a host of more general topics: clothing and physical appearance; food and diet; cultural norms and national character; manufacturing and handicrafts; education, roads, and electric streetlights; marriage and death; and finally, Buddhism and the arrival of Christianity in Japan.[43] At one point in this overview, he reflects on the fundamental contribution of Japan to world history: in a discussion of the country's "heroism and ingenuity," he observes that "The Japanese, in times of war, are cruel and decisive. For this reason, it is said, 'Beauty to the Greeks, holiness to Israel, candor to the Romans, and heroism to the Japanese.'"[44] In his estimation, Japan was a worthy foreign nation that informed Ethiopians could admire. Less categorical but no less educational descriptions of the worlds' peoples can also be found in his

Figure 4.2. Ḫeruy and companions visiting Nikko, Japan. Ḫeruy Wäldä Sellasé, *Madhärä berhan*, 36.

accounts of the crown prince's travels in the Holy Land and Europe, which describe Jerusalem and various European capitals, and of his own 1930s adventures in Greece and the Eastern Mediterranean, which include several chapters on the Hellenic heritage.

This innovative approach to semibiographical, instructive, and historically inflected travelography was first developed in Ḫeruy's account of *wäyzäro* Mänän's journey to the Levant. This study is doubly pioneering: it is Ḫeruy's first published effort at travel writing, containing many of the methodological innovations found in his later works; and it is his first description of a region with a distinctive pride of place in the Ethiopian historical imagination—indeed, two of his other travelogues described return visits to the Holy Land. Put simply, Japan and Europe were culturally distant and modern, while the Holy Land was nearby and the imagined crucible of Ethiopian Christian society. For this reason, the present discussion will focus on this early work while drawing parallels to Ḫeruy's later travel accounts.

The Journey of le'ult wäyzäro Mänän is a book of forty-two pages, abundantly illustrated with photos of its subjects and their tour destinations. On one level, it consists of Ḫeruy's basic description of life in the lands of the interwar Middle East. He maps its geography, political institutions, and religious communities, and he occasionally addresses contemporary issues like sectarian tensions, colonial rule, and the beneficial consequences of new technologies. In some respects, these informative sections resemble the era's newspaper reports and Ṗawlos Män Amäno's guide to Jerusalem and the Holy Places. But Ḫeruy occasionally goes beyond descriptive reportage to offer subtle lessons on the nature of progress, especially when Ethiopians meet representatives of other nations who are grappling with modern ideas and questions. Ḫeruy uses these moments of cross-cultural encounter to present arguments about the stages of historical development, the appropriate relationship between foreign and indigenous knowledge, and the place of faith in an increasingly secular world.

One such episode occurs at sea, shortly after *wäyzäro* Mänän and her entourage departed from Djibouti for Port Said. Ḫeruy sets the stage as follows:

> And on this boat were people of different states, and the ones that stood out to us were [some] very wealthy people of America. Among these there was one of very great wealth, [and] because of the amount [of his] wealth he traveled the world. Many months were devoted to this. His wife came from him to *le'ult wäyzäro* Mänän because she had a desire to know her [Mänän], and after she was introduced, news of Ethiopia was heard and we gave [them] much counsel. And the counsel grew deep[,] and religion, freedom, and slavery were discussed.[45]

This was a timely conversation, for Ethiopia's foreign relations were then dominated by questions of freedom and slavery. In 1922, one year before *wäyzäro* Mänän's journey, and the same year Egypt obtained conditional independence from Britain and the League of Nations ratified the draft of the British Mandate in Palestine, Ethiopia became embroiled in an international controversy that jeopardized its political sovereignty. The affair began when a member of the British legation in Addis Ababa penned a series of explosive newspaper articles on the ubiquity of slavery in Ethiopia, mobilizing two British humanitarian organizations, the League of Nations Union and the Anti-slavery and Aboriginals Protection Society, to bring the matter to the British Parliament and Foreign Office, and eventually, the League of Nations Mandates Section.[46] In September of that same year, the League Assembly passed a resolution on the resurgence of slavery in Africa, mentioning Ethiopia by name, and in November, Frederick Lugard (1858–1945), the famed British authority on colonial Africa and a member of the League's Permanent Mandates Commission, produced a widely read memorandum on the matter. In it, he argued that the persistence of slavery in Ethiopia—in his estimation "the only country in Africa in which slave-raids and the slave trade are still openly practiced"—constituted grounds for foreign intervention and the creation of a League-administered Mandate in the country, effectively a variant of those established in the former German colonies in July of that same year.[47] The questions of Ethiopian sovereignty and slavery were thus more closely intertwined than ever before, and Lugard's plan seemed the portent of a renewed imperial scramble for Ethiopia that would be sanctioned by international law.

Crown Prince Täfäri Mäkonnen launched a vigorous response to these developments. In a February 1922 interview with the British Minister in Addis Ababa, he rejected the humanitarians' claims and derided the continued international challenge to Ethiopian independence. To refute the accusation of his government's complicity in the slave trade, he pointed to a 1918 decree that had formally abolished slavery in Ethiopia.[48] As a further measure, in July of that same year his government issued a second decree requiring governors to ban all slavery in their districts.[49] A more dramatic counter followed roughly one year later, in August 1923, when Täfäri Mäkonnen formally petitioned the League of Nations for Ethiopian membership, hoping to obtain international protection for its territorial integrity and decisively end the debate over Lugardian intervention. In September, Ethiopia was conditionally admitted after the erosion of British and Italian opposition; its sovereignty now had the theoretical backing of international law. But the whole affair had raised the issue of the discrepancy between the reformist image of the crown prince and the Ethiopian government, on the one hand, and the tacit support for slavery that was then widespread among the Ethiopian elite, on the other.[50] Was Ethiopia a land of injustice? And were its leaders as modern as they claimed?

Writing in the immediate context of these heated international controversies, Ḫeruy uses *wäyzäro* Mänän's conversations on the boat to address the general problem of slavery and Ethiopia's precise relationship with it. First, the wealthy American traveller explains the importance of personal freedom and describes the threat that slavery and religious intolerance pose to a modern state and society:

> [In the United States,] everyone is entitled to choose their wives, and no one could impose on them the faith or wives that they do not want. Whence the need for you to grant freedom to slaves and [of] religion. If you fail to do that, the people you have subjected to slavery and religious oppression will hate the state. Foreigners would find a motive to rise against you. Slavery and faith are also sensitive issues to us Americans. There are more than fifty different faiths in America, but in view of the freedom given by the government, they live in harmony.[51]

Next, the American elaborates on how to secure this freedom:

> Another thing you will have to [do is] open schools in all your provinces, hire teachers, and send your children to school. In the event your people do not want any white teachers, there are many black teachers who are as competent and whose blood is the same as yours that you can hire and bring here [to Ethiopia] so that your children will learn many things. The reason I tell you all this is because we Americans are keen to see people all over the world living with knowledge and freedom.[52]

Wäyzäro Mänän then responds to these proposals, in the process describing the state of Ethiopian progress: "*Le'ult wäyzäro* Mänän replied, assuring him that slavery was a thing of the past and was now banned under a government decree, [and] that as regards religion, the state does not engage in any form of coercion unless the [religion in question] is enemy propaganda."[53]

For Ḫeruy's Ethiopian reader, this conversation between *wäyzäro* Mänän and the wealthy American would have several salient points. We learn that slavery is "a thing of the past" and therefore archaic or premodern, and that it can cause both domestic unrest and criticism from abroad—all conclusions that spoke directly to the public controversy of the day. We also learn that modern nations like the United States protect individual freedoms, whether freedom from coercion or the freedom of religion, and that they secure these freedoms through educational institutions that reduce ignorance. And finally, we hear that the American believes that Ethiopia still has much to learn from the progress of the United States—indeed, so much that African-Americans might be appropriate educators for Ethiopia. As much as this conversation on the boat is about slavery and education, it is also about the characteristics of political modernity and the measurement of Ethiopia against these. For Ḫeruy's American traveler, the United States had achieved a historic stage of civilization that Ethiopia had yet to reach. *Wäyzäro* Mänän corrected this mistaken view by pointing to the relevant facts of recent Ethiopian history. The humanitarian concerns of the American, like those of the international observers at the League of Nations, were simply misdirected. Ethiopia was part of the family of modern and free nations.

Another instructive cross-cultural encounter occurs during the travelers' visit to Luxor in Upper Egypt, where European archaeologists had just unearthed the tomb of Tutankhamun in the Valley of the Kings. This discovery tapped a torrent of international "Egyptomania" and a renewed stream of nationalist pride in Egypt, for it came at a time when many Egyptian writers sought to rehabilitate and celebrate the Pharaonic past as part of their collective national heritage.[54] Ḫeruy takes great interest in this new discovery and its implications for the present, discussing it at some length in his narrative. He describes how *wäyzäro* Mänän and her companions toured the site and tombs, and he gives the reader some description of its interior appearance, noting that the "paintings, writings, and other ornaments" seem "as though they were made today, though they were made two thousand years before the birth of Christ."[55] He then provides a detailed history of Tutankhamun's life and family, the political situation of the New Kingdom, and the then-current understanding of Egyptian burial customs. He concludes by discussing the discovery of the tomb in the 1920s.

Ḫeruy takes a great interest in Lord Carnarvon, the British financier and amateur Egyptologist who sponsored the excavation of Tutankhamun's crypt only to die of mysterious causes shortly after its opening. After outlining the dramatic events surrounding the discovery, Ḫeruy explains the prevailing interpretation of Carnarvon's demise: "The death of Lord . . . [Carnarvon], the man who had opened the tomb, was received [by everyone] with emotional feeling. The peasants of Egypt spoke of many people who were yet to die because of the magic put into the tombs by the ancient philosophers. However, they said this because they were angry with the French and the English who had taken their antiquities away."[56] The Ethiopians were so interested in this topic that they struck up a conversation with some of the Egyptian peasants, or *balagär*, who surrounded them at Luxor:

> Many of these Egyptians were among us, and we put to them that they could have excavated and extracted the antiquities themselves. [We asked,] "Why did they let *färänǧ* hollow out [the tomb] and take the antiquities with them?" And one of the Egyptians answered, "We do not like to dig into the

> graves of our ancestors, that is the reason why." Another one retorted, "They were taken from us by the French and English because we had no knowledge and skill, not because of [our] respect for the graves of our ancestors."[57]

Like their conversation with the American, the Ethiopians' discussion with the Egyptian *balagär* allows Ḫeruy to introduce the reader to a larger problem, in this case the dangers of rigid traditionalism. But the Luxor episode also illustrates the potential for foreign expertise to serve indigenous purposes: it was European Egyptologists who had opened the tomb and produced important insights into Egypt's past. While Ḫeruy offers the progress of freedom in the United States as an idealized model, this passage presents the superstitious Egyptian *balagär* as an example of what Ethiopians ought to avoid.

These object lessons on progress complemented a related discussion of the place of faith in the modern world. For Ḫeruy, historical progress involved spiritual renewal, not secularization or disenchantment—an anti-historicist view that Gäbrä Krestos would have wholeheartedly endorsed. The broad contours of this position emerge from Ḫeruy's discussions of the human and physical landscape of Palestine, which are saturated with scriptural references. Upon the pilgrims' arrival in Gaza, for example, he noted that they were where the Acts of the Apostles reported that a pious Ethiopian traveler, the eunuch-treasurer of Queen Candace, or Hendäké, had once discussed the scriptures with the apostle Philip, who baptized him.[58] This episode is in fact the sole mention of Ethiopia in the New Testament. A deluge of similar biblical references fills his narration of *wäyzäro* Mänän's tour of the Holy Land and its pilgrimage sites. Ḫeruy took particular care to situate contemporary places within the sacred history and geography of scripture: he cites biblical verses while describing the party's visit to Nazareth and the tomb of Sarah, and in Nablus, he notes how "in the Gospels, the city was called Sikar [Shechem]."[59] He uses full-verse quotations to describe Capernaum, and he includes eight scriptural references related to the Sea of Galilee.[60] By presenting the landscape of the modern Middle East through the lens of its scriptural past, Ḫeruy showed the persistence of holiness into the present, and its power to strengthen the faith of the modern pilgrim. The ancient epochs described in the scriptures and vernacular historiography were alive.

Significantly, Ḫeruy suggests that the Ethiopians shared this understanding of a living sacred history with other Christians. In his telling, *wäyzäro* Mänän's travels from Bethlehem to Golgotha are opportunities for her foreign co-religionists to recognize their common bonds of faith and ritual. The Ethiopians' time in the Holy Land was punctuated by encounters with other Christians: they explored a site "frequented by the Latins" at Nazareth, witnessed the burial of a child at a "Greek and Roman" church in Jerusalem, and attended an ecumenical celebration of Palm Sunday by Greek, Syrian, Armenian, and Egyptian Orthodox Christians.[61] In addition, the Coptic, Armenian, Greek, Catholic, and Protestant churches of Palestine and Egypt all issued invitations to the Ethiopians to join them in their ceremonies of worship, many of which they accepted. The complement to these invitations came, as Ḫeruy described with pride, with the many foreign visitors who attended the celebration of Easter at Dér Śelṭan, the Ethiopian monastery in Jerusalem: the regent of Jerusalem, foreign notables, and even American tourists.[62] The point of all this was significant: though the world's Christians came from diverse nations, they were nonetheless united in a universal community of the one true faith. Like the Ethiopian pilgrims, the Levantine and European Christians of the Holy Land saw the land of the scriptures as their own, and they treated one another with the fellowship and pious charity their co-religiosity required.[63] In this respect, their relations were altogether unlike those of the Muslims and Jews of Mandatory Palestine, whose tensions Ḫeruy noted.[64] Among Christians, Ḫeruy had found a true and capacious ecumenism.

Though the Ethiopian quest for inter-Christian solidarity began with the diplomatic and religious missions of the medieval and early modern eras, which were largely fruitless from an Ethiopian perspective, Ḫeruy's particular brand of Christian fraternity was no atavistic relic. It was in fact a distinctly modern vision. Discussing similar phenomena in other settings, Sugata Bose suggests that

> universalism was hardly a quest over which European modernity had any kind of monopoly. Local, regional, and national cultures in different parts of the globe were not just jealous guardians of their own distinctiveness, but also wished to participate in and contribute to larger arenas of cultural exchange . . . A certain sense of nostalgia for the bonds of the past need not be seen as a simple longing for a pre-colonial refuge in the hostile environment of the colonial world. It was very much part of the struggle in the present to try to influence the shape of a global future.[65]

This fraternal nostalgia helps to explain why Ḫeruy took such pains to emphasize Ethiopia's historic and contemporary solidarity with the larger ecumene. As much as he wanted to anatomize the modern world for readers, he was well aware of the challenges it posed to his own Orthodox Christian faith. Indeed, these threats were particularly acute at the time of his writing: the dangers of apostasy posed by growing number of European missionaries in Ethiopia, the simmering tensions with the Egyptian Copts, the Ethiopians' closest Orthodox co-religionists, and the stormy relationship with the would-be imperialists of European Christendom.[66] To these could be added the more abstract danger that technological and institutional innovations—like printing and public schools—might disrupt traditional values.[67] All these fissures threatened to pit Ethiopian Orthodox Christians against the rest of the ecumene.

Ḫeruy's expansive vision of Christian fellowship can be read as a response to these challenges. His travelogue documents the extent to which the world's different Christians respected Ethiopia's historic faith, whether they were Orthodox Copts and Armenians or European Catholics and Protestants, and the sacred geography and forms of worship they shared suggested that a historical and spiritual fellowship underpinned this respect. The many invitations, gifts, and compliments that *wäyzäro* Mänän received from these foreign Christians were a dramatic counterpoint to the inter-Christian sectarian tensions of the day. Her journey to the Holy Land thus affirmed the importance of historic bonds of faith in the modern world. Progress required continuity as well as change.

Living History

Ḫeruy's outward looking historical arguments contextualized another set of claims about the pedigree of Ethiopia's rulers-in-waiting, Crown Prince Täfäri Mäkonnen and *wäyzäro* Mänän.[68] These also involved historical themes. While the crown prince saw himself as an enlightened monarch tasked with transforming Ethiopia into a modern nation, he invoked Solomonic ideology in his public discourse and state pageantry to legitimate his program of carefully managed development, thereby employing a venerable langauge and iconography of power. In the eyes of his subjects and the wider world, he was a modern head of state from an ancient dynasty. In order to cultivate this political image, the crown prince carefully orchestrated and monitored his depiction in journalistic and historical writing, even going so far as to censor works that threatened his idealized vision of himself.[69] He also fused European and Ethiopian rituals of power, an invention of tradition that reached its apex with his extravagant 1930 coronation.[70] The message of this complex strategy was clear: though Täfäri Mäkonnen/Ḫaylä Śellasé was the munificent patron of reformers and the *śelleṭṭané* movement, he was also a good Solomonid.

Travel writing helped manufacture this politico-historical posture. Some works did so through empirical documentation of Täfäri Mäkonnen's majesty. This is certainly true of Ḫeruy's *Happiness and Honor*, a glowing description of the crown prince's 1924 diplomatic grand tour of Europe and the Levant. After an introduction in which Ḫeruy surveys the sources of Ethiopian history and the *longue durée* of Ethiopian foreign relations—from the era of Grañ and Emperor Gälawdéwos through Emperor Menilek and his international fame, the Ethiopian victory at Adwa, the arrival of European merchants, consuls, and tourists in the nineteenth century, and finally the admission of Ethiopia into the League of Nations in the twentieth century—the narrative relates Täfäri Mäkonnen's odyssey through Djibouti, Jerusalem, Egypt, France, Belgium, Sweden, Italy, England, Switzerland, and Greece; his many speeches to dignitaries along the way; and countless mundane details of commendation and protocol, such as the seating arrangements of notable meals. It is a document of a great leader on the world stage. Equally celebratory is Marse'é Ḫazan's post-liberation account of the imperial couple's triumphal return to their homeland. Filled with lavish photographs and detailed descriptions of their visits to Gondär's notables and students, this work offered a past-due historical reckoning of sorts: the emperor's visit was the vehicle for an eleven-page alphabetized list of Ethiopia's anticolonial patriots, or *arbäñas*.[71]

Ḫeruy made complementary claims through historical comparison in his account of his own journey to Japan. One of these appeared in an episode that recalls *wäyzäro* Mänän's earlier dialogues on the Red Sea and in Egypt. Shortly after Ḫeruy's arrival in Japan, he attended a large reception in honor of his visit and the related Ethiopian-Japanese trade agreement. The event was the occasion for a tremendous amount of national pageantry, which culminated in a speech by the retired Admiral Arima Ryokitsu (1861–1944). The latter began by discussing the similarities between Japan and Ethiopia: these were the antiquity and uninterrupted lineage of their ruling dynasties; their commitment to the freedom of their respective geographic arenas; and their similarly strong ideas and spirit.[72] These parallels, he suggested, underpinned the deep friendship that was instantiated in their new diplomatic agreements. After Admiral Ryokitsu issued a rousing three cheers for Emperor Ḫaylä Śellasé, it was Ḫeruy's turn for a speech. He began by affirming the Admiral's characterization of the similarities between Japan and Ethiopia, noting that "the two nations' customs and heroism are similar," and then went on to offer his own view on the past and present parallels between their ruling dynasties. He observed that their founders, the Queen of Sheba and Emperor Jimmu—the legendary first emperor of Japan, and the object of considerable modern nationalist veneration—were contemporaries nearly three thousand years before, and that the Ethiopian and Japanese people were justifiably proud of these illustrious ancestors. No less impressive was the fact that both dynasties had endured "without being interrupted even once" into the present day, as Ḫeruy explained: Emperor Ḫaylä Śellasé was Sheba's 126th descendent, while Emperor Hirohito was Jimmu's 124th successor. This historical perserverance was all the more remarkable in Ethiopia's case, he noted, because its past heroes had defended their land and freedom not with cannons and rifles but with swords and shields. This was an achievement to be remembered by future generations, just as posterity would recall the names of Japan's kings and heroes. If Ḫeruy's historical analysis rested on rather murky lineal claims, his larger point could not have been clearer: like Japan, Ethiopia was home to a magnificent ruling line and a heroic martial nation, and its modern head of state—Emperor Ḫaylä Śellasé—was the bearer of a great historical inheritance.

The connection between travelography and the ideology of imperial power asserted in these accounts of Europe and Japan is also quite evident in *The Journey of le'ult wäyzäro Mänän*, which moves beyond epic celebration and historical comparison to empirically document the presence of the Solomonid dynasty in the modern era. This genealogy is symbolically signaled by the fact that its protagonist is a woman, *wäyzäro* Mänän—the modern Makedda, as we have already seen. Within the narrative, this historical comparison is further bolstered by *wäyzäro* Mänän's own words and deeds. While in Egypt and Palestine, she gives many speeches and greetings that dutifully extol the august greatness of the Ethiopian empire, and on several occasions, she provides her audiences—both actual and reading—with a condensed Solomonid interpretation of Ethiopian history.[73] These symbolic and literal associations publicly assert the continuity between Ethiopia's past and current rulers.

Ḫeruy offers concrete historical proof of *wäyzäro* Mänän's Solomonid credentials by demonstrating that she is a suitably moral ambassador for Ethiopia. He pays particular attention to her charitable support for schools, churches, religious orders, and servants. In Jerusalem, we learn that she went to see a school for Armenian orphans, where she made a donation to "these poor ones."[74] She also visited a local school for the blind, to which she similarly donated money: the students' achievements suggested that "it was as though these blind men see with eyes."[75] In Egypt, she continued to visit and aid worthy institutions: in Cairo, she stopped at the schools of the Coptic and Armenian Orthodox churches, a school for girls, and another school for orphans, and in Alexandria, she visited the British-run Victoria College.[76] *Wäyzäro* Mänän, known for her commitment to education and charity in Ethiopia, was thus a paragon of both Solomonic dignity and Christian virtue abroad.[77] Even her own chronicle cited the significance of her charitable giving on this journey.[78] She was a modern who lived up to the historical ideal.

Beyond her own actions, *wäyzäro* Mänän's grandeur was also confirmed by her warm reception in these foreign lands. Ḫeruy notes how dignitaries and the general population alike unfailingly greet her with respect throughout her journey, beginning with the great welcome she received in Djibouti, where the French Consul and all the notables greeted her and celebrated their international fraternity with champagne. Such episodes occurred again and again. She was personally honored by powerful individuals: the Armenian Patriarch of Jerusalem gave her a gift of a gold cross; Herbert Samuel, the British High Commissioner for Palestine, invited her to his house to attend a dinner party; and King Fu'ad of Egypt personally opened her car door exclaiming, "You [yourself] have opened the door of state, *le'ult wäyzäro* Mänän, by coming here [to Egypt]."[79] She was also adored by the masses: everywhere she went, the roads were crowded with onlookers and adorned with silk fabrics, and the men greeted her in Arabic "shouting *amira* Mänän" while the women ululated with joy.[80] When she arrived in Jerusalem, the crowds at the station were such that she was forced to greet the local dignitaries inside the train, and at the train station in Cairo "many people and journalists were gathered, over seven thousand it has been said and written," though Ḫeruy modestly noted that "we estimate it was [only] four thousand."[81] Her life and travels were thus a new and still unfolding chapter in Solomonid history—one that could be added to the saga previously described in royal biography, dynastic history, and universal chronology. The inherited historical tradition now encompassed an eminently modern genre.

Through these references, Ḫeruy was in effect converting the mythic *Kebrä nägäśt* into documented history. This effort resembles several other creative historical projects of the era, which also blurred generic lines and flaunted distinctions between history and myth, fact and fiction. Bankimchandra Chattopadhyay, the Bengali writer, and Jurji Zaydan, the Egyptian journalist and novelist, both used similarly "nonhistorical" literary genres to explore historical themes.[82] Ḫeruy's historicized travelography is a variant on such "factual fiction," in that it fuses biography and reportage with stylized macro-historical arguments and mytho-historical metaphors. Travel writing allowed him to reconcile past and present, the ancient and the modern, and the sacred and the profane, in a single text. It also allowed him to conceptualize the wider world without recourse to historicism and its analytic categories. His contemporary Tä'ammrat Amanu'el—an equally peripatetic, cosmopolitan, and creative intellectual—considered Ḫeruy's work to be literature that verged on "mastery" in its use of language and its ability to clearly convey complex knowledge to the layman.[83] Arguably, Ḫeruy's travel narratives were equally masterful in their innovative approach to the historian's craft.

5

The Triumph of Historicism?

In the years after the liberation of Ethiopia in 1941, the playwright, author, and civil servant Käbbädä Mika'él (1916–98) wrote a series of studies that recalled the pioneering histories of the years before 1935. The first of these was his 1947 work *Ityopyanna me'erabawi śelleṭṭané*, or *Ethiopia and Western Civilization*, which was issued in a joint Amharic-English edition by Berhanenna Sälam. Dedicated to the restored Emperor Ḫaylä Śellasé, its frontispiece announced Käbbädä's threefold desire to "enlighten his countrymen," "lead the general reader to a better understanding of Western Civilization," and "make known to the outside world the efforts put forth by the New Ethiopia in striving to attain modernization."[1] Yet Käbbädä's purpose was more polemical than these anodyne pronouncements implied. After an opening quotation from Goethe, he presents a systematic analysis of the tension between the West's myriad accomplishments and its use of slavery. He opened with juxtaposing chapters on "the Formation of States" and "the Meaning of Slavery," followed by "the Greek Philosophers" and "Slaves Among the Greeks," in which he reflected on the irony that Plato boasted of his freedom only to be enslaved himself.[2] Käbbädä continued with treatments of "The Renaissance" and "Slavery in the Middle Ages," and then turned to the more modern topics of American plantations, the Haitian and French Revolutions, the abolitionist movements in the United States and Britain, the "Troubled Century" of nationalist foment, and the "Mechanical Age" of industrial achievement. These last two eras, he judged, had jointly contributed to the end of slavery.[3] He then went on to demonstrate—with documentary evidence—that Emperor Ḫaylä Śellasé had formally abolished slavery in his own country, and thus "Ethiopia had found her Lincoln," as *etégé* Mänän had suggested many years before.[4] In recognition of this fact, Käbbädä concluded his work with a chapter on "The Great Achievements of Haile Selassie." His new world history was an ambitious and assertively corrective study of Western civilization, one that traced the antagonism between philosophical ideals and historical realities.

Though Käbbädä's work offered its readers a provocative critique of the West, its argument rested upon strong historicist foundations. In many respects, this was an Ethiopian version of a Hegelian story. Since Käbbädä's world history was defined by the evolution of Western civilization, Ethiopia and Africa were comparatively marginal actors on the world-historical stage. True, Ethiopia was possibly unrivalled in its "moral civilization," but it was nonetheless still following its emperor "on the march toward a greater civilization" of knowledge and material prosperity, along a course set by the West.[5] It was for precisely this reason that Käbbädä could compare the emancipator Ḫaylä Śellasé with his counterpart Abraham Lincoln. The implications of this point are revealed by the catalog of "Men of Genius" that concludes the work. Though Käbbädä's list includes Homer, Rousseau, Schopenhauer, and Darwin, among others, he noted that his own nation had "not yet reached that evolutionary stage which produces men of genius," though he allowed that *blattén géta* Ḫeruy was a near-candidate.[6] More than a decade later, in 1960, Käbbädä wrote a second world history that reasserted this claim. This was his *Talalaq säwoč*, or *Great Men*, an instructive prosopography whose subjects included Homer, Cleopatra, Shakespeare, Frederick the Great, Napoleon, and finally Goethe.[7] The historical pantheon still did not include any native sons or daughters.

These omissions suggest the basic architecture of Käbbädä's historical imagination. In his assessment, the modernization of Ethiopia was a historical process that was underway but not yet complete, and the path forward had been clearly if imperfectly marked. Though the West might learn from the moral example of Ethiopia, Ethiopia had to learn from the West. In making this point, Käbbädä's 1947 study of Western civilization—translated for foreign readers, filled with references to European history and culture (including an account of the European inheritance from classical Greece, Plato's boasts aside), and printed by the emperor's state press—asserted Ethiopia's new Cold War political identity as a modernizing and sovereign African ally of the United States. It did so by surveying the past while looking toward an approaching future, much like Gabra Krestos Täklä Haymanot's earlier *Short History*. One day soon, it was hoped, Ethiopia would produce its own great men.

Yet the Eurocentric historicism of Käbbädä's two works belies the true breadth of his historical ambitions. In 1952 he became the director of the National Library's newly formed archaeological section, which he aimed to make "not just a center of scientific research and documentation, but [a] veritable conservatory of the past."[8] It would be an institutional guardian of the national heritage. He and the section staff systematically surveyed the ancient and medieval archaeological sites of Ethiopia and disseminated their findings in a new French-Amharic biannual academic journal, *Annales d'Éthiopie*, which Käbbädä co-edited after 1955.[9] These institutions supported major advances in the scholarly reconstruction of the Northeast African past, most notably in the areas of archaeology and manuscript studies.

That same year, in 1955, he produced the first volume of a new Amharic world history that offered a rather different vista from the one presented in his two studies of Western civilization.[10] Ambitiously ranging from "the beginning of world history" to the early modern era of the British Atlantic, his *Yä'aläm tarik* inserted the topical foci of a *tarikä nägäśt* into a more general narrative of human civilization. If Käbbädä's chronology was rather erratic in this work, his scope was impressive. The first half of the book examined prehistory and antiquity, with chapters on China, India, Egypt, and Israel, a series on the attainments of the Greeks and Romans, and an extended discussion of pre-Christian Ethiopia, the Queen of Sheba, and early relations between Ethiopia and Europe. The second half of the book discussed Muhammad and the emergence of Islam; Ethiopia and its rulers, from the Aksumites through the Solomonids; Ethiopian-Portuguese relations and their repercussions; and finally, the course of Western history. Despite the Eurocentric implications of his earlier studies, in this work, Käbbädä forcefully asserted Ethiopia's significance on the world historical stage. It was no longer confined to the wings until the final act.

The disjuncture between these two perspectives emerged in the introduction to his 1955 world history, in which Käbbädä attempted to address the "great difficulty" of the historical enterprise. He observed that sound scholarship was based on three varieties of evidence: the oral tradition, or "history delivered by mouth from generation to generation"; material culture, such as obelisks and coins; and finally, written sources, published or otherwise.[11] It was only upon this comprehensive tripartite basis that history could be properly written and judged, and he believed that mankind had too often erred by allowing politics and religion to shape historical analysis and judgment. Moreover, many historians lacked daring because of their fear of error. Käbbädä did not share these flaws, in his estimation, and it was for this reason that he could attempt to so boldly combine the old and the new, fusing vernacular history and institutionalized, academic world-history. In this respect, Käbbädä—like his predecessors Gäbrä Krestos, Gäbrä Mika'él, and Ḫeruy—became modern through the past.

Käbbädä's histories reveal much about the changing nature of historiography in post-liberation Ethiopia. In addition to his studies of Western civilization and world history, he wrote a host of other books on more Ethiopian-centered topics,[12] and he devoted much of his career to the institutional preservation of Ethiopia's material patrimony. His breadth of interests and professional roles highlight the rich complexity of the postwar historical scene, and in particular, the growing influence of Western varieties of historical thinking upon Ethiopian scholars. This new turn was widespread in early postcolonial Africa and Asia, where many leaders of newly independent Third World states endeavored to document and preserve their national and multinational heritage by employing the tools of academic history.[13] Liberation required systematic historical recuperation, and accordingly, vernacular history—variously perceived by modernizing states as traditional, amateur, unsophisticated, or unscientific—ceased to be the principal avenue for investigating the past. In short, the politics of decolonization brokered shifts in Third World historical practice.

In postcolonial Ethiopia and Eritrea, two key developments exemplified this change. The first was the institutionalization of the interdisciplinary area studies paradigm. This process began in 1944 with the establishment of the National Library, a lending and research facility directed by the foreign-trained Sereke Berhan Gäbrä Egzi'abḥér and with a main reading room fittingly named for *blattén géta* Ḫeruy. Its collection of 15,000 books, manuscripts, and cultural artifacts, many originating from the private library of the emperor, ensured that "the ancient civilization . . . [was] wedded to the new," in the assessment of director Sereke Berhan.[14] This new historical turn continued in the 1950s with the creation of the Ethnological Society and Museum of the University College Addis Ababa, the future Haile Selassie I/Addis Ababa University,[15] and reached its apogee in 1963, with the creation of the Institute of Ethiopian Studies. Housed in a former imperial residence and directed by the expatriate British academic Richard Pankhurst, the Institute aimed to promote area-specific research by publishing new scholarship, building a library and manuscript collection, managing a museum, hosting foreign scholars and conferences, and showcasing Ethiopia's past to visiting heads of state.[16] One of its most noteworthy achievements was the publication of the annual *Journal of Ethiopian Studies*.[17] The preservative efforts of the Institute were complemented by the National Museum of Addis Ababa, directed by Käbbädä's colleague Gezäw Ḫaylä Maryam (1910–89), and the Archeological Museum and Institute of Ethiopian Studies of Asmära, led by Vincenzo Franchini (1914–n.d.), an expatriate resident since 1941.[18] These entities created a new multidisciplinary framework for research and scholarship related to the Ethiopian (and Eritrean) past, one that encompassed history, philology, archeology, anthropology, linguistics, bibliography, and art history. Ethiopian studies was now institutionalized.

A second key development was the emergence of a cohort of Ethiopian historians trained in western graduate programs. This pioneering group of Western-trained historians included Bairu Tafla, Berhanou Abbebe (1932–2008), Getatchew Haile, Merid Wolde Aregay (1934–2008), Sergew Hable Selassie (1929–2003), Taddesse Tamrat (n.d.–2013), and numerous others.[19] Many of these scholars obtained positions at Haile Selassie University and in government, and their rigor and creativity jointly produced a

Figure 5.1. Inside the National Library, ca. 1945. *Ethiopian Review* 1 (1945): 14.

watershed moment in the study of Ethiopia and the Horn of Africa. They made enduring contributions to scholarship by fusing new methods and conceptual tools with native linguistic competencies and deep cultural understanding, and as educators, they trained generations of undergraduate and graduate students. Through their efforts, Ethiopian studies was effectively indigenized.

But academic history was not the only game in town, though it may have enjoyed the most state largesse. Vernacular historiography continued to flourish amid these momentous developments, and its exponents moved in—and wrote for—somewhat different circles than their academic counterparts. One of the most prominent postwar exemplars of this school was Yäréd Gäbrä Mika'él, who unofficially assumed the role of royal biographer in the 1940s and served in this capacity for several decades.[20] Throughout his career he produced a large number of histories in traditional genres, from a *tarikä nägäśt* to biographies of members of the imperial family, such as Emperor Ḫaylä Śellasé, *etégé* Mänän, and Crown Prince Asfa Wässän (1916–97), their eldest son.[21] These works exemplify the annalistic, observational, and laconic tendencies in vernacular historical writing, eschewing narrative and explicit analysis for a rigorous chronography of the actions of the biographical subject(s). Rather more innovative was Yäréd's detailed study of Addis Ababa, certainly one of the first vernacular experiments with urban history.[22] This copiously illustrated work consists of three parts: a discussion of the development of the city, in multiple chapters; a collection of poems on urban and modern themes; and an extensive index of Addis Ababa's most notable past and current residents, including titles and photos. Yäréd also wrote books on spiritual topics.[23]

Blattén géta Marse'é Ḫazan Wäldä Qirqos was another prominent postwar exponent of vernacular history. A civil servant and the author of a very large number of works, historical and otherwise, he attempted to elaborate and develop the tradition rather like his predecessor Ḫeruy. One of his most intriguing efforts to this end was a detailed documentary history of the Italian occupation, commissioned by the imperial government and titled *Yä'amestu yämäkära a'mätat aččer tarik*, or *Short History of the Five Years of Hardship*.[24] This was a pioneering if preliminary treatment of a complex topic, as Marse'é Ḫazan noted in its introduction.[25] He and coauthor Berhanu Denqé addressed such matters as the fall of Addis Ababa; the speeches of Emperor Ḫaylä Śellasé and Viceroy Rodolfo Graziani; the role of newspapers, propaganda, and the tools of war; the resistance movement and refugees, with a special chapter on Ḫeruy; and finally, Italy's entry into the Second World War, the British-Ethiopian reconquest of Ethiopia, and the emperor's reentry into Addis Ababa. This was likely one of the first published Amharic accounts of the colonial interregnum, and it coincided with the Ethiopian government's effort to submit historical evidence for

Italian war crimes in Ethiopia to the United Nations War Crimes Commission.[26] Marse'é Ḫazan's other historical works include a series of memoirs, an Amharic translation of Herodotus's *Histories,* and an account of the emperor's journey to Gondär, essentially a travel narrative with biographical and prosopographical elements.[27] He also wrote an introduction to an edition of *ṣäḥafé te'ezaz* Gäbrä Śellasé's chronicle of Emperor Menilek.[28]

Numerous other intellectuals remained devotees of vernacular history. Though they were no longer direct observers of power or transmitters of an official tradition, they wrote history in a style that would have been largely recognizable to their forebears. The most prominent of these figures include Maḫtämä Sellasé Wäldä Mäsqäl and Käbbädä Tessema, and lesser-known examples are Berhanu Denqé, Berhan Mäsqäl Dästa, and Gärima Taffärä.[29] The goals of these writers varied. For some, memoir-as-history was a tool for preserving their personal recollections; for others, it was one branch of the larger field of traditional knowledge that needed to be preserved. On the latter point, it is significant that several of these vernacular historians—most notably Yäréd Gäbrä Mika'él, Marse'é Ḫazan, and Maḫtämä Sellasé—contributed to other branches of traditional scholarship. The opposite was also true: some traditionalist intellectuals occasionally considered historical topics through quasi-historical works. Thus Tässäma Häbtä Mika'él produced an Amharic dictionary that included etymologies and a host of historical entries, while Aklilä Berhan Wäldä Qirqos wrote a highly eclectic linguistic study touching on numerous historical questions.[30] In this respect, vernacular historians were quite distinct from their academic counterparts, who tended to treat traditional scholarship as source material or an object of discipline-based inquiry, and not a field to which they themselves contributed. Effectively, academic history aimed to assimilate the vernacular tradition into itself.

A few scholars contributed to both schools. One was Täklä Ṣadeq Mäkʷeriya (1913–2000), arguably the most prolific and long-lived historian of the postwar era.[31] A traditionally educated civil servant who spoke French, Italian, and English, Täklä Ṣadeq produced a massive oeuvre of histories in Amharic and foreign languages over the course of his near-half-century career. His many Amharic works include a host of monographs and two magisterial multivolume surveys: a four-volume study of Ethiopian history from antiquity to the reign of Emperor Ḫaylä Śellasé, published in the 1940s and 1950s, and a three-volume study on late-nineteenth-century Ethiopian emperors and the unity of Ethiopia, written in the 1980s.[32] These efforts were complemented by Täklä Ṣadeq's contributions to the international fields of Ethiopian and African studies. He produced several French works on topics ranging from church history to royal genealogy, and contributed two English chapters on the Horn of Africa to the *UNESCO General History of Africa,* a major scholarly and educational reference.[33] He was also very active in academic societies, most notably the International Conference of Ethiopian Studies and the International Congress of Orientalists. He was lauded in life and after death by his Ethiopian and foreign colleagues for his achievements.[34]

It is difficult to gauge the interplay between the two varieties of history. One arena to consider is government educational curricula, where the situation was decidedly mixed. On the one hand, the study of Ethiopian history at the secondary level rested upon firm vernacular foundations.[35] Most notable in this respect was Täklä Ṣadeq's multivolume survey of Ethiopian history, a popular text written with the aim of making Ethiopian history accessible to students and the general reader. Some volumes in the series were eventually edited by the Ministry of Education and subsequently used in the secondary-school curriculum.[36] Another vernacular history textbook was *aläqa* Tayyä's history of the Ethiopian people, which was reprinted multiple times in the postwar period and used by the Ministry of Education in the 1960s.[37] On the other hand, several history textbooks merged vernacular and Ethiopian topics with Western historical material, like Käbbädä's 1955 world history. Somewhat similar was a 1947/8 world history by Yoḥannes Wäldä Maryam, which presented the general contours of Western civilization with a cursory treatment of Ethiopia and the Horn of Africa.[38] In terms of public education, then, the kind of history deemed suitable for instructing the nation's youth combined old and new, vernacular and academic.

In the early 1970s, the Ministry of Education attempted to impose order on this heterogeneity with a rigorous new history curriculum called "History for Young Ethiopians," written by a team of Ethiopian academics and civil servants.[39] Some of the results of this initiative were commendable and sophisticated attempts to ground pedagogical materials in the latest research of academic specialists. Notable in this regard are the efforts of Bairu Tafla, who wrote a textbook for tenth-grade students that presented Ethiopian history within the broader context of African, European, and Islamic history.[40] Its Foreword asked instructors to place "special emphasis" on the Ethiopian and African chapters, because: "Ethiopia is part of Africa, and it could be treated in our textbook as one of the African countries. But it is our country, and we are concerned more with its history, culture, civilization, politics, economy, and religion throughout our life than with any other country. For us, to know Ethiopia's past is to know ourselves."[41] The series was published with limited distribution in 1974.[42]

By that point, though, a new variety of historicism had transformed the Ethiopian historical imagination: Marxism. The radical student movement that fueled the 1974 revolution also generated a distinctive historical culture that reconsidered the Ethiopian—and Eritrean—past, present, and future through the analytic prisms of historical materialism, productive forces, and class and ethnic conflict. In the later 1960s and early 1970s, the leading student leftist organizations—notably the Ethiopian People's Revolutionary Party (EPRP) and the All Ethiopia Socialist Movement (AESM)—produced a considerable body of polemical writings that addressed the origins of feudalism, class conflict, ethnic oppression, and patriarchy.[43] Many of these works were more theoretical than empirical, and some tended toward acute ahistoricism and presentism.[44] After 1974, this radical historical culture entered into mainstream public discourse through a variety of media—from the proclamations of the Provisional Military Administrative Council, or Därg, which regularly justified its policies through references to past injustices, to the newspaper articles that examined historical topics with revolutionary significance, such as Russo-Ethiopian relations.[45] Broadly speaking, this turn to Marxism had historicist implications, since the variety of doctrinaire scientific socialism that was ultimately embraced by the Därg and its allies required the assimilation of Ethiopian specificities to orthodox Marxist-Leninist models. It is precisely for this reason that Ethiopian Marxist thought has been termed Eurocentric, impoverished, and superficial.[46]

Though the revolutionary generation has been critiqued for its failure to generate a sufficiently rigorous and creative analysis of Ethiopian society, some intellectuals of the era did produce serious works of history. The most systematic and lucid analysis in this vein is that of Addis Hiwet, whose groundbreaking *Ethiopia: From Autocracy to Revolution* examined the emergence of the modern Ethiopian social formation, which in his view was produced by the interplay between Ethiopian "feudal imperialism" and European "capitalist imperialism" in the late nineteenth and early twentieth centuries. This historical dialectic generated a new social order—which he termed somewhat cumbersomely "military-feudal-colonialism"—that was, in turn, toppled by the 1974 revolution.[47] The author explores these dynamics through focused, inter-linked discussions, considering Emperor Menilek's imperial conquests in the nineteenth century, the development and features of Ethiopian feudalism, its impact upon the newly conquered peripheral societies, the concomitant emergence of a nascent and externally oriented capitalism in the early twentieth century, the political ascendency of Täfäri Mäkonnen/Ḫaylä Śellasé ("the First Autocrat of All Ethiopia"), and the ideas of the radical "Japanizing" and "antifeudal" intellectuals of the 1920s and '30s—whose cause, Addis argued, should be taken up by the revolutionaries of the 1970s.[48] His study concludes with short chapters narrating events up to the 1960 coup attempt, the causes and course of the revolution, and finally the ascendency of the Därg military dictatorship, which the author critiqued from the left as "Bonapartist" and "bourgeois," in that it liquidated feudalism but preserved imperialism in the guise of state capitalism.

Addis Hiwet's work is notable for several important achievements. It offered an empirically grounded, ethnically inflected, and relatively dynamic model of Ethiopian feudalism, a topic that was widely discussed in the student movement and became the subject of considerable debate among academics interested in theorizing what was termed "the Abyssinian Mode of Production."[49] His study is also notable for its close attention to concretizing the specific agents and social categories of this system, focusing on their specific historical forms rather than abstract ideal types. Finally, Addis Hiwet's study was a pioneering contribution to the modern intellectual history of Ethiopia through its consideration of the reformist culture of *Berhanenna sälam* in the years prior to the Italian occupation, a topic that until that point had attracted little attention. His work was lauded at the time of its publication, and it can still be read with profit today.[50]

Comparable in approach if not influence are the writings of the Howard University-educated Lapiso Gétahun Delébo. The most substantial of these is his two-volume social history of Ethiopia, written in Amharic using a wide range of foreign sources.[51] Like Addis Hiwet, Lapiso takes a synchronic approach: his study considers the overlapping historical processes of "the rise and fall of the *gäbbar* system," the origins of capitalism and communism, and "the revolutionary uprising of the people." He focuses on the ethnic and peripheral roots of the 1974 revolution, with chapters devoted to the history of Balé, the Gédé'o, and the Guragé, and the impact of the *gäbbar* system upon these. The author concludes by considering the forces that contributed to "the Explosion of the Revolution."

A rather different perspective is offered by Legesse Lemma, whose 1979 doctoral dissertation at the University of Notre Dame explored the economic history of core-periphery relations in the Horn of Africa.[52] Employing a theoretical apparatus rooted in modes of production, and especially the distinction between the colonial and neocolonial phases of its capitalist variety, his work examines Ethiopia's political economy and external relations from the late nineteenth century to 1974. Its chapters consider the conquests of Emperor Menilek, the developments of the interwar period, British and then American dominance in the postwar era, and finally Ethiopia's educational system and its relationship to "the interests of the Monarchy" and "the interests of Imperialism." Rather like Addis Hiwet, and with echoes of Gäbrä Ḥeywät, he characterizes the imperial government of the twentieth century as a neocolonial regime, in which the Nkrumahesque "junior and senior partners" were the monarchy and the foreign imperialists, who shared a collective interest in "the strengthening of the central government and development of human and physical infrastructure."[53] Legesse is careful, however, to qualify his analysis by acknowledging the limited penetration of foreign capital in the first half of the twentieth century,[54] and he considers the antagonisms and contradictions of the imperial system, such as those produced by its hegemonic ideology of paternalism, per Eugene Genovese.[55] Legesse's work is a nuanced and by no means doctrinaire examination of neocolonialism and underdevelopment in Ethiopia grounded in an impressive range of empirical data and archival materials. He went on to write several articles on related topics.[56]

These Marxist-inflected histories were complemented by New Left analyses of Ethiopia and the Horn that began to appear in international academic journals after 1974, most notably *African Review of Political Economy, New Left Review, Northeast African Studies, Politique Africaine,* and *Peasant Studies.*[57] Monographs in foreign languages added to this specialist work.[58] At the same time, Marxist studies of Ethiopia and its revolution developed within the institutional and academic framework of Soviet area studies, and became embroiled in debates about the nature of Third World revolutions and the role of superpower interventions therein.[59] Some of this work was translated from Russian into Amharic.[60] As a result of all this literature, historical materialism entered the Ethiopian historical repertoire.

These developments are the subject of a fraught public conversation in Ethiopia and its diaspora today. The generation of student radicals who brought down the imperial order only to usher in the bloody Därg dicatorship have begun to critically examine their achievements and failings, and the nature of their historical outlook has come under close scrutiny. Though spurred by academic publications and conference presentations, this conversation has spilled into the public sphere through blog posts and radio programs. The historical reckoning is particularly passionate because most of the participants were personally involved in the student movement or connected to the Därg.

For some, the revolutionaries' renunciation of their cultural patrimony was an over-determined but critical error. Messay Kebede has argued that the sterile intellectual culture and poor educational system of the postwar period fostered a Eurocentric outlook that led students to categorically reject their heritage and uncritically adopt internationalist varieties of Marxism.[61] In his view, their eventual "infatuation" with Marxism-Leninism reflected "[the] mental disorientation imparted by exposure to Western education," which demeaned indigenous knowledge and achievements.[62] Had the student radicals been more attuned to the value of Ethiopian traditions and institutions, their revolutionary project might have taken a different and possibly less tragic course. Thus the revolutionaries' cultural alienation—their historical ignorance—was both their motive and their downfall.

Others have forcefully critiqued this position. Bahru Zewde has offered a response to Messay by systematically examining the historical causes of radicalization. He notes that the Ethiopian student movement confronted the same structural inequalities that mobilized leftist student protest elsewhere in the 1960s and '70s, and further, that it was part of a longer history of oppositional student politics at Addis Ababa University that began in the 1950s—the silencing of which, in the context of more general governmental intransigence on a host of social and political grievances, fueled the students' radicalization. Absent a visible domestic tradition of dissent, or an institutional forum for legitimate political opposition, the student movement became increasingly exogenetic in its search for liberatory models, looking to the New Left, Marxism-Leninism, and Pan-Africanism. The students eagerly adopted these foreign movements' sophisticated, ready-made intellectual tools wholesale, and in the process, Bahru suggests, "Marxism-Leninism became a dogma that could intepret the Ethiopian reality, not a theory that could be deployed intelligently to analyze it."[63] Put simply, there was no Ethiopian Lenin or Mao, though there were certainly many theoreticians who embraced their ideas. The overall course of radicalization, however, was not a symptom of cultural alienation or historical ignorance; rather, it was a consequence of the structural features of the authoritarian postwar order.

Similarly, Gebru Tareke asserts that the student movement was uniquely authentic in its commitment to Ethiopian emancipation, and as a riposte to Messay, that the educational system did not in fact disparage all things Ethiopian and non-Western. Instead, it simply offered an incomplete historical perspective focused on the agency and culture of dominant ethnic groups, adopting the "Greater Ethiopia" narrative that was then ubiquitous in the academic literature. The student radicals' more significant error, in his view, was their blind acceptance of a Russian revolutionary model that focused on the transformative power of a revolutionary vanguard.[64] Their flaw was thus their strategy, not their mindset.[65]

Teshale Tibebu explains this flawed course by noting that Ethiopian Marxism was Eurocentric because it was insufficiently developed. This was a consequence of its relatively short lifespan before 1974. Though the radical students and intellectuals grappled with multiple strands of political and historical analysis—relating to class, ethnicity, gender, and the varieties of imperialism—the violence of the revolution halted their efforts. This historically conditioned theoretical poverty, in his view, stands in stark contrast to the intellectually sophisticated approach to modernization held by the radicals' more vernacularly attuned and traditionally educated contemporaries, and it contributed to the Därg's general disregard for custom and culture. In his view, Ethiopian Marxism ultimately "rejected Ethiopia's past as being one reactionary pile of refuse badly in need of cleaning."[66]

The nature of the rich and dynamic dual historical culture of the postwar period is surely relevant to this debate. It is true that the prerevolutionary era witnessed the flourishing of academic and institutionalized historical inquiry, and that the development of Ethiopian studies tended to privilege the Western disciplinary framework. Some intellectuals even wrote histories that could be called Eurocentric, and Western historical models became prominent—most notably single-path modernization theory, though this was often only latent in historiography proper. But two other points are perhaps more significant. First, the new generation of Western-trained historians who emerged in the postwar period incomparably deepened and enriched our understanding of the Ethiopian past, which is precisely why their works remain classic studies today. They uncovered new sources and reinterpreted old ones, and though they might have said little about subaltern ethnic and religious groups, it is difficult to see how such enduring contributions could be understood as the product of "colonized" or "alienated" minds. Second, vernacular history remained a vibrant counter-tradition to academic history throughout the postwar period, and some of its exponents aimed to develop and transmit Ethiopia's rich historical inheritance to future generations. Like their predecessors of the early twentieth century, they were defenders of the tradition—they were bulwarks against cultural alienation, not products of it.

This dualism was not the weakness of postwar historical culture—it was its strength. The years before the revolution saw the flourishing of a new historiography and historical culture that was rich and variegated, not Eurocentric and impoverished. If the era's academic historians sought to overcome the perceived limitations of the vernacular tradition, they did not seek to destroy it, but instead to develop a new way of thinking about the Ethiopian past. The Marxist activists and historians who followed them took up this same project, though they employed different tools for other purposes. It is thanks to the collective efforts of all these individuals that history in the vernacular is alive and well in Ethiopia today.

Conclusion

This book has examined the creative zenith of vernacular historiography in Ethiopia and Eritrea, a moment that coincided with the flourishing of the Ethiopianist branch of Semitic studies in Europe and North America. In light of this parallel, it is fitting to conclude this study with a brief reflection on the precise relationship between Ethiopian and Eritrean intellectuals and their Western counterparts. As this book has shown, the former made great use of the latter's published scholarship, while the latter relied to a considerable extent upon indigenous sources and so-called native informants. But what of actual intellectual collaboration?

This is a complex question. Until the second half of the twentieth century, the two groups interacted within the context of formal and informal imperialism in the Horn of Africa, and this setting influenced the dynamics of their relationships. The connection between knowledge and power is most overtly manifest in Italian anthropological scholarship that had intelligence or administrative dimensions.[1] But a subtler tendency was also widespread. Although foreign specialists depended upon the testimony, tutelage, and research of their indigenous colleagues, they often minimized or failed to acknowledge the significance of these relationships in their academic publications. This practice effaced these early indigenous contributions to the field of Ethiopian studies, over-westernizing the genealogy of the field and institutionalizing an unequal intellectual partnership.

This situation was by no means unique. In 1938, Jomo Kenyatta (1894–1978), the Kenyan intellectual and British-trained social anthropologist, castigated "the professional [academic] friends of the African," who in his view "monopolize the office of interpreting his mind and speaking for him," and who believe that "an African who writes a study of . . . [their] kind is encroaching on their preserves. He is a rabbit turned poacher."[2] In Kenyatta's estimation, anthropologists like Louis Leakey (1903–1972) were thus not the moderate or even radical critics of the colonial situation they believed themselves to be, since their own profession replicated its inequalities through a de facto race-based glass ceiling. Kenyatta hoped to shatter this barrier with his own study of the Kikuyu, *Facing Mount Kenya*, which he believed was an authoritative, rigorously scientific, and politically useful account of his society and the harmful impact of British colonial policy upon it. But this attempt at objective auto-ethnography, possibly the first anthropological study published by an African in the English language, was ignored by most of his contemporaries, British and Kenyan alike.[3] This mute reception would seem to confirm his critique: his scholarly poaching was unwelcome.

In more recent years, the general problem Kenyatta identified has become the subject of increased scrutiny and debate. The central question is this: during the colonial era, to what extent could indigenous intellectuals substantively contribute to the academic study of their own societies? Were their voices silenced by—or assimilated into—colonial knowledge? Or was this knowledge in fact co-produced? Different versions of these questions have emerged across African, South Asian, and Middle Eastern studies, with implications for debates about the strength and constitution of colonial power.[4]

Answers to the question of the balance of power in foreign-indigene relations vary in time and place. This is well illustrated by the complex situation that prevailed in British India.[5] Two episodes reveal its contours. One is that of Colin Mackenzie (1754–1821), the British East India Company agent who undertook a monumental geographic and historical survey of Mysore and Deccan in the early nineteenth century.[6] Lacking the requisite linguistic training, he supervised a large number of native intermediaries who collected oral traditions, inscriptions, and manuscripts with precolonial origins. This vernacular material was then translated for the company's use and for future publication, with Mackenzie's indigenous colleagues occasionally adding prefatory and interpretive comments to their efforts.[7] The wide-ranging archive that resulted was a massive and unprecedented contribution to the documentary history of South Asia, and Mackenzie lauded the research talents of his native colleagues, whose "penetrating acute genius" he considered essential to the entire endeavor.[8] He had particular esteem for his first collaborator, a Brahmin from Andhra Pradesh named Kavelli Venkata Boria (n.d.–1803), whom he deemed "of the quickest genius and disposition."[9]

In holding these views, though, Mackenzie distinguished himself from many of his contemporaries and successors, who tended to see indigenes as unsuitable for anything beyond the "technical" tasks of fieldwork, source-procurement, and translation. As the Indologist branch of orientalism became increasingly state-funded, instrumentalist, and official in constitution, it allowed considerably less room for Indian voices.[10] The impact of this development is illustrated by the case of Ram Gharib Chaube (n.d.–1914), a Pandit from Gorakhpur who was employed by the folklorist and civil servant William Crooke (1848–1923). In the last decades of the nineteenth century, Chaube collected oral traditions in central India, which he translated and commented upon for Crooke, whom he considered an intellectual associate and patron. However, despite Chaube's tremendous respect for Crooke, and Crooke's deep intellectual indebtedness to Chaube, Crooke failed to mention him in his two published works.[11] The chasm between the two widened after 1900, when Crooke returned to England, where he became a distinguished scholar and obtained an honorary doctorate from Oxford. Although Chaube continued to send reports to his former employer, Crooke failed to respond to his requests for professional recommendations and financial assistance. Thereby deprived of income and perhaps more significantly of the scholarly recognition that was his due, Chaube became penniless, obsessed and angry with Crooke, who became known to Chaube's acquaintances as "crooked sahib."[12] He was driven to insanity, and he died in relative obscurity in 1914.

If Mackenzie refused to treat his indigenous colleagues as threatening poachers, Crooke certainly made up for it through his exploitative behavior. Yet despite their different approaches to acknowledging their collaborators, Mackenzie and Crooke both devoted their careers to assimilating indigenous research and learning into the archive and conceptual language of Western scholarship, and in both cases—though to different degrees—their own academic stature overshadowed that of their indigenous colleagues. A host of similar kinds of unequal academic relationships have been described in other African and Asian settings.[13] Kenyatta's rabbit/poacher dualism, however categorical, therefore seems correct in its broad strokes.

So what of the Ethiopian and Eritrean case? Were there more Mackenzies or more Crookes in the field? To the extent that the intercultural lineage of Ethiopian studies has been noted in the academic literature, it has been seen as an equitable and positivist collaboration between partners.[14] This optimistic view is at odds with at least one Ethiopian assessment from the period in question. In 1935, during the tumultuous first weeks of the Italian invasion of Ethiopia, an anonymous contributor to *Berhanenna sälam* offered a scathing critique of the political dangers of foreign scholarship. He or she began by noting the importance of scrutinizing the motivations of strangers—regardless of whether they professed friendship or enmity—and offered as a cautionary example the cases of Ignazio Guidi, Carlo Conti Rossini, Enrico Cerulli, Nello Puccioni, and various other Italian scholars. The author wrote that these men, "who were not born to us and who are not related to us," were in fact "workers for the Italian government" who endeavored "to know the history [of Ethiopia] . . . because they planned to take over our land." Their duplicity had not only aided the Italian colonial project; it had also imparted a bias to Italian writings on Ethiopia, which were consequently riddled with "impurities and lies."[15] Politically motivated foreign scholarship thus threatened freedom as well as truth. This public exposé of the bellicose dimensions of purportedly neutral scholarship, which was accompanied by a corrective history of Ethiopian-Italian relations, was made more ominous by the fact that it appeared alongside articles discussing the mobilization of Ethiopian military forces and the prevailing "spirit of war."[16] It was not the only contemporary assessment of this kind. Shortly after the cataclysmic Italian conquest of Addis Ababa in 1936, Tä'ammrat Amanu'el said of Mario Moreno, "Now he is no longer a scholar of the Orient or of Ethiopia: I have seen him dressed as a warrior."[17]

In point of fact, a number of Italian Ethiopianists were directly involved in colonial projects, fusing academic analysis with administration, intelligence-gathering, and even military command. Tä'ammrat and the author of the *Berhanenna sälam* article only named the most prominent exemplars. The most extreme case is surely that of Enrico Cerulli, the distinguished historian, folklorist, and linguist who served as a civil servant in Italian Somalia, as the Director of Political Affairs in the Ministry of Italian Africa, and finally as Vice-Governor General and occasional Viceregal Regent in Italian East Africa—in the latter capacity assuming the highest executive position in the colony.[18] A similarly engaged scholar was Alberto Pollera, the ethnographer of the Eritrean lowlands who provided intelligence assessments for colonial administrators, and who published articles extolling the civilizing mission in colonial newspapers.[19]

Like their counterparts in other colonial settings, these scholar-conquerors depended upon collaboration with Ethiopians and Eritreans. Yet few of these indigenous scholars received the academic esteem posthumously accorded to *abba* Täklä Maryam, who, as we have seen, pursued his own research agenda within the disciplinary framework of Ethiopian and Eastern Christian studies. It would appear that these pioneering *etiopianistas* were formidable gamekeepers indeed. Were Kenyatta and his Ethiopian contemporaries thus correct? To what extent could Ethiopians and Eritreans contribute to the development of the Ethiopianist branch of Semitic studies? Two dramatic and well-documented case studies help to elucidate these questions. They do not provide clear answers, but they do permit some speculative conclusions.

Littmann and Näffa'e

The first is that of Enno Littmann (1875–1958), the German Semiticist, and Näffa'e Wäd Etman (c. 1882–1909), his Eritrean language teacher and research assistant.[20] Littmann first visited the Italian colony in 1905 as head of a Princeton research expedition. His principal goals were to study Tegré and Tigrinya, copy epigraphic texts, and acquire manuscripts, and it was these aims that led him to Näffa'e. The latter was originally a Muslim from Sänḥit who spoke Tegré, Tigrinya, and Amharic. He had been educated by his father until the age of thirteen, at which point he began attending the EFS mission school in Gäläb, where he converted to Christianity, expeditiously completed his course of study, and worked as a teacher for thirteen years.[21] Littmann met him briefly in the last months of 1905, when Näffa'e taught him Tegré and assisted with the expedition's research. In 1907, more than a year after Littmann's departure from the colony, Näffa'e then travelled to meet him in Strasbourg, where he resided for two years. Under Littmann's direction, he studied German, Italian, and Arabic. He apparently believed that knowing Italian would help his community upon his return to Eritrea, and that Arabic would allow him to read the Quran and debate Muslims.[22]

The two scholars became close colleagues over the course of this period. Each day, they worked together in the morning on Littmann's projects, with Näffa'e's language studies occupying the afternoons and evenings.[23] According to Littmann, Näffa'e possessed a complex personality: he was spiritual, humorous, and intensely studious, but also inclined toward solitude. He also found his distance from home difficult to bear. As Littmann later recalled, "Even though he was glad to gain so much knowledge and to get to collect so many different impressions, he still did not feel happy. He did not talk much about it, but one could tell. It was like a flower being planted into different soil."[24] Näffa'e became increasingly homesick, and after a failed bid to attend a school in Sweden with EFS sponsorship, he decided to return to Eritrea.[25] Unfortunately, after departing from Genoa by ship, he died at sea under mysterious circumstances. Littmann subsequently attempted to determine what had happened through inquiries with the crew, even threatening to take the matter to the press, but his efforts proved inconclusive. In Näffa'e's final letter to Littmann, he had reported that the other passengers were severely mistreating him, and this led Littmann to speculate that he had been murdered, or that he had become deranged and killed himself. Littmann subsequently wrote an extremely detailed and personal obituary for his late Eritrean colleague, which he published in the German journal *Der Neue Orient*.[26]

Yet this sad episode was followed by a coda of sorts. Littmann's years of research and collaboration with Näffa'e eventually led to a monumental four-volume study of Tegré names, songs, and oral traditions, published one year after Näffa'e's death. Littmann freely acknowledged that his Eritrean colleague had been instrumental to the work, and that his contributions were numerous and significant.[27] In Eritrea, Näffa'e had obtained nearly all the texts that were published by Littmann. He transcribed dirges as they were sung, and identified their places of origin when these were unclear.[28] This project apparently involved a not-insignificant breach of custom: dirge-singing was reserved for women, and Näffa'e's female relatives reportedly questioned his motive for recording their words.[29] But his contributions went far beyond fieldwork. Littmann also observed that Näffa'e "explained narrations, traditions, and songs of his tribe, and has written [down] a great part of the literature, to this point unknown and only orally delivered, in his language himself."[30] Littmann cited these explanations in footnotes throughout the four-volume work, especially on linguistic matters.[31] Finally, and perhaps most significantly, Näffa'e wrote an introduction in Tegré to the third volume of this work.[32] Surveying all these contributions, Littmann frankly concluded that "his services in copying manuscripts, explaining the texts, collecting words[,] and interpreting them . . . have been invaluable to me," and "the volumes of my Publications of the Princeton University Expedition to Abyssinia would have not been written nor published without him."[33]

As these accolades suggest, Näffa'e posthumously received the recognition that his contemporary Chaube had been denied. For this reason, it is difficult to see Littmann as an intellectual gamekeeper like Crooke, even if he was occasionally prone to patronizing characterizations of African culture.[34] Indeed, he worked to reify Näffa'e's authorial identity and academic legacy after the latter's death. He dedicated the Princeton publications to his Eritrean counterpart, and he observed that "[Näffa'e's] death is a very great loss not only to his own nation, but also to European science."[35] In his laudatory obituary for Näffa'e, Littmann elaborated on the nature of this loss: "He had the ability to see what matters when exploring a language; he also had the intention to draw more down for me. If he had stayed alive he could have helped us learn much more about his people and his home country."[36] Näffa'e was an esteemed colleague, not an importunate rival.

Coon and Mäkonnen

At the opposite extreme is the case of Carleton Coon (1904–81), the American physical anthropologist, and Mäkonnen Dästa (c. 1910–68), his Ethiopian research assistant. The two met in the early 1930s at Harvard, where they both studied with Earnest Hooton (1887–1954), the rival of Columbia's Franz Boas (1858–1942). Coon was completing a doctorate in anthropometry, or metrical racial morphology, and Mäkonnen was pursuing an undergraduate degree in anthropology.[37] In 1933, Coon enlisted Mäkonnen as an interpreter for a university research expedition to Ethiopia, and the two departed from New York and arrived in Dire Dawa via Marseilles, the Suez Canal, Aden, and finally Djibouti.[38] Coon found the journey a pleasant adventure, but it was ominously marred by several tense clashes with Mäkonnen.

Upon their arrival in Dire Dawa, they were delayed for several days, during which time Mäkonnen dutifully inquired about official introductions.

Remarkably, he managed to secure a meeting with *blattén géta* Ḫeruy, then the Foreign Minister, who was in transit with *etégé* Mänän on a journey to the Levant, and thus Coon—a graduate student—had the opportunity to discuss his developing racial theories with Ethiopia's foremost man of letters. He reported that Ḫeruy found his research a promising avenue for uncovering possible biological links between Ethiopia and Japan, and bizarrely, he attempted to enlist Ḫeruy as his first anthropometric subject.[39] Heruy declined, and with typical tact, he ignored the encounter in his own account of his sojourn in Dire Dawa.[40] But Mäkonnen had begun his service in a promising fashion, introducing Coon to an important and extremely well-connected contact.

Despite this early success, the mood darkened considerably on the train to Addis Ababa, as the antagonism between two men intensified. Coon became fixated on Mäkonnen's psychology, later recalling "I was more concerned with the perversity of the human mind than with the scenery," in reference to his Ethiopian colleague.[41] He began to obsessively catalog minor episodes that in his view discredited Mäkonnen.[42] Things worsened upon their arrival in the capital. Coon disregarded Mäkonnen's lodging arrangements, which led the latter to accuse him of racism, and further insulted his Ethiopian colleague by hiring a young boy as his assistant even though Mäkonnen took the effort to introduce him to several qualified, American-educated Ethiopian candidates.[43] Another setback came when the group visited the American Legation, where some mysterious incident connected to Mäkonnen led the consular representative to write a letter to the State Department asserting that Coon was "not fit to be abroad."[44] Finally—and from Coon's perspective most alarmingly—Mäkonnen was unable to secure a meeting with the emperor. The American came to believe that he was being deliberately misled, and after a confrontation between the two men, Mäkonnen resigned from his position.

Freed of his supposedly difficult native guide, Coon now believed his research would proceed unhampered. He couldn't have been more wrong. The acting Foreign Minister refused to allow Coon to travel in the countryside but granted him permission to study military recruits, who came from varied backgrounds. The Minister had two stipulations, however: the results of Coon's work could only be published in an academic venue, and Coon was required to rehire Mäkonnen to coordinate the transfers of soldiers to Coon's team. Coon grudgingly accepted this plan, rented a building, and began preparing for the research. Yet Mäkonnen and the promised military subjects did not appear, and after Coon met with the Foreign Minister to discuss the matter, he was told that Mäkonnen had disappeared with Coon's permit, and thus the research could not proceed. Frustrated, Coon decided to leave the country. As he arranged his departure, he made a final effort to measure some city residents outside his facility, which led to an altercation with an Ethiopian police officer. He was restrained at gunpoint and reprimanded, and after a final angry meeting with the Foreign Minister, Coon and the rest of the expedition left for the Arabian peninsula, abandoning the research project altogether.

In a formal report to Harvard's Peabody Museum, the expedition's sponsor, Coon attributed his abrupt change of plans to "political conditions" in Ethiopia, and made no mention of Mäkonnen in a roster of the expedition's participants.[45] This was disingenuous, since the fraught relationship between the two men—the principal subject of his published account of these events—had clearly destroyed the project. In his later writings, Coon attributed his troubles to Mäkonnen's obstructionism. For this, he offered three explanations. At one point, he claimed that Mäkonnen had become fixated upon Coon's racism upon their arrival in the Horn of Africa, by which point "all his feelings about the Negro–white question had now risen up to colour his every speech and action."[46] Later, Coon suggested that Mäkonnen suffered from some form of mental illness.[47] Finally, many years after the expedition, toward the end of his life, Coon attributed their youthful troubles to the idiosyncrasies of Mäkonnen's "noble blood and social position."[48]

Based on Coon's own account, the first explanation seems most likely. Despite his claims to the contrary, Coon clearly harbored disparaging views of Ethiopians and Africans more generally. Perhaps most damningly from an Ethiopian perspective, Coon openly and unreservedly approved of the colonial civilizing mission, much to Mäkonnen's dismay.[49] He mocked Mäkonnen, contested his descriptions and explanations, insulted an Ethiopian government official in Mäkonnen's company, refused to honor the latter's requests to avoid photographing potentially embarrassing cultural practices, and generally displayed open contempt for matters of protocol and decorum—manifest most bizarrely in his surprise that the emperor would not meet with him, a foreign graduate student.[50] He even tried to tell a taxi driver how to navigate the streets of Addis Ababa.[51] Coon's casual description of these episodes reveals the very prejudice he claimed Mäkonnen had falsely attributed to him.

This fissure reared its head methodologically. At one point, while training Mäkonnen and another American assistant in caliper measurement and physiognomic description, Coon concluded that Mäkonnen was incompetent. Mäkonnen responded that "our standards were all wrong; that we based our observations on white standards and that hence many important variations among non-whites would be lumped indiscriminately as 'thick' or 'everted.'"[52] Of this objection, Coon later wrote, "Although there was some justice in his argument, I nevertheless insisted on adhering to conventional principles."[53] His junior colleague was right, but it didn't matter. One can imagine that this early episode alone could have undermined their working relationship. More generally, the methodological shoddiness this story suggests was typical of the era's racial science.[54]

The aborted Ethiopian expedition produced some curious results. Coon delivered hundreds of acquisitions to Harvard's Peabody Museum, where they were catalogued and incorporated into the collection. These acquisitions included jewelry, household items, crosses, musical instruments, farm implements, and prehistoric obsidian blades. A few years later, in 1936, Coon produced an autobiographical account of his time in Ethiopia, *Measuring Ethiopia and Flight into Arabia*, which he intended as a realistic description of the difficulties of fieldwork, written for the general reader. Since this popular work describes some of Coon's theories about the biological features of Ethiopia's racial identity, it represents a breach of Coon's promise to the Ethiopian government. His disrupted fieldwork in Addis Ababa next played a minor role in a misleadingly titled 1939 work, *The Races of Europe*. In it, he argued that Ethiopians constituted a Mediterranean "sub-race" based on the fusion of diverse elements, with each of Northeast Africa's principal ethnic groups reflecting a distinct racial admixture.[55] His discussion made extensive use of the 1933–34 expedition's anthropometric data, which he presented through metrical discussions of body types and facial features. He also included an aside presenting what he described as an indigenous Ethiopian taxonomy of skin color and hair type, which, he noted, could not be reconciled with his own schema.[56] It is easy to imagine this taxonomy coming from Mäkonnen, his anthropologically inclined and critically minded native informant.

Ultimately, Coon went on to become an eminent but increasingly anachronistic exponent of a deterministic, race-focused school of physical anthropology. In 1961, he began serving as the President of the American Association of Physical Anthropology, while also lending informal and covert support to the segregationist cause. His 1962 magnum opus, *The Origin of Races*, offered a polygenic, biological explanation for different levels of civilizational attainment among the world's five races, which he argued were independently evolved subspecies of *Homo sapiens*. Seized upon by segregationists as a scientific demonstration that people of African descent were less evolved than whites, the work—and Coon's reluctance to acknowledge its patent political implications—was attacked by cultural anthropologists as well as physical anthropologists influenced by evolutionary biology and who eschewed the older methods of racial morphology and taxonomy.[57] The book, the ensuing debate about it, and Coon's unwillingness to distance himself from the odious racist arguments based on his writings effectively destroyed his academic career.

While Coon's scholarship approached its evolutionary dead end, Mäkonnen rose to achieve considerable distinction in Ethiopian political and intellectual life. Following a brief exile, he returned to participate in the resistance to the Italian occupation. In the years after 1941, he was appointed the head of the Ministry of Education, which he was credited with organizing, and he was a founder of the Anthropology Department at Haile Selassie University, where he achieved some distinction for his curiously Coonian arguments about the meta-racial nature of the greater Ethiopian nation.[58] He thus followed through on his early undergraduate dream to spend his life studying the people of Ethiopia.[59] In addition to these roles, the now *däǧǧazmač* Mäkonnen also served as Minister of Posts, Telephones, and Telegraphs (1944), President of the Chamber of Deputies (1946), Governor General of Wälläga (1949), and in various other ministerial positions, eventually joining the Senate in 1958. A few years later, he returned to Harvard to complete his long-interrupted undergraduate degree, which he finished in 1964.[60] Two years later, he succumbed to leukemia while in the United States.[61] He is remembered in Ethiopia today as a pioneer of Ethiopian anthropology.[62]

These are two extreme cases, and between them lie a range of possibilities. If taken as archetypes, the examples of Littmann, Näffa'e, Coon, and Mäkonnen suggest several general—if admittedly speculative—points about the nature of Ethiopian studies before 1941. The first is that while sustained scholarly collaboration could be tremendously productive, it was also rather exceptional. Very few Ethiopian/Eritrean and European scholars had—or at least acknowledged—the kind of close intellectual relationship that Littmann and Näffa'e enjoyed. They appear to have been most common in mission-related settings. Absent these kinds of personal ties, there were few opportunities for Ethiopian and Eritrean scholars to formally contribute to the academic study of their own societies, even though a considerable number of Ethiopians and Eritreans studied abroad during this period. Some of those who found foreign patrons, like Näffa'e, Tä'ammrat, and *abba* Täklä Maryam, managed to move in Western academic institutions and publish in Western academic fora, though these cases were rare.[63] On the whole, it would seem that until the postwar period, the academic field of Ethiopian studies remained a private preserve with nonnative wardens.

Second, this exclusionary and arrogant dynamic hindered the development of the field. Our two cases illustrated this point starkly. The collaboration of Littmann and Näffa'e was tremendously fruitful, generating a large corpus of source material that served as a bedrock for subsequent research. Other similar collaborations had an equally enduring significance, from *abba* Gorgoryos (n.d.–1658) and Hiob Ludolf (1624–1704) to Johannes Kolmodin (1884–1933) and his many Eritrean contacts.[64] In comparison, the dysfunctional partnership of Coon and Mäkonnen was fruitless, at least in terms of scholarship, even though both men subsequently enjoyed long careers in academic and public life. Ultimately, the failed Harvard expedition produced antiquities for the Peabody Museum and a handful of skull measurements of little scientific significance. If Coon had been willing to heed Mäkonnen's criticisms of his method, the outcome of the expedition might have been different.

Third, Western and Ethiopian/Eritrean scholars generally considered each others' work in isolation—as source material—rather than as opportunities for joint or collaborative inquiry. If Coon and Mäkonnen's fractious relationship was atypical in its drama, the social distance between the two scholars was probably not uncommon. This point is illustrated by the nonrelationship of the two most prominent and prolific intellectuals of the period, Ḫeruy and Cerulli. In the 1920s, they briefly lived in the same city, Addis Ababa, and Cerulli regularly reviewed and translated excerpts from Ḫeruy's Amharic publications in the Italian academic journal *Oriente moderno.*[65] Ḫeruy, in turn, noted two of Cerulli's works in his second bibliography.[66] At that time, Cerulli's career was still in its early stages: his most significant publication was his 1922 *Folk Literature of the Galla of Southern Abyssinia,* which was published by Harvard's Peabody Museum in a series edited by Hooton, Coon's mentor. Yet despite their similar stature, mutual awareness, occasional geographical proximity, and shared scholarly interests, Ḫeruy and Cerulli effectively contributed to different intellectual communities, and this surely goes some of the way toward explaining why Ḫeruy's achievements—which were substantial, in Cerulli's estimation—were entirely within the domain of vernacular history and traditional learning, and not academic Ethiopian studies *per se,* Cerulli's formal field of study. Put simply, the era's greatest Ethiopian scholar did not feel the need to contribute to the international field of Ethiopian studies.

Within a few years, these academic matters were overtaken by more worldly events. By 1936, Ḫeruy was in exile in Britain, where he briefly taught at the School of Oriental and African Studies. One year later, in 1937, Cerulli became the Vice-Governor General of Italian East Africa.

Guardians of the Tradition

This book has surveyed the evolution of Ethiopian and Eritrean historical writing. Though this tradition has the distinction of being Africa's oldest form of historiography, it is largely unknown outside the societies that produced it, a situation that has impoverished our general historical understanding. Why have debates about orality, literacy, and history in Africa disregarded the vast realm of Ethiopian scholarship and its unique historical and pseudo-historical literatures? And how can arguments about the genesis of historical consciousness and the modernity of historical thinking proceed without reference to this sustained non-Western effort to describe and understand the past? The neglect of the Ethiopian and Eritrean tradition of historical writing is a byproduct of the latent Eurocentrism of the contemporary historical discipline, on the one hand, and the continued marginalization of Ethiopia and Eritrea within the fields of African and Middle Eastern studies, on the other. If we wish to correct it, we must also be willing to reconsider some universal claims.[67]

One involves the parochialism of some of the theory regarding the historical enterprise. Over the last two decades, numerous scholars—from historians and anthropologists to philosophers and literary critics—have described history as a uniquely Western and specifically modern form of knowledge. This book has offered a different view, one that is in keeping with several recent comparative studies of historiography.[68] It has argued that the Ethiopian and Eritrean historical tradition is a fact-based field of learning with deep local roots, a stable canon of texts, a coherent set of genres and methods, and a tremendous capacity for exogenous assimilation. Though it was often invigorated by the region's connection to the Arab world and the West, the tradition was an autochthonous cultural product, and not a gift from without. It was, moreover, created by successive generations of local specialists who collectively preserved the work of their forebears, and who elaborated on their inheritance by endeavoring to truthfully describe the witnessed present. These intellectuals wrote—in many cases anonymously—for themselves, their patrons, their society, and posterity. The result of their efforts is history, or *tarik*, and it was perceived as such by those who produced it, studied it, and listened to it. For all these reasons, this vernacular historical tradition fundamentally challenges the theoretical binary of a historical West and a mythic or ahistorical "Other." History can emerge anywhere, and it can be written in many genres and modes.

This book has also outlined the complex interactions between the Ethiopian and Eritrean vernacular historical tradition and its Western disciplinary counterpart. In contrast to those who see the latter as hegemonic, the present work argues that these interactions are best conceptualized as a dialogue produced by two distinct voices. Over the course of the nineteenth and twentieth centuries, Ethiopian and Eritrean intellectuals adopted and synthesized the methods and insights of Western scholars, selectively incorporating these into their received historical toolkit. At the same time, their own representations of the local past entered into Western academic discourse through the efforts of foreign scholars, and eventually, the domestication of the area studies and Marxist historical paradigms. In this evolving dialogue, each side saw its counterpart as a source, and though the exchanges between vernacular and Western historians were shaped by intercultural schisms, institutional gamekeeping, and imperial and postcolonial politics, one side did not silence the other. Instead, history was translated, both literally and conceptually, for different audiences—often with tremendous skill and creativity. It is therefore imprecise to describe history as a sign of modernity, following Nicholas Dirks. In Ethiopia and Eritrea, history was reimagined in the modern era, not clearly glimpsed for the first time.

Ultimately, while this book has explored the changing nature of history in the Horn of Africa, it has also endeavored to show how shifts in historical practice illuminate broader patterns of intellectual and social change. Creative work is obviously conditioned by real historical forces, and microhistory has a special capacity to document this connection. The primary subjects of this study—Gäbrä Krestos, Gäbrä Mika'él, and *blattén géta* Ḫeruy—were each products of a new political, economic, and cultural environment that can be described with some precision as modern, and this distinguished them from the archetypal chronicler of centuries past. Like many of the other subjects of this book, the trajectories of their lives and thought were altered by these new dynamics. The politics of nationalism and colonialism, the tension between traditionalism and reform, and the emergence of new educational institutions and career paths profoundly shaped their intellectual outlook and informed the ideas and questions they explored. They number among the first generation of public figures who participated in popular debates that were sustained by the new medium of print, and this task required them to perform an exquisite balancing act, reconciling ideas old and new by rethinking the historian's craft. In meeting this challenge, they served as guardians of the tradition in an era of change.

Abbreviations

Archivio Storico del Ministero dell'Africa Italiana	ASMAI
Hill Monastic Manuscript Library, St. John's University	EMML
Institute of Ethiopian Studies, Manuscript Section	IES
Annales d'Éthiopie	*AE*
Bulletin of the School of Oriental and African Studies	*BSOAS*
Bulletin de la maison des études éthiopiennes	*BMEE*
Encyclopaedia Aethiopica	*EA*
Journal asiatique	*JA*
Journal of Ethiopian Studies	*JES*
Northeast African Studies	*NEAS*
Oriente moderno	*OM*
Rassegna di studi etiopici	*RSE*
Rendiconti della reale accademia dei lincei	*RRAL*
Review of African Political Economy	*ROAPE*
Revue de l'orient chrétien	*ROC*
Revue sémitique	*RS*

Notes

Introduction

1. Ḫeruy Wäldä Śellasé, *Bä'ityopya yämmigäñu bäge'ezenna bamariña qʷanqʷa yätäṣafu yämäṣaḥeft katalog* (Addis Ababa: Täfäri Mäkonnen Press, 1920EC). The earlier work is *Bä'ityopya yämmigäñu yämäṣaḥeft quṭer* (Addis Ababa: 1904EC). A few years earlier, *aläqa* Tayyä Gäbrä Maryam had attempted a fairly modest survey of the manuscripts and printed books he found during his travels in Europe. The list is reprinted in Aleme Eshete, "Alaqa Taye Gabra Mariam," *RSE* 25 (1971–72): 26–28.

2. A notable exception is Ḫeruy's 1927 notation of *Qädinna mufti*, or "Qadis and Muftis," likely a reference to Abd al-Fattah Abdallah, *Yä'ityopya qäddämotenna tallaq ulamoč tarik* (Addis Ababa: Chamber Printing Press, 2005), an Amharic translation of an Arabic work.

3. One of Ḫeruy's subjects approvingly noted the inclusion of international works in the catalog: Enrico Cerulli, "Nuovi libri pubblicati in Etiopia," *OM* XII (1932): 174.

4. Lynn Hunt, *Measuring Time, Making History* (New York: Central European University, 2008), 54.

5. Ḫeruy, *Katalog*, 7.

6. Ḫeruy, *Katalog*, 8.

7. Vinay Lal, *The History of History: Politics and Scholarship in Modern India* (New Delhi: Oxford University, 2003), 15.

8. Yoav Di-Capua, *Gatekeepers of the Arab Past: Historians and History Writing in Twentieth Century Egypt* (Berkeley: University of California Press, 2009), 52.

9. Andreas Eckert, "Historiography on a 'Continent without History: Anglophone West Africa, 1880s–1940s," in *Across Cultural Borders: Historiography in Global Perspective*, ed. Eckhardt Fuchs and Benedikt Stuchtey (New York: Rowman and Littlefield, 2002), 99–117; Karin Barber, "I. B. Akinyẹle and Early Yoruba Print Culture," in *Recasting the Past: History Writing and Political Work in Modern Africa*, ed. Derek Peterson and Giacomo Macola (Athens: Ohio University, 2009), 31–49; and Toyin Falọla, "Yoruba Town Histories," in *A Place in the World: New Local Historiographies from Africa and South Asia*, ed. Axel Harneit-Sievers (Boston: Brill, 2002), 65–85.

10. Di-Capua, *Gatekeepers*, 19–65; T. C. McCaskie, "Asante Origins, Egypt, and the Near East," in *Recasting the Past*, ed. Peterson and Macola, 125–48.

11. Ali Salih Karrar, Yahya Muhammad Ibrahim, and R. S. O'Fahey, "The Life and Writings of a Sudanese Historian: Muḥammad ʿAbd al-Raḥīm (1878–1966)," *Sudanic Africa* 6 (1995): 125–36; and Derek Peterson and Giacomo Macola, "Homespun Historiography and the Academic Profession," in *Recasting the Past*, ed. Peterson and Macola, 1–28.

12. Michael Twaddle, "On Ganda Historiography," *History in Africa* 1 (1974): 85–100.

13. Ashis Nandy, "History's Forgotten Doubles," *History and Theory* 34, no. 2 (1995): 44–66. For a discussion of Ashis Nandy's "critical traditionalist" approach to the past, see Dipesh Chakrabarty, *Habitations of Modernity: Essays in the Wake of Subaltern Studies* (Chicago: University of Chicago Press, 2002), 38–47.

14. Lal, *The History of History*, esp. 27–78.

15. Mohandas Gandhi, *Hind Swaraj or Indian Home Rule* (Ahmedabad: Navajivan Publishing, 2003), 67. From this, he concluded that "History, then, is a record of an interruption of the course of nature": Gandhi, *Hind Swaraj*, 68. Chattopadhyay similarly explained India's lack of history, adding "the Europeans are extremely proud. They think that even when they yawn, the achievement should be recorded as a memorable deed in the annals of world history. Proud nations have an abundance of historical writing; we have none." See Partha Chatterjee, *Nationalist Thought and the Colonial World: A Derivative Discourse?* (Minneapolis: University of Minnesota Press, 1998), 82, fn. 9.

16. For an example from Middle East studies, see Di-Capua, *Gatekeepers*; for literary criticism, consider Patrick Joyce's observation "Contemporary history is itself the offspring of modernity," discussed in Richard J. Evans, *In Defence of History* (London: Granta, 2000), 8.

17. V. S. Naipaul, *A Bend in the River* (New York: Vintage, 1980), 12.

18. Thus Joseph Conrad's character Charles Marlow says of the Congolese: "I don't think a single one of them had any clear idea of time, as we at the end of countless ages have. They still belonged to the beginnings of time—had no inherited experience to teach them as it were." See Joseph Conrad, *Heart of Darkness and the Secret Sharer* (New York: Doubleday, 1950), 111. For an implicit critique of this imputed ahistoricism, see Chinua Achebe, *Arrow of God* (New York: Anchor, 1989), 14–17, and 32–35.

19. Velcheru Narayana Rao, David Shulman, and Sanjay Subrahmanyam, *Textures of Time: Writing History in South India 1600–1800* (New York: Other Press, 2003). See also the forum devoted to this work in *History and Theory* 46, no. 3 (2007), esp. Rao, Shulman, and Subrahmanyam, "A Pragmatic Response," 409–27.

20. Rao, Shulman, and Subrahmanyam, "A Pragmatic Response," 427.

21. A perceptive early discussion of this problem is J. G. A. Pocock, "The Origins of the Study of the Past: A Comparative Approach," *Comparative Studies in Society and History* 2, no. 4 (1962): 209–46. In Pocock's view, all societies have a generalized awareness of their own past, and this relationship varies among groups and institutions, from myth to ritual, genealogy, or legal precedent. History emerges when this awareness encounters a challenge that tradition cannot resolve, at which point specialists sometimes attempt to address the problem by explaining the relationship between past and present through evidence. Pocock considers these figures to be historians, regardless of whether or not their arguments employ writing, narrative, or even an exclusively defined genre of historical scholarship. From this it follows that (1) the Rankean, critical historian is but a European variant of a general pattern, (2) all societies can produce historians given certain conditions, and (3) historians can perform their work in a variety of ways. For a complementary discussion of law and the origins of history, see also Carlo Ginzburg, *The Judge and*

the Historian: Marginal Notes on a Late-Twentieth Century Miscarriage of Justice, trans. Antony Shugaar (New York: Verso, 1999), 12–18.

22. Peter Burke, "Western Historical Thinking in a Global Perspective—10 Theses," in *Western Historical Thinking: An Intercultural Debate*, ed. Jörn Rüsen (Berghahn: New York, 2002), 15–30. This edited volume contains a number of provocative responses to Burke's arguments.

23. Hayden White, "The Westernization of History," in Rüsen, *Western Historical Thinking*, 111–18; and Dipesh Chakrabarty, "A Global and Multicultural 'Discipline' of History?," *History and Theory* 45, no. 1 (2006): 101–9.

24. Ranajit Guha, *History at the Limit of World-History* (New York: Columbia University, 2002). See also Hunt, *Measuring Time*, esp. 93–128. Guha's analysis is highly abstract and somewhat reductive, especially in his treatment of Hegel and "world-history" as glosses for nineteenth century European intellectual history. However, for a discussion of one such antagonistic assimilation (the looting of the Cairo Geniza, the largest archive of the medieval world), see Amitav Ghosh, *In An Antique Land: History in the Guise of a Traveler's Tale* (New York: Vintage, 1994).

25. Guha, *History at the Limit of World-History*, 16.

26. The German historian Leopold von Ranke (1795–1886) is generally described as the founder of the modern historical profession, since his ideas about objectivity and scientific historical inquiry became widely influential in Europe and North America. For discussions, see Georg Iggers, *Historiography in the Twentieth Century: From Scientific Objectivity to Postmodern Challenge* (Hanover: Wesleyan University Press, 1997), 23–30; and Peter Novick, *That Noble Dream: The "Objectivity Question" and the American Historical Profession* (New York: Cambridge University Press, 1988), 26–31.

27. For Guha, this historical shift was a critical political task: in India, intellectuals had to reclaim their "appropriated past" from Britain before they could contest colonial power. See Ranajit Guha, *Dominance without Hegemony: History and Power in Colonial India* (Cambridge, MA: Harvard University Press, 1997).

28. Representative of this view is David C. Gordon, *Self-Determination and History and the Third World* (Princeton, NJ: Princeton University Press, 1973). See also the discussion of perceptions of Dike as "the father of modern African historiography" in Toyin Falola, *Nationalism and African Intellectuals* (Rochester, NY: University of Rochester Press, 2001), 228–45.

29. For an interesting discussion of the political context of these efforts, see Vijay Prashad, *The Darker Nations: A People's History of the Third World* (London: New Press, 2007), 85–88.

30. Kumkum Chatterjee, "The King of Controversy: History and Nation-making in Late-Colonial India," *American Historical Review* 110, no. 5 (2005): 1454–75.

31. Sumit Guha, "Speaking Historically: The Changing Voices of Historical Narration in Western India, 1400–1900," *American Historical Review* 109, no. 4 (2004): 1084–1103.

32. Purnima Dhavan, "Reading the Texture of History and Memory in Early-Nineteenth-Century Punjab," *Comparative Studies of South Asia, Africa and the Middle East* 29, no. 3 (2009): 515–27.

33. Youssef M. Choueiri, *Modern Arab Historiography: Historical Discourse and the Nation-State* (London: Routledge, 2003).

34. For an example of an analysis of African historiography that does not account for the vernacular tradition, see Joseph Miller, "History and Africa/Africa and History," *American Historical Review* 104, no. 1 (1999): 1–32. For an analysis of this phenomenon, see Adam Jones, "Epilogue: Academic and Other Historians—An Uneasy Relationship," in *A Place in the World*, ed. Harneit-Sievers, 366–74.

35. Peterson and Macola, "Homespun Historiography," in *Recasting the Past*, ed. Peterson and Macola, 1–28.

36. This topic is discussed in Axel Harneit-Sievers, "Introduction: New Local Historiographies in Africa and Asia: Approaches and Issues," in *A Place in the World*, ed. Harneit-Sievers, 1–30.

37. A brief discussion of this issue is offered by Bairu Tafla, "A Turning Point in Ethiopian Historiography from Within," in *Die aethiopischen Studien im 20. Jahrhundert*, ed. Rainer Maria Voigt (Aachen: Shaker Verlag, 2003), 159–82. I am indebted to its author for his detailed comments on the present work.

38. For a useful discussion of this approach, see Carlo Ginzburg and Carlo Poni, "The Name and the Game: Unequal Exchange and the Historiographical Marketplace," in *Microhistory and the Lost Peoples of Europe*, ed. Edward Muir and Guido Ruggiero, trans. Eren Branch (Baltimore, MD: Johns Hopkins University Press, 1991), 1–10.

39. For a taxonomy of the stages of globalization, see A. G. Hopkins, ed., *Globalization in World History* (New York: Norton, 2002). Though the Mediterranean and Indian Oceans were once seen as unified historical spaces cleft by early modern imperial projects—the Ottoman-Hapsburg contest and the maritime company empires of the British and Dutch, respectively—a newer literature emphasizes the endurance of older arena-wide patterns and structures and the role of modern imperial networks in brokering new forms of integration and schism. Cf. Fernand Braudel, *The Mediterranean and the Mediterranean in the Age of Philip II*, trans. Siân Reynolds, 2 Vols. (New York: Harper Collins, 1966) and K. N. Chaudhuri, *Trade and Civilization in the Indian Ocean: An Economic History from the Rise of Islam to 1750* (New York: Cambridge University, 1985); with Sugata Bose, *A Hundred Horizons: The Indian Ocean in the Age of Global Empire* (Cambridge, MA: Harvard University Press, 2006); Thomas Metcalf, *India and the Indian Ocean Arena, 1860–1920* (Berkeley: University of California Press, 2007); Faruk Tabak, *The Waning of the Mediterranean, 1550–1870: A Geohistorical Approach* (Baltimore, MD: Johns Hopkins University Press, 2008); Julia Clancy Smith, *Mediterraneans: North Africa and Europe in an Age of Migration, 1800–1900* (Berkeley: University of California Press, 2012); Christopher Bayly and Leila Tarazi Fawaz, eds. *Modernity and Culture: From the Mediterranean to the Indian Ocean* (New York: Columbia University Press, 2003); and Edmund Burke III, "Towards a Comparative History of the Modern Mediterranean, 1750–1919," *Journal of World History* 23, no. 4 (2012): 907–39. The most developed application of this more recent work to the Horn of Africa to date is Jonathan Miran, *Red Sea Citizens: Cosmopolitan Society and Cultural Change in Massawa* (Bloomington: Indiana University, 2009).

40. Ulrike Freitag and Achim von Oppen, "Introduction: 'Translocality': An Approach to Connection and Transfer in Area Studies," in *Translocality: The Study of Globalising Processes from a Southern Perspective*, ed. Ulrike Freitag and Achim von Oppen (Leiden: Brill, 2010), 1–24. See also Jonathan Miran, "Space, Mobility, and Translocal Connections across the Red Sea Area since 1500," *NEAS* 12, no. 1 (2012): ix–xxvi.

Chapter 1

1. William Conzelman, ed. and trans., *Chronique de Galâwdêwos (Claudius), Roi d'Éthiopie* (Paris: Librairie Émile Bouillon, 1895), 121.

2. The term "chronicle" is often used to describe a variety of historical writing that lacks certain literary or analytic features. Hayden White, for example, distinguishes it from history proper through its lack of plot: see his *The Content of the Form: Narrative Discourse and Historical Representation* (Baltimore, MD: Johns Hopkins University Press, 1984), esp. 2–23. I here employ "chronicle" in its more general sense of chronological narratives or records, or historical writing, and without generic or epistemological implications.

3. Jim McCann, "The Ethiopian Chronicles: An African Documentary Tradition," *NEAS* 1, no. 2 (1979): 47–61; and Pietro Toggia, "History Writing as a State Ideological Project in Ethiopia," *African Identities* 6, no. 4 (2008): 319–43. See also Paulos Milkias, "Traditional Institutions and Traditional Elites: The Role of Education in the Ethiopian Body-Politic," *African Studies Review* 19, no. 3 (1976): 79–93.

4. On the connection between individual and collective or social memory, see Maurice Hawlbachs, *The Collective Memory* (New York: Harper & Row, 1980), esp. 50–87.

5. For a discussions of oral and written history in this vein, see Anaïs Wion, *Paradis pour une reine: le monastère de Qoma Fasilädäs, Éthiopie, XVIIe siècle* (Paris: Sorbonne, 2012), and Witold Witakowski, "Coptic and Ethiopic Historical Writing," in *Oxford History of Historical Writing, Vol. 2: 400–1400*, ed. Sarah Foot, Daniel R. Woolf, and Chase F. Robinson (New York: Oxford University, 2012), 138–54.

6. The framework presented follows Ḫeruy's comprehensive outline of the vernacular tradition, found in his second bibliography: Ḫeruy, *Katalog*, 24–25. It does so by synthesizing a rich but highly specialized secondary literature, making particular use of the groundbreaking work of Manfred Kropp and Sevir Chernetsov. I have also profited greatly from the approach of Chase Robinson, *Islamic Historiography* (New York: Cambridge University Press, 2003) and John Burrow, *A History of Histories: Epics, Chronicles, Romances, and Inquiries from Herodotus and Thucydides to the Twentieth Century* (New York: Penguin, 2009).

7. On these links, see Timothy Power, *The Red Sea from Byzantium to the Caliphate* (New York: American University in Cairo Press, 2012).

8. For discussions, see Sergew Hable Sellassie, *Ancient and Medieval Ethiopian History to 1270* (Addis Ababa: Haile Selassie University, 1972); G. W. Bowersock, *The Throne of Adulis: Red Sea Wars on the Eve of Islam* (New York: Oxford University Press, 2013); and George Hatke, "Africans in Arabia Felix: Aksumite Relations with Ḥimyar in the Sixth Century CE" (PhD diss., Princeton University, 2011).

9. Ḫeruy, *Katalog*, 24. After the *Kebrä nägäśt*, Ḫeruy lists Emperor Kaléb as the beginning of Ethiopian historiography. This is presumably a reference to his epigraphic descriptions of his sixth-century campaign in South Arabia. For a discussion of this text, see Hatke, "Africans in Arabia Felix," 191.

10. Alessandro Bausi, "La *Collezione aksumita* canonico-liturgica," *Adamantius* 12 (2006): 43–70.

11. Bausi, "*Collezione aksumita*," 55–56.

12. This point is attested to by the recent discovery of parchment-manufacturing materials from the Aksumite and pre-Aksumite eras: Laurel Phillipson, "Parchment Production in the First Millennium BC at Seglamen, Northern Ethiopia," *African Archaeological Review* 30, no. 3 (2013): 285–303.

13. Bowersock, *Adulis,* 63–64.

14. On Yeḥa and its various communities, see Rodolfo Fattovich, "Reconsidering Yeha: c. 800–400 BC," *African Archaeological Review* 26, no. 4 (2009): 275–90; and more generally *EA* 5:42–43. On the Ptolemaic stele, see Bowersock, *Adulis,* 34–43.

15. David Phillipson, *Ancient Ethiopia, Aksum: its Antecedents and Successors* (London: British Museum, 1998), 65–67, 126–28; Derek Welsby, *The Medieval Kingdoms of Nubia: Pagans, Christians, and Muslims along the Middle Nile* (London: British Museum Press, 2002), 14; and Powers, *Red Sea,* 38–41.

16. One less certain speculation is that Aksum's historical texts are fragmentary traces of a documentary culture of sorts, one in which historical writing informed administration. Another is that the numeracy and temporality of the epigraphic texts implies a more general awareness of chronology as an organizing principle of the past. For an interesting discussion of these points, see Sergew Hable Sellassie, *History,* 90.

17. For a discussion of similarities between Aksumite epigraphy and later historiography, see Enrico Cerulli, *Storia della letteratura etiopica* (Milan: Nuova Accademia, 1956), esp. 16–17 and 21–23.

18. A medieval reference to the Alexandrian History can be found in the work of Giyorgis of Sägla, a saint and fifteenth-century theologian. See *EA* 2:812. This relationship was rather more complex in the area around the town of Aksum, where local scholars preserved the memory of the Aksumite era as a variety of local history attuned to the material culture and ruins that surrounded them. For a discussion, see Bertrand Hirsch and François-Xavier Fauvelle-Aymar, "Aksum après Aksum. Royauté, archéologie et herméneutique chrétienne de Ménélik II (r. 1865–1913) à Zära Yaqob (r. 1434–1468)," *AE* 17 (2001): 59–109. This situation can be contrasted with the more widely available chronologies of the Aksumite rulers, discussed in E. Drouin, "Les listes royales éthiopiennes et leur autorité historique," *Revue Archaéologique* 44 (1882): 99–224. See also Sergew Hable Selassie, *History,* 82.

19. For a discussion of this point, see Hatke, "Africans," 354, n. 546.

20. Alessandro Bausi, "The Aksumite Background of the Ethiopic 'Corpus Canonum,'" in *Proceedings of the XV Conference of Ethiopian Studies,* ed. Siegbert Uhlig (Wiesbaden: Harrassowitz Verlag, 2006), 532–41.

21. On this connection, see Phillipson, *Ethiopia,* 140–43. See also the discussion of "the Aksumite paradigm" in Teshale Tibebu, *The Making of Modern Ethiopia, 1896–1974* (Lawrenceville: Red Sea Press, 1995), esp. 3–18.

22. This began with Emperor Zä'ra Ya'eqob in 1439: *EA* 1: 802–3. I thank Getatchew Haile for calling my attention to this point.

23. For an overview of the arguments, see *EA* 3: 364–68. Getatchew Haile argues for a tenth-century date of composition: Getatchew Haile, "The *Kəbrä Nägäśt* Revisited," *Oriens Christianus* 93 (2009): 131. For a critique of early dating, see Stuart Munro-Hay, "A Sixth Century Kebra Nagast?" *AE* 17 (2001): 43–58; for a sympathetic view, see David Johnson, "Dating the Kebra Nagast: Another Look," in *Peace*

and War in Byzantium: Essays in Honor of George T. Dennis, ed. Timothy Miller and John Nesbitt (Washington: Catholic University of America, 1995), 197–208. The literary backdrop of the work is assessed in Robert Beylot, "Du Kebra Nagast," *Aethiopica* 7 (2004): 74–83.

24. For a discussion, see Cerulli, *Letteratura*, 44–45, and Hatke, "Africans," 353–405. Its comments on the spread of Islam are brief and confined to North Africa and the Near East. Getatchew Haile argues that if the Arabic original was not written with the Zagwe and Solomonid dynasties in mind, but instead an earlier pagan queen, it was adapted from Arabic into Ge'ez in the thirteenth century because of its significance in the changed political context: Getatchew Haile, "The *Kəbrä Nägäśt* Revisited," 127–34.

25. Burrow, *History*, 232–38. Like the *Kebrä nägäśt*, Geoffrey's *History* was supposedly translated (from Welsh to Latin) from an ancient book that is otherwise unattested.

26. Ḫeruy, *Katalog*, 24.

27. Jules Perruchon, trans., "Histoire des Guerres d'ʿAmda Ṣyon, Roi d'Éthiopie," *Journal Asiatique* 8, no. 14 (1889): 271–363, 381–493. For a discussion, see *EA* 3:41.

28. Amdä Ṣeyon was renowned in the Ethiopian tradition for these victories, and there was at least some awareness of them abroad; he is, for example, referred to in *Orlando Furioso*. See *EA* 1: 229.

29. *EA* 3:40–45. Like many, Cerulli asserts that the detailed nature of the text suggests that its author was a contemporary to the events described, likely an ecclesiastic close to the court: Cerulli, *Letteratura*, 37–38.

30. Manfred Kropp, "La réédition des chroniques éthiopiennes: perspéctives et premiers resultats," *Abbay* 12 (1983–84): 57.

31. Jules Perruchon, ed. and trans., *Les chroniques de Zar'a Yâqôb et de Ba'eda Mâryâm, Rois d'Éthiopie de 1434 a 1478* (Paris: Émile Bouillon, 1893), 3–103.

32. For this point and a discussion of these works, see Marie-Laure Derat, "'Do Not Search for Another King, One Whom God Has Not Given You': Questions on the Elevation of Zärʾä Yaʿeqob (1434–1468)," *Journal of Early Modern History* 8, no. 3–4 (2004): 210–28.

33. *Zar'a Yâqôb*, 105–82.

34. Jules Perruchon, trans., "Histoire d'Eskender, d'`Amda-Ṣeyon II et de Nâ'od, rois d'Éthiopie, texte éthiopien inédit comprenant en outre un fragment de la chronique de Ba'eda-Mâryâm, leur prédécesseur, et traduction," *JA* 3 (1894): 319–66.

35. *Zar'a Yâʿqôb*, 3, 13, 14. The attribution is suggested by Perruchon: "Eskender," 342.

36. For a discussion, see Cerulli, *Letteratura*, 82–85.

37. Jules Perruchon, ed. and trans., *Vie de Lalibala, roi d'Éthiopie. Texte éthiopien publié d'après un manuscrit du Musée Britannique et traduction française avec un résumé de l'histoire des Zagüés et la description des églises monolithes de Lalibala* (Paris: Ernest Laroux, 1892). Ḫeruy correctly described this as hagiography (*gädl*), not history (*tarik*): Ḫeruy, *Katalog*, 18. However, since this hagiography deals with the life of a medieval ruler and appears to contain observational elements, it seems fruitful to consider it in this discussion of early medieval historiography.

38. *Lalibala,* 71, 101.

39. For a discussion, see Marie-Laure Derat, "The Acts of King Lalibäla," in *Proceedings of the XVth International Conference of Ethiopian Studies,* ed. Siegbert Uhlig (Wiesbaden: Harrassowitz Verlag, 2006), 561–68. See also Maimire Mennasemay, "Utopia and Ethiopia: The Chronicles of Lalibela as Critical Reflection," *NEAS* 12, no. 2 (2013): 95–121.

40. André Caquot once suggested that the political and religious tumult of the era stimulated "an awakening of historical curiosity" in Christian Ethiopia. If this was not a first stirring per se, it is certainly true that the era's historiography began to display new and distinctive features. See André Caquot, "Les 'chroniques abrégées' d'Éthiopie," *AE* 2 (1957): 189.

41. Jules Perruchon, trans., "La règne de Lebna-Dengel: Texte éthiopien tiré du ms. 131 de la Bibliothèque nationale de Paris et traduction," *RS* 1 (1893): 274–86.

42. Manfred Kropp points to citations of this work in the later chronicle of Minas that identify the author of the Gälawdéwos chronicle as Sennä Krestos: see Kropp, "Réédition," 52. This attribution is at variance with the earlier suggestions of Perruchon and others that its author was Enbaqom: see the brief discussion in *Galâwdêwos,* vii. There is some textual evidence that complicates the attribution to Sennä Krestos: this includes the chronicler's references to *Anqäṣä amin,* Enbaqom's polemic against Islam; the author's distinctive description of the Portuguese as "the sons of Japhet," a reference to the scriptural understanding of the repopulation of the earth after the Flood; his familiarity with Catholic theology; and his occasional use of the Islamic calendar and Arabicisms like *al Habesh* and *fellah.* On Enbaqom more generally, see Emeri Johannes van Donzel, trans., *Anqaṣa amin (La Porte de la Foi): Apologie éthiopienne du Christianisme, contre l'Islam à partir du Coran* (Leiden: Brill, 1969), 17–34; on the Arabicisms in this text, see Ignazio Guidi, "La cronaca di Galāwdēwos o Claudio re di Abissinia (1540–1559)," *Actes du douzième congrès international des orientalistes, Rome 1899* (Florence: Société Typographique Florentine, 1899), Vol. 3, 111–15.

43. *Galâwdêwos,* 123, 136, 138–39, 164–66.

44. For a succinct overview of Portuguese activities, see Andreu Martínez d'Alòs-Moner, "Conquistadores, Mercenaries and Missionaries: The Failed Portuguese Dominion of the Red Sea," *NEAS* 12, no. 1 (2012): 1–28. Ottoman efforts are detailed in Giancarlo Casale, *The Ottoman Age of Exploration* (Oxford: Oxford University Press, 2010), esp. 107–9.

45. Francisco Maria Esteves Pereira, trans., *Zênā Minās/Historia de Minás 'Además Sagad rei de Ethiopia* (Lisbon: Imprensa Nacional, 1888).

46. Carlo Conti Rossini, trans., *Historia Regis Sarṣa Dengel (Malak Sagad)* (Paris: Republic Press, 1907). The authorship of this work is disputed. Sevir Chernetsov attributes it to Baḥrey on the basis of the chronicle's stylistic and evidentiary similarities to *The History of the Galla*: see Sevir Chernetsov, "Who Wrote 'the History of King Sarsa Dengel'—Was it the Monk Bahrey?" in *Proceedings of the Eight International Conference of Ethiopian Studies,* ed. Taddesse Beyene (Addis Abeba: Institute of Ethiopian Studies, 1988), 131–36. Against this attribution, Denis Nosnitsin proposes that the chronicle was written by several authors: chapters 1–7 were produced upon the emperor's coronation in 1579; chapter 8 was written in 1580 after a campaign in Semén; and chapter 9 relates events during 1587–90. See *EA* 4: 544–47.

The problem is explored in Manfred Kropp, "Un cas de censure politique au XVIIe siècle: la chronique de Śarṣa-Dəngəl," *AE* XVII (2001): 257–77.

47. Manfred Kropp, trans., *Die Geschichte des Lebna-Dengel, Claudius und Minās* (Leuven: E. Peeters, 1988). The chapters dealing with Lebnä Dengel and Minas were previously published in Carlo Conti Rossini, "Storia di Lebna Dengel re d'Etiopia, fino alle prime lotte contro Ahmad Ben Ibrahim," *RRAL* Ser. 5, no. 3 (1894): 617–40; and *Minās,* op. cit.

48. I employ this term following Georg Simmel, "The Stranger," in *The Sociology of Georg Simmel,* trans. Kurt Wolff (New York: Free Press, 1950), 402–8. For discussions of strangerhood in the Northeast African context, see Donald Levine, "Simmel at a Distance: On the History and Systematics of the Sociology of the Stranger," and William Shack, "Open Systems and Closed Boundaries: The Ritual Process of Stranger Relations in New African States," both in *Strangers in African Societies,* ed. William Shack and Elliot Skinner (Berkeley: University of California Press, 1979), 21–36, and 37–47.

49. Getatchew Haile, ed. and trans., *Yä'abba baḥrey dersätoč oromočen kämmim-mäläkkätu léloč sänädoč gara* (Avon: 2002). See also Mohammed Hassen, "Revisiting Abba Bahrey's 'the News of the Galla,'" *International Journal of African Historical Studies* 45, no. 2 (2012): 273–94; and Sevir Chernetsov, "The 'History of the Galla' and Death of Za-Dengel, King of Ethiopia (1603–1604)," in *IV Congresso internazionale di studi etiopici* (Rome: Accademia Nazionale dei Lincei, 1974), 803–8.

50. André Caquot, "Histoire amharique de Grāñ et des Gallas," *AE* 2 (1957): 123–43. For a discussion of this literature, see Ekaterina Gusarova, "The Oromo as Recorded in Ethiopian Literature," in *Proceedings of the 16th International Conference of Ethiopian Studies,* ed. Svein Ege, Harald Aspen, Birhanu Teferra, and Shiferaw Bekele (Trondheim, Norway: Norwegian University of Science and Technology, 2009), 1323–31. Carlo Conti Rossini argued that one such text served as the basis for the Keflä Maryam *tarikä nägäśt*: see this section, below.

51. Murad Kamil, "Translations from Arabic into Ethiopian Literature," *Bulletin de la société d'archéologie Copte* 7 (1941): 61–71.

52. Paolo Marrassini, "'I possenti di Rom': i turchi ottomani nella letteratura etiopica," in *Turcica et Islamica: Studia in memoria di Aldo Gallota,* ed. Ugo Marazzi (Naples: Università degli Studi di Napoli "L'Orientale," 2003), 593–622; and Abraham Demoz, "Moslems and Islam in Ethiopian Literature," *JES* 10, no. 1 (1972): 1–11.

53. This discussion of the *ṣäḥafé te'ezaz* is based on the short study in Marse'é Ḫazan Wäldä Qirqos, unpublished manuscript, 397–98. See also *EA* 4: 460–61; and Täsämma Häbtä Mika'él, *Yä'amareña mäzgäb qalat* (Addis Ababa: 1951EC), 1350.

54. Francisco Maria Esteves Pereira, trans., *Chronica de Susenyos, rei de Ethiopia* (Lisbon: Imprensa Nacional, 1900).

55. Ignazio Guidi, trans., *Annales Iohannis I, Iyāsu I, Bakāffā* (Paris: Republic Press, 1903).

56. Hawaryatä Krestos relates how he came to replace Sinoda in his section of the chronicle: "On this day, the king said to Sinoda, 'Bring me a man whom you trust, so that I can give you the charge you desire, naming this person in your place.' Sinoda said, 'The word of the king is good, but I do not have another person whom I trust: that which I trust is my head—me, it is my head you speak of.' After this the king said

to him, 'I give you the charge of the head of the church of Qeddus Mika'él that is in the chamber of the king; tomorrow you will pay me homage.' This secret was not revealed or expressed to anyone, until it was made manifest in its time, for the word of the king was sharp, like the flame of a fire." See *Iohannis*, 306.

57. Ignazio Guidi, trans., *Annales Regum Iyasu II et Iyo'as* (Paris: 1910). This work, really a *tarikä nägäśt*, is discussed in the next section of this chapter.

58. Shiferaw Bekele, "The Chronicle of Takla Giyorgis (first r. 1779–84): An Introductory Assessment," in *Studia Aethiopica in Honour of Siegbert Uhlig on the Occasion of his 65th Birthday*, ed. Verena Boll et al. (Wiesbaden: Harrassowitz Verlag, 2004), 247–58.

59. For a discussion of this development, see Sevir Chernetsov, "The Crisis of Ethiopian Official Royal Historiography and its Consequences in the Eighteenth Century," in *Proceedings of the Eleventh International Conference of Ethiopian Studies*, ed. Bahru Zewde, Richard Pankhurst, and Taddese Beyene (Addis Ababa: Institute of Ethiopian Studies, 1991), Vol. 1, 87–101.

60. René Basset, trans., *Études sur l'histoire d'Éthiopie* (Paris: Imprimerie Nationale, 1882). The literature on this text is considerable. For overviews, see Caquot, "Chroniques abrégées," 187–92; and Manfred Kropp, "An Hypothesis Concerning an Author or Compiler of the 'Short Chronicle' of the Ethiopian Kings," in *Proceedings of the Sixth International Conference of Ethiopian Studies, Tel Aviv, 14–17 April, 1980*, ed. Gideon Goldenberg (Boston: Balkema, 1986), 359–72.

61. This attribution has been speculatively advanced by Manfred Kropp: see his "Hypothesis," 365.

62. It also appears to be closely related to the biography of Iyasu II, which begins with a similar prefatory genealogy.

63. Caquot, "Chroniques abrégées."

64. The Israelites, the Ethiopians, and the Church more generally.

65. For a brief discussion of these three works, see Witold Witakowski, "Ethiopic Universal Chronography," in *Julius Africanus und die christliche Weltchronik*, ed. Martin Wallraff (Berlin: 2006), 285–301. For later examples of Giyorgis Wäldä Amid, see EMML 192 and EMML 511.

66. Cf. EMML 144, EMML 1202, EMML 1313, EMML 1466, EMML 4042, EMML 4634, EMML 4875, EMML 5730, and EMML 5731.

67. EMML 1313. The work is dated to the reign of Susenyos, 1606–32: 68.

68. Cf. Carlo Conti Rossini, "Les listes des rois d'Aksoum," *JA* 10, no. 14 (1899): 263–320; Enrico Cerulli, "Gli abbati di Dabra Libānos, capi del monachismo etiopico, secondo la 'lista rimata' (sec. XIV–XVIII)," *Orientalia* 12 (1943): 226–53; and Ignazio Guidi, "Le liste dei metropoliti d'Abissinia," *Bessarione: Pubblicazione periodica di studi orientali* 4, no. 37–38 (July–August 1899): 1–16.

69. For a discussion of this point, see Marilyn Robinson Waldman, "'The Otherwise Unnoteworthy Year 711': A Reply to Hayden White," *Critical Inquiry* 7, no. 4 (1981): 784–92.

70. On the interface between orality and historiography, see Wion, *Paradis*, 73–99; and Didier Morin, "Orality in the Chronicle of King Tewodros II," in *Proceedings of the 16th International Conference of Ethiopian Studies*, ed. by Svein Ege, Harald Aspen, Birhanu Teferra, and Shiferaw Bekele (Trondheim, Norway: Norwegian University of Science and Technology, 2009), 1333–38.

71. On listening to history, see the discussion of prefatory addresses in the next section of this chapter.

72. Donald Crummey, *Land and Society in the Christian Kingdom of Ethiopia* (Urbana-Champaign: University of Illinois, 2000). See also Anaïs Wion and Paul Bertrand, "Production, Preservation, and Use of Ethiopian Archives (Fourteenth–Eighteenth Centuries)," *NEAS* 11, no. 2 (2011): vii–xvi.

73. Cf. Śärṣä Dengel's oral lineage ceremony at Aksum, described in *Sarṣa Dengel*, 89–91, and the coronation ceremony of Iyyasu II at Gondär, described in *Iyāsu II*, 29–31.

74. For an example, see Tekle Tsadik Mekouriya, "Histoire abregée de Haylou Esheté (Degiazmatche)," in *Proceedings of the Eighth International Congress of Ethiopian Studies*, ed. Taddese Beyene (Addis Ababa: Institute of Ethiopian Studies, 1988–89), 203. See also the case of poetic lamentation (*engʷergʷero*): *EA* 2: 305–6.

75. For an interesting case of a royal biographer who was also a painter, see Shiferaw Bekele, "Chronicle," 248.

76. Marilyn Heldman, "Architectural Symbolism, *Sacred Geography*, and the Ethiopian Church," *Journal of Religion in Africa* 22, no. 3 (1992): 222–41. See also the discussion in chapter 5.

77. Cf. Enno Littmann, ed., *Yätéwodros tarik* (New York: Scribner, 1902); Luigi Fusella, ed., *Yaṭé téwodros tarik* (Rome: Sénāto [?], 1959); Casimir Mondon-Vidalhait, trans., *Chronique de Théodoros II roi des rois d'Éthiopie* (Paris: E. Guilmoto, 1905); Bairu Tafla, trans., *A Chronicle of Emperor Yoḥannes IV (1872–89)* (Wiesbaden: Franz Steiner Verlag, 1977); and Gäbrä Śellasé, *Tarik zämän zädagmawi Menilek neguśä nägäśt zä'ityoṗya* (Addis Ababa: Artistic Press, 1959EC).

78. Haggai Erlich, trans., "A Contemporary Biography of Ras Alula: A Ge'ez Manuscript from Manawe, Tamben—I," *BSOAS* 39, no. 1 (1976): 1–46; Erlich, trans., "A Contemporary Biography of Ras Alula: A Ge'ez Manuscript from Manawe, Tamben—II," *BSOAS* 39, no. 2 (1976): 287–327; and Brian Yates, "Christian Patriot or Oromo Traitor? The Ethiopian State in the Memories of *Ras* Gobäna Dače," *NEAS* 13, no. 2 (2013): 195–222.

79. Girma Getahun, "The Goǧǧam Chronicle: Introduction with Edition, Translation, and Annotation of Select Chapters" (PhD diss., Oxford University, 1991); and Hussein Ahmed, "The Chronicle of Menilek II of Ethiopia: A Brief Assessment of its Versions," *JES* 16 (1983): 78–79. The examples of Aksum and Ḥamasén historiography are discussed in the next section of this chapter and in chapter 4, respectively.

80. Maḫtämä Sellasé Wäldä Mäsqäl, *Zekrä nägär* (Addis Ababa: Berhanenna Sälam, 1962), 646; and Marse'é Ḫazan, unpublished manuscript, 397–98. Menilek's longtime chronicler Gäbrä Śellasé was the first *ṣäḥafé te'ezaz* to serve in this formal ministerial function; *blattén géta* Maḫtämä Sellasé's father, Wäldä Masqäl Tariku, served Empress Zäwditu and then Emperor Ḫaylä Śellasé in this role. On the latter, see Sergew Hable Selassie, "Two Leading Ethiopian Writers," *Journal of Semitic Studies* 25, no. 1 (1980): 85.

81. For a discussion, see Roger Chartier, *The Cultural Origins of the French Revolution* (Durham, NC: Duke University Press, 1991), 67–91.

82. On this point, see Burrow, *History*, 179–87.

83. For a discussion of some of these ideas, see Sevir Chernetsov, "Medieval Ethiopian Historiographers and their Methods," in *Proceedings of the Ninth International*

Congress of Ethiopian Studies, ed. Anatolii Andreevich Gromyko (Moscow: Nauka Publishers, 1988), 191–200.

84. Cf. *Iohannis*, 289; *Minas*, 37; *Sarṣa Dengel*, 3, 93; and *Iyāsu II*, 3.

85. *Sarṣa Dengel*, 115.

86. *Galâwdêwos*, 186,

87. *Iyāsu II*, 13.

88. *Iyāsu II*, 11. Other historians more matter-of-factly indicated the limitations of their knowledge: see for example *Zara Yaqob*, 4, 14.

89. *Sarṣa Dengel*, 25.

90. *Ba'eda Maryam* [being out of town]; and *Bakāffā* [the episode of Sinoda's replacement].

91. *Sarṣa Dengel*, 37, 92; *Iohannis*, 288; and *Zara Yaqob*, 12, 80.

92. *Sarṣa Dengel*, 92.

93. Cf., *Iohannis*, 294 ("I will unfortunately speak of the great anger of this king Bakkäffa, terrible and terrifying, and of his great clemency for the Ǧawi, for next to his anger was his great clemency"), 297 ("the goodness, honesty, and humility of this great Bakkäffa"), 310 ("the oppression of Bakkäffa"), and 316 ("I am obliged to discuss the virtues of this king, which were more numerous than those of the kings [who were] his fathers.").

94. Carlo Conti Rossini, trans., "L'autobiografia di Pāwlos, monaco abissino del secolo XVI," *RRAL* 5a, no. 27 (1918): 279–96; see also *EA* 4:125.

95. Manfred Kropp, *Die äthiopischen Königschroniken in der Sammlung des Däğğazmač Haylu* (New York: Peter Lang, 1989).

96. Tekle-Tsadiq Mekouria, "Haylou Esheté," 204.

97. Manfred Kropp, "Petite histoire de Yohannès Ier 'Retrouvée dans un autre pays,'" *AE* 15 (1990): 85–109; and Tekle-Tsadiq Mekouria, "Haylou Esheté," 203–5.

98. See for example his claim that, of some rulers, "nothing else is known": *Études*, 102.

99. This is the Emar episode, discussed later in this section: *Études*, 108–9.

100. *Études*, 101, 153.

101. Cf. *Études*, 111, 113, 131, 132–38.

102. Kropp, "Short Chronicle," 372, n. 37; and *EA* 1: 382–83.

103. *EA* 1: 386, 5: 246.

104. *Iohannis*, 328.

105. Cf. Robert George Collingwood, who described medieval compilatory historiography as "scissors and paste" history: see his *The Idea of History* (Oxford: Oxford University, 1946), 251.

106. Anaïs Wion, "Le Liber Aksumae selon le manuscrit Bodleian Bruce 93: le plus ancien témoin d'un project historiographique sans cesse réactivé," *Oriens Christianus* 93 (2009): 135–71.

107. Manfred Kropp, "La théologie au service de la rébellion: Chroniques inédites du ras Mika'él," in *Actes de la Xe conférence internationale des études éthiopiennes, Paris 24–28 Août 1988*, ed. Claude Lepage and Étienne Delage (Paris: Société française pour les études éthiopiennes, 1994), 225–36; and Ignazio Guidi, "Due nuovi manoscritti della 'cronaca abbreviata' di Abissinia," *RRAL* 6, no. 2 (1926): 357–421.

108. A copyist could achieve the same with an almost invisible subtlety. For one example, see Kropp, "Un cas de censure politique," 255–75.

109. *Lalibela,* 77.
110. *Lalibela,* 129.
111. *Iohannis,* 1.
112. *Iohannis,* 287–88.
113. "'Amda Ṣyon," 358; and *Galâwdêwos,* 128.
114. *Iohannis,* 309; and *Sarṣa Dengel,* 60, 87.
115. *Iohannis,* 316–17.
116. Chernetsov suggests that Ethiopian historians sought the ideal, not the fact, and that this is what distinguishes them from their modern counterparts. As I have suggested here, ideals and facts need not be mutually exclusive. See Chernetsov, "Historiographers."
117. "'Amda Ṣyon," 330.
118. Similarly potent imagery is evident in many other works. The Gälawdéwos chronicle, for example, compares the Muslim invasions of the Christian domains to the destruction of the Second Temple, and casts the struggle against Adal as the epitome of Christian virtue. See *Galâwdêwos,* 123.
119. *Sarṣa Dengel,* 3.
120. This is a hallmark of epic writing more generally. For a discussion, see Mikhail Bakhtin, *The Dialogic Imagination,* trans. Caryl Emerson and Michael Holquist (Austin: University of Texas Press, 1981), 13–18.
121. *Iohannis,* 297.
122. *Iohannis,* 299.
123. "Eskender," 347, 363.
124. "Eskender," 363–66.
125. This argument is all the more conspicuous given that it follows the author's rather negative assessment of the reign of Eskender, Na'od's brother and predecessor on the throne.
126. *Iohannis,* 291.
127. For discussions of this aspect of *etégé* Mentewwab and *ras* Mika'él's histories, see Chernetsov, "Crisis," 87–90, and 94–96.
128. "Lebna-Dengel," 284–85.
129. For a similar observation related to the accession of Śärṣä Dengel, see *Sarṣa Dengel,* 6.
130. For another example, see the accounts of the views of the camp followers (*aqétzar*) in Baḥrey's royal biography: *Sarṣa Dengel,* 35, 60. On this group more generally, see *EA* 1: 290.
131. *Galâwdêwos,* 158.
132. *Galâwdêwos,* 184.
133. *Iyasu II,* 71; and *Études,* 103. For another example, see the prefatory statements in *Zar'a Yâ'qôb,* 2.
134. EMML 1313, 75.
135. Baḥrey, "Galla," 111. Baḥrey also analyses and explains the Oromo's military successes against the Solomonids. He notes that all Oromo are trained for warfare, and that this sets the Oromo apart from their rivals, who are more broadly engaged in agriculture, commerce, scholarship, and artisanal production. See Baḥrey, "Galla," 125–27.
136. *Sarṣa Dengel,* 11, 83, 58–60.

137. "'Amda Ṣyon," 334.

138. Ezekiel, 40–48.

139. Chernetsov suggests it was written by Baḥrey. The published edition excludes the earlier chapters on Lebnä Dengel, Gälawdéwos, and Minas.

140. *Sarṣa Dengel*, 39.

141. For a discussion, see *Sarṣa Dengel*, 34–35.

142. *Sarṣa Dengel*, 16, 22, 24–5, 27, 34–35; 40–48, 60; 68–69, 76, 86.

143. *Sarṣa Dengel*, 45, 35, 48.

Chapter 2

1. Gäbrä Krestos Täklä Haymanot, *Aččer yä'aläm tarik bamareña* (Addis Ababa: Berhanenna Sälam, 1924).

2. Keflä Egzi'e Yeḫdägu, "Yä'ato Gäbrä Krestos yäḥeywät tarik," *Berhanenna sälam*, October 27, 1932.

3. Dämessé Wäldä Gäbr'él, "Tarikenna mätasäbiya," *Berhanenna sälam*, November 24, 1932; Tämanu Rämeha, "Yäḥeywät tarik," *A'emro*, February 4, 1933; Keflä Egzi'e Yeḫdägu, "Yäheywät tarik"; and Karl Johan Lundström and Ezra Gebremedhin, *Kenisha: The Roots and Development of the Evangelical Church of Eritrea, 1866–1935* (Trenton: Red Sea Press, 2011), 491.

4. Ḫeruy Wäldä Śellasé, *Yäḥeywät tarik (Biographie) bäḫʷala zämän lämminäśu leğoč mastawäqiya* (Addis Ababa: 1922), 93; and Nils Nilsson, "Gebra Kristus Tekle Hajmanot: *In Memoriam*," *Missions-Tidning*, January 1, 1933.

5. *EA* 1: 374–75.

6. See "Map of Asmära, 1910," in *EA* 1: 376–77. A contemporary description of the city and its inhabitants can be found in Renato Paoli, *Nella colonia Eritrea* (Milan: Fratelli Treves, 1908), 52–99.

7. Jonas Iwarson and Alessandro Tron, *Notizie storiche e varie sulla missione evangelica svedese dell'Eritrea, 1866–1916* (Asmära: Missione Evangelica Svedese, 1918), 9. In 1905, an Italian visitor noted that the mission schools served over 144 indigenous students: Rufillo Perini, *Di qua dal Mareb* (Florence: Tipografica Cooperativa, 1905), 350–54.

8. Iwarson and Tron, *Notizie*, 42; and Lundström and Gebremedhin, *Kenisha*, 304.

9. Lundström and Gebremedhin, *Kenisha*, 475.

10. An example is Jonas Iwarson, "A Moslem Mass Movement Toward Christianity in Abyssinia," *The Muslim World* 14, no. 3 (1924): 286–89.

11. Gäbrä Krestos, *Yä'aläm tarik*, 6.

12. The Waldensians, or Valdesi, are an Italian Christian minority with late-medieval origins. Following the Reformation, they allied themselves with the mainline Protestant churches. Some of the Swedes took great interest in the tradition of their Italian brethren: see *Missions-Tidning*, November 15, 1926, 315–17. Waldensian-EFS relations are briefly outlined in Lundström and Gebremedhin, *Kenisha*, 211–13.

13. *Missions-Tidning*, August 15, 1926, 221–21.

14. *Missions-Tidning*, November 15, 1926, 315–17.

15. Giuseppe Puglisi, *Chi è? dell' Eritrea 1952. Dizionario biografico con una cronologia* (Asmära: Agenzia Regina, 1952), 291.

16. Paoli, *Eritrea,* 181–87, which relates a hostile dialogue between Iwarson and an Italian visitor to the mission.

17. See discussion in this section below.

18. Lundström and Gebremedhin, *Kenisha,* 413.

19. Iwarson and Tron, *Notizie,* 41.

20. Lundström and Gebremedhin, *Kenisha,* 413.

21. Nilsson, "Gebra Kristus."

22. Iwarson and Tron, *Notizie,* 25.

23. Keflä Egzi'e Yeḫdägu, "Yäḫeywät tarik"; and Nilsson, "Gebra Kristus."

24. Iwarson and Tron, *Notizie,* 25–26.

25. Iwarson and Tron, *Notizie,* 38.

26. For a full list, see Stephen Wright, *Ethiopian Incunabula* (Addis Ababa: 1967), 72–88, supplemented by Stefan Strelcyn, "'Incunables' Éthiopiens des principales bibliothèques romaines," *RSE* 25 (1971–72): 469–70, 472–81, and 513–14.

27. Iwarson and Tron, *Notizie,* 42.

28. *EA* 3: 695; and *Berhan yeḥun sebkät zanta wédo nehezbi ityopya/Sia la Luce! Prediche, racconti, e spiegazioni edificanti per il popolo etiopico* (Asmära: Tipografia della Missione Svedese, 1912).

29. Alessandro Tron, *Scuole elementari della Missione Svedese in Eritrea. Consigli ai maestri e programma d'insegnamento,* trans. by Gäbrä Krestos Täklä Haymanot (Asmära: Tipografia della Missione Svedese, 1917). Gabra Krestos's contribution to this work is noted in Iwarson and Tron, *Notizie,* 37.

30. Alessandro Tron, *Manuale di aritmetica, temherti qʷeṣeri,* trans. by Gäbrä Krestos Täklä Haymanot (Asmära: Tipografia della Missione Svedese, 1923).

31. Population estimate from *EA* 1: 79–85. For discussions, see Shimelis Bonsa, "City as Nation: Imagining and Practicing Addis Ababa as a Modern and National Space," *NEAS* 13, no. 1 (2013): 168–213; and Peter Garretson, *A History of Addis Ababa from its Foundation in 1886 to 1910* (Wiesbaden: Harrassowitz Verlag, 2000).

32. On the Eritrean evangelical congregation in Addis Ababa, see Johannes Launhardt, *Evangelicals in Addis Ababa (1919–1991): With Special Reference to the Ethiopian Evangelical Church Mekane Yesus and the Addis Ababa Synod* (Münster: Lit Verlag, 2004), 34–35.

33. Gustav Arén, *Envoys of the Gospel in Ethiopia: In the Steps of the Evangelical Pioneers, 1898–1936* (Stockholm: EFS Förlaget, 1999), 182–87. See also Lundström and Gebremedhin, *Kenisha,* 412–13.

34. Keflä Egzi'e Yeḫdägu, "Yäḫeywät tarik."

35. Dämessé Wäldä Gäbr'él, "Tarikenna mätasäbiya."

36. Arén, *Pioneers,* 190–92. One of Gäbrä Krestos's obituaries states that he "served a couple of years in the mission school" in Addis Ababa: Nilsson, "Gebra Kristus."

37. The change of name is discussed in *Yäberhanenna sälam q.ḥ.ṣ matämiya bét yäwärq iyubélyi/Berhanena Selam H.S.I. Printing Press Golden Jubilee* (Addis Ababa: Berhanenna Sälam, 1971), 54.

38. Bahru Zewde, *Pioneers of Change in Ethiopia: The Reformist Intellectuals of the Early Twentieth Century* (Oxford: James Currey Press, 2002), 209.

39. Marse'é Ḫazan Wäldä Qirqos, *Of What I Saw and Heard: The Last Years of Emperor Menilek II and the Brief Rule of Iyassu,* intro. Gérard Prunier and trans. Hailu

Habtu (Addis Ababa: Centre Français des Études Éthiopiennes and Zamra Publishers, 2006), 29. See also National Archives, Letter dated April 14, 1911, Ethiopia Consulate, Addis Ababa, USDS Archives, Box 004.

40. For a discussion of *A'emro*, see *EA* 1: 111. *Yäṭor wäré* has received little attention and is difficult to find: a number of issues were available at the Istituto Italiano per l'Africa e l'Oriente (ISIAO), Rome. Other early newspapers include the French *Semeur d'Éthiopie*, published by the Lazarist missionaries in Harär, and the handwritten Amharic daily produced by Gäbrä Egzi'abḥér Gilay for Emperor Menilek. On these, see Richard Pankhurst, "The Foundations of Education, Printing, Newspapers, Book Production, Libraries, and Literacy in Ethiopia," *Ethiopia Observer* 6, no. 3 (1962): 241–92; and his "Two Early Periodical Publications 'Djibouti' and 'Le Semeur d'Éthiopie' as Sources for Late 19th Century and Early 20th Century Ethiopian history," *AE* 19 (2003): 231–56.

41. *EA* 1: 810–11.

42. *Jubilee*, 50; Gäbrä Egzi'abḥér Elyas, *Prowess, Piety, and Politics: The Chronicle of Abeto Iyasu and Empress Zäwditu of Ethiopia, 1909–1930*, trans. Reidulf Molvaer (Cologne: Rüdiger Köppe Verlag, 1994), 309.

43. For a complete list, see Wright, *Incunabula*, 26–43; supplemented by Strelcyn, "Incunables." For accounts of the press by involved parties, see Ḫaylä Śellasé, *Ḥeywäténna yä'ityopya ermeǧǧa*, Vol. 1 (Addis Ababa: Berhanenna Sälam, 1965EC), 47–48; Maḫtämä Śellasé, *Zekrä nägär*, 683–84; and the short history of the press by Habte Wäldä in *Berhanenna sälam*, January 8, 1925.

44. For a discussion, see Tim Carmichael, "Bureaucratic Literacy, Oral Testimonies, and the Study of Ethiopian History," *Journal of African Cultural Studies* 18, no. 1 (2006): 23–42.

45. On the "informalization" of learning, see Irma Taddia, "Correspondence as a New Source for African History: Some Evidence from Colonial Eritrea," *Cahiers des études africaines* 157 (2000): 109–34.

46. Gäbrä Krestos Täklä Haymanot, *Yäquṭer temhert bamareña* (Addis Ababa: Täfäri Mäkonnen Press, 1921).

47. For descriptions of the various editions, see Wright, *Incunabula*, 27, 39, and 79.

48. On these, see Strelcyn, "Incunables," 514; and also Marcel Cohen, "La naissance d'une littérature imprimée en amharique," *JA* CCVL (1925): 361–62.

49. Ḫeruy Wäldä Śellasé, *Yäheywät tarik*, 94–95.

50. *Jubilee*, 54.

51. *Jubilee*, 56. The new newspapers included *Käśśaté berhan* (Revealer of Light), an Amharic monthly, *Aṭbiya kokäb* (Morning Star), a bilingual French-Amharic weekly, and *Correspondance d'Éthiopie/Aethiopien-Korrespondenz*, a French-language monthly that aimed to foster "the economic and social rapprochement of Ethiopia and Abroad." The latter paper was edited by Ḫeruy and Erich Weinzinger, who was tangentially involved in the 1927 newspaper scandal involving the Italian Legation, discussed later in this section.

52. Dämessé Wäldä Gäbr'él, "Tarikenna mätasäbiya."

53. Marse'é Ḫazan, unpublished manuscript, 245.

54. Ḫeruy, *Katalog*, 6.

55. Ḫaylä Śellasé, *Ḥeywäté*, 48.

56. *Jubilee*, 44–45, 65.

57. "Knowledge" (*A'emro*), "Light and Peace" (*Berhanenna sälam*), "Guide to Wisdom" (Märḥa Ṭebäb), and "Dawn" (Goh Ṣebah). On this point, see also the acrostic poem based upon the words "Berhanenna sälam" by *qés* Badma Yalläw, in *Berhanenna sälam*, July 9, 1925.

58. Gäbrä Egzi'abḥér, *Prowess*, 477.

59. Berhanou Abebbe, *Haymanot abbaw qäddämot: La foi des pères anciens* (Stuttgart: Steiner Verlag, 1986), 37–40. The decidedly less conservative Tä'ammrat Amanu'el made similar arguments: see his famous "Selä ityopya därasyan," published as "An Early Essay on Amharic Literature," *BMEE*, No. 11 (1997): 58.

60. *Jubilee*, 46, 65.

61. IES Ms. 1996 [*aläqa* Kenfé diary].

62. It was perhaps in part because of these assorted apprehensions that Empress Zäwditu created a royal scribal house as a more traditional counterpart to Täfäri Mäkonnen's new state press. Under the direction of Sahle Maryam, its 250 copyists reproduced and illuminated manuscripts for the royal library: Gäbrä Egzi'abḥér, *Prowess*, 456–57; and Ḫaylä Śellasé, *Ḥeywäté*, 48.

63. *Jubilee*, 66.

64. Dämessé Wäldä Gäbr'él, "Tarikenna mätasäbiya."

65. *Jubilee*, unpaginated prefatory chapter, entitled "Previous General Managers."

66. Keflä Egzi'e Yeḫdägu, "Yäḥeywät tarik."

67. Marse'é Ḫazan, unpublished manuscript.

68. Keflä Egzi'e Yeḫdägu, "Yäḥeywät tarik"; and Dämessé Wäldä Gäbr'él, "Tarikenna mätasäbiya."

69. For a contemporary Ethiopian account, see Gäbrä Egzi'abḥér, *Progress*, 488.

70. Harold Marcus, *Haile Selassie I: The Formative Years, 1892–1936* (Trenton: Red Sea Press, 1995), 39–96.

71. *Berhanenna sälam*, March 17, 1927. The original French article is by R. Louzon, "Le fascisme risquera-t-il la guerre? Le dogue en cage," *La révolution prolétarienne: revue mensuelle syndicaliste communiste*, No. 24 (December, 1926): 1–6.

72. *Berhanenna sälam*, March 17, 1927.

73. *Berhanenna sälam*, March 17, 1927.

74. Pankhurst, "Printing," 271.

75. Letter from Tä'ammrat Amanu'el to Jacques Faitlovitch, dated March 20, 1927, reproduced in *L'epistolario di Taamrat Emmanuel: Un intellettuale ebreo d'Etiopia nella prima metà del XX secolo*, ed. Emanuela Trevisan Semi (Turin: L'Harmattan Italia, 2000), 126.

76. Weinzinger was also involved in the affair in some way, so the government closed his small Addis Ababa press and suspended the publication of its pro-Ethiopian newsletter *Correspondance d'Éthiopie*, which subsequently resumed publication in Hanover, Germany. On this, see ASMAI I, Pos. 181, fasc. 54, Intercepted Telegram from Addis Ababa, January 6, 1929.

77. Cf. "Abyssinian Newspaper and Fascismo," *The Times*, March 25, 1927, and "Incidente italo-abissino prontamente liquidato," *La Tribuna*, March 26, 1927. The latter argued that the piece aimed to "unsettle the amicable existing relations between Ethiopia and Italy."

78. Letter from Tä'ammrat to Jacques Faitlovitch, dated April 9, 1927, reproduced in *L'epistolario*, ed. Trevisan Semi, 127.

79. IES Ms. 1996, 156–57.
80. *Jubilee*, 54–56; and *EA* 4: 1103.
81. Peter Garretson, *A Victorian Gentleman and Ethiopian Nationalist: The Life and Times of Hakim Wärqenäh* (Woodbridge, UK: James Currey, 2012), 138–39; and Arén, *Pioneers*, 241.
82. Nilsson, "Gebra Kristus."
83. Keflä Egzi'e Yeḫdägu, "Yäheywät tarik."
84. Wäldä Giyorgis Wäldä Yoḥannes, Poem, *Berhanenna sälam*, October 27, 1932.
85. Dämessé Wäldä Gäbr'él, "Yäheywät tarik." The song appears at the end of this text, with the title "Teneš yäḫazän mäzmur."
86. Tämanu Rämeha, "Yäheywät tarik."
87. Nilsson, "Gebra Kristus."
88. *Missions-Tidning*, August 13, 1933.
89. Wäldä Giyorgis, poem.
90. Gäbrä Krestos, *Yä'aläm tarik*, 5.
91. For overviews of historiography in this period, see Bahru, *Pioneers*, 141–57; and Bairu, "Turning Point."
92. Ḫeruy, *Yäheywät tärik*, 47.
93. Gäbrä Ḥeywät Baykädañ, "Aṭé Menilekenna ityoṗya," in *Berhan yeḥun*, 336–55. The republished and translated edition is Gäbrä Ḥeywät Baykädañ, "L'empereur Menilek et Éthiopie," trans. Beletou Kebede and Jacques Bureau, *BMEE*, No. 2 (1993): 1–56, cited hereafter.
94. Gäbrä Ḥeywät, "Menilek," 29.
95. Gäbrä Ḥeywät, "Menilek," 36.
96. Gäbrä Ḥeywät, "Menilek," 34–35.
97. These include the interpretation of Emperor Téwodros as a national unifier and the idea that Ethiopian development was slowed by chronic conflict. For a discussion of this point, see Shiferaw Bekele, "Gäbrä-Heywät Baykädañ and the Emergence of a Modern Intellectual Discourse," *Sociology Ethnology Bulletin*, No. 1 (1994): 106–21.
98. Gäbrä Ḥeywät Baykädañ, *Mängeśtenna yäḥezb astädadär* (Addis Ababa: Berhanenna Sälam, 1923). It has been translated with commentary as Gäbrä Ḥeywät Baykädañ, *The State and Economy in Early Twentieth Century Ethiopia: Gabrahiwot Baykadagn*, trans. Tenkir Bonger (Lawrenceville: Red Sea Press, 1995), cited hereafter.
99. This is not surprising given the prominence and influence of Marxist and anti-Marxist arguments circa 1900 in Austrian academia, where Gäbrä Ḥeywät studied. For a discussion, see Eric Hobsbawm, *How to Change the World: Reflections on Marx and Marxism* (New Haven: Yale, 2011), 211–60.
100. The implications of Gäbrä Ḥeywät's conceptual borrowing have been the subject of considerable debate: Messay Kebede, "Gebrehiwot Baykedagn, Eurocentrism, and the Decentering of Ethiopia," *Journal of Black Studies* 36, no. 6 (2006): 815–32; Tenkir Bonger, "Introduction," in *Government*, 15–46; and Matteo Salvadore, "A Modern African Intellectual: Gabre-Heywat Baykadan's Quest for Ethiopia's Sovereign Modernity," *Africa* LXIII, no. 1 (2008): 560–79. See also Richard Caulk, "Dependency, Gebre Heywet Baykedagn, and the Birth of Ethiopian Reformism," in *Proceedings of the Fifth International Conference of Ethiopian Studies*, ed. Robert Hess (Chicago: University of Illinois, 1979), 569–81.

101. This work is not usually considered historiography proper, despite the fact that Gäbrä Ḥeywät's analysis focuses on change over time. It has often been described as an early work of developmental economics. Using contemporary disciplinary and methodological distinctions, it most closely approximates historical sociology in the vein of Barrington Moore, Perry Anderson, and Immanuel Wallerstein. In early-twentieth-century Ethiopia, however, it surely would have been seen as historiography. Indeed, like a universal historian, Gäbrä Ḥeywät begins his analysis with a discussion of human origins.

102. Emanuela Trevisan Semi, "Taamrat Emmanuel between Colonized and Colonizer," and Brook Abdu, "Taamrat Emmanuel in Post-Italian Ethiopia," papers presented at the seminar "Ethiopian Jews under Fascist Rule," New York University Casa Italiana, October 23, 2014.

103. Tä'ammrat Amanu'el, "Episodi della storia dei Falascià (dalle Chronache del Negusé-Neghèst Seltan-Seghed," *La rassegna mensile di Israel* 11, no. 3 (1936): 83–92. This journal was founded in 1925 as a supplement to the weekly *Israel.* For a detailed history of the journal in this period, see Bruno Di Porto, "La rassegna mensile di Israel in epoca fascista," *La rassegna mensile di Israel* 61, no. 1 (1995): 7–60. In later years, Tä'ammrat wrote a considerable number of other works, including a pioneering study of Amharic literature. See Tä'ammrat, "Essay," 29–68, with approximate date of writing on 55.

104. For a brief discussion, see *EA* 2: 730.

105. Tä'ammrat discusses the biases of the chronicler in his introduction: Tä'ammrat, "Episodi," 84.

106. The closest pre-twentieth-century analogue would be *abba* Baḥrey's study of the Oromo. However, this work was based on observation and oral accounts, and not on the careful analysis of various, possibly distorted sources. See the discussion in chapter 1.

107. Western awareness of Ethiopia's Jews was relatively limited at this time: for a discussion, see James Quirin, *The Evolution of the Ethiopian Jews: a History of the Beta Israel (Falasha) to 1920* (Philadelphia: University of Pennsylvania, 1992), 191–98.

108. Tä'ammrat's piece was framed by a contributor named "N. d. R" as evidence of the merit of new colonial projects: since Tä'ammrat displayed such cultural and intellectual elevation, and since he additionally sought to elevate his people in the same way, this suggested that Italy could fruitfully bring other similarly advanced Jews into the Italian empire through conquest. See Tä'ammrat, "Episodi," 84. In light of Tä'ammrat's anticolonial activities before and during the Italian occupation, he would have surely objected to this.

109. The press was destroyed, paradoxically, by Italian Jewish fascists who hoped to win the favor of Mussolini: see Jonathan Steinberg, *All or Nothing: The Axis and the Holocaust, 1941–43,* 2nd ed. (Routledge: New York, 2002), 227–28.

110. Tä'ammrat, "Episodi," 88n1.

111. Tä'ammrat, "Episodi," 92.

112. For a succinct overview of these narratives, see Joel Beinin, *The Dispersion of Egyptian Jewry: Culture, Politics, and the Formation of a Modern Diaspora* (Berkeley: University of California Press, 1998), 1–28.

113. Faitlovitch hoped to develop these sympathies among his Ethiopian protégés: see Quirin, *Beta Israel,* 197–98.

114. Richard Pankhurst, "Tedla Haile and the Problem of Multi-ethnicity in Ethiopia," *NEAS* 5, no. 3 (1998): 81–96.

115. Tedla Hailé Modjà Guermami, "Pourquoi et comment pratiquer une politique d'assimilation en Éthiopie" (Thesis, Université Coloniale d'Anvers, 1930).

116. Tedla Hailé, "Pourquoi," 8.

117. Tedla Hailé, "Pourquoi," 13, 23.

118. Tedla Hailé, "Pourquoi," 24–25, 30.

119. Tedla Hailé, "Pourquoi," 31.

120. See for example his critique of Coulbeaux's reproach of Emperor Lebnä Dengel for not recognizing the value of a European alliance: "To our eyes, the rejection of the Portuguese alliance makes more dear the memory of Lebne-Denghel[,] who alone struggled against the Muslims." Tedla Hailé, "Pourquoi," 20.

121. Yäğägnoč mätasäbiya," *Berhanenna sälam*, February 6, 1930; "Selä hagär feqer selä mäśariyanna selä ğägnoč ṭeneqaqé massasäbiya," *Berhanenna sälam*, February 13, 1933; untitled article, *Berhanenna sälam*, October 31, 1935; and "Addis zämän bä'ityopya tarik," *Berhanenna sälam*, December 24, 1930.

122. An interesting and timely example is the article on Ethiopia's historical unity that appeared on the eve of the Italian invasion: *A'emro*, July 27, 1935.

123. "Les souvenirs d'un Ancien," *Courrier d'Éthiopie*, December 11, 1931; "Les recherches archéologiques," *Courrier d'Éthiopie*, November 8, 1929; "La Pénétration Européenne en Éthiopie à travers les âges," *Courrier d'Éthiopie*, January 6, 1933; "Évolution," *Courrier d'Éthiopie*, September 11, 1931; and "Les origines de l'université de Paris," *Courrier d'Éthiopie*, November 27, 1931. For an assessment of one of these reports, see Gäbrä Egzi'abḥér, *Progress*, 484–86.

124. For example, "Melkam tarik," *Berhanenna sälam*, March 31, 1932; and "Revue littéraire," *Courrier d'Éthiopie*, September 1, 1931.

125. Ḫeruy, *Katalog*, 27.

126. Olle Eriksson, *Alämen eney/Voyons le monde* (Asmära: Imprimerie évangélique, 1924).

127. Olle Eriksson, *Ahunenna ṭent/Présent et passé* (Asmära: Imprimerie évangélique, 1926).

128. Karl Heden, *Yäḥezboč ameleko anwänwäračäwenna yäwängél śera käšanqelločenna kähendoč käčinočem käğapanočem käléloč ḥezbočem zänd endét mähonun yämminager*, trans. Olle Eriksson (Addis Ababa: Goh Ṣebah, 1935).

129. Stockholm, Stadsarkiv, EFS Särarkiv, 815: U10, 3–7, "Eriksson manuscripts."

130. Bahru, *Pioneers*, 73–75.

131. Gäbrä Egzi'abḥér, *Progress*, 303. In the introduction to this work, the author explained that it was based on an earlier history that had been destroyed during the Italian invasion. It was apparently requested by Empress Zäwditu and printed, but not distributed. See Reidulf Molvaer, introduction to Gäbrä Egzi'abḥér, *Progress*, 17–18.

132. IES Ms. 1996. *Aläqa* Kenfé later collaborated with the Italian orientalist Mario Moreno on a collection of Amharic folktales: see *däbtära* Kenfé, *Cent Fables Amhariques*, trans. and ann. by Martino Mario Moreno (Paris: Imprimerie Nationale, 1948).

133. EMML 1610.

134. Girma Getahun, "The Goǧǧam Chronicle: Introduction with Edition, Translation, and Annotation of Select Chapters" (PhD diss., Oxford University, 1991); and Jacques Bureau, "Un fragment de l'histoire du peuple Wollaita d'Afework Gebre-Sellassie," *AE* 15 (1990): 47–81.

135. EMML 1202.

136. Afäwärq Gäbrä Iyäsus, *Dagmawi aṭé Menilek* (Addis Ababa: United Printers, 1973). The translated edition is Luigi Fusella, "Il Dāgmāwi Měnilěk di Afawarq Gabra Iyasus," *RSE* 17 (1961): 11–44. His other major historical work is his account of Crown Prince Täfäri Mäkonnen's visit to Aden, discussed in chapter 4.

137. Tä'ammrat, "An Early Essay," 59.

138. See discussion in Alain Rouaud, *Afä-wärq 1868–1947: Un intellectuel éthiopien témoin de son temps* (Paris: Éditions CNRS, 1991), 246.

139. Ḫeruy, *Yäheywät tarik*, 37–38; and Aleme Eshete, "Alaqa Tayyä," 14–30.

140. This and all subsequent quotes come from the critical edition: Tayyä Gebre Medhin, *Yä'ityopya hezb tarik*, trans. Grover Hudson and Tekeste Negash (Uppsala: Centre for Multiethnic Research, 1988), 3.

141. For a perceptive discussion, see Ezra Gebremedhin, "Aleqa Tayye: The Missionary Factor in his Scholarly Work," in *The Missionary Factor in Ethiopia: Papers from a Symposium on the Impact of European Missions on Ethiopian Society, Lund University, August 1996*, ed. by Getatchew Haile, Aasulv Lande, and Samuel Rubenson (New York: Peter Lang, 1998), 101–20.

142. Tayyä, *History*, 39.

143. Private manuscript, cited in Bahru, *Pioneers*, 147.

144. Tayyä, *History*, 51–57. For a similar discussion of the origins of the Queen of Sheba, see Tedla Hailé, "Pourquoi," 13.

145. Bahru, *Pioneers*, 145–48.

146. See my discussion of these studies in chapter 1.

147. Luigi Fusella, "Abissinia e Metemma in uno scritto di Bělāttā Hěruy," *RSE* 3, no. 2 (1943): 200–213. These are in all likelihood references to the disparaging comments made by Afäwärq Gäbrä Iyäsus in the introduction to his biography of Emperor Menilek.

148. Fusella, "Abissinia," 202–3.

149. Fusella, "Abissinia," 212–13.

150. Fusella, "Abissinia," 202.

151. Ḫeruy, *Yäheywät tarik*.

152. Two examples of these shorter works are the introductions to his European and Japanese travel narratives, discussed in chapter 4; another is Ḫeruy, *Katalog*, 4–9.

153. Ḫeruy Wäldä Śellasé, *Wazéma: Bämagestu yä'ityopyan nägäśtat yätarik bä'al lämakbär* (Addis Ababa: Goh Ṣebah, 1926EC).

154. Ḫeruy Wäldä Śellasé, *Yä'ityopya tarik känegeśt saba esk tallaqu yä'adwa del* (Addis Ababa: Central Printing Press, 2006). This recent edition includes commentaries and academic articles on Ḫeruy by several authors. For a discussion, see Bahru, *Pioneers*, 150–51.

155. This has been published as Bairu Tafla, ed. and trans., *Asma Giyorgis and his Work: History of the Galla and the Kingdom of Sawa* (Stuttgart: Franz Steiner Verlag Wiesbaden, 1987).

156. Marse'é Ḫazan, unpublished manuscript. A translated excerpt from this work has been published as Marse'é Ḫazan Wäldä Qirqos, *Of What I Saw and Heard.*

157. IES Ms. 1136, *Mäṣḥafä tarik* by Märägéta Berhanu. This work is a two-column historical notebook, possibly from the 1920s. The author begins with the Church fathers and proceeds through the Solomonids. He mentions his use of "Yäliti tarik" in the conclusion, possibly a reference to Littmann.

158. His closest counterpart in this regard might be Mika'él Tässäma, who produced an introduction to political economy that was serially published in *Berhanenna sälam.* For one example, see *Berhanenna sälam,* February 7, 1929; a brief discussion appears in Bahru, *Pioneers,* 188.

159. Gäbrä Krestos, *Yä'aläm tarik,* 1–2. On Éfrem, see Lundström and Gebremedhin, *Kenisha,* 485.

160. Erikkson was also prone to adding French alternate titles to his published works; see the examples in the previous section of this chapter.

161. Gäbrä Krestos, *Yä'aläm tarik,* 6, 10.

162. See for example his discussion of Adwa, which uses both calendars: Gäbrä Krestos, *Yä'aläm tarik,* 101–5.

163. For other explanations of human origins in this period, see Tayyä, *History,* 31; Bairu Tafla, *Asma Giyorgis,* 259; and Gäbrä Ḥeywät, *Government,* 57–71.

164. Gäbrä Krestos, *Yä'aläm tarik,* 10.

165. Gäbrä Krestos, *Yä'aläm tarik,* 10. In this assessment, Gäbrä Krestos agreed with Tedla.

166. See Gäbrä Krestos, *Yä'aläm tarik,* 19, fn.; and Philip Van Ness Meyers, *Ancient History* (Boston: Ginn and Company, 1904), esp. 14–19. One of the principal debates among ethnologists in this period concerned the question of human origins: monogenists endorsed a single original population, while polygenists held that there were multiple original populations whose variations produced racial difference.

167. For a somewhat similar attempt at reclassifying the world's people, see the critical discussion of *aläqa* Tayyä's use of the category *nägäd* ("people" or "lineage") in Bahru, *Pioneers,* 148. A discussion of Tayyä's understanding of western political and social categories can be found in Aleme Eshete, "Tayyä."

168. Gäbrä Krestos, *Yä'aläm tarik,* 11–12, 16–18.

169. For a discussion, see Meyers, *Ancient History,* 12.

170. Gäbrä Krestos, *Yä'aläm tarik,* 12–14.

171. Gäbrä Krestos, *Yä'aläm tarik,* 15–16. On the significance of Japan in Ethiopian intellectual life, see Bahru Zewde, "The Concept of Japanization in the Intellectual History of Modern Ethiopia," in *Society, State, and History: Selected Essays,* ed. Bahru Zewde (Addis Ababa: Addis Ababa University, 2008), 198–214.

172. Gäbrä Krestos, *Yä'aläm tarik,* 94–96.

173. Gäbrä Krestos, *Yä'aläm tarik,* 99.

174. Gäbrä Krestos, *Yä'aläm tarik,* 100–105. For a contemporary description of this celebration, see Gäbrä Egzi'abḥér, *Prowess,* 463–64.

175. Gäbrä Krestos, *Yä'aläm tarik,* 102.

176. Gäbrä Krestos, *Yä'aläm tarik,* 103. See also Psalms 68:31.

177. For a discussion, see Arif Dirlik, "Is There History after Eurocentrism?: Globalism, Postcolonialism, and the Disavowal of History," *Cultural Critique* 42 (1999):

1–34. More generally, see Dipesh Chakrabarty, *Provincializing Europe: Postcolonial Thought and Historical Difference* (Princeton, NJ: Princeton University Press, 2000), esp. 27–47; Immanuel Wallerstein, *European Universalism: The Rhetoric of Power* (New York: New Press, 2006); and Samir Amin, *Eurocentrism: Modernity, Religion, and Democracy*, trans. Russell Moore and James Membrez (New York: Monthly Review Press, 2009).

178. Chakrabarty, *Provincializing Europe*, 7.

179. White, *The Content of the Form*, 2.

180. Gäbrä Krestos, *Yä'aläm tarik*, 26.

181. Gäbrä Krestos, *Yä'aläm tarik*, 24–25.

182. Gäbrä Krestos, *Yä'aläm tarik*, 12–13.

183. Gäbrä Krestos, *Yä'aläm tarik*, 13–15. These sections were likely partially based on EFS publications.

184. Gäbrä Krestos, *Yä'aläm tarik*, 100.

185. For discussion of some of these concepts, see Messay Kebede, *Survival and Modernization, Ethiopia's Enigmatic Present: a Philosophical Discourse* (Lawrenceville: Red Sea Press, 1999). The system is more generally described in Crummey, *Land*.

186. For key comparisons of the *gäbbar* system and European feudalism, see Tsegaye Tegenu, *The Evolution of Ethiopian Absolutism: The Genesis and Making of the Fiscal Military State, 1696–1913* (Uppsala: Uppsala University Press, 1996); and Donald Crummey, "Abyssinian Feudalism," *Past and Present* 89 (November 1980): 115–38. These draw upon Perry Anderson, *Lineages of the Absolutist State* (London: Verso, 1979).

187. Gäbrä Krestos, *Yä'aläm tarik*, 31, 12–13, respectively.

188. Gäbrä Krestos, *Yä'aläm tarik*, 31.

189. Gäbrä Krestos, *Yä'aläm tarik*, 35.

190. In this regard, see especially his attention to the alliance structures of the Napoleonic wars and the issues of royal lineage, such as Napoleon's coronation of his brother as the King of Naples. Gäbrä Krestos, *Yä'aläm tarik*, 32–33.

191. Chakrabarty, *Provincializing Europe*, especially his discussion of capital and barter, 72–96.

192. François Hartog, "Time, History and the Writing of History: The *Order* of Time," *KVHAA Konferenser* 37 (1996): 95–113.

193. Hartog offers Tocqueville as an exemplar of this regime, quoting the latter's *Democracy in America*: "When the past no longer throws light on the future, the spirit walks in darkness." See Hartog, "Time," 96.

Chapter 3

1. See Dane Kennedy, *Islands of White: Settler Society and Culture in Kenya and Southern Rhodesia, 1890–1939* (Durham, NC: Duke University Press, 1987), 1–8; and David Prochaska, *Making Algeria French: Colonalism in Bône, 1870–1920* (New York: Cambridge University Press, 1990), 6–11.

2. Bäraqit had been a key Italian position during the Adwa campaign in the years immediately before Gäbrä Mika'él's birth. On this, see Raymond Jonas, *The Battle of Adwa: African Victory in the Age of Empire* (Cambridge, MA: Harvard University Press, 2011), 154.

3. IES Ms. 323, frontispiece.

4. Berhan Abreha, "Mäqdem," in Gäbrä Mika'él Germu, *Dägyat bahta ḥagos sägänäyti* (1997), 5.

5. IES Ms. 323, frontispiece.

6. Earlier Catholic missionary efforts were led by Iberian Jesuits and French Lazarists. The latter were expelled from Eritrea in 1894 and replaced by the more suitably Italian Capuchins.

7. On Carrara and these achievements, see the special issue of *Annali Francescani* 55, no. 14–15 (1924): 404–88, with Da Iseo's memorials, 410, 414–18; Metodio da Nembro, *Missione dei Minori Cappuccini in Eritrea (1894–1952)* (Rome: Bibliotheca Seraphico-Capuccina, 1953), 57–94; and Puglisi, *Chi è*, 72.

8. These developments are surveyed in Jonathan Miran, "Missionaries, Education, and the State in the Italian Colony of Eritrea," in *Christian Missionaries and the State in the Third World*, ed. Holger Bernt Hansen and Michael Twaddle (Athens: Ohio University Press, 2002), 121–35; Silvana Palma, "Educare alla subalternità: Prassi e politiche scholastiche nella colonia eritrea," in *L'Africa orientale italiana nel dibattito storico contemporaneo*, ed. Bianca Maria Carcangiu and Tekeste Negash (Rome: Carocci, 2007), 211–38; and Matteo Pretelli, "Education in the Italian Colonies during the Interwar Period," *Modern Italy* 16, no. 3 (2011): 275–93.

9. In 1912, one Capuchin historian estimated that Bäraqit Abbay was "two thirds" Catholic, with 410 parishioners and 15 adult baptisms, an unusually high number. Carrara himself visited the town on at least one occasion. On both points, see Galdino da Mezzana, *La Missione Eritrea affidata ai Frati Minori Cappucini di Milano* (Milan: Tipografia Lanzani, 1912), 40–42. For a description of a Capuchin journey from Asmära to Bäraqit via Sägänäyti in the mid-1890s, see Francesco da Offeio, *I Cappucini nella colonia Eritrea: Ricordi del P. Francesco da Offeio* (Rome: Tipografia SS. Concez, 1910), 61–65.

10. For details on these three schools, see Da Nembro, *Missione*, 461–62, and 467.

11. Da Nembro, *Missione*, 77; and Da Mezzana, *Missione*, 82–84.

12. Da Nembro, *Missione*, 75, n. 77; and Da Mezzana, *Missione*, 87–88.

13. Da Nembro, *Missione*, 78.

14. Puglisi, *Chi è*, 120; and Da Nembro, *Missione*, 62, 450.

15. Puglisi, *Chi è*, 148.

16. Da Mezzana, *Missione*, 34; and Da Nembro, *Missione*, 448.

17. Puglisi, *Chi è*, 22.

18. For a discussion, see Gianni Dore, "Catechisti e evangelisti come intermediari culturali nella Colonia Eritrea," in *Governare l'Oltremare: Istituzioni, funzionari e società nel colonialismo italiano*, ed. Gianni Dore, Chiara Giorgi, Antonio Morone, and Massimo Zaccaria (Rome: Carocci, 2013), 133–50.

19. Da Mezzana, *Missione*, 27.

20. *Pagine d'Apostolato nell' Eritrea: Omaggio ai nostri Benefattori* (Asmära: Tipografia Francescana, 1917), 46.

21. Da Mezzana, *Missione*, 26, 72–78; *Pagine*, 7. For a contemporary discussion of the colonial significance of telegraphy, see Luigi Solari, "La radiotelegrafia e le nostre colonie," *Rivista coloniale* 1 (1906): 206–9.

22. See for example the day of remembrance, prayers, and patriotic speeches for Italian soldiers who died in Libya, "a land bathed in much Italian blood": Da

Mezzana, *Missione*, 29–30. On the aims of colonial education more generally, see Tekeste Negash, "The Ideology of Italian Colonial Educational Policy in Eritrea," in *Italian Colonialism*, ed. Ruth Ben-Ghiat and Mia Fuller (New York: Palgrave, 2005), 109–20; and Pretelli, "Education," 275–93.

23. Ezechio da Iseo, *Manuale d'industrie, arti e mestieri ad uso degli indigeni nelle due lingue italiano e tigrigna per cura della missione cattolica* (Asmära: Tipografia Francescana, 1914), 6–7.

24. Da Mezzana, *Missione*, 21.

25. *Pagine*, 46.

26. *Pagine*, 46.

27. Berhan Abreha, "Mäqdem," 5. The author of this short biography, who apparently knew Gäbrä Mika'él, describes his job as *scrivano* and *ṣäḥafi*.

28. Taddia, "Correspondence," 109–34.

29. ASMAI II, Pos. 181, fasc. 48, "Elenco dei permessi di porto d'armi concessi in occasione del Mascal 1934-XII," September 19, 1934. According to this document, his subordinates were Kidanä Wäldämäsqäl, an orderly, and Habtu Bahta and Täsfagäbrä Mika'él, both assistant typists.

30. Several issues of this gazette from this period can be found in ASMAI II, Pos. 181, fasc. 48. For some of the many newspaper summaries from this same period, see *Il Quotidiano Eritreo*, July 5, 1933; July 23, 1933; August 24, 1933; and September 7, 1933. On occasion, Mosconi and his office produced short Italian and Tigrinya articles for this publication: see *Il Quotidiano Eritreo*, November 24, 1933, and June 10, 1934.

31. Gäbrä Mika'él Germu, "Beza'eba qeteläten śerqen mellaš," *Il Quotidiano Eritreo*, July 1, 1934. I have been unable to locate a complete series of this newspaper, so it possible that Gäbrä Mika'él wrote other articles prior to this one.

32. For a contemporary Italian description of this affair, see *Il Quotidiano Eritreo*, September 30, 1934; see also the earlier accounts in Pier Ludovico Occhini, *Viaggi* (Città di Castello: S. Lapi, 1908), 87–102; and Paoli, *Eritrea*, 192–94.

33. From lowest to highest in terms of rank, the four permits awarded were pistol, hunting rifle, Mod. 79/87 military rifle (*moschetto*), and Mod. 91 military rifle: ASMAI II, Pos. 181, fasc. 48, memo with the title "Meschel 1934 – Proposte di concessioni di titoli onorifici e di permessi di porte d'armi," August 31, 1934.

34. See for example *Il Quotidiano Eritreo*, October 1, 1933; and September 30, 1934.

35. On the politics of Italian native policy more generally, see Tekeste Negash, "Resistance and Collaboration, 1882–1914," in *No Medicine for the Bite of a White Snake: Notes on Nationalism and Resistance in Eritrea, 1890–1940*, ed. Tekeste Negash (Uppsala: University of Uppsala Reprocentralen, 1986), 37–54; and Uoldelul Chelati Dirar, "Colonialism and the Construction of National Identities: The Case of Eritrea," *Journal of East African Studies* 1, no. 2 (2007): 256–76. On colonial ritual and traditionalism more generally, see Terence Ranger, "The Invention of Tradition in Colonial Africa," in *The Invention of Tradition*, ed. Eric Hobsbawm and Terence Ranger (Cambridge: Cambridge University Press, 1983), 211–62; and also his "The Invention of Tradition Revisited: The Case of Colonial Africa," in *Inventions and Boundaries: Historical and Anthropological Approaches to the Study of Ethnicity and Nationalism*, ed. Preban Kaarsholm and Jan Hultin (Roskilde: Roskilde University, 1994), 5–50.

36. ASMAI II, Pos. 181, fasc. 48, "Elenco dei permessi di porto d'armi concessi in occasione del Mascal 1934-XII," September 19, 1934.

37. On these intermediaries and their fraught "bargain of collaboration," see Benjamin Lawrance, Emily Lynn Osborn, and Richard Roberts, eds., *Intermediaries, Interpreters, and Clerks: African Employees in the Making of Colonial Africa* (Madison: University of Wisconsin, 2006).

38. Private, self-representative texts written by African intermediaries during the colonial era are relatively rare. For a discussion of this issue and the relationship between the depictions of intermediaries in colonial archives and private writings, see Ralph Austin, "Colonialism from the Middle: African Clerks as Historical Actors and Discursive Subjects," *History in Africa* 38 (2011): 21–33.

39. IES Ms. 324/EMML 1470.

40. IES Ms. 324, notes on 79 and 80, with signature on 90.

41. IES Ms. 325, with date on cover. See also page 44, which contains signatures by acquaintances of the author that are dated 1933/34.

42. IES Ms. 325, 1–20, with notes on 5 and 6.

43. IES Ms. 325, 21–30; reference to Littmann appears on 22.

44. IES Ms. 325, 35–44.

45. Edward Ullendorff, *The Two Zions: Reminiscences of Jerusalem and Ethiopia* (New York: Oxford University Press, 1988), 167. This observation overlooks the earlier writings of Eritrean intellectuals in *Il Quotidiano Eritreo*, discussed below.

46. Nicole Saulsberry, "The Life and Times of Woldeab Woldemariam, 1905–1995" (PhD diss., Stanford University, 2001), 95–138; and Puglisi, *Chi è*, 144; for Gäbrä Mäsqäl's earlier writings, see *Il Quotidiano Eritreo*, January 14, 1934, and April 17, 1934. These two individuals were friends who initially shared an anticolonial nationalism, but later splintered into pro-independence and pro-union positions.

47. Abbebe Kifleyesus, correspondence with author, December 5, 2012.

48. Puglisi, *Chi è*, 146.

49. Puglisi, *Chi è*, 174.

50. Gäbrä Mika'él Germu, "Selä nay temeherti wäq^{w}emi (bäkäbur däğğazmač bäyen bäraki zetänägerä qal radiyo)," *Nay értra sämunawi gazéṭa*, September 27, 1944. Another early short article is Gäbrä Mika'él Germu, "Zenäb kab dämäna fetḥi kab daña," *Nay értra sämunawi gazéṭa*, July 13, 1944.

51. Gäbrä Mika'él Germu, "Ḥegi zebäzeho äddi yenäddi mesar zebäzeho gundi yebädi," *Nay értra sämunawi gazéṭa*, October 12, 1944.

52. Gäbrä Mika'él Germu, "Iyärusalém hagärä – dawit akusem [aksum] hagärä – menilek wäldä – solomon wäkaléb," *Nay értra sämunawi gazéṭa*, December 28, 1944.

53. Gäbrä Mika'él Germu, "Nay bozäné – n belḥaté – n tärät," *Nay értra sämunawi gazéṭa*, February 22, 1945. See also Gäbrä Mika'él Germu, "Ğegna ğegna yefätu qenu'e mängedi äddi yä'etu, ṣebuq šetu ensäsak^{w}a yefätu," *Nay értra sämunawi gazéṭa*, October 24, 1945.

54. See, for example, "Zanta ḥezb[i] ḥabäšat," *Nay értra sämunawi gazéṭa*, Megäbit 20, 1945 (?) and "Haṣäy yoḥännes," *Nay értra sämunawi gazéṭa*, Yekätit 15, 1945 (?), both based on the work of Wallace Budge.

55. Bairu Tafla, correspondence with author, January 8, 2008.

56. Puglisi, *Chi è*, 146.

57. Tom Killion, *Historical Dictionary of Eritrea* (Lanham: Scarecrow, 1998), 229.

58. See for example Gäbrä Mika'él Germu, "Gäbrä egzi'abḥér ḫamasénay," *Ityopya*, no. 853–6 (1961).

59. IES Ms. 326, 36. Gäbrä Mika'él notes that the Téwodros chronicle was completed in 1946 EC, and the rest of the work appears to have been written in several stages.

60. IES Ms. 326, 2.

61. EMML 1467.

62. Gäbrä Mika'él Germu, *Bahta ḥagos*; and Gäbrä Mika'él Germu, "Blatta Gäbrä egzi'abḥér gilay ṣä'eda krestyan," unpublished Tigrinya manuscript from the collection of Ammanuel Germu, Asmära.

63. *EA* 3: 97.

64. This is the IES copy of *aläqa* Tayyä's dictionary and grammar, which is signed in *fidäl* and Italian cursive by *blatta* Gäbrä Mika'él Germu, its former owner: Tayyä Gäbrä Maryam, *Mäṣḥafä säwasew* (Monkullu: Mission Press, 1889).

65. Richard Pankhurst, correspondence with author, January 23, 2009.

66. For an overview and analysis of these positions, see Richard Reid, "The Trans-Mereb Experience: Perceptions of the Historical Relationship between Eritrea and Ethiopia," *Journal of Eastern African Studies* 1, no. 2 (2007): 238–55; and Alemseged Abbay, "The Trans-Mareb Past in the Present," *Journal of Modern African Studies* 35, no. 2 (1997): 321–34.

67. Exceptions to this tendency can be found in some of the Tigrinya articles that appear in *Il Quotidiano Eritreo*: see, for example, *abba* Yoḥannes Gäbrä Egzi, "Menkusena," in *Il Quotidiano Eritreo*, September 26, 1934.

68. Gäbrä Egzi'abḥér is easily the most studied Eritrean intellectual of the era: see Irma Taddia, *Un intelletuale tigrino nell'Etiopia di Menilek: Blatta Gäbrä Egzi'abḥēr Gilay (1860–1914)* (Milan: Giuffrè Editore, 1990); Irma Taddia, "Ethiopian Source Material and Colonial Rule in the Nineteenth Century: The Letter to Menilek (1899) by Blatta Gäbrä Egzi'abeḥēr," *Journal of African History* 34 (1993): 493–516; and Tekeste Negash, "Blatta Gebre Egziabeher Gila Mariam and His Works: A Sketch Towards a Political Biography of a Nationalist," in *Nationalism and Resistance*, ed. Tekeste Negash, 1–21.

69. Taddia, *Intelletuale tigrino*, 9–11.

70. Taddia, *Intelletuale tigrino*, 7.

71. Taddia, "Source Material," 497.

72. The plot is described in detail in Taddia, *Intelletuale tigrino*, 16–38.

73. His discovery, imprisonment, escape, and subsequent career in Ethiopia is described in detail in Taddia, *Intelletuale tigrino*, 41–107.

74. Archivio Eritrea, 1888–1917, busta 78, "Interprete Blata Garesghear Ghilèmariam, sue memorie, 1899." The actual title of this work is on the following page, the original frontispiece: *Zämäṣḥaf blätta gäbrä egzi'abḥér wäldä lägila maryam.*

75. For a synopsis, discussion, and chapter outline, see Tekeste Negash, "Blatta Gebre Egziabeher," 4–12, 21.

76. Quotation taken from Tekeste Negash, "Blatta Gebre Egziabeher," 8.

77. Quotation taken from Tekeste Negash, "Blatta Gebre Egziabeher," 12.

78. For the text, see Taddia, "Source Material," 509–15.

79. Quotation taken from Tekeste Negash, "Blatta Gebre Egziabeher," 11.

80. These were subsequently published in J. I. Eadie, ed., *An Amharic Reader* (Cambridge: Cambridge University Press, 1924). For a discussion, see Tekeste Negash, "Blatta Gebre Egziabeher," 12–16.

81. For a discussion emphasizing these themes, see Taddia, *Intelletuale tigrino,* 1–3, 105–9.

82. Gäbrä Mika'él Germu, "Gäbrä egzi'abḥér," which contains two biographies. Gäbrä Egzi'abḥér was not mentioned by Puglisi, making Gäbrä Mika'él's piece one of the earliest discussions of him. For a later depiction, see Yesḥaq Yoséf, *Qäddamot ğeganu értran bahlenan* (Asmära: 1997), 16–31.

83. On his education, see his aside about his teacher studying with Téwodros in Gondär: Feśśeḥa Giyorgis, *Storia d'Etiopia,* trans. and intro. Yaqob Beyene (Naples: Istituto Universario Orientale, 1987), 208. See also *AE,* Vol. 2, 532–33.

84. Yaqob Beyene, "Introduzione," in *Storia,* viii, and n. 4.

85. Feśśeḥa, *Storia.* Although unpublished during his lifetime, Feśśeḥa apparently intended for this work to be published. See his comments to this effect in the introduction to his later work: Hailu Habtu, "The Voyage of Däbtära Fesseha Giyorgis to Italy at the End of the 19th Century," *AE* 16 (2000): 362.

86. "Zäwäld," *Fitäñaytunna ḥʷalañaytu ityopya. L'Etiopia antica e moderna* (Rome: Tipografia della Casa Editrice Italiana, 1899). Following Lanfranco Ricci, Yaqob Beyene persuasively attributes this work to Feśśeḥa: see Yaqob Beyene, "Introduzione," in Feśśeḥa, *Storia,* vii, n. 3.

87. Hailu Habtu, "Fesseha Giyorgis," 361–68; according to Feśśeḥa, this was to be part of a projected larger work. For a discussion, see chapter 5.

88. Feśśeḥa Giyorgis, *Enkab aräbeña etägälbäṭä qäta qäddamot a'eraben enkab iṭalya etägälbäṭä tarik egebäṣen, Storia degli Arabi e degli Egiziani tradotta in lingua tigrai* (Rome: 1897), cited in *EA* 2: 533.

89. Though provisional, there is both internal and external evidence for this dating. First, the author focuses on the nineteenth century but concludes his narrative before the battle of Adwa in 1896, a turning point that figures in many Ethiopian and Eritrean histories from this period. Second, in 1895 Feśśeḥa referred to an unpublished work "on the ancient genealogies Ethiopians reckon their own; on their ancient cities with indications on their toponyms; on the lives of some of their famous emperors and princes, and on the customs of the country." This is surely a version of his *Tarik ityopya.* For the quotation, see Haile Habtu, "Fesseha Giyorgis," 362.

90. See his observations on Yoḥannes's defeat by the Mahdists, after which "Menilek had everything in his hands"; his metaphorical descriptions of the fearsomeness of Tigrayan soldiers and the embarrassing gaffes of Tigrayan disputants before *ras* Mäkonnen; and his refutation of European arguments about the Greek and Egyptian construction of Lalibäla: respectively, Feśśeḥa, *Storia,* 239, 218, 234, and 190.

91. Feśśeḥa, *Storia,* 192, 202–8. Tayyä also pioneered the study of Tigrinya etymologies: see his discussion of Khartoum, Tayyä, *History,* 31.

92. For example, Feśśeḥa describes the rationale behind the Tegrayans' hatred for *ras* Wäbé and love for Téwodros, and then explains why his countrymen ultimately turned upon the doomed emperor. See Feśśeḥa, *Storia,* 203.

93. Feśśeḥa, *Storia,* 206–8; for a subsequent oath-related episode, see 235.

94. On the latter, see Giulia Barrera, "Colonial Affairs: Men, Women, and the Construction of Racial Hierarchies in Colonial Eritrea (1885–1941)" (PhD diss., Northwestern University, 2002).

95. "Yä'éretra gezat ḥezb," in Zäwäld, *Ityopya*, 1–2. This is one the few times Feśśeḥa employs this term.

96. Zäwäld, *Ityopya*, 4–16.

97. Zäwäld, *Ityopya*, 16–20.

98. For examples, see Zäwäld, *Ityopya*, 1, and 9, n. 1.

99. Ḫeruy, *Katalog*, 25; and IES Ms. 326. For additional perspectives on the reception of Feśśeḥa's work, see the various annotations on the manuscript by its readers: Feśśeḥa, *Storia*, 257–58. It is curious that Feśśeḥa lacks an entry in Puglisi, *Chi è*.

100. Ghirmai Negash, *A History of Tigrinya Literature in Eritrea: The Oral and the Written, 1890–1991* (Leiden: Research School of Asian, African, and Amerindian Studies, 1999).

101. For an overview of his life and writings, see *EA* 4: 841–42. Uqbagaber Woldeghiorghis, the author of this entry, has also produced a more comprehensive annotated bibliography: "Abba Takla Maryam Semheray," available at http://eparchyofkeren.com/liturgy/articles.php.

102. This dispute is described in Da Nembro, *Missione*, 384–92.

103. Täklä Maryam Sämḥaray Sälim, *La messe éthiopienne* (Rome: École Typographique, 1937), 3.

104. Täklä Maryam, *Messe*, 2–3. According to the author, this publication was occasioned by the fact that René Graffin, the founder and editor of *ROC*, lost his submissions to the journal. See Täklä Maryam, *Messe*, n.p., "Avant-Propos."

105. Täklä Maryam, *Messe*, 2–3, 8.

106. Täklä Maryam, *Messe*, 9–12. For an example of the prevailing contemporary view, see Donald Attwater, *Eastern Catholic Worship* (New York: Devin-Adair Company, 1945), 94–95. See also *EA* 4: 271–75. For examples of his analysis, see Täklä Maryam, *Messe*, 22, 24, 26–28, 30, 37, and 39.

107. Täklä Maryam, *Messe*, 1, 12. By implication, this meant that his Eritrean Ge'ez Catholic Rite was thus the purest form of Ethiopian Christianity.

108. Täklä Maryam Sämḥaray Sälim, "La Messe Éthiopienne" and "La Messe Éthiopienne (Suite) (I)," *ROC* IX (1933–34): 187–95, 425–44; "La Messe Éthiopienne (Suite) (I[I])" and "La Messe Éthiopienne (fin)," *ROC* X (1935–36): 170–215, 421–32; Täklä Maryam Sämḥaray Sälim, *Messe*; and Täklä Maryam Sämḥaray Sälim, *Règles spéciales de la messe éthiopienne* (Rome: École Typographique, 1936), a supplement to the previous work. Täklä Maryam was one of a handful of non-Western contributors to this journal: see the lists of contributors in *Tables de la troisième série: Tomes I à X (XXI à XXX)* [Contents of *ROC*] (Mesnil: Firmin-Didot et Cie., 1946), n.p., "Table alphabétique des auteurs."

109. Enrico Cerulli, "'Abba' Takla Māryām Samḥārāy ed i suoi studi etiopici," *OM* 22, no. 12 (1942): 516; and Sylvain Grébaut "Abba Takla-Maryam Semharay Selim," *ROC* X (1935–36): 421. Both men knew Täklä Maryam personally.

110. Bairu Tafla, *Troubles and Travels of an Eritrean Aristocrat: A Presentation of Kantibā Gilāmikā'él's Memoirs* (Aachen: Shaker Verlag, 2007). See also Tekeste Negash, "Blatta Gebre Egziabeher," 13; and Taddia, *Intelletuale tigrino*, 22, n. 38.

111. Johannes Kolmodin, *Traditions de Tsazzega et Hazzega: Annales et Documents* (Uppsala: Imprimerie E. Berling, 1914), Vol. 1.

112. *Qäši* Solomon and *qäši* Zär'a Ṣeyon, "Nay wängél berhan ab ḥamasén kämäy ilu käm ze'eton käm etägäleṣän," *Berhan yehun*, ed. Erikksson, 174–86; Lündstrom and Gebremedhin, *Kenisha*, 464–67; and Aren, *Envoys*, 538.

113. Bairu Tafla, *Yoḥannes*, 15–16.

114. Puglisi, *Chi è*, 285.

115. According to Puglisi, Fioretti was an agricultural entrepreneur, restaurateur, and philanthropist who in 1911 acquired a press that had arrived in the colony in 1885. He then started the firm Stabilimento Tipografia Colonial M. Fioretti, a press that specialized in Ethiopian and Arabic scripts. *Il Quotidiano Eritreo* was preceded by *Annuncio Eritrea* and *Notizario Telegrafico Quotidiano*, and after 1935 it became *Nuova Eritrea* and finally *Corriere Eritreo*. For a discussion, see Puglisi, *Chi è*, 130.

116. *Il Quotidiano Eritreo*, December 24, 1933; January 16, 1934; January 21, 1934; and April 29, 1934.

117. *Il Quotidiano Eritreo*, October 22, 1933; and August 19, 1934.

118. *Il Quotidiano Eritreo*, October 22, 1933; November 19, 1933; and September 26, 1934.

119. *Il Quotidiano Eritreo*, October 24, 1933; June 17, 1934; October 28, 1934; and December 16, 1934.

120. *Il Quotidiano Eritreo*, January 14, 1934; and April 17, 1934.

121. Review of *La Grande Illusion* by Norman Angel, *Il Quotidiano Eritreo*, July 27, 1933; "I precursori di Cristofero Colombo," *Il Quotidiano Eritreo*, November 24, 1933; and "Cesare e Cleopatra, amante o prigionera?" *Il Quotidiano Eritreo*, September 8, 1934.

122. "Il Generale Ettore Viganò," *Il Quotidiano Eritreo*, August 26, 1933; "I Rapporti fra l'Italia e l'Etiopia," *Il Quotidiano Eritreo*, November 24, 1933.

123. See for example the obituaries for *käntiba* Gilazgi Uqbaṣeyon and *baḥernägasi* Täwelday Uq^{w}ar, both in *Il Quotidiano Eritreo*, September 3, 1933.

124. On this point, it is significant that this newspaper occasionally published responses to articles that appeared in *Berhanenna sälam*. See for example *Il Quotidiano Eritreo*, September 17, 1934.

125. Kolmodin, *Traditions*, Vol. 1, 111.

126. Kolmodin, *Traditions*, Vol. 2, 198–99.

127. Kolmodin, *Traditions*, Vol. 2, 187–92.

128. Bairu Tafla, *Gilamikael*, 26–27.

129. On this last point, see his discussion of the French merchants "Ḥadino" and "Bulān": Feśśeḥa, *Storia*, 219–21.

130. EMML 1470, 137–44, and 145–200.

131. Respectively, EMML 1470, 154 ("Bäroma yänägäśu qéśaroč käledätä krestos eskä motä pawlos deräs"); 181–84; and 189–94.

132. EMML 1470, 154.

133. For a somewhat similar view, see the brief account of Adwa and its consequences by Kelete, who observed that after Menilek's treaty with the Italians, "we others, [the] men of Ḥamasén, we remain lost." See Kolmodin, *Traditions*, Vol. 2, 202.

134. EMML 1470, 145, 153.

135. EMML 1470, 157.

136. EMML 1470, 155.
137. EMML 1470, 140.
138. EMML 1470, 172.
139. EMML 1470, 173–79.
140. Reid, "The Trans-Mereb Experience," 238–55.
141. EMML 1470, 158.
142. EMML 1470, 158. For the consequences of this turning point, see EMML 1470, 161.
143. EMML 1470, 165.
144. For study of the revolt, see Richard Caulk, "'Black Snake, White Snake': Bāhtā Ḥāgos and his revolt against Italian overrule in Eritrea, 1894," in *Banditry, Rebellion, and Social Protest in Africa*, ed. Donald Crummey (Portsmouth: Heinemann, 1986), 293–310. Bahta does not appear in Afäwärq, *Dägmawi menilek*, or Ḫeruy, *Yäheywät tarik*. He is, however, discussed by Ḫeruy in *Yä'ityopya tarik*, 228–29. For examples of his later significance for Eritreans, see Yeseḥaq Yoséf, *Qäddamot ǧegnu*, 59–72; Puglisi, *Chi è*, 30; and "Skeletal Remains of Dagiat Bahta Ḥāgos Laid to Rest," *Eritrea Profile*, March 10, 2007.
145. For other early but brief treatments, see the accounts of Merid and Kelete: Kolmodin, *Traditions*, Vol. 2, 192–93, 201–2. In the postcolonial period, Gäbrä Mika'él offered a much more detailed study: Gäbrä Mika'él Germu, *Bahta ḥagos.*
146. EMML 1470, 180.
147. EMML 1470, 185.
148. EMML 1470, 187.
149. EMML 1470, 187.
150. EMML 1470, 187–88.
151. This is now a common view among scholars of colonialism: see Douglas Hayes and Gyan Prakash, "Introduction: The Entanglement of Power and Resistance," in *Contesting Power: Resistance and Everyday Social Relations in South Asia*, ed. Hayes and Prakash (Berkeley: University of California Press, 1991), 1–22; and Dagmar Engels and Shula Marks, "Introduction: Hegemony in a Colonial Context," *Contesting Colonial Hegemony: State and Society in Africa and India*, ed. Engels and Marks (New York: I. B. Tauris, 1994), 1–18.
152. EMML 1470, 162–3.
153. EMML 1470, 174.
154. EMML 1470, 142. See also his account of Ethiopian bravery that was delivered by an Italian: EMML 1470, 163–4.
155. EMML 1470, 142.
156. EMML 1470, 199.
157. EMML 1470, 194.
158. EMML 1470, 171.
159. EMML 1470, 137.
160. EMML 1470, 198.
161. Though Gäbrä Mik'a'él had a large personal collection of books, he also makes at least one cryptic reference that suggests he may have used the Asmära mission library, named for Giuglielmo Massaia. The name of the library can be found in the biography of its director, Aquilino da Bergamo: Puglisi, *Chi è*, 22.
162. These can be found in the IES European language collection.

163. Carlo Conti Rossini, *Italia ed Etiopia dal trattato d'Uccialli alla battaglia di Adua* (Rome: Istituto per l'Oriente, 1935). Curiously, this work was not reviewed in *Oriente Moderno*; see only the notice in "Libri sull'Etiopia e sul conflitto Italo-Etiopico," *OM* 16, no. 9 (1936): 534. A contemporary American reviewer called it "the most definitive treatment of the subject that we are likely to get for a very long time." See Robert Gale Woolbert, "Review of *Le origini della colonia Eritrea* by Carlo Zaghi; *Italia ed Etiopia dal trattato d'Uccialli alla battaglia di Adua* by Carlo Conti Rossini; *Ethiopia: A Pawn in European Diplomacy* by Ernest Work," *Journal of Modern History* 9, no. 3 (1937): 387–88.

164. On this, see Conti Rossini, *Italia ed Etiopia*, v: "È la storia degli avvenimenti che ebbero epilogo in Adua."

165. The two works explored a historical reality that was also described in a variety of other sources. This results in a number of similarities between the two, including the role of Yoséf (Conti Rossini, *Italia ed Etiopia* 6, no. 1); Emperor Menilek's response to Weččale (463–464); *ras* Alula (464: "the first and most open adversary of the Italians"); and Italian prestige (57).

166. Conti Rossini, *Italia ed Etiopia.*

167. EMML 1470, 147.

168. Conti Rossini, *Italia ed Etiopia*, 110–18. Conti Rossini sees this episode in terms of regional politics, focusing on its implications for Menilek, Mengeša, and Baratieri. He does, however, mention the "black snake, white snake" aphorism in 114, n. 2.

169. Some would argue that this has political implications. Speaking about the capacity of colonialism to enforce a regime of historical truth, Ranajit Guha suggests that "the discourse of history, hardly distinguished from policy, ends up by absorbing the concerns and objectives of the latter." This means that challenges to colonial knowledge can be seen as challenges to colonial power. See Ranajit Guha, "The Prose of Counter-Insurgency," in *Selected Subaltern Studies*, ed. Ranajit Guha and Gayatri Chakravorty Spivak (New York: Oxford University Press, 1988), 70. Conti Rossini certainly wrote history with a political aim. In *Italia ed Etiopia*, he explains that he sought to understand a national tragedy, and in his preface, he added that he hoped to write a second work that would celebrate the triumph of Italy's civilizing mission in newly conquered Ethiopia. See Conti Rossini, *Italia ed Etiopia*, ix.

170. One of the few discussions of this transitional stage is Alemseged Abbay, "The Assumption of 'A *Colony Equals* to a *Nation*' and the Political Accident in Eritrea," *Africa* 61, no. 2 (2006): 159–88, esp. 182–86.

171. Berhan Abreha, "Mäqdem," 5.

172. The extent to which this is the case is demonstrated by a comparison of Gäbrä Mika'él's work with that of later Eritrean historians. Gäbrä Iyasus Abbay, for example, discussed Emperor Menilek II's struggle with the Italians in generally flattering terms, though he included a poem that subtly critiqued his abandonment of Eritrea; see his *Mäśärät asét ḥezbi märäb mällaš* (Asmära: Kokäb Ṣebaḥ, 1960), 171–75. Uthman Salih Sabbi instead emphasized the primordial nature of Eritrean identity, its historic distinction from Ethiopia, and its many ties to the Muslim world, and showed little interest in the colonial period as a historical subject. See his *The History of Eritrea*, trans. Muhamad Fawaz al-Azem (Beirut: Dar al-Masirah, 1970).

173. Arjun Appadurai, *Modernity at Large: Cultural Dimensions of Globalization* (Minneapolis: University of Minnesota Press, 1996), 178–99.

174. I derive this term from the discussion in Harneit-Sievers, "Introduction," 1–30. This edited collection introduces a typology of the African and Asian "new local historian" and offers numerous case studies.

Chapter 4

1. Ḫeruy Wäldä Śellasé, *Yäle'ult wäyzäro mänän mänged bä'iyärusalémenna bämesr* (Addis Ababa: Täfäri Mäkonnen Press, 1915EC), 10.

2. Ḫeruy Wäldä Śellasé, *Madhärä berhan hagärä ğapan* (Addis Ababa: Goh Ṣebah, 1924 EC), 1–2.

3. Hailu Habtu, "Voyage," 366. The phrasing comes from 1 Kings 10:7.

4. The literature is vast but remains deeply influenced by Mary Louise Pratt, *Imperial Eyes: Transculturation and Travel Writing* (New York: Routledge, 1992).

5. Most famously, Edward Said, *Orientalism* (New York: Vintage, 1979).

6. Mohamad Tavakoli-Targhi, *Refashioning Iran: Orientalism, Occidentalism, and Historiography* (New York: Palgrave, 2001), 35–76; Antoinette Burton, *At the Heart of the Empire: Indians and the Colonial Encounter in Late-Victorian Britain* (Berkeley: University of California Press, 1998); Lisa Pollard, "The Habits and Customs of Modernity: State Scholarship, Foreign Travel, and the Construction of a New Egyptian Nationalism," *Arab Studies Journal* 7, no. 2 (1999/2000): 45–74; Scott Reese, "The Adventures of Abu Harith: Muslim Travel Writing and Navigating the Modern in Colonial East Africa," in *The Transmission of Learning in Islamic Africa*, ed. Scott Reese (Leiden: Brill, 2004), 244–56; Thomas Geider, "The Paper Memory of East Africa: Ethnohistories and Biographies Written in Swahili," in *A Place in the World*, ed. Harnet-Sievers, 255–88; and *Afrique et Histoire* 4, no. 2 (2005), special issue on "Voyageurs Africains."

7. Cf. Muzaffar Alam and Sanjay Subrahmanyam, *Indo-Persian Travels in the Age of Discoveries, 1400–1800* (Cambridge: Cambridge University Press, 2007); and Nabil Matar, ed., *In the Lands of the Christians: Arabic Travel Writing in the Seventeenth Century* (New York: Routledge, 2003).

8. Cf. *Zar'a Yâ'qôb*, 114–18; *Eskender*, 355; *Yohannis*, 7, 295–96, 302.

9. For example, *Sarṣa Dengel*, Vol. 2, 12–16; and *Iyāsu II*, 22. According to Bruce, the latter was also the subject of a derogatory text that described his travels in the city of Gondär as ersatz military campaigns. For a discussion, see Chernetsov, "Crisis," 91.

10. Enrico Cerulli, "Eugenio IV e gli Etiopi al Concilio di Firenze," *RRAL* 6, IX (1933): 353. I thank Matteo Salvadore for alerting me to this reference.

11. Several itineraries were described by the Venetian scholar Alessandro Zorzi (ca. 1470–n.d.), who learned of them from interviews with Ethiopian informants. See O. G. S. Crawford, ed., *Ethiopian Itineraries circa 1400–1524* (Cambridge: Hakluyt Society, 1958).

12. For a comprehensive survey of these contacts, see Matteo Salvadore, *Prester John and the Birth of Ethiopian-European Relations, 1402–1555* (Surrey, UK: Ashgate, forthcoming).

13. *Kebrä nägäśt*, 78, 84.

14. *EA* 3: 364–68.

15. See for example the Solomonic imagery in Meläku Bäyyän's travel poetry: EMML 1610, 41–42.

16. *Lalibala*, xxvii; *EA* 4: 484–88, 2: 469–72.

17. Ernest Wallace Budge, trans., *The Alexander Book in Ethiopia* (London: Oxford University Press, 1933); Cerulli, *Letteratura*, 58–62; and *EA* 1: 195.

18. Getatchew Haile, "Journey to Heaven: The Popular Belief in Reward and Punishment in Ethiopian Christianity," in *Studia Aethiopica in Honour of Siegbert Uhlig*, ed. Verena Böll (Wiesbaden: Harrassowitz Verlag, 2004), 41–65.

19. *Berhanenna sälam*, January 9, 1925, and March 10, 1932, respectively.

20. *A'emro*, September 23, 1933, and November 4, 1933.

21. See for example "S. A. I. le Prince Asfaou héritier du Trône d'Éthiopie s'est embarqué sur le d'Artagnan des Messageries Maritimes," *Courrier d'Éthiopie*, December 11, 1931; and "Voyage a l'exploration forestière de Djam-Djam," *Courrier d'Éthiopie*, November 22, 1929. Lists of arrivals and departures were also common. See for example "L'ambassade Pontificale," *Courrier d'Éthiopie*, November 15, 1929; and the list of departures for Europe that appears in *Berhanenna sälam*, July 15, 1926.

22. For example, "Viaggio in Mare," *Il Quotidiano Eritreo*, December 7 and 14, 1933; "Le avventure Africane di un giornalista Tedesco," *Il Quotidiano Eritreo*, December 22, 1933; and "Dalla Colonia Primogenita alla Città Eterna," *Il Quotidiano Eritreo*, December 27, 1933. This same paper also routinely featured notices on maritime arrivals and departures.

23. Ghirmai Negash has observed that this work is possibly the first printed Tigrinya text: Ghirmai Negash, *Tigrinya Literature*, 77–87. A complete translation of the work can be found in Hailu Habtu, "Voyage"; more general information on the author is provided by Yaqob Beyene, "Introduzione," in Feśśeḥa Giyorgis, *Storia*, vii–xii.

24. See his introductory comments: Hailu, "Voyage," 362. Gallina helped publish several works by Ethiopian and Eritrean authors: see *EA* 2: 662.

25. Afäwärq Gäbrä Iyäsus, *Yä'ityopya mängeśt alga wärašenna endärasé le'ul täfäri mäkonnen yä'aden mängädačäw ak^{w}aḥwan*, 2nd ed. (Addis Ababa: Täfäri Mäkonnen Press, 1918 EC). The precise date of publication is unclear, since this work went through three editions. Rouaud cites both 1922 and 1923 as original dates of publication: Rouaud, *Afä-wärq*, 259 and 340. Wright has it appearing after Ḫeruy, *Mänän:* see Wright, *Incunabula*, 34. Though perhaps academic, the precise chronology would establish which of these is the first published Amharic travel narrative.

26. Ḫeruy Wäldä Śellasé, *Dässetanna keber. Yä'ityopya mängeśt alga wärašenna endärasé le'ul täfäri mäkonnen wädä awropa sihédunna simäläsu yämängädačäw ak^{w}aḫ^{w}an* (Addis Ababa: Täfäri Mäkonnen Press, 1916 EC).

27. Ḫeruy, *Ǧapan*; and Ḫeruy Wäldä Śellasé, *Bä'ädmé mäsänbät hulun lämayät* (Addis Ababa: 1926 EC).

28. Ḫaylä Śellasé, *Ḥeywäténna yä'ityopya ermeğğa*, Vol. 1 (Addis Ababa: Berhanenna Sälam, 1965 EC), especially 61–97.

29. Marse'é Ḫazan, *Germawi neguśä nägäśt qäddamawi ḫaylä śellasé gondären yämägobeñätačäw tarik* (Addis Ababa: Berhanenna Sälam, 1939EC).

30. Many of the era's intellectuals discussed their experiences abroad in diaries, autobiographies, and annalistic notes. Ḫeruy attended the coronation of George V

in 1911: for a discussion of this trip and his account of it, see Bahru Zewde, "Ethiopians Abroad: The Ethiopian Delegation to the Coronation of King George V," in *Proceedings of the XV Conference of Ethiopian Studies, Hamburg 2003*, ed. Siegbert Uhlig (Wiesbaden: Harrassowitz Verlag, 2006), 201–9. *Aläqa* Tayyä kept a journal that partially described his 1905 visit to Europe: it is discussed in Aleme Eshete, "Alaqa Taye," 16–17. Sarkis Terzian, the Armenian advisor to Emperor Menilek, wrote about some of his business trips abroad: his account was printed in Eadie, *Amharic*, 134–62. Rather different are the private letters of Ethiopian and Eritrean prisoners of war, who wrote to friends and family at home from their prison camps in wartime Italy. Many of these are preserved in ASMAI II, Pos. 181, fasc. 54.

31. Ḫeruy Wäldä Śellasé, *Selä awropa mängäd yämeker qal* (Addis Ababa: Täfäri Mäkonnen Press, 1924). For a discussion, see Alain Rouaud, "Le Voyage d'Europe," *Bulletin des études africaines* 17/18 (1992): 51–89.

32. P̣awlos Män Amäno, *Yä'iyärusalémenna yäqeddusat botawoč tarik* (Addis Ababa: Goh Ṣebaḥ, 1925 EC). Map follows the introduction. For details on his work with Gäbrä Krestos, see Strelcyn, "Incunables," 514; and Cohen, "Naissance," 361–62.

33. Afäwärq Gäbrä Iyäsus, *Ityop̣ya: guide du voyageur en Abyssinie* (Rome: Imprimerie C. de Luigi, 1908).

34. For a perceptive discussion, see Rouaud, *Afä-Wärq*, 235–50.

35. Ḫeruy Wäldä Śellasé, *Addis aläm* (Addis Ababa: Goh Ṣebaḥ, 1932).

36. Ḫeruy, *Addis aläm*, 1–4. On the work more generally, see *EA* 1: 91–92.

37. Gebreyesus Hailu, *The Conscript: A Novel of Libya's Anticolonial War*, trans. Ghirmai Negash (Athens: Ohio University Press, 2013).

38. Rouaud, *Afä-wärq*, 144.

39. Ten percent was common. See the following samples from *Berhanenna sälam*: January 1, 1925 (three out of twenty); September 26, 1929 (five out of thirty-seven); and July 25, 1934 (five out of fifty-nine).

40. Lucien Febvre and Henri-Jean Martin, *The Coming of the Book: The Impact of Printing, 1450–1800*, trans. David Gerard (London: Verso, 1997). See also Elizabeth Eisenstein, *The Printing Press as an Agent of Change: Communications and Cultural Transformations in Early Modern Europe* (New York: Cambridge University, 1979), Vol. 1, 71–80.

41. Isabel Hofmeyr, Preben Kaarsholm, and Bodil Folke Frederiksen, "Introduction: Print Cultures, Nationalisms and Publics of the Indian Ocean," *Africa* 81, no. 1 (2011): 1–22. See also Juan Cole, "Printing and Urban Islam in the Mediterranean World, 1890–1920," in *Modernity and Culture*, ed. Bayly and Fawaz, 344–64.

42. For a discussion, see Bahru Zewde, "Japanization," 198–214, esp. 199–201.

43. Ḫeruy, *Ǧapan*, 147–78. According to a citation on page 157, Ḫeruy derived some of this "manners and customs" style information from two sources: H. G. Wells, *The Outline of History* (New York: Macmillan, 1921), and James Scherer, *The Romance of Japan through the Ages* (New York: Japan Society/Doubleday, 1928).

44. Ḫeruy, *Ǧapan*, 157.

45. Ḫeruy, *Mänän*, 8.

46. The articles and their reception are detailed in Antoinette Iadarola, "Ethiopia's Admission into the League of Nations: An Assessment of Motives," *The International Journal of African Historical Studies* 8, no. 4 (1975): 601–22; and Amalia Ribi, "'The Breath of a New Life'? British Anti-slavery Activism and the League of

Nations," in *Internationalism Reconfigured: Transnational Ideas and Movements Between the World Wars,* ed. Daniel Laqua (London: I. B. Tauris, 2011), 101–2.

47. These developments are discussed in Jean Allain, "Slavery and the League of Nations: Ethiopia as a Civilized Nation," *Journal of the History of International Law* 8 (2006): 213–44; the quotation is from the contemporaneous Frederick Lugard, *The Dual Mandate in British Tropical Africa* (Edinburgh and London: Blackwood, 1922), 388.

48. Iadarola, "Ethiopia's Admission," 608.

49. Marcus, *Haile Sellassie,* 48–55.

50. Local debates about slavery are discussed in Bahru Zewde, *Pioneers,* 127–30. One prominent opponent of slavery in Ethiopia was Hakim Wärqäneh, whose wife Q^{w}ä'äla Wärqäneh accompanied Mänän on this trip.

51. Ḫeruy, *Mänän,* 8–9.

52. Ḫeruy, *Mänän,* 9.

53. Ḫeruy, *Mänän,* 9.

54. See Donald Malcolm Reid, *Whose Pharaohs? Archaeology, Museums, and Egyptian National Identity from Napoleon to World War I* (Berkeley: University of California Press, 2002); Israel Gershoni and James Jankowski, *Egypt, Islam, and the Arabs: the Search for Egyptian Nationhood, 1900–1930* (New York: Oxford University Press, 1986), 270–74; and Lisa Pollard, *Nurturing the Nation: The Family Politics of Modernizing, Colonizing, and Liberating Egypt, 1805–1923* (Berkeley: University of California Press, 2005), 53–57, 181–82.

55. Ḫeruy, *Mänän,* 28.

56. Ḫeruy, *Mänän,* 28.

57. Ḫeruy, *Mänän,* 28.

58. Ḫeruy, *Mänän,* 10. The verse Ḫeruy referred to is Acts 8:27. Many centuries earlier, *abba* Ṗetros noted this same episode in his Vatican address: Cerulli, "Eugenio IV," 353.

59. Ḫeruy, *Mänän,* 12–13.

60. Ḫeruy, *Mänän,* 11.

61. Ḫeruy, *Mänän,* 12, 14.

62. Ḫeruy, *Mänän,* 16.

63. On other perceptions of the sacred geography of Palestine, see Ussama Makdisi, "Reclaiming the Land of the Bible: Missionaries, Secularism, and Evangelical Modernity," *The American Historical Review* 102, no. 3 (1997): 680–713. For a discussion of its significance in Ethiopia, see Heldman, "Architectural Symbolism," 222–41.

64. Ḫeruy, *Mänän,* 14.

65. Bose, *A Hundred Horizons,* 268–70.

66. Taddesse Tamrat, "Evangelizing the Evangelized: The Root Problem Between Missions and the Ethiopian Orthodox Church," in *The Missionary Factor in Ethiopia: Papers from a Symposium on the Impact of European Missions on Ethiopian Society, Lund University, August 1996,* ed. Getatchew Haile, Aasulv Lande, and Samuel Rubenson (New York: Peter Lang, 1998), 17–30.

67. Crummey, "The Politics of Modernization: Protestant and Catholic Missionaries in Modern Ethiopia," in *The Missionary Factor in Ethiopia,* ed. Getatchew Haile, Lande, and Rubenson, 85–99.

68. Täfäri Mäkonnen was a paternal cousin of Menilek II, whose grandson and appointed heir *leǧ* Iyyasu was deposed in 1916. Menilek's eldest daughter was then crowned Empress Zäwditu, with Täfäri Mäkonnen serving as the crown prince (*alga wäraš*) and de facto head of government until Zäwditu's death in 1930.

69. Hannah Rubinkowska, "The History that Never Was: Historiography by Ḫaylä Śəllase I," in *Studia Aethiopica in Honour of Siegbert Uhlig on the Occasion of his 65th Birthday*, ed. Verena Böll *et al* (Wiesbaden: Harrassowitz Verlag, 2004), 221–31.

70. For an account, see Marcus, *Haile Selassie*, 97–114.

71. Marse'é Ḫazan, *Gondären yämagobeñataččäw tarik*, 86–97.

72. Ḫeruy, *Ǧapan*, 56–57.

73. Ḫeruy, *Mänän*, 31.

74. Ḫeruy, *Mänän*, 16.

75. Ḫeruy, *Mänän*, 17.

76. Ḫeruy, *Mänän*, 26.

77. Mänän offered financial support to churches and monasteries, and was instrumental in the creation of the Ethiopian Red Cross and the Ethiopian Women's Charitable Association. The steering committee of the latter organization included many Ethiopian women who had traveled to Europe: "Association de Bienfaisance des Femmes Éthiopiennes," *Courrier d'Éthiopie*, August 23, 1935. On Mänän's charitable activities more generally, see Yaréd Gäbrä Mika'él, *Germawit etégé mänän* (Addis Ababa: Artistic Printing Press, 1950EC).

78. Yaréd Gäbrä Mika'él, *Mänän*, 21.

79. Ḫeruy, *Mänän*, 19.

80. Ḫeruy, *Mänän*, 19.

81. Ḫeruy, *Mänän*, 10, 18.

82. Chatterjee, *Nationalist Thought*, 54–84; Lal, *The History of History*, 42; and Di-Capua, *Gatekeepers*, 52–59.

83. Tä'ammrat, "Essay," 63–64.

Chapter 5

1. Käbbädä Mika'él, *Ityopyanna me'erabawi śelləṭṭané, Ethiopia and Western Civilization*, trans. Marcel Hassid (Addis Ababa: Berhanenna Sälam Press, 1941 EC), frontispiece.

2. Käbbädä Mika'él, *Ityopyanna me'erabawi śelləṭṭané*, 15–21.

3. Käbbädä Mika'él, *Ityopyanna me'erabawi śelləṭṭané*, 41–57.

4. Käbbädä Mika'el, *Ityopyanna me'erabawi śelləṭṭané*, 64.

5. Käbbädä Mika'el, *Ityopyanna me'erabawi śelləṭṭané*, 97–103.

6. Käbbädä Mika'él, *Ityopyanna me'erabawi śelləṭṭané*, 92–104.

7. Käbbädä Mika'él, *Talalaq säwoč* (Addis Ababa: Artistic Press, 1963).

8. Käbbädä Mika'él and Jean Leclant, "La Section d'Archéologie (1952–1955)," *AE* 1 (1955): 1–8.

9. The journal featured articles in French and English, with abstracts in Amharic, and its contributors were predominantly foreign scholars, with some exceptions. For contemporary assessments, see "Présentation des *Annales d'Éthiopie*,

par la Direction," *AE* 1 (1955): 15–19; and Lanfranco Ricci, Review of *Annales d'Éthiopie*, *RSE* 17 (1961): 123–41.

10. Käbbädä Mika'él, *Yä'aläm tarik* (Addis Ababa: Artistic Press, 1955). For a glowing review, see Pierre Comba, "Une année de publications en langue amharique," *AE* 2 (1957): 258.

11. Käbbädä Mika'él, *Yä'aläm tarik*, 1–3.

12. One of these was an account of the emperor's visit to North America: Käbbädä Mika'él, *Germawinätačäw bä'amérika agär* (Addis Ababa: Artistic Press, 1951EC).

13. For a perceptive discussion, see Prashad, *Darker Nations*, 65–94, esp. 86–87.

14. Sereke Berhan Gäbrä Egzi'abḥér, "The National Ethiopian Library," *Ethiopian Review* 1 (1945): 17. More generally, see Stephen Wright, "Book and Manuscript Collections in Ethiopia," *Journal of Ethiopian Studies* 2, no. 1 (1964): 22–23; Stephen Wright, "National Libraries in Ethiopia," *University College Review* 1, no. 1 (1961): 13–17; and Stephen Wright, "The National Library of Ethiopia," *Ethiopian Review* 1 (1945): 13–17.

15. Stanislaw Chojnacki, "Some Notes on the Occasion of the 25th Anniversary of the Institute of Ethiopian Studies," in *Silver Jubilee Anniversary of the Institute of Ethiopian Studies*, ed. Richard Pankhurst and Taddese Beyene (Addis Ababa: Addis Ababa University Press, 1990), 27–38.

16. For an overview, see Richard Pankhurst, "I.E.S. Foundation and the First Decade: A Personal View by Dr. Richard Pankhurst, the Founding Director," in *Silver Jubilee*, ed. Pankhurst and Taddese, 11–26.

17. Numerous other journals appeared in this period, including *Tarik* and *Abba Salama*.

18. Francis Anfray, "Le Musée Archéologique d'Asmara," *RSE* 21 (1965): 5–15; and Puglisi, *Chi è*, 133.

19. For a discussion focused on the role of the History Department, see Bahru Zewde, "Ethiopian Historiography: Retrospect and Prospect," in *Silver Jubilee*, ed. Pankhurst and Taddese, 89–95.

20. According to Marṣe'é Ḫazan, Ḫaylä Śellasé had five official *ṣäḥafé te'ezazs*: Wäldä Mäsqäl, Ḥaylé Wäldä Rufé, Wäldä Giyorgis Wäldä Yoḥannes, Täfara Wärq Engeda Wärq, and Aklilu Häbtä Wäld. See the table in chapter 1.

21. Yäréd Gäbrä Mika'él, *Yätarik säw* (Addis Ababa: 1948EC); Yäréd Gäbrä Mika'él, *Mänän*; and Yäréd Gäbrä Mika'él, *Yä'arba amät gʷelmasa aç̌ç̌er tarik* (Addis Ababa: Artistic Press, 1948EC).

22. Yäréd Gäbrä Mika'él, *Yemeṭu bäzena addis abäba* (Addis Ababa: Berhanenna Sälam, 1958EC).

23. Yäréd Gäbrä Mika'él, *Yäfeqer merkoña* (Addis Ababa: Artistic Press, 1950EC).

24. *Yä'amestu yämäkära a'mätat aç̌ç̌er tarik* (Addis Ababa: Berhanenna Sälam, 1937 EC). See also his effort to complete the Goğğam chronicle of *aläqa* Täklä Iyasus, EMML 4802: Girma Getahun, "Goğğam," 8.

25. Marse'é Ḫazan, *Yämäkära a'mätat*, unpaginated introduction. Numerous studies of the colonial period appeared after this work; see also Abdiśśa Aga, *Bä'iṭaliya bärähawoč* (Addis Ababa: New Press, 1969); Mogäs Keflé, *Yämussolini meṣṭir* (Addis Ababa: 1959); and Gärima Taffärä, *Gondäré bägaššaw* (Addis Ababa: Täsfa Gäbrä Śellasé Press, 1959).

26. See for example *La civilisation de l'Italie Fasciste en Éthiopie* (Addis Ababa: Press and Information Office, 1938EC). The charges are detailed in Richard Pankhurst, "Italian Fascist War Crimes in Ethiopia: A History of Their Discussion, from the League of Nations to the United Nations (1936–1949)," *NEAS* 6, no. 1–2 (1999): 83–140.

27. Marse'é Ḫazan, unpublished manuscript; Herodotus, *Yäṭent tarik ḥérodotus*, trans. Marse'é Ḫazan Wäldä Qirqos (Addis Ababa: Artistic Press, 1951 EC); and Marse'é Ḫazan Wäldä Qirqos, *Tarik*. The Herodotus translation went through several editions.

28. Marse'é Ḫazan Wäldä Qirqos, "Mäqdem," in Gäbrä Śellasé, *Menilek*, 5–11.

29. Mahteme Sellasé Wäldä Mäsqäl, *Zekrä nägär*, a massive compilation of documents from the first half of the twentieth century; Käbbädä Tässäma, *Yätarik mastawäša* (Addis Ababa: 1970), an autobiography; Berhanu Denqé, *Yä'ityopya aččer tarik* (Addis Ababa: 1952EC), essentially a *tarikä nägäśt* from Saba and the introduction of Christianity through the Solomonids to the reign of Emperor Ḫaylä Śellasé; and Berhan Mäsqäl Dästa, *Zéna lal yebälal* (Addis Ababa: Berhanenna Sälam, 1951EC), a detailed study of Emperor Lalibäla. On Gärima Taffärä, see above and *EA* 2: 706.

30. Tässäma Häbtä Mika'él, *Yä'amareña mäzgäb qalat* (Addis Ababa: 1951 EC), and Aklilä Berhan Wäldä Qirqos, *Mäṣhét ṭebäb selä ge'ezenna amareña qʷanqʷa tarik* (Addis Ababa: Commercial Press, 1957). The latter also translated a German history of philosophy: *Yäfälasfoč tarikenna śera: yäwäṭatočen a'emro wädä ewqät yämmimära*, trans. Aklilä Berhan Wäldä Qirqos (Addis Ababa: Merḥa Ṭebäb Press, 1954). See also EMML 1368, a history of the Amharic language by Bä'emnat Gäbr Amlak that included a chapter on the history of printing in Ethiopia, discussing the early mission presses, Märḥa Ṭebäb, Goh Ṣebah, and Berhanenna Sälam. According to the author, this work was published by Berhanenna Sälam in 1955.

31. Another was Gezäw Ḫaylä Maryam, director of the National Museum and a contributor to *Annales d'Éthiopie*. He was the author of numerous published and unpublished Amharic histories, and the translator of several archaeological studies. See his "Objects Found in the Neighbourhood of Aksum," *AE* 1 (1955): 47–51; and also *EA* 2: 782.

32. Täklä Ṣadeq Mäkʷeriya, *Yä'ityopya tarik*, 2 Vol. (Addis Ababa: Tenśa'é Zäguba'é, 1951–53EC); and Täklä Ṣadeq Mäkʷeriya, *Aṣé téwodros enna yä'ityopya andenät* (Addis Ababa: Artistic Press, 1981), *Aṣé yoḥannes enna yä'ityopya andenät* (Addis Ababa: Bolé, 1982), and *Aṣé menilek enna yä'ityopya andenät* (Addis Ababa: Bolé, 1983).

33. T. T. Mekouria, "Christian Aksum," *UNESCO General History of Africa*, Vol. 2, ed. G. Mokhtar (London: Heinemann, 1981), 401–22; and T. T. Mekouria, "The Horn of Africa," *UNESCO General History of Africa*, Vol. 3, ed. Ivan Hrbek (London: Heinemann, 1988), 559–74.

34. Beletu Kebede, "Tekle-Tsadiq Mekuria: un grand historien contemporain de langue amharique," *BMEE* 1 (1992): 53–61; and Lanfranco Ricci, "In memoriam: Taklaṣādèq Makuriyà," *RSE* 43 (1999): 213–15. These should be compared with the more critical assessment of him as a "state historian": see Toggia, "History," 322–23.

35. For a discussion of an early debate about the teaching of history at the university level, see Bahru Zewde, *The Quest for Socialist Utopia: The Ethiopian Student Movement, c. 1960–1974* (Woodbridge, UK: James Currey, 2014), 195.

36. Beletu, "Tekle-Tsadiq Mekuria"; Rubinkowska, "Historiography," 229–31.

37. Hudson and Tekeste, "Introduction," in Tayyä, *History*, ii.

38. Yoḥannes Wäldä Maryam, *Yä'aläm tarik käğiwografi gar yätäyayazä* (Addis Ababa: Berhanenna Sälam, 1940EC). See also Asfaw Täfära, *Aččer yä'alem tarik* (Addis Ababa: Neged Press, 1957).

39. Bairu Tafla, correspondence with author, December 4, 2011.

40. IES Ms. 851, proofs of Bairu Tafla, "History for Young Ethiopians."

41. IES Ms. 851, 126. Note about "special emphasis" can be found on page 3.

42. Bairu Tafla, correspondence with author, December 4, 2011.

43. For a survey of this literature, see Bahru Zewde, *Quest*.

44. Thus the EPRP decried the AESM as "fascist," equating it with the Italian colonizer, and its supporters as *banda*, or colonial collaborators. See Teshale Tibebu, "Modernity, Eurocentrism, and Radical Politics in Ethiopia, 1961–1991," *African Identities* 6, no. 4 (2008): 353.

45. The pages of *The Ethiopian Herald* contain countless articles of this sort: for one example, see Aleme Eshete, "Ethiopia and the Bolshevik Revolution (1917–1935)," *Ethiopian Herald*, January 1, 1975.

46. Teshale Tibebu, "Modernity"; and Messay Kebede, *Radicalism and Cultural Dislocation in Ethiopia, 1960–1974* (Rochester, NY: University of Rochester Press, 2008).

47. Addis Hiwet, *Ethiopia: From Autocracy to Revolution* (London: Review of African Political Economy, 1975). The same author subsequently wrote an article that examined the course of the student movement and revolution, surveyed the international situation, called for a revival of the Left Marxist opposition, and critically assessed the emerging literature on the revolution by Ethiopian/Eritrean and foreign analysts. See Addis Hiwet, "Analysing the Ethiopian Revolution," *ROAPE* 11, no. 30 (1984): 32–48.

48. Addis Hiwet, *Ethiopia*, 67, and 83, n. 32.

49. For example, Donald Crummey, "Abyssinian Feudalism," *Past and Present* 89 (1980): 115–38. On the early writings of Dessalegn Rahmato and Eshetu Chole, see Bahru Zewde, *Quest*, 125–27.

50. For early assessments, see John Markakis, Review of *Ethiopia: from Autocracy to Revolution*, by Addis Hiwet, *ROAPE* 2, no. 4 (1975): 122–23; and Bahru Zewde, "Economic Origins of the Absolutist State in Ethiopia (1916–1935)," *Journal of Ethiopian Studies* 17 (1984): 1–29, esp. 4–6.

51. Lapiso Gétahun Delébo, *Yä'ityopya yägäbbar śer'atenna ğemmer kapitalizem 1900–1966* (Addis Abeba: Neged, 1983 EC). See also his *Yä'ityopya rägem yäḥezbenna yämängeśt tarik* (Addis Abeba: Neged, 1982 EC), and "Land Tenure: Underlying Cause of the Ethiopian Revolution," *Proceedings of the Fifth International Conference of Ethiopian Studies*, ed. Robert Hess (Chicago: University of Illinois, 1979), 713–28.

52. Legesse Lemma, "Political Economy of Ethiopia 1875–1974: Agricultural, Educational, and International Antecedents of the Revolution" (PhD diss., University of Notre Dame, 1979).

53. Legesse Lemma, "Political Economy," 146, 151.

54. See for example his discussion of the limited nature of foreign investment in Ethiopia by the imperial aspirants of the late nineteenth century: Legesse Lemma, "Political Economy," 73–74.

55. Legesse Lemma, "Political Economy," 141–45; see also 150, for a discussion of the growing awareness of racism in the United States, as documented in an article in *Berhanenna sälam*, June 16, 1927.

56. See also by the same author, "The Ethiopian Student Movement in 1960–1974: A Challenge to the Monarchy and Imperialism in Ethiopia," *NEAS* 1, no. 2 (1979): 31–46; and "United States Imperialism in Revolutionary Ethiopia: An Illustration of Imperialist Machinations in the Present Epoch," in *The Centenary of Dogali: Proceedings of the International Symposium, Addis Ababa-Asmara, January 24–25, 1987*, ed. Taddesse Beyene, Taddesse Tamrat, and Richard Pankhurst (Addis Ababa: Institute of Ethiopian Studies, 1988), 301–22.

57. Local counterparts to these academic journals also emerged, like the government-sponsored *Meskerem*. It is striking that the venerable *Journal of Ethiopian Studies* continued to produce relatively apolitical scholarship throughout these years, though its publication schedule was erratic.

58. John Markakis and Nega Ayele, *Class and Revolution in Ethiopia* (Nottingham: Spokesman, 1978), Fred Halliday and Maxine Molyneux, *The Ethiopian Revolution* (London: Verso, 1981), and René Lefort, *Ethiopa: An Heretical Revolution?* (London: Zed, 1981).

59. For a discussion of this debate, see Odd Arne Westad, *Global Cold War: Third World Interventions and the Making of Our Times* (Cambridge: Cambridge University Press, 2005), 378–87.

60. For one example, see *Yä'ityopya abyot aśer amätat*, trans. Fantu Śahlé (Moscow and Addis Ababa: Progress Press and Kuraz Press, 1987, which contains translated studies of the Ethiopian revolution, Ethiopian-Soviet relations, and Därg policy by Russian Africanists.

61. Messay Kebede, *Radicalism*.

62. Messay Kebede, *Radicalism*, 3, 37.

63. Bahru Zewde, *Quest*, 271.

64. Gebru Tareke, "The Genesis of Student Radicalism in Ethiopia," *African Review of Books* (March 2009), 4–5.

65. On this point and its relationship to the optimism of "scientific socialism," see also Andreas Eshete, "Modernity: Its Title to Uniqueness and its Advent in Ethiopia," *NEAS* 13, no. 1 (2013): 1–18.

66. Teshale Tibebu, "Modernity," 345.

Conclusion

1. There is some debate about the extent to which anthropological research had direct utility. See Talal Asad, "From the History of Colonial Anthropology to the Anthropology of Western Hegemony," in *Colonial Situations: Essays on the Contextualization of Ethnographic Knowledge*, ed. George Stocking (Madison: University of Wisconsin, 1991), 314–24.

2. Jomo Kenyatta, *Facing Mount Kenya* (New York: Vintage, 1962), xviii. For a discussion, see Wendy James, "The Anthropologist as Reluctant Imperialist," in *Anthropology and the Colonial Encounter*, ed. Talal Asad (Atlantic Highlands: Humanities, 1973), 41–69.

3. Bruce Berman and John Lonsdale, "Custom, Modernity, and the Search for *Kihooto*: Kenyatta, Malinowski, and the Making of Facing Mount Kenya," in *Ordering Africa: Anthropology, European Imperialism, and the Politics of Knowledge*, ed. Helen Tilley and Robert Gordon (Manchester: Manchester University Press, 2007), 173–98. The authors suggest that Kenyatta had Leakey in mind when he spoke of gamekeepers.

4. In part, this debate reflects Edward Said's claim that colonial discourse and knowledge silenced the voices of colonial subjects, advanced in his *Orientalism*. For an overview and critique of this argument, see Daniel Varisco, *Reading Orientalism: Said and the Unsaid* (Seattle: University of Washington Press, 2007), esp. 141–55.

5. See Philip Wagoner, "Precolonial Intellectuals and the Production of Colonial Knowledge," *Comparative Study of Society and History* 45, no. 4 (2003): 783–814.

6. Nicholas Dirks, "Colonial Histories and Native Informants: Biography of an Archive," in *Orientalism and the Postcolonial Predicament: Perspectives on South Asia*, ed. Carol Breckenridge and Peter van der Veer (Philadelphia: University of Pennsylvania, 1993), 279–313.

7. One of them, Narrain Row, a Brahmin from Tamil Nadu, independently wrote an original study of South Indian epigraphy: Wagoner, "Precolonial Intellectuals," 797–804.

8. Quoted in Dirks, "Colonial Histories," 306.

9. Quoted in Dirks, "Colonial Histories," 293.

10. On this process more generally, see Bernard S. Cohn, *Colonialism and its Forms of Knowledge: The British in India* (Princeton, NJ: Princeton University Press, 1996), 16–56.

11. Sadhana Naithani, "To Tell a Tale Untold: Two Folklorists in Colonial India," *Journal of Folklore Research* 39, no. 2/3 (2002): 201–16; and Shahid Amin, "The Marginal Jotter: Scribe Chaube and the Making of the Great Linguistic Survey of India c. 1890–1920," *Occasional Publications of the India International Center* 27 (2011): 1–17.

12. Amin, "The Marginal Jotter," 16.

13. Cf. Tavakoli-Targhi, *Refashioning Iran*, 18–34; Jean-Hervé Jezequel, "Voices of their Own? African Participation in the Production of Colonial Knowledge in French West Africa, 1910–1950," in *Ordering Africa*, ed. Tilley and Gordon, 145–72; and Sekibakiba Peter Lekgoathi, "'Colonial' Experts, Local Interlocutors, Informants, and the Making of an Archive on the Transvaal Ndebele, 1930–1989," *Journal of African History* 50, no. 1 (2009): 61–80.

14. Eike Haberland, *Three Hundred Years of Ethiopian-German Academic Collaboration* (Frankfurt: Frobenius Institute, 1986).

15. "Mäqdem," *Berhanenna sälam*, October 31, 1935. The article is untitled.

16. See the articles "Yäṭor śärawit mäsäbsäb bä'addis abeba" and "Yäṭornat mänfas," both in the same issue, *Berhanenna sälam*, October 31, 1935.

17. Cited in Emanuela Trevisan Semi, "Ethiopian Jews in Europe: Taamrat Emmanuel in Italy and Makonnen Levi in England," in *The Jews of Ethiopia: the Birth*

of an Elite, ed. Tudor Parfitt and Emanuela Trevisan Semi (London: Routledge, 2005), 87.

18. His activities are documented in the ASMAI records of the ministry and governorship; for brief discussions of his career, see Alberto Sbacchi, *Legacy of Bitterness: Ethiopia and Fascist Italy* (Trenton: Red Sea Press, 1997).

19. See for example his series of telegraphs to the Italian Legation on *ras* Gugsa, dated August 27, 1926, September 11, 1926, September 13, 1926, October 2, 1926, and 10 November, 1926, ASMAI I, Pos. 54, fasc. 4; and also his article on General Ettore Viganò, in *Il Quotidiano Eritreo,* August 26, 1933.

20. For a brief discussion, see *EA* 3:1097.

21. For details on this small school, see Lundstrom and Ezra Gebremedhin, *Kenisha,* 236.

22. Enno Littmann, "Erinnerungen an Naffa' wad 'Etmân," *Der Neue Orient* 2 (1918): 588–89.

23. Littmann, "Erinnerungen," 589.

24. Littmann, "Erinnerungen," 589.

25. Lundstrom and Ezra Gebremedhin, *Kenisha,* 230.

26. Littmann, "Erinnerungen," 587–91.

27. Enno Littmann, *Publications of the Princeton Expedition to Abyssinia,* Vol. 1 (Leiden: Brill, 1910), especially xii–xiii.

28. Enno Littmann, *Publications of the Princeton Expedition to Abyssinia,* Vol. 2 (Leiden: Brill, 1910), 285, n. 1; and Littmann, *Publications,* Vol. 1, 305, n. 1.

29. Littmann, *Publications,* Vol. 2, xv.

30. Littmann, "Erinnerungen," 587.

31. Littmann, *Publications,* Vol. 1, 138, fn. 1.

32. Näffa'e Wäd Etman, "Mä'ätäyi," in Enno Littmann, *Publications of the Princeton Expedition to Abyssinia,* Vol. 3 (Leiden: Brill, 1913), xi–xxiv.

33. Littmann, *Publications,* Vol. 2, xiii; and Littmann, "Erinnerungen," 587.

34. Cf. Littmann, *Publications,* Vol. 2, xii: "Although the Abyssinians are very fond of telling and hearing stories and, as I often witnessed myself, pass many a lonely night at their campfires doing so, they are by no means great story-tellers. The dramatic power, the creative imagination, which lend the Persian-Arabian stories their undying charm, are not met with here. These tales are simple, often indeed quite primitive and naive."

35. Littmann, *Publications,* Vol. 2, xiii.

36. Littmann, "Erinnerungen," 589.

37. *Ethiopian Herald,* October 22, 1966 [Mäkonnen Dästa obituary].

38. Carleton Coon, *Measuring Ethiopia and Flight into Arabia* (London: Jonathan Cape, 1936), 28. Coon later explained that he had used a pseudonym for Mäkonnen: Carleton Coon, *Adventures and Discoveries: The Autobiography of Carleton Coon* (Englewood: Prentice-Hall, 1981), 126. They were accompanied on this venture by Coon's wife, Mary, and Waldo Forbes, a Harvard colleague who knew Mäkonnen.

39. The physical measurements of Ḫeruy's skull would have had a dual significance for physical anthropology at that time: they would indicate both racial group and intelligence, then believed to be connected to cranial capacity.

40. Ḫeruy, *Bä'admé,* 2.

41. Coon, *Measuring Ethiopia*, 59.
42. Coon, *Measuring Ethiopia*, 53, 59–61.
43. Coon, *Measuring Ethiopia*, 66–67.
44. Coon, *Adventures*, 97.
45. "Abyssinia and Arabia," *Official Register of Harvard University* 32, no. 3 (1935): 308.
46. Coon, *Measuring Ethiopia*, 60.
47. Coon, *Measuring Ethiopia*, 112.
48. Coon, *Adventures*, 96.
49. On one occasion, Mäkonnen criticized the linguistic incompetence of some British colonial officials who were in their company, and Coon responded by affirming his support for colonial rule in Africa: "we were not ourselves enthusiasts for a glorious emergence of Africa." Mäkonnen viewed this insult as a betrayal, and while the Americans continued to socialize with the British, he retreated to his private quarters to listen to records. See Coon, *Measuring Ethiopia*, 31.
50. For examples, see Coon, *Measuring Ethiopia*, 41, 49, 53, and 62.
51. Coon, *Measuring Ethiopia*, 68.
52. Coon, *Measuring Ethiopia*, 33.
53. Coon, *Measuring Ethiopia*, 33.
54. See Stephen Jay Gould, *The Mismeasure of Man* (New York: Norton, 1981).
55. Carleton Coon, *The Races of Europe* (New York: Macmillan, 1939), 444–58. In this discussion, the author mentions an unpublished article in manuscript, with the title "Contribution to the Study of the Physical Anthropology of the Ethiopians and Somalis," which he describes as "based on a series of 100 Ethiopians and 80 Somalis measured in 1933–1934." See Coon, *Races*, 448, fn. 60.
56. Coon, *Races*, 453.
57. For an overview of the debate surrounding this work, see John Jackson, "'In Ways Unacademical': The Reception of Carleton S. Coon's *The Origin of Races*," *Journal of the History of Biology* 34 (2001): 247–85.
58. These are described in Thomas Zitelmann, "Anthropology and Empire in Post-Italian Ethiopia: Makonnen Desta and the Imagination of an Ethiopian 'We-Race,'" *Paideuma* 47 (2001): 161–79.
59. Coon, *Measuring*, 21.
60. Harvard University Archives, Correspondence with author, January 8, 2013.
61. *Ethiopian Herald*, October 22, 1966.
62. Gebre Yntsino, "The Growing Prominence of Anthropology in Ethiopian Studies: Reflections on Research by Ethiopian Anthropologists," Plenary paper presented at Seventeenth International Conference of Ethiopian Studies, November 2, 2009, Addis Ababa.
63. Täklä Maryam himself noted that he faced numerous difficulties with the publication of his work, most notably the loss of his submitted manuscripts by a journal editor. See his introductory comments in his *Messe*, unpaginated "Avant-Propos."
64. On some of these earlier exchanges, see James De Lorenzi "Red Sea Travelers in Mediterranean Lands: Ethiopian Scholars and Early Modern Orientalism, ca. 1500–1668," in *World-Building in the Early Modern Imagination*, ed. Allison Kavey (New York: Palgrave Macmillan, 2010), 173–200; and Osvaldo Raineri, "Gli studi

etiopici nell'età del Giovio," in *Atti del convegno Paolo Giovio. Il Rinascimento e la memoria* (Como: Soc. Villa Gallia, 1985), 117–31.

65. For one of many examples, see Enrico Cerulli, "Nuove idee nell'Etiopia e nuova letteratura amarica," *OM* 6, no. 3 (1926): 167–73. In this work, Cerulli suggests that Ḫeruy's writing illustrates the features of new Amharic literature and "above all, the mentality of the Abyssinians." See Cerulli, "Nuove idee," 68.

66. Ḫeruy, *Katalog*, 23.

67. On this point more generally, see Steven Feierman, "African Histories and the Dissolution of World History," in *Africa and the Disciplines: the Contributions of Research in Africa to the Social Sciences and Humanities*, ed. Robert Bates, V. Y. Mudimbe, and Jean F. O'Barr (Chicago: University of Chicago Press, 1993), 167–212.

68. Most notably, Georg G. Iggers and E. Q. Wang, with Supriya Mukherjee, *A Global History of Historiography* (New York: Pearson, 2008); Daniel Woolf, *A Global History of History* (New York: Cambridge University Press, 2011); and the five volume *Oxford History of Historical Writing*, ed. Daniel Woolf (New York: Oxford University Press, 2011–12). It must be said, however, that none of these works adequately treat the historical tradition of Ethiopia and Eritrea.

Glossary

(Amharic, Tigrinya, and Ge'ez, unless otherwise noted)

abba	Religious title or term of address, lit. "Father"
abéto	Lord; term of address for someone of importance
abun/abunä	Bishop of Ethiopian Orthodox Church
aläqa	Priest, or honorific denoting learning
amira	Wife of a prince or ruler, feminine form of *amir* (Arabic)
arbäña	Patriot, partisan
aṣé/aṭé	Term of address for emperor
askari	Colonial conscript (Italian, Arabic)
azmač	Military commander or leader
azzaž	Court official
baḥrä ḥassab	Computus
balambaras	Imperial title of sixth rank, lit. "Head of the Mountain/Settlement"
banda	Eritrean irregular militia (Italian)
bašša	Minor imperial title
blatta	Learned title for government officials, second rank
blattén géta	Learned title for government officials, first rank
capo	Chief (Italian)
däbtära	Unordained clergy
däǧǧazmač	Imperial title of second rank, lit. "Commander of the Gate"
eč̣č̣ägé	Administrative head of the Ethiopian Orthodox Church
etégé	Title of the emperor's spouse, as distinct from ruling empress
färänǧ	European or white foreigner, lit. "Frank"
fitawrari	Imperial title of third rank, lit. "Commander of Vanguard"
gäbbar	Tribute payer
gädl	Hagiography
grazmač	Imperial title of fifth rank, lit. "Commander of the Left"

imam	Title of leadership, used in various Islamic contexts (Arabic)
käntiba	Mayor
leğ	Honorific for a young male royal or noble
le'ul/le'ult	Title of member of royal family, "Highness"
liq/liqawent	Senior church scholar(s)
liqä p̣ap̣p̣asat	Archbishop of Ethiopian Orthodox Church
mängeśt	Government, polity
negeśt	Queen
neguś	King
neguśä nägäśt	Emperor, lit. "King of Kings"
qadi	Judge or specialist in Islamic law (Arabic)
qäññazmač	Imperial title of fourth rank, lit. "Commander of the Right"
qés/qäši	Priest
ras	Imperial title of first rank, lit. "Head"
ṣäḥafé te'ezaz	Court historian, later Minister of the Pen
tarik	History
tarikä nägäśt	Dynastic history, lit. "History of Kings"
wäyzäro	Lady
yäḥeywät tarik	Biography, lit. "History of Life"
yä'aläm tarik	World or universal history, lit. "History of the World"
yäneguś näfs abbat	Royal confessor
zämänä mäsafent	Period of imperial disintegration that lasted from the mid-eighteenth to mid-nineteenth centuries, lit. "Era of the Princes"

Bibliography

Archives and Special Collections

Archivio Storico del Ministero dell'Africa Italiana, Ministero degli Affari Esteri, Rome, Italy.
Archivio Eritrea, Ministero degli Affari Esteri, Rome, Italy.
Hill Museum and Manuscript Library, St. John's University, Collegeville, MN, United States.
Institute of Ethiopian Studies, Addis Ababa University, Addis Ababa, Ethiopia.
National Archives, College Park, MD, United States.
Stockholm Stadsarkiv, Stockholm, Sweden.

Published and Unpublished Works

Abdallah, Abd al-Fattah. *Yä'ityopya qäddämotenna tallaq ulamoč tarik.* Addis Ababa: Chamber Press, 2005.
Abdiśśa Aga. *Bä'ṭaliya bärähawoč.* Addis Ababa: New Press, 1969.
Abraham Demoz. "Moslems and Islam in Ethiopian Literature." *JES* 10, no. 1 (1972): 1–11.
"Abyssinia and Arabia." *Official Register of Harvard University* 32, no. 3 (1935): 308.
Achebe, Chinua. *Arrow of God.* New York: Anchor, 1989.
Addis Hiwet. "Analysing the Ethiopian Revolution." *ROAPE* 11, no. 30 (1984): 32–48.
———. *Ethiopia: From Autocracy to Revolution.* London: Review of African Political Economy, 1975.
Afäwärq Gäbrä Iyäsus. *Dagmawi aṭé Menilek.* Addis Ababa: United Printers, 1973.
———. *Ityopya: guide du voyageur en Abyssinie.* Rome: Imprimerie C. de Luigi, 1908.
———. *Yä'ityopya mängeśt alga wärašenna endärasé le'ul täfäri mäkonnen yä'aden mängädačäw ak^{w}aḫ^{w}an.* 2nd ed. Addis Ababa: Täfäri Mäkonnen Press, 1918EC.
Aklilä Berhan Wäldä Qirqos. *Mäṣhét ṭebäb selä ge'ezenna amareña q^{w}anq^{w}a tarik.* Addis Ababa: Commercial Press, 1957.
———, trans. *Yäfälasfoč tarikenna śera: yäwäṭatočen a'emro wädä ewqät yämmimära.* Addis Ababa: Merḥa Ṭebäb Press, 1954.
Alam, Muzaffar, and Sanjay Subrahmanyam. *Indo-Persian Travels in the Age of Discoveries, 1400–1800.* Cambridge: Cambridge University Press, 2007.
Aleme Eshete. "Alaqa Taye Gabra Mariam." *RSE* 25 (1971–72): 26–28.

Alemseged Abbay. "The Assumption of 'A Colony Equals to a Nation' and the Political Accident in Eritrea." *Africa* 61, no. 2 (2006): 159–88.

———. "The Trans-Mareb Past in the Present." *Journal of Modern African Studies* 35, no. 2 (1997): 321–34.

Allain, Jean. "Slavery and the League of Nations: Ethiopia as a Civilized Nation." *Journal of the History of International Law* 8 (2006): 213–44.

Amin, Samir. *Eurocentrism: Modernity, Religion, and Democracy.* Translated by Russell Moore and James Membrez. New York: Monthly Review Press, 2009.

Amin, Shahid. "The Marginal Jotter: Scribe Chaube and the Making of the Great Linguistic Survey of India c. 1890–1920." *Occasional Publications of the India International Center* 27 (2011): 1–17.

Anderson, Perry. *Lineages of the Absolutist State.* London: Verso, 1979.

Andreas Eshete. "Modernity: Its Title to Uniqueness and its Advent in Ethiopia." *NEAS* 13, no. 1 (2013): 1–18.

Anfray, Francis. "Le Musée Archéologique d'Asmara." *RSE* 21 (1965): 5–15.

Appadurai, Arjun. *Modernity at Large: Cultural Dimensions of Globalization.* Minneapolis: University of Minnesota Press, 1996.

Arén, Gustav. *Envoys of the Gospel in Ethiopia: In the Steps of the Evangelical Pioneers, 1898–1936.* Stockholm: EFS Förlaget, 1999.

Asad, Talal. "From the History of Colonial Anthropology to the Anthropology of Western Hegemony." In *Colonial Situations: Essays on the Contextualization of Ethnographic Knowledge,* edited by George Stocking, 314–24. Madison: University of Wisconsin Press, 1991.

Asfaw Täfära. *Aç̣ç̣er yä'aläm tarik.* Addis Ababa: Neged Press, 1957.

Attwater, Donald. *Eastern Catholic Worship.* New York: Devin-Adair Company, 1945.

Austin, Ralph. "Colonialism from the Middle: African Clerks as Historical Actors and Discursive Subjects." *History in Africa* 38 (2011): 21–33.

Bahru Zewde. "The Concept of Japanization in the Intellectual History of Modern Ethiopia," in *Society, State, and History: Selected Essays,* edited by Bahru Zewde, 198–214. Addis Ababa: Addis Ababa University Press, 2008.

———. "Economic Origins of the Absolutist State in Ethiopia (1916–1935)." *JES* 17 (1984): 1–29.

———. "Ethiopian Historiography: Retrospect and Prospect." In *Silver Jubilee Anniversary of the Institute of Ethiopian Studies,* edited by Richard Pankhurst and Taddese Beyene, 89–95. Addis Ababa: Addis Ababa University Press, 1990.

———. "Ethiopians Abroad: The Ethiopian Delegation to the Coronation of King George V." In *Proceedings of the XV Conference of Ethiopian Studies, Hamburg 2003,* edited by Siegbert Uhlig, 201–9. Wiesbaden: Harrassowitz Verlag, 2006.

———. *Pioneers of Change in Ethiopia: The Reformist Intellectuals of the Early Twentieth Century.* Oxford: James Currey Press, 2002.

———. *The Quest for Socialist Utopia: The Ethiopian Student Movement, c. 1960–1974.* Woodbridge, UK: James Currey, 2014.

Bairu Tafla, ed. and trans. *Asma Giyorgis and his Work: History of the Galla and the Kingdom of Sawa.* Stuttgart: Franz Steiner Verlag, 1987.

———, ed. and trans. *A Chronicle of Emperor Yoḥannes IV (1872–89).* Wiesbaden: Franz Steiner Verlag, 1977.

———. *Troubles and Travels of an Eritrean Aristocrat: A Presentation of Kantibā Gilāmikā'él's Memoirs.* Aachen: Shaker Verlag, 2007.

———. "A Turning Point in Ethiopian Historiography from Within," In *Die aethiopischen Studien im 20. Jahrhundert*, edited by Rainer Maria Voigt, 159–82. Aachen: Shaker Verlag, 2003.

Bakhtin, Mikhail. *The Dialogic Imagination.* Translated by Caryl Emerson and Michael Holquist. Austin: University of Texas Press, 1981.

Barber, Karin. "I. B. Akinyẹle and Early Yoruba Print Culture." In *Recasting the Past: History Writing and Political Work in Modern Africa*, edited by Derek Peterson and Giacomo Macola, 31–49. Athens: Ohio University Press, 2009.

Barrera, Giulia. "Colonial Affairs: Men, Women, and the Construction of Racial Hierarchies in Colonial Eritrea (1885–1941)." PhD dissertation, Northwestern University, 2002.

Basset, René, trans. *Études sur l'histoire d'Éthiopie.* Paris: Imprimerie Nationale, 1882.

Bausi, Alessandro. "The Aksumite Background of the Ethiopic 'Corpus Canonum.'" In *Proceedings of the XV Conference of Ethiopian Studies*, edited by Siegbert Uhlig, 532–41. Wiesbaden: Harrassowitz Verlag, 2006.

———. "La *Collezione aksumita* canonico-liturgica." *Adamantius* 12 (2006): 43–70.

Bayly, Christopher, and Leila Tararzi Fawaz, eds. *Modernity and Culture: From the Mediterranean to the Indian Ocean.* New York: Columbia University Press, 2003.

Beinin, Joel. *The Dispersion of Egyptian Jewry: Culture, Politics, and the Formation of a Modern Diaspora.* Berkeley: University of California Press, 1998.

Beletu Kebede. "Tekle-Tsadiq Mekuria: un grand historien contemporain de langue amharique." *BMEE* 1 (1992): 53–61.

Berhan Mäsqäl Dästa. *Zéna lal yebälal.* Addis Ababa: Berhanenna Sälam, 1951EC.

Berhan yeḥun sebkät zanta wédo nehezbi ityopya/Sia la Luce! Prediche, racconti, e spiegazioni edificanti per il popolo etiopico. Asmära: Tipografia della Missione Svedese, 1912.

Berhanou Abebbe. *Haymanot abbaw qäddämot: La foi des pères anciens.* Stuttgart: Steiner Verlag, 1986.

Berhanu Denqé. *Yä'ityopya aççer tarik.* Addis Ababa: 1952EC.

Berman, Bruce, and John Lonsdale. "Custom, Modernity, and the Search for *Kihooto*: Kenyatta, Malinowski, and the Making of Facing Mount Kenya." In *Ordering Africa: Anthropology, European Imperialism, and the Politics of Knowledge*, edited by Helen Tilley and Robert Gordon, 173–98. Manchester: Manchester University Press, 2007.

Beylot, Robert. "Du Kebra Nagast." *Aethiopica* 7 (2004): 74–83.

Bose, Sugata. *A Hundred Horizons: The Indian Ocean in the Age of Global Empire.* Cambridge, MA: Harvard University Press, 2006.

Bowersock, G. W. *The Throne of Adulis: Red Sea Wars on the Eve of Islam.* New York: Oxford University Press, 2013.

Braudel, Fernand. *The Mediterranean and the Mediterranean in the Age of Philip II.* 2 Vols. Translated by Siân Reynolds. New York: Harper Collins, 1966.

Brook Abdu. "Taamrat Emmanuel in Post-Italian Ethiopia." Paper presented at the seminar "Ethiopian Jews under Fascist Rule," New York University Casa Italiana, October 23, 2014.

Budge, Ernest Wallace, trans. *The Alexander Book in Ethiopia.* London: Oxford University Press, 1933.
Bureau, Jacques. "Un fragment de l'histoire du peuple Wollaita d'Afework Gebre-Sellassie." *AE* 15 (1990): 47–81.
Burke III, Edmund. "Towards a Comparative History of the Modern Mediterranean, 1750–1919." *Journal of World History* 23, no. 4 (2012): 907–39.
Burke, Peter. "Western Historical Thinking in a Global Perspective—10 Theses." In *Western Historical Thinking: An Intercultural Debate,* edited by Jörn Rüsen, 15–30. New York: Berghahn, 2002.
Burrow, John. *A History of Histories: Epics, Chronicles, Romances, and Inquiries from Herodotus and Thucydides to the Twentieth Century.* New York: Penguin, 2009.
Burton, Antoinette. *At the Heart of the Empire: Indians and the Colonial Encounter in Late-Victorian Britain.* Berkeley: University of California Press, 1998.
Caquot, André. "Histoire amharique de Grāñ et des Gallas." *AE* 2 (1957): 123–43.
———. "Les 'chroniques abrégées' d'Éthiopie." *AE* 2 (1957): 187–92.
Carmichael, Tim. "Bureaucratic Literacy, Oral Testimonies, and the Study of Ethiopian History." *Journal of African Cultural Studies* 18, no. 1 (2006): 23–42.
Casale, Giancarlo. *The Ottoman Age of Exploration.* Oxford: Oxford University Press, 2010.
Caulk, Richard. "'Black Snake, White Snake': Bāhtā Ḥāgos and his Revolt Against Italian Overrule in Eritrea, 1894." In *Banditry, Rebellion, and Social Protest in Africa,* edited by Donald Crummey, 293–310. Portsmouth, NH: Heinemann, 1986.
———. "Dependency, Gebre Heywet Baykedagn, and the Birth of Ethiopian Reformism." In *Proceedings of the Fifth International Conference of Ethiopian Studies,* edited by Robert Hess, 569–81. Chicago: University of Illinois Press, 1979.
Cerulli, Enrico. "'Abba' Takla Māryām Samḥārāy ed i suoi studi etiopici." *OM* 22, no. 12 (1942): 516–17.
———. "Eugenio IV e gli Etiopi al Concilio di Firenze," *RRAL* 6, IX (1933): 347–68.
———. "Gli abbati di Dabra Libānos, capi del monachismo etiopico, secondo la 'lista rimata' (sec. XIV–XVIII)." *Orientalia* 12 (1943): 226–53.
———. "Nuove idee nell'Etiopia e nuova letteratura amarica." *OM* 6, no. 3 (1926): 167–73.
———. "Nuovi libri pubblicati in Etiopia." *OM* XII (1932): 170–75.
———. *Storia della letteratura etiopica.* Milan: Nuova Accademia, 1956.
Chakrabarty, Dipesh. "A Global and Multicultural "Discipline" of History?" *History and Theory* 45, no. 1 (2006): 101–9.
———. *Habitations of Modernity: Essays in the Wake of Subaltern Studies.* Chicago, University of Chicago Press, 2002.
———. *Provincializing Europe: Postcolonial Thought and Historical Difference.* Princeton, NJ: Princeton University Press, 2000.
Chartier, Roger. *The Cultural Origins of the French Revolution.* Durham, NC: Duke University Press, 1991.
Chatterjee, Kumkum. "The King of Controversy: History and Nation-making in Late-Colonial India." *American Historical Review* 110, no. 5 (2005): 1454–75.
Chatterjee, Partha. *Nationalist Thought and the Colonial World: A Derivative Discourse?* Minneapolis: University of Minnesota Press, 1998.

Chaudhuri, K. N. *Trade and Civilization in the Indian Ocean: An Economic History from the Rise of Islam to 1750.* New York: Cambridge University Press, 1985.

Chernetsov, Sevir. "The Crisis of Ethiopian Official Royal Historiography and its Consequences in the Eighteenth Century." In *Proceedings of the Eleventh International Conference of Ethiopian Studies*, edited by Bahru Zewde, Richard Pankhurst, and Taddese Beyene, Vol. 1, 87–101. Addis Ababa: Institute of Ethiopian Studies, 1991.

———. "The 'History of the Galla' and Death of Za-Dengel, King of Ethiopia (1603–1604)." In *IV Congresso internazionale di studi etiopici*, 803–8. Rome: Accademia Nazionale dei Lincei, 1974.

———. "Medieval Ethiopian Historiographers and their Methods." In *Proceedings of the Ninth International Congress of Ethiopian Studies*, edited by Anatolii Andreevich Gromyko, 191–200. Moscow: Nauka Publishers, 1988.

———. "Who Wrote 'the History of King Sarsa Dengel'—Was it the Monk Bahrey?" In *Proceedings of the Eight International Conference of Ethiopian Studies*, edited by Taddesse Beyene, 131–36. Addis Ababa: Institute of Ethiopian Studies, 1988.

Chojnacki, Stanislaw. "Some Notes on the Occasion of the 25th Anniversary of the Institute of Ethiopian Studies." In *Silver Jubilee Anniversary of the Institute of Ethiopian Studies*, edited by Richard Pankhurst and Taddese Beyene, 27–38. Addis Ababa: Addis Ababa University Press, 1990.

Choueiri, Youssef M. *Modern Arab Historiography: Historical Discourse and the Nation-State.* London: Routledge, 2003.

Clancy Smith, Julia. *Mediterraneans: North Africa and Europe in an Age of Migration, 1800–1900.* Berkeley: University of California Press, 2012.

Cohen, Marcel. "La naissance d'une littérature imprimée en amharique." *Journal asiatique* CCVL (1925): 348–63.

Cohn, Bernard S. *Colonialism and its Forms of Knowledge: The British in India.* Princeton, NJ: Princeton University Press, 1996.

Cole, Juan. "Printing and Urban Islam in the Mediterranean World, 1890–1920." In *Modernity and Culture: From the Mediterranean to the Indian Ocean*, edited by Christopher Bayly and Leila Tarazi Fawaz, 344–64. New York: Columbia University Press, 2003.

Collingwood, Robert George. *The Idea of History.* Oxford: Oxford University Press, 1946.

Comba, Pierre. "Une année de publications en langue amharique." *AE* 2 (1957): 253–64.

Conrad, Joseph. *Heart of Darkness and the Secret Sharer.* New York: Doubleday, 1950.

Conti Rossini, Carlo, trans. "L'autobiografia di Pāwlos, monaco abissino del secolo XVI." *RRAL* 5a, no. 27 (1918): 279–96.

———, trans. *Historia Regis Sarṣa Dengel (Malak Sagad).* Paris: Republic Press, 1907.

———. *Italia ed Etiopia dal trattato d'Uccialli alla battaglia di Adua.* Rome: Istituto per l'Oriente, 1935.

———. "Les listes des rois d'Aksoum." *JA* 10, no. 14 (1899): 263–320.

———. "Storia di Lebna Dengel re d'Etiopia, fino alle prime lotte contro Ahmad Ben Ibrahim." *RRAL* Ser. 5, no. 3 (1894): 617–40.

Conzelman, William, ed. and trans. *Chronique de Galâwdêwos (Claudius), Roi d'Éthiopie.* Paris: Librairie Emile Bouillon, 1895.

Coon, Carleton. *Adventures and Discoveries: The Autobiography of Carleton Coon.* Englewood Cliffs, NJ: Prentice-Hall, 1981.

———. *Measuring Ethiopia and Flight into Arabia.* London: Jonathan Cape, 1936.

———. *The Races of Europe.* New York: Macmillan, 1939.

Crawford, O. G. S., ed. *Ethiopian Itineraries circa 1400–1524.* Cambridge: Hakluyt Society, 1958.

Crummey, Donald. "Abyssinian Feudalism." *Past and Present* 89 (1980): 115–38.

———. *Land and Society in the Christian Kingdom of Ethiopia.* Urbana-Champaign: University of Illinois Press, 2000.

———. "The Politics of Modernization: Protestant and Catholic Missionaries in Modern Ethiopia." In *The Missionary Factor in Ethiopia: Papers from a Symposium on the Impact of European Missions on Ethiopian Society, Lund University, August 1996,* edited by Getatchew Haile, Aasulv Lande, and Samuel Rubenson, 85–99. New York: Peter Lang, 1998.

Da Iseo, Ezechio. *Manuale d'industrie, arti e mestieri ad uso degli indigeni nelle due lingue italiano e tigrigna per cura della missione cattolica.* Asmära: Tipografia Francescana, 1914.

Da Mezzana, Galdino. *La Missione Eritrea affidata ai Frati Minori Cappucini di Milano.* Milan: Tipografia Lanzani, 1912.

Da Nembro, Metodio. *Missione dei Minori Cappuccini in Eritrea (1894–1952).* Rome: Bibliotheca Seraphico-Capuccina, 1953.

Da Offeio, Francesco. *I Cappucini nella colonia Eritrea: Ricordi del P. Francesco da Offeio.* Rome: Tipografia SS. Concez, 1910.

De Lorenzi, James. "Red Sea Travelers in Mediterranean Lands: Ethiopian Scholars and Early Modern Orientalism, ca. 1500–1668." In *World-Building in the Early Modern Imagination,* edited by Allison Kavey, 173–200. New York: Palgrave Macmillan, 2010.

Derat, Marie-Laure. "'Do Not Search for Another King, One Whom God Has Not Given You': Questions on the Elevation of Zärʾä Yaʿeqob (1434–1468)." *Journal of Early Modern History* 8, no. 3–4 (2004): 210–28.

Derat, Marie-Laure. "The Acts of King Lalibala." In *Proceedings of the XVth International Conference of Ethiopian Studies,* edited by Siegbert Uhlig, 561–68. Wiesbaden: Harrassowitz Verlag, 2006.

Dhavan, Purnima. "Reading the Texture of History and Memory in Early-Nineteenth-Century Punjab." *Comparative Studies of South Asia, Africa and the Middle East* 29, no. 3 (2009): 515–27.

Di Porto, Bruno. "La rassegna mensile di Israel in epoca fascista." *La rassegna mensile di Israel* 61, no. 1 (1995): 7–60.

Di-Capua, Yoav. *Gatekeepers of the Arab Past: Historians and History Writing in Twentieth Century Egypt.* Berkeley: University of California Press, 2009.

Dirks, Nicholas. "Colonial Histories and Native Informants: Biography of an Archive." In *Orientalism and the Postcolonial Predicament: Perspectives on South Asia,* edited by Carol Breckenridge and Peter van der Veer, 279–313. Philadelphia: University of Pennsylvania Press, 1993.

Dirlik, Arif. "Is There History after Eurocentrism?: Globalism, Postcolonialism, and the Disavowal of History." *Cultural Critique* 42 (1999): 1–34.

Dore, Gianni. "Catechisti e evangelisti come intermediari culturali nella Colonia Eritrea." In *Governare l'Oltremare: Istituzioni, funzionari e società nel colonialismo italiano,* edited by Gianni Dore, Chiara Giorgi, Antonio Morone, and Massimo Zaccaria, 133–50. Rome: Carocci, 2013.

Drouin, E. "Les listes royales éthiopiennes et leur autorité historique." *Revue Archaéologique* 44 (1882): 99–224.

Eadie, J. I., ed. *An Amharic Reader.* Cambridge: Cambridge University Press, 1924.

Eckert, Andreas. "Historiography on a 'Continent without History: Anglophone West Africa, 1880s–1940s." In *Across Cultural Borders: Historiography in Global Perspective,* edited by Eckhardt Fuchs and Benedikt Stuchtey, 99–117. New York: Rowman and Littlefield, 2002.

Eisenstein, Elizabeth. *The Printing Press as an Agent of Change: Communications and Cultural Transformations in Early Modern Europe.* New York: Cambridge University Press, 1979.

Engels, Dagmar, and Shula Marks. "Introduction: Hegemony in a Colonial Context." *Contesting Colonial Hegemony: State and Society in Africa and India,* edited by Dagmar Engels and Shula Marks, 1–18. New York: I. B. Tauris, 1994.

Eriksson, Olle. *Ahunenna ṭent/Présent et passé.* Asmära: Imprimerie évangélique, 1926.

———. *Alämen eney/Voyons le monde.* Asmära: Imprimerie évangélique, 1924.

Erlich, Haggai, trans. "A Contemporary Biography of Ras Alula: A Ge'ez Manuscript from Manawe, Tamben—I." *BSOAS* 39, no. 1 (1976): 1–46.

———, trans. "A Contemporary Biography of Ras Alula: A Ge'ez Manuscript from Manawe, Tamben—II." *BSOAS* 39, no. 2 (1976): 287 - 327.

Evans, Richard J. *In Defence of History.* London: Granta, 2000.

Ezra Gebremedhin. "Aleqa Tayye: The Missionary Factor in his Scholarly Work." In *The Missionary Factor in Ethiopia: Papers from a Symposium on the Impact of European Missions on Ethiopian Society, Lund University, August 1996,* edited by Getatchew Haile, Aasulv Lande, and Samuel Rubenson, 101–20. New York: Peter Lang, 1998.

Falola, Toyin. *Nationalism and African Intellectuals.* Rochester, NY: University of Rochester Press, 2001.

———. "Yoruba Town Histories." In *A Place in the World: New Local Historiographies from Africa and South Asia,* edited by Axel Harneit-Sievers, 65–85. Boston: Brill, 2002.

Fantu Śahlé, trans. *Yä'ityopya abyot aśer amätat.* Moscow and Addis Ababa: Progress Press and Kuraz Press, 1987.

Fattovich, Rodolfo. "Reconsidering Yeha: c. 800–400 BC." *African Archaeological Review* 26, no. 4 (2009): 275–90.

Febvre, Lucien, and Henri-Jean Martin. *The Coming of the Book: The Impact of Printing, 1450–1800.* Translated by David Gerard. London: Verso, 1997.

Feśśeḥa Giyorgis. *Storia d'Etiopia.* Translated and introduced by Yaqob Beyene. Naples: Istituto Universario Orientale, 1987.

Freitag, Ulrike, and Achim von Oppen. "Introduction: 'Translocality': An Approach to Connection and Transfer in Area Studies." In *Translocality: The Study of Globalising Processes from a Southern Perspective,* edited by Ulrike Freitag and Achim von Oppen, 1–24. Leiden: Brill, 2010.

Fusella, Luigi. "Abissinia e Metemma in uno scritto di Bĕlāttā Hĕruy." *RSE* 3, no. 2 (1943): 200–213.

———. "Il Dāgmāwi Mĕnilĕk di Afawarq Gabra Iyasus." *RSE* 17 (1961): 11–44.

———, ed. *Yaṭé téwodros tarik.* Rome: Sénāto [?], 1959.

Gäbrä Egzi'abḥér Elyas. *Prowess, Piety, and Politics: The Chronicle of Abeto Iyasu and Empress Zäwditu of Ethiopia, 1909–1930.* Translated by Reidulf Molvaer. Cologne: Rüdiger Köppe Verlag, 1994.

Gäbrä Ḥeywät Baykädañ. "L'empereur Menilek et Éthiopie." Translated by Beletou Kebede and Jacques Bureau. *BMEE,* No. 2 (1993): 1–56.

———. *Mängeśtenna yäḥezb astädadär.* Addis Ababa: Berhanenna Sälam, 1923.

———. *The State and Economy in Early Twentieth Century Ethiopia: Gabrahiwot Baykadagn.* Translated by Tenkir Bonger. Lawrenceville, NJ: Red Sea Press, 1995.

Gäbrä Iyasus Abbay. *Mäśärät asét ḥezbi märäb mällaš.* Asmära: Kokäb Ṣebaḥ, 1960.

Gäbrä Krestos Täklä Haymanot. *Aç̣ç̣er yä'aläm tarik bamareña.* Addis Ababa: Berhanenna Sälam, 1924.

———. *Yäquṭer temhert bamareña.* Addis Ababa: Täfäri Mäkonnen Press, 1921.

Gäbrä Mika'él Germu. "Blatta gäbrä egzi'abḥér gilay ṣä'eda krestyan." Copy of an unpublished manuscript from the collection of Ammanuel Germu, Asmära.

———. *Dägyat bahta ḥagos sägänäyti.* 1997.

Gäbrä Śellasé. *Tarik zämän zädagmawi Menilek neguśä nägäśt zä'ityoṗya.* Addis Ababa: Artistic Press, 1959EC.

Gale Woolbert, Robert. "Review of *Le origini della colonia Eritrea* by Carlo Zaghi; *Italia ed Etiopia dal trattato d'Uccialli alla battaglia di Adua* by Carlo Conti Rossini; *Ethiopia: A Pawn in European Diplomacy* by Ernest Work." *Journal of Modern History* 9, no. 3 (1937): 387–88.

Gandhi, Mohandas. *Hind Swaraj or Indian Home Rule.* Ahmedabad: Navajivan Publishing, 2003.

Gärima Taffärä. *Gondäré bägaššaw.* Addis Ababa: Täsfa Gäbrä Śellasé Press, 1959.

Garretson, Peter. *A History of Addis Ababa from its Foundation in 1886 to 1910.* Wiesbaden: Harrassowitz Verlag, 2000.

———. *A Victorian Gentleman and Ethiopian Nationalist: The Life and Times of Hakim Wärqenäh.* Woodbridge, UK: James Currey, 2012.

Gebre Yntsino. "The Growing Prominence of Anthropology in Ethiopian Studies: Reflections on Research by Ethiopian Anthropologists." Plenary paper presented at Seventeenth International Conference of Ethiopian Studies, November 2, 2009, Addis Ababa.

Gebreyesus Hailu. *The Conscript: A Novel of Libya's Anticolonial War.* Trans. Ghirmai Negash. Athens: Ohio University Press, 2013.

Gebru Tareke. "The Genesis of Student Radicalism in Ethiopia." *African Review of Books* (March 2009), 4–5.

Geider, Thomas. "The Paper Memory of East Africa: Ethnohistories and Biographies Written in Swahili," in *A Place in the World,* edited by Axel Harneit-Sievers, 255–88. Boston: Brill, 2002.

Gershoni, Israel, and James Jankowski. *Egypt, Islam, and the Arabs: the Search for Egyptian Nationhood, 1900–1930.* New York: Oxford University Press, 1986.

Getatchew Haile. "Journey to Heaven: The Popular Belief in Reward and Punishment in Ethiopian Christianity." In *Studia Aethiopica in Honour of Siegbert Uhlig,* edited by Verena Böll, 41–65. Wiesbaden: Harrassowitz Verlag, 2004.

———. "The *Kəbrä Nägäśt* Revisited." *Oriens Christianus* 93 (2009): 127–34.

———, ed. and trans. *Yä'abba baḥrey dersätoč oromočen kämmimmäläkkätu léloč sänädoč gara.* Avon, MN: self published, 2002.

Gezäw Ḫaylä Maryam. "Objects Found in the Neighbourhood of Aksum." *AE* 1 (1955): 47–51.

Ghirmai Negash. *A History of Tigrinya Literature in Eritrea: The Oral and the Written, 1890–1991.* Leiden: Research School of Asian, African, and Amerindian Studies, 1999.

Ghosh, Amitav. *In An Antique Land: History in the Guise of a Traveler's Tale.* New York: Vintage, 1994.

Ginzburg, Carlo. *The Judge and the Historian: Marginal Notes on a Late-Twentieth Century Miscarriage of Justice.* Translated by Antony Shugaar. New York: Verso, 1999.

Ginzburg, Carlo, and Carlo Poni. "The Name and the Game: Unequal Exchange and the Historiographical Marketplace." In *Microhistory and the Lost Peoples of Europe,* edited by Edward Muir and Guido Ruggiero, 1–10. Translated by Eren Branch. Baltimore, MD: Johns Hopkins University Press, 1991.

Girma Getahun. "The Goǧǧam Chronicle: Introduction with Edition, Translation, and Annotation of Select Chapters." PhD dissertation, Oxford University, 1991.

Gordon, David C. *Self-Determination and History and the Third World.* Princeton, NJ: Princeton University Press, 1973.

Gould, Stephen Jay. *The Mismeasure of Man.* New York: Norton, 1981.

Grébaut, Sylvain. "Abba Takla-Maryam Semharay Selim," *ROC* X (1935–36): 421.

Guha, Ranajit. *Dominance without Hegemony: History and Power in Colonial India.* Cambridge, MA: Harvard University Press, 1997.

———. *History at the Limit of World-History.* New York: Columbia University Press, 2002.

———. "The Prose of Counter-Insurgency," in *Selected Subaltern Studies,* edited by Ranajit Guha and Gayatri Chakravorty Spivak, 45–86. New York: Oxford University Press, 1988.

Guha, Sumit. "Speaking Historically: The Changing Voices of Historical Narration in Western India, 1400–1900." *American Historical Review* 109, no. 4 (2004): 1084–1103.

Guidi, Ignazio, trans. *Annales Iohannis I, Iyāsu I, Bakāffā.* Paris: Republic Press, 1903.

———, trans. *Annales Regum Iyasu II et Iyo'as.* Paris: 1910.

———. "Due nuovi manoscritti della 'cronaca abbreviata' di Abissinia." *RRAL* 6, no. 2 (1926): 357–421.

———. "La cronaca di Galāwdēwos o Claudio re di Abissinia (1540–1559)." In *Actes du douzième congrès international des orientalistes, Rome 1899,* Vol. 3, 111–15. Florence: Société Typographique Florentine, 1899.

———. "Le liste dei metropoliti d'Abissinia." *Bessarione: Publicazione periodica di studi orientali* 4, no. 37–38 (July–August 1899): 1–16.

Gusarova, Ekaterina. "The Oromo as Recorded in Ethiopian Literature." In *Proceedings of the 16th International Conference of Ethiopian Studies*, edited by Svein Ege, Harald Aspen, Birhanu Teferra, and Shiferaw Bekele, 1323–31. Trondheim, Norway: Norwegian University of Science and Technology, 2009.

Haberland, Eike. *Three Hundred Years of Ethiopian-German Academic Collaboration.* Frankfurt: Frobenius Institute, 1986.

Hailu Habtu. "The Voyage of Däbtära Fesseha Giyorgis to Italy at the End of the 19th Century." *AE* 16 (2000): 361–68.

Halliday, Fred, and Maxine Molyneux. *The Ethiopian Revolution.* London: Verso, 1981.

Harneit-Sievers, Axel. "Introduction: New Local Historiographies in Africa and Asia: Approaches and Issues." In *A Place in the World: New Local Historiographies from Africa and South Asia*, edited by Axel Harneit-Sievers, 1–30. Boston: Brill, 2002.

Hartog, François. "Time, History and the Writing of History: The *Order* of Time." *KVHAA Konferenser* 37 (1996): 95–113.

Hassen, Mohammed. "Revisiting Abba Bahrey's 'the News of the Galla.'" *International Journal of African Historical Studies* 45, no. 2 (2012): 273–94.

Hatke, George. "Africans in Arabia Felix: Aksumite Relations with Ḥimyar in the Sixth Century CE." PhD dissertation, Princeton University, 2011.

Hawlbachs, Maurice. *The Collective Memory.* New York: Harper & Row, 1980.

Hayes, Douglas, and Gyan Prakash. "Introduction: The Entanglement of Power and Resistance." In *Contesting Power: Resistance and Everyday Social Relations in South Asia*, edited by Douglas Hayes and Gyan Prakash, 1–22. Berkeley: University of California Press, 1991.

Ḫaylä Śellasé. *Ḥeywäténna yä'ityopya ermeǧǧa.* Vol. 1. Addis Ababa: Berhanenna Sälam, 1965EC).

Heden, Karl. *Yäḥezboč ameleko anwänwäračäwenna yäwängél śera käšanqelločenna kähendoč käčinočem käǧapanočem kälélož ḥezbočem zänd endét mahonun yämminager.* Translated by Olle Eriksson. Addis Ababa: Goh Ṣebah, 1935.

Heldman, Marilyn. "Architectural Symbolism, *Sacred Geography*, and the Ethiopian Church." *Journal of Religion in Africa* 22, no. 3 (1992): 222–41.

Herodotus. *Yäṭent tarik ḥérodotus.* Translated by Marse'é Ḫazan Wäldä Qirqos. Addis Ababa: Artistic Press, 1951EC.

Ḫeruy Wäldä Śellasé. *Addis aläm.* Addis Ababa: Goh Ṣebaḥ, 1932.

———. *Bä'ädmé mäsänbät hulun lämayät.* Addis Ababa: 1926EC.

———. *Bä'ityopya yämmigäñu bäge'ezenna bamariña $q^{w}anq^{w}a$ yätäṣafu yämäṣaḥeft katalog.* Addis Ababa: Täfäri Mäkonnen Press, 1920EC.

———. *Bä'ityopya yämmigäñu yämäṣaḥeft quṭer.* Addis Ababa: 1904EC.

———. *Dessetanna keber. Yä'ityopya mängeśt alga wärašenna endärasé le'ul täfäri mäkonnen wädä awropa sihédunna simäläsu yämängädačäw $ak^{w}aḫ^{w}an$.* Addis Ababa: Täfäri Mäkonnen Press, 1916EC.

———. *Madhärä berhan hagärä ǧapan.* Addis Ababa: Goh Ṣebah, 1924.

———. *Selä awropa mängäd yämeker qal.* Addis Ababa: Täfäri Mäkonnen Press, 1924.

———. *Wazéma: Bämagestu yä'ityopyan nägäśtat yätarik bä'al lämakebbär.* Addis Ababa: Goh Ṣebah: 1926EC.

———. *Yä'ityopya tarik känegešt saba esk tallaqu yä'adwa del.* Addis Ababa: Central Printing Press, 2006.

———. *Yäheywät tarik (Biographie) bäḫʷala zämän lämminäšu leğoč mastawäqiya.* Addis Ababa: 1922.

———. *Yäle'ult wäyzäro mänän mänged bä'iyärusalémenna bämesr.* Addis Ababa: Täfäri Mäkonnen Press, 1915EC.

Hirsch, Bertrand, and François-Xavier Fauvelle-Aymar. "Aksum après Aksum. Royauté, archéologie et herméneutique chrétienne de Ménélik II (r. 1865–1913) à Zära Yaqob (r. 1434–1468)." *AE* 17 (2001): 59–109.

Hobsbawm, Eric. *How to Change the World: Reflections on Marx and Marxism.* New Haven, CT: Yale University Press, 2011.

Hofmeyr, Isabel, Preben Kaarsholm, and Bodil Folke Frederiksen. "Introduction: Print Cultures, Nationalisms and Publics of the Indian Ocean." *Africa* 81, no. 1 (2011): 1–22.

Hopkins, A. G., ed., *Globalization in World History.* New York: Norton, 2002.

Hunt, Lynn. *Measuring Time, Making History.* New York: Central European University Press, 2008.

Hussein Ahmed. "The Chronicle of Menilek II of Ethiopia: A Brief Assessment of its Versions." *JES* 16 (1983): 75–86.

Iadarola, Antoinette. "Ethiopia's Admission into the League of Nations: An Assessment of Motives." *The International Journal of African Historical Studies* 8, no. 4 (1975): 601–22.

Iggers, Georg. *Historiography in the Twentieth Century: From Scientific Objectivity to Postmodern Challenge.* Hanover: Wesleyan University, 1997.

Iwarson, Jonas, and Alessandro Tron. *Notizie storiche e varie sulla missione evangelica svedese dell'Eritrea, 1866–1916.* Asmära: Missione Evangelica Svedese, 1918.

Iwarson, Jonas. "A Moslem Mass Movement Toward Christianity in Abyssinia." *The Muslim World* 14, no. 3 (1924): 286–89.

Jackson, John. "'In Ways Unacademical': The Reception of Carleton S. Coon's *The Origin of Races.*" *Journal of the History of Biology* 34 (2001): 247–85.

James, Wendy. "The Anthropologist as Reluctant Imperialist." In *Anthropology and the Colonial Encounter,* edited by Talal Asad, 41–69. New York: Humanities, 1973.

Jezequel, Jean-Hervé. "Voices of their Own? African Participation in the Production of Colonial Knowledge in French West Africa, 1910–1950." In *Ordering Africa: Anthropology, European Imperialism, and the Politics of Knowledge,* edited by Helen Tilley and Robert Gordon, 145–72. Manchester: Manchester University Press, 2007.

Johnson, David. "Dating the Kebra Nagast: Another Look." In *Peace and War in Byzantium: Essays in Honor of George T. Dennis,* edited by Timothy Miller and John Nesbitt, 197–208. Washington, DC: Catholic University of America Press, 1995.

Jonas, Raymond. *The Battle of Adwa: African Victory in the Age of Empire.* Cambridge, MA: Harvard University Press, 2011.

Jones, Adam. "Epilogue: Academic and Other Historians—An Uneasy Relationship." In *A Place in the World: New Local Historiographies from Africa and South Asia,* edited by Axel Harneit-Sievers, 366–74. Boston: Brill, 2002.

Käbbädä Mika'él. *Ityopyanna me'erabawi śellaṭané, Ethiopia and Western Civilization.* Translated by Marcel Hassid. Addis Ababa: Berhanenna Sälam Press, 1941EC.

———. *Talalaq säwoč.* Addis Ababa: Artistic Press, 1963.

———. *Yä'aläm tarik.* Addis Ababa: Artistic Press, 1955.

Käbbädä Mika'él, and Jean Leclant. "La Section d'Archéologie (1952–1955)." *AE* 1 (1955): 1–8.

Käbbädä Tässäma. *Yätarik mastawäša.* Addis Ababa: 1970.

Kamil, Murad. "Translations from Arabic into Ethiopian Literature." *Bulletin de la société d'archéologie Copte* 7 (1941): 61–71.

Karrar, Ali Salih, Yahya Muhammad Ibrahim, and R. S. O'Fahey. "The Life and Writings of a Sudanese Historian: Muḥammad ʿAbd al-Raḥīm (1878–1966)." *Sudanic Africa* 6 (1995): 125–36.

Kenfé [*aläqa*]. *Cent fables amhariques.* Translated and annotated by Martino Mario Moreno. Paris: Imprimerie Nationale, 1948.

Kennedy, Dane. *Islands of White: Settler Society and Culture in Kenya and Southern Rhodesia, 1890–1939.* Durham, NC: Duke University Press, 1987.

Kenyatta, Jomo. *Facing Mount Kenya.* New York: Vintage, 1962.

Killion, Tom. *Historical Dictionary of Eritrea.* Lanham: Scarecrow, 1998.

Kolmodin, Johannes. *Traditions de Tsazzega et Hazzega: Annales et Documents.* Uppsala: Imprimerie E. Berling, 1914.

Kropp, Manfred, trans. *Die äthiopischen Königschroniken in der Sammlung des Däğğazmač Haylu.* New York: Peter Lang, 1989.

———, trans. *Die Geschichte des Lebna-Dengel, Claudius und Minās.* Leuven: E. Peeters, 1988.

———. "An Hypothesis Concerning an Author or Compiler of the 'Short Chronicle' of the Ethiopian Kings." In *Proceedings of the Sixth International Conference of Ethiopian Studies, Tel Aviv, 14–17 April, 1980,* edited by Gideon Goldenberg, 359–72. Boston: Balkema, 1986.

———. "La réédition des chroniques éthiopiennes: perspéctives et premiers resultats." *Abbay* 12 (1983–84): 49–72.

———. "La théologie au service de la rébellion: Chroniques inédites du ras Mika'él." In *Actes de la Xe conférence internationale des études éthiopiennes, Paris 24–28 Août 1988,* edited by Claude Lepage and Étienne Delage, 225–36. Paris: Société française pour les études éthiopiennes, 1994.

———, trans. "Petite histoire de Yohannès Ier 'Retrouvée dans un autre pays.'" *AE* 15 (1990): 85–109.

———. "Un cas de censure politique au XVIIe siècle: la chronique de Śarṣa-Dəngəl." *AE* XVII (2001): 257–77.

La civilisation de l'Italie fasciste en Éthiopie. Addis Ababa: Press and Information Office, 1938EC.

Lal, Vinay. *The History of History: Politics and Scholarship in Modern India.* New Delhi: Oxford University Press, 2003.

Lapiso Gétahun Delébo. "Land Tenure: Underlying Cause of the Ethiopian Revolution." In *Proceedings of the Fifth International Conference of Ethiopian Studies,* edited by Robert Hess, 713–28. Chicago: University of Illinois Press, 1979.

———. *Yä'ityopya rägem yäḥezbenna yämängeśt tarik.* Addis Abeba: Neged, 1982EC.

———. *Yä'ityopya yägäbbar šer'atenna ǧemmer kapitalizem 1900–1966.* Addis Abeba: Neged, 1983EC.

Launhardt, Johannes. *Evangelicals in Addis Ababa (1919–1991): With Special Reference to the Ethiopian Evangelical Church Mekane Yesus and the Addis Ababa Synod.* Münster: Lit Verlag, 2004.

Lawrance, Benjamin, Emily Lynn Osborn, and Richard Roberts, eds. *Intermediaries, Interpreters, and Clerks: African Employees in the Making of Colonial Africa.* Madison: University of Wisconsin Press, 2006.

Lefort, René. *Ethiopia: An Heretical Revolution?* London: Zed, 1981.

Legesse Lemma. "The Ethiopian Student Movement in 1960–1974: A Challenge to the Monarchy and Imperialism in Ethiopia." *NEAS* 1, no. 2 (1979): 31–46.

———. "Political Economy of Ethiopia 1875–1974: Agricultural, Educational, and International Antecedents of the Revolution." PhD dissertation, University of Notre Dame, 1979.

———. "United States Imperialism in Revolutionary Ethiopia: An Illustration of Imperialist Machinations in the Present Epoch." In *The Centenary of Dogali: Proceedings of the International Symposium, Addis Ababa-Asmara, January 24–25, 1987,* edited by Taddesse Beyene, Taddesse Tamrat, and Richard Pankhurst, 301–22. Addis Ababa: Institute of Ethiopian Studies, 1988.

Lekgoathi, Sekibakiba Peter. "'Colonial' Experts, Local Interlocutors, Informants, and the Making of an Archive on the Transvaal Ndebele, 1930–1989." *Journal of African History* 50, no. 1 (2009): 61–80.

Levine, Donald. "Simmel at a Distance: On the History and Systematics of the Sociology of the Stranger." In *Strangers in African Societies,* edited by William Shack and Elliot Skinner, 21–36. Berkeley: University of California Press, 1979.

Littmann, Enno. "Erinnerungen an Naffa' wad 'Etmân." *Der Neue Orient* 2 (1918): 588–89.

———, ed. *Publications of the Princeton Expedition to Abyssinia.* 3 Vols. Leiden: Brill, 1910–13.

———, ed. *Yätéwodros tarik.* New York: Scribner, 1902.

Louzon, R. "Le fascisme risquera-t-il la guerre? Le dogue en cage." *La révolution prolétarienne: revue mensuelle syndicaliste communiste.* No. 24 (December, 1926): 1–6.

Lugard, Frederick. *The Dual Mandate in British Tropical Africa.* London: Blackwood, 1922.

Lundström, Karl Johan and Ezra Gebremedhin. *Kenisha: The Roots and Development of the Evangelical Church of Eritrea, 1866–1935.* Trenton, NJ: Red Sea Press, 2011.

Maḫtämä Sellasé Wäldä Mäsqäl. *Zekrä nägär.* Addis Ababa: Berhanenna Sälam, 1962.

Maimire Mennasemay. "Utopia and Ethiopia: The Chronicles of Lalibela as Critical Reflection." *NEAS* 12, no. 2 (2013): 95–121.

Makdisi, Ussama. "Reclaiming the Land of the Bible: Missionaries, Secularism, and Evangelical Modernity." *The American Historical Review* 102, no. 3 (1997): 680–713.

Marcus, Harold. *Haile Selassie I: The Formative Years, 1892–1936.* Trenton, NJ: Red Sea Press, 1995.

Markakis, John. Review of *Ethiopia: from Autocracy to Revolution*, by Addis Hiwet. *ROAPE* 2, no. 4 (1975): 122–23.

Markakis, John, and Nega Ayele. *Class and Revolution in Ethiopia*. Nottingham: Spokesman, 1978.

Marrassini, Paolo. "'I possenti di Rom': i turchi ottomani nella letteratura etiopica." In *Turcica et Islamica: Studia in memoria di Aldo Gallota*, edited by Ugo Marazzi, 593–622. Naples: Università degli Studi di Napoli "L'Orientale," 2003.

Marse'é Ḫazan Wäldä Qirqos. *Germawi neguśä nägäśt qäddamawi ḫaylä śellasé gondären yämägobeñätačäw tarik*. Addis Ababa: Berhanenna Sälam, 1939EC.

———. *Of What I Saw and Heard: The Last Years of Emperor Menilek II and the Brief Rule of Iyassu*. Introduced by Gérard Prunier and translated by Hailu Habtu. Addis Ababa: Centre Français des Études Éthiopiennes and Zamra Publishers, 2006.

———. Unpublished manuscript. In author's collection.

———. *Yä'amestu yämäkära a'mätat aččer tarik*. Addis Ababa: Berhanenna Sälam, 1937EC.

Martínez d'Alòs-Moner, Andreu. "Conquistadores, Mercenaries and Missionaries: The Failed Portuguese Dominion of the Red Sea." *NEAS* 12, no. 1 (2012): 1–28.

Matar, Nabil, ed. *In the Lands of the Christians: Arabic Travel Writing in the Seventeenth Century*. New York: Routledge, 2003.

McCann, Jim. "The Ethiopian Chronicles: An African Documentary Tradition." *NEAS* 1, no. 2 (1979): 47–61.

McCaskie, T. C. "Asante Origins, Egypt, and the Near East." In *Recasting the Past: History Writing and Political Work in Modern Africa*, edited by Derek Peterson and Giacomo Macola, 125–48. Athens: Ohio University Press, 2009.

Messay Kebede. "Gebrehiwot Baykedagn, Eurocentrism, and the Decentering of Ethiopia." *Journal of Black Studies* 36, no. 6 (2006): 815–32.

———. *Radicalism and Cultural Dislocation in Ethiopia, 1960–1974*. Rochester, NY: University of Rochester Press, 2008.

———. *Survival and Modernization, Ethiopia's Enigmatic Present: a Philosophical Discourse*. Lawrenceville, NJ: Red Sea Press, 1999.

Metcalf, Thomas. *India and the Indian Ocean Arena, 1860–1920*. Berkeley: University of California Press, 2007.

Miller, Joseph. "History and Africa/Africa and History." *American Historical Review* 104, no. 1 (1999): 1–32.

Miran, Jonathan. "Missionaries, Education, and the State in the Italian Colony of Eritrea." In *Christian Missionaries and the State in the Third World*, edited by Holger Bernt Hansen and Michael Twaddle, 121–35. Athens: Ohio University Press, 2002.

———. *Red Sea Citizens: Cosmopolitan Society and Cultural Change in Massawa*. Bloomington: Indiana University Press, 2009.

———. "Space, Mobility, and Translocal Connections across the Red Sea Area since 1500." *NEAS* 12, no. 1 (2012): ix–xxvi.

Mogäs Keflé. *Yämussolini meṣṭir*. Addis Ababa: 1959.

Mondon-Vidalhait, Casimir, trans. *Chronique de Théodoros II roi des rois d'Éthiopie*. Paris: E. Guilmoto, 1905.

Morin, Didier. "Orality in the Chronicle of King Tewodros II." In *Proceedings of the 16th International Conference of Ethiopian Studies*, edited by Svein Ege, Harald Aspen, Birhanu Teferra, and Shiferaw Bekele, 1333–38. Trondheim, Norway: Norwegian University of Science and Technology, 2009.

Munro-Hay, Stuart. "A Sixth Century Kebra Nagast?" *AE* 17 (2001): 43–58.

Näffa'e Wad Etman. "Mä'atäyi." In *Publications of the Princeton Expedition to Abyssinia*, edited by Enno Littmann, Vol. 3, xi–xxiv. Leiden: Brill, 1913.

Naipaul, V. S. *A Bend in the River.* New York: Vintage, 1980.

Naithani, Sadhana. "To Tell a Tale Untold: Two Folklorists in Colonial India." *Journal of Folklore Research* 39, no. 2/3 (2002): 201–16.

Nandy, Ashis. "History's Forgotten Doubles." *History and Theory* 34, no. 2 (1995): 44–66.

Novick, Peter. *That Noble Dream: The "Objectivity Question" and the American Historical Profession.* New York: Cambridge University Press, 1988.

Occhini, Pier Ludovico. *Viaggi.* Città di Castello: S. Lapi, 1908.

Pagine d'Apostolato nell' Eritrea: omaggio ai nostri benefattori. Asmära: Tipografia Francescana, 1917.

Palma, Silvana. "Educare alla subalternità: Prassi e politiche scholastiche nella colonia eritrea." In *L'Africa orientale italiana nel dibattito storico contemporaneo*, edited by Bianca Maria Carcangiu and Tekeste Negash, 211–38. Rome: Carocci, 2007.

Pankhurst, Richard. "The Foundations of Education, Printing, Newspapers, Book Production, Libraries, and Literacy in Ethiopia." *Ethiopia Observer* 6, no. 3 (1962): 241–92.

———. "I.E.S. Foundation and the First Decade: A Personal View by Dr. Richard Pankhurst, the Founding Director." In *Silver Jubilee Anniversary of the Institute of Ethiopian Studies*, edited by Richard Pankhurst and Taddese Beyene, 11–26. Addis Ababa: Addis Ababa University Press, 1990.

———. "Italian Fascist War Crimes in Ethiopia: A History of Their Discussion, from the League of Nations to the United Nations (1936–1949)." *NEAS* 6, no. 1–2 (1999): 83–140.

———. "Tedla Haile and the Problem of Multi-ethnicity in Ethiopia." *NEAS* 5, no. 3 (1998): 81–96.

———. "Two Early Periodical Publications 'Djibouti' and 'Le Semeur d'Éthiopie' as Sources for Late 19th Century and Early 20th Century Ethiopian history." *AE* 19 (2003): 231–56.

Paoli, Renato. *Nella colonia Eritrea.* Milan: Fratelli Treves, 1908.

Paulos Milkias. "Traditional Institutions and Traditional Elites: The Role of Education in the Ethiopian Body-Politic." *African Studies Review* 19, no. 3 (1976): 79–93.

P̣awlos Män Amäno. *Yä'iyärusalémenna yäqeddusat botawoč tarik.* Addis Ababa: Goḥ Ṣebaḥ, 1925EC.

Pereira, Francisco Maria Esteves, trans. *Chronica de Susenyos, rei de Ethiopia.* Lisbon: Imprensa Nacional, 1900.

Pereira, Francisco Maria Esteves, trans. *Zénā Minās/Historia de Minás 'Además Sagad rei de Ethiopia.* Lisbon: Imprensa Nacional, 1888.

Perini, Rufillo. *Di qua dal Mareb.* Florence: Tipografica Cooperativa, 1905.

Perruchon, Jules, trans. "Histoire des Guerres d''Amda Şyon, Roi d'Éthiopie." *JA* 8, no. 14 (1889): 271–363, 381–493.

———, trans. "Histoire d'Eskender, d'`Amda-Şeyon II et de Nâ'od, rois d'Éthiopie, texte éthiopien inédit comprenant en outre un fragment de la chronique de Ba'eda-Mâryâm, leur prédécesseur, et traduction." *JA* 3 (1894): 319–66.

———, trans. "La règne de Lebna-Dengel: Texte éthiopien tiré du ms. 131 de la Bibliothèque nationale de Paris et traduction." *RS* 1 (1893): 274–86.

———, ed. and trans. *Les chroniques de Zar'a Yâqôb et de Ba'eda Mâryâm, Rois d'Éthiopie de 1434 a 1478.* Paris: Émile Bouillon, 1893.

———, ed. and trans. *Vie de Lalibala, roi d'Éthiopie. Texte éthiopien publié d'après un manuscrit du Musée Britannique et traduction française avec un résumé de l'histoire des Zagüés et la description des églises monolithes de Lalibala.* Paris: Ernest Laroux, 1892.

Peterson, Derek, and Giacomo Macola. "Homespun Historiography and the Academic Profession." In *Recasting the Past: History Writing and Political Work in Modern Africa,* edited by Derek Peterson and Giacomo Macola, 1–28. Athens: Ohio University Press, 2009.

Phillipson, David. *Ancient Ethiopia: Aksum—its Antecedents and Successors.* London: British Museum, 1998.

Phillipson, Laurel. "Parchment Production in the First Millennium BC at Seglamen, Northern Ethiopia." *African Archaeological Review* 30, no. 3 (2013): 285–303.

Pocock, J. G. A. "The Origins of the Study of the Past: A Comparative Approach." *Comparative Studies in Society and History* 2, no. 4 (1962): 209–46.

Pollard, Lisa. "The Habits and Customs of Modernity: State Scholarship, Foreign Travel, and the Construction of a New Egyptian Nationalism." *Arab Studies Journal* 7, no. 2 (1999/2000): 45–74.

———. *Nurturing the Nation: The Family Politics of Modernizing, Colonizing, and Liberating Egypt, 1805–1923.* Berkeley: University of California Press, 2005.

Power, Timothy. *The Red Sea from Byzantium to the Caliphate.* New York: American University in Cairo Press, 2012.

Prashad, Vijay. *The Darker Nations: A People's History of the Third World.* London: New Press, 2007.

Pratt, Mary Louise. *Imperial Eyes: Transculturation and Travel Writing.* New York: Routledge, 1992.

"Présentation des *Annales d'Éthiopie,* par la Direction." *AE* 1 (1955): 15–19.

Pretelli, Matteo. "Education in the Italian Colonies during the Interwar Period." *Modern Italy* 16, no. 3 (2011): 275–93.

Prochaska, David. *Making Algeria French: Colonalism in Bône, 1870–1920.* New York: Cambridge University Press, 1990.

Puglisi, Giuseppe. *Chi è?: dell' Eritrea 1952. Dizionario biografico con una cronologia.* Asmära: Agenzia Regina, 1952.

Quirin, James. *The Evolution of the Ethiopian Jews: a History of the Beta Israel (Falasha) to 1920.* Philadelphia: University of Pennsylvania Press, 1992.

Raineri, Osvaldo. "Gli studi etiopici nell'età del Giovio." In *Atti del convegno Paolo Giovio. Il Rinascimento e la memoria,* 117–31. Como: Soc. Villa Gallia, 1985.

Ranger, Terence. "The Invention of Tradition in Colonial Africa." In *The Invention of Tradition*, edited by Eric Hobsbawm and Terence Ranger, 211–62. Cambridge: Cambridge University Press, 1983.

———. "The Invention of Tradition Revisited: The Case of Colonial Africa." In *Inventions and Boundaries: Historical and Anthropological Approaches to the Study of Ethnicity and Nationalism*, edited by Preban Kaarsholm and Jan Hultin, 5–50. Roskilde, Denmark: Roskilde University Press, 1994.

Rao, Velcheru Narayana, David Shulman, and Sanjay Subrahmanyam. "A Pragmatic Response." *History and Theory* 46, no. 3 (2007): 409–27.

———. *Textures of Time: Writing History in South India 1600–1800.* New York: Other Press, 2003.

Reese, Scott. "The Adventures of Abu Harith: Muslim Travel Writing and Navigating the Modern in Colonial East Africa." In *The Transmission of Learning in Islamic Africa*, edited by Scott Reese, 244–56. Leiden: Brill, 2004.

Reid, Donald Malcolm. *Whose Pharaohs? Archaeology, Museums, and Egyptian National Identity from Napoleon to World War I.* Berkeley: University of California Press, 2002.

Reid, Richard. "The Trans-Mereb Experience: Perceptions of the Historical Relationship between Eritrea and Ethiopia." *Journal of Eastern African Studies* 1, no. 2 (2007): 238–55.

Ribi, Amalia. "'The Breath of a New Life'? British Anti-slavery Activism and the League of Nations." In *Internationalism Reconfigured: Transnational Ideas and Movements Between the World Wars*, edited by Daniel Laqua, 93–114. London: I. B. Tauris, 2011.

Ricci, Lanfranco. "In memoriam: Taklaṣādèq Makuriyà." *RSE* 43 (1999): 213–15.

———. Review of *Annales d'Éthiopie. RSE* 17 (1961): 123–41.

Robinson Waldman, Marilyn. "'The Otherwise Unnoteworthy Year 711': A Reply to Hayden White." *Critical Inquiry* 7, no. 4 (1981): 784–92.

Robinson, Chase. *Islamic Historiography.* New York: Cambridge University Press, 2003.

Rouaud, Alain. *Afä-wärq 1868–1947: un intellectuel éthiopien témoin de son temps.* Paris: Éditions CNRS, 1991.

———. "Le Voyage d'Europe." *Bulletin des études africaines* 17/18 (1992): 51–89.

Rubinkowska, Hannah. "The History that Never Was: Historiography by Ḥaylä Śəllase I." In *Studia Aethiopica in Honour of Siegbert Uhlig on the Occasion of his 65th Birthday*, edited by Verena Böll et al., 221–31. Wiesbaden: Harrassowitz Verlag, 2004.

Said, Edward. *Orientalism.* New York: Vintage, 1979.

Salvadore, Matteo. "A Modern African Intellectual: Gabre-Heywat Baykadan's Quest for Ethiopia's Sovereign Modernity." *Africa* LXIII, no. 1 (2008): 560–79.

Saulsberry, Nicole. "The Life and Times of Woldeab Woldemariam, 1905–1995." PhD dissertation, Stanford University, 2001.

Sbacchi, Alberto. *Legacy of Bitterness: Ethiopia and Fascist Italy.* Trenton, NJ: Red Sea Press, 1997.

Scherer, James. *The Romance of Japan through the Ages.* New York: Japan Society/Doubleday, 1928.

Sereke Berhan Gäbrä Egzi'abḥér. "The National Ethiopian Library." *Ethiopian Review* 1 (1945): 17.

Sergew Hable Selassie. *Ancient and Medieval Ethiopian History to 1270.* Addis Ababa: Haile Selassie University Press, 1972.

———. "Two Leading Ethiopian Writers." *Journal of Semitic Studies* 25, no. 1 (1980): 85–93.

Shack, William. "Open Systems and Closed Boundaries: The Ritual Process of Stranger Relations in New African States." In *Strangers in African Societies,* edited by William Shack and Elliot Skinner, 37–47. Berkeley: University of California Press, 1979.

Shiferaw Bekele. "The Chronicle of Takla Giyorgis (first r. 1779–84): An Introductory Assessment." In *Studia Aethiopica in Honour of Siegbert Uhlig on the Occasion of his 65th Birthday,* edited by Verena Böll et al., 247–58. Wiesbaden: Harrassowitz Verlag, 2004.

———. "Gäbrä-Heywät Baykädañ and the Emergence of a Modern Intellectual Discourse." *Sociology Ethnology Bulletin,* No. 1 (1994): 106–21.

Shimelis Bonsa. "City as Nation: Imagining and Practicing Addis Ababa as a Modern and National Space." *NEAS* 13, no. 1 (2013): 168–213.

Simmel, Georg. "The Stranger." In *The Sociology of Georg Simmel,* Translated by Kurt Wolff, 402–8. New York: Free Press, 1950.

Solari, Luigi. "La radiotelegrafia e le nostre colonie." *Rivista coloniale* 1 (1906): 206–9.

Steinberg, Jonathan. *All or Nothing: The Axis and the Holocaust, 1941–43.* 2nd ed. New York: Routledge, 2002.

Strelcyn, Stefan. "'Incunables' Éthiopiens des principales bibliothèques romaines." *RSE* 25 (1971–72): 456–519.

Subrahmanyam, Sanjay. "On World Historians in the Sixteenth Century." *Representations* 91 (2005): 26–57.

Tä'ammrat Amanu'el. "An Early Essay on Amharic Literature." Translated by Hailu Habtu. *BMEE,* No. 11 (1997): 29–68.

———. "Episodi della storia dei Falascià (dalle Chronache del Negusé-Neghèst Seltan-Seghed." *La rassegna mensile di Israel* 11, no. 3 (1936): 83–92.

Tabak, Faruk. *The Waning of the Mediterranean, 1550–1870: A Geohistorical Approach.* Baltimore, MD: Johns Hopkins University Press, 2008.

Tables de la troisième série: Tomes I à X (XXI à XXX) [Contents of *ROC*]. Mesnil: Firmin-Didot et Cie., 1946.

Taddesse Tamrat. "Evangelizing the Evangelized: The Root Problem Between Missions and the Ethiopian Orthodox Church," in *The Missionary Factor in Ethiopia: Papers from a Symposium on the Impact of European Missions on Ethiopian Society, Lund University, August 1996,* edited by Getatchew Haile, Aasulv Lande, and Samuel Rubenson, 17–30. New York: Peter Lang, 1998.

Taddia, Irma. "Correspondence as a New Source for African History: Some Evidence from Colonial Eritrea." *Cahiers des études africaines* 157 (2000): 109–34.

———. "Ethiopian Source Material and Colonial Rule in the Nineteenth Century: The Letter to Menilek (1899) by Blatta Gäbrä Egzi'abeḥēr." *Journal of African History* 34 (1993): 493–516.

———. *Un intelletuale tigrino nell'Etiopia di Menilek: Blatta Gäbrä Egzi'abḥēr Gilay (1860–1914).* Milan: Giuffrè Editore, 1990.

Täklä Maryam Sämḥaray Sälim. "La Messe Éthiopienne." *ROC* IX (1933–34): 187–95.

———. *La messe éthiopienne.* Rome: École Typographique, 1937.

———. "La Messe Éthiopienne (fin)." *ROC* X (1935–36): 421–32.

———. "La Messe Éthiopienne (Suite) (I)." *ROC* IX (1933–34): 425–44.

———. "La Messe Éthiopienne (Suite) (I[I])." *ROC* X (1935–36): 170–215.

———. *Règles speciales de la messe éthiopienne.* Rome: École Typographique, 1936.

Täklä Ṣadeq Mäkʷeriya [Tekle Tsadik Mekouria]. *Aṣé menilek enna yä'ityopya andenät.* Addis Ababa: Bolé, 1983.

———. *Aṣé téwodros enna yä'ityopya andenät.* Addis Ababa: Artistic Press, 1981.

———. *Aṣé yoḥannes enna yä'ityopya andenät.* Addis Ababa: Bolé, 1982.

———. "Christian Aksum." In *UNESCO General History of Africa,* edited by G. Mokhtar, Vol. 2, 401–22. London: Heinemann, 1981.

———. "Histoire abregée de Haylou Esheté (Degiazmatche)." In *Proceedings of the Eighth International Congress of Ethiopian Studies,* edited by Taddese Beyene, 189–213. Addis Ababa: Institute of Ethiopian Studies, 1988–89.

———. "The Horn of Africa." In *UNESCO General History of Africa,* edited by Ivan Hrbek, Vol. 3, 559–74. London: Heinemann, 1988.

———. *Yä'ityopya tarik.* 2 Vols. Addis Ababa: Tenśa'é Zäguba'é, 1951–53EC.

Täsämma Häbtä Mika'él. *Yä'amareña mäzgäb qalat.* Addis Ababa: 1951EC.

Tavakoli-Targhi, Mohamed. *Refashioning Iran: Orientalism, Occidentalism, and Historiography.* New York: Palgrave, 2001.

Tayyä Gäbrä Maryam. *Mäṣḥafä säwasew.* Monkullu: Mission Press, 1889.

———. *Yä'ityopya hezb tarik/History of the People of Ethiopia.* Translated by Grover Hudson and Tekeste Negash. Uppsala: Centre for Multiethnic Research, 1988.

Tedla Hailé Modjà Guermami. "Pourquoi et comment pratiquer une politique d'assimilation en Éthiopie." Thesis, Université Coloniale d'Anvers, 1930.

Tekeste Negash, "Blatta Gebre Egziabeher Gila Mariam and His Works: A Sketch Towards a Political Biography of a Nationalist," In *No Medicine for the Bite of a White Snake: Notes on Nationalism and Resistance in Eritrea, 1890–1940,* edited by Tekeste Negash, 1–21. Uppsala: University of Uppsala Reprocentralen, 1986.

———. "The Ideology of Italian Colonial Educational Policy in Eritrea." In *Italian Colonialism,* edited by Ruth Ben-Ghiat and Mia Fuller, 109–20. New York: Palgrave, 2005.

———. "Resistance and Collaboration, 1882–1914." In *No Medicine for the Bite of a White Snake: Notes on Nationalism and Resistance in Eritrea, 1890–1940,* edited by Tekeste Negash, 37–54. Uppsala: University of Uppsala Reprocentralen, 1986.

Teshale Tibebu. *The Making of Modern Ethiopia, 1896–1974.* Lawrenceville, NJ: Red Sea Press, 1995.

———. "Modernity, Eurocentrism, and Radical Politics in Ethiopia, 1961–1991." *African Identities* 6, no. 4 (2008): 345–71.

Toggia, Pietro. "History Writing as a State Ideological Project in Ethiopia." *African Identities* 6, no. 4 (2008): 319–43.

Trevisan Semi, Emanuela, ed. *L'epistolario di Taamrat Emmanuel: un intellettuale ebreo d'Etiopia nella prima metà del XX secolo.* Turin: L'Harmattan Italia, 2000.

Trevisan Semi, Emanuela. "Ethiopian Jews in Europe: Taamrat Emmanuel in Italy and Makonnen Levi in England." In *The Jews of Ethiopia: the Birth of an Elite,* edited by Tudor Parfitt and Emanuela Trevisan Semi, 74–100. London: Routledge, 2005.

———. "Taamrat Emmanuel between Colonized and Colonizer." Paper presented at the seminar "Ethiopian Jews under Fascist Rule." New York University Casa Italiana, October 23, 2014.

Tron, Alessandro. *Manuale di aritmetica, temherti qʷəṣeri.* Translated by Gäbrä Krestos Täklä Haymanot. Asmära: Tipografia della Missione Svedese, 1923.

———. *Scuole elementari della Missione Svedese in Eritrea. Consigli ai maestri e programma d'insegnamento.* Translated by Gäbrä Krestos Täklä Haymanot. Asmära: Tipografia della Missione Svedese, 1917.

Tsegaye Tegenu. *The Evolution of Ethiopian Absolutism: The Genesis and Making of the Fiscal Military State, 1696–1913.* Uppsala: Uppsala University Press, 1996.

Twaddle, Michael. "On Ganda Historiography." *History in Africa* 1 (1974): 85–100.

Ullendorff, Edward. *The Two Zions: Reminiscences of Jerusalem and Ethiopia.* New York: Oxford University Press, 1988.

Uoldelul Chelati Dirar. "Colonialism and the Construction of National Identities: The Case of Eritrea." *Journal of East African Studies* 1, no. 2 (2007): 256–76.

Uthman Salih Sabbi. *The History of Eritrea.* Translated by Muhamad Fawaz al-Azem. Beirut: Dar al-Masirah, 1970.

Van Donzel, Emeri Johannes, trans. *Anqaṣa amin (La Porte de la Foi): Apologie éthiopienne du Christianisme, contre l'Islam à partir du Coran.* Leiden: Brill, 1969.

Van Ness Meyers, Philip. *Ancient History.* Boston: Ginn and Company, 1904.

Varisco, Daniel. *Reading Orientalism: Said and the Unsaid.* Seattle: University of Washington Press, 2007.

Wagoner, Philip. "Precolonial Intellectuals and the Production of Colonial Knowledge." *Comparative Study of Society and History* 45, no. 4 (2003): 783–814.

Wallerstein, Immanuel. *European Universalism: The Rhetoric of Power.* New York: New Press, 2006.

Wells, H. G. *The Outline of History.* New York: Macmillan, 1921.

Welsby, Derek. *The Medieval Kingdoms of Nubia: Pagans, Christians, and Muslims along the Middle Nile.* London: British Museum Press, 2002.

Westad, Odd Arne. *Global Cold War: Third World Interventions and the Making of Our Times.* Cambridge: Cambridge University Press, 2005.

White, Hayden. "The Westernization of History." In *Western Historical Thinking: An Intercultural Debate,* edited by Jörn Rüsen, 111–18. New York: Berghahn, 2002.

———. *The Content of the Form: Narrative Discourse and Historical Representation.* Baltimore, MD: Johns Hopkins University Press, 1984.

Wion, Anaïs. "Le Liber Aksumae selon le manuscrit Bodleian Bruce 93: le plus ancien témoin d'un project historiographique sans cesse réactivé." *Oriens Christianus* 93 (2009): 135–71.

———. *Paradis pour une reine: le monastère de Qoma Fasilädäs, Éthiopie, XVIIe siècle.* Paris: Sorbonne, 2012.

Wion, Anaïs, and Paul Bertrand. "Production, Preservation, and Use of Ethiopian Archives (Fourteenth–Eighteenth Centuries)." *NEAS* 11, no. 2 (2011): vii–xvi.

Witakowski, Witold. "Coptic and Ethiopic Historical Writing." In *Oxford History of Historical Writing, Vol. 2: 400–1400*, edited by Sarah Foot, Daniel R. Woolf, and Chase F. Robinson, 138–54. New York: Oxford University Press, 2012.

———. "Ethiopic Universal Chronography." In *Julius Africanus und die christliche Weltchronik*, edited by Martin Wallraff, 285–301. Berlin: 2006.

Wright, Stephen. "Book and Manuscript Collections in Ethiopia." *JES* 2, no. 1 (1964): 11–24.

———. *Ethiopian Incunabula*. Addis Ababa: 1967.

———. "National Libraries in Ethiopia." *University College Review* 1, no. 1 (1961): 13–17.

———. "The National Library of Ethiopia." *Ethiopian Review* 1 (1945): 13–17.

Yäberhanenna sälam q.ḥ.ṣ matämiya bét yäwärq iyubélyi/Berhanena Selam H.S.I. Printing Press Golden Jubilee. Addis Ababa: Berhanenna Sälam, 1971.

Yaréd Gäbrä Mika'él. *Germawit etégé mänän*. Addis Ababa: Artistic Printing Press, 1950EC.

———. *Yä'arba amät g^{w}elmasa aç̌ç̌er tarik*. Addis Ababa: Artistic Press, 1948EC.

———. *Yäfeqer merkoña*. Addis Ababa: Artistic Press, 1950EC.

———. *Yätarik säw*. Addis Ababa: 1948EC.

———. *Yemeṭu bäzena addis abäba*. Addis Ababa: Berhanenna Sälam, 1958EC.

Yates, Brian. "Christian Patriot or Oromo Traitor? The Ethiopian State in the Memories of *Ras* Gobäna Dače." *NEAS* 13, no. 2 (2013): 195–222.

Yeseḥäq Yoséf. *Qäddamot ğegnu értran bahelnan*. Asmära: Commercial Press, 1997.

Yoḥannes Wäldä Maryam. *Yä'aläm tarik käğiwografi gar yätäyayazä*. Addis Ababa: Berhanenna Sälam, 1940EC.

Zäwäld [Feśśeḥa Giyorgis]. *Fitäñaytunna ḥ^{w}alañaytu ityopya. L'Etiopia antica e moderna*. Rome: Tipografia della Casa Editrice Italiana, 1899.

Zitelmann, Thomas. "Anthropology and Empire in Post-Italian Ethiopia: Makonnen Desta and the Imagination of an Ethiopian 'We-Race.'" *Paideuma* 47 (2001): 161–79.

Index

Abägaz, *abéto*, 27, 58
Abbās b. Ibrāhīm, 19
ʿAbd al-Raḥīm, Muḥammad, 6
ʿAbduh, Muḥammad, 6
Achebe, Chinua, 146n18
Adal, 18–19, 27, 30, 33–35
Addis Ababa University, 76, 117, 125. *See also* Haile Selassie University; University College of Addis Ababa
Addis Ababa, 1, 37, 42–43, 45, 47–48, 51, 54–55, 59–62, 77, 94, 105, 119, 130, 133–35, 137
Addis Hiwet, 122–23
Aden, 99, 132
Adulis, 15–16
Adwa (town), 49, 68, 78, 86
Adwa, Battle of, 38, 53, 55, 58, 62–63, 67, 81, 83, 86–87, 89, 91, 110
Afäwärq Gäbrä Iyäsus, 2, 55, 59, 87, 99
Aḥmad Ibrāhīm al-Ġāzī, 19, 79
Akinyẹle, Isaac Babalola, 5
Akkälä Guzay, 76, 87–89
Aksum (ancient empire): 4, 15–18, 150n16; historical discussions of, 22–24, 27–28, 53, 56, 75, 77, 79, 116, 149n9
Aksum (town), 28, 39, 73
Aklilä Berhan Wäldä Qirqos, 120
ʿAlī, Muḥammad, 6
Alula, *ras*, 24, 81, 83–84, 87–88, 92
Amba Alagé, Battle of, 62
Amdä Ṣeyon, Emperor, 17–19, 30, 35, 55, 57
American Revolution, 65
Annales d'Éthiopie, 115–16
anthropology, 117, 132, 135, 136
anthropometry, 132
Anti-Slavery and Aboriginals Protection Society, 105. *See also* League of Nations
Antonelli, Pietro, 78, 84, 90
Arabian peninsula, 4, 15, 16, 17, 73, 134, 135
Arabic (language and literature), 8, 17, 18, 23, 77, 78–79, 82, 97, 113, 131
Arabs, 8, 53, 60, 78, 95, 100, 138
Armenians, 20, 42, 109–10, 112, 179n30
askari, 70, 72, 83, 98, 100
Aṣmä Giyorgis, 2, 58
Asmära, 38–43, 49, 51–52, 54, 59, 69, 71, 75–76, 81–83, 87, 96, 99, 117
Assäb, 38, 61, 67, 83–84, 91
Aṭbiya kokäb, 160
Austria, 47, 49, 162n99

Bä'edä Maryam, Emperor, 18, 32
baḥrä ḥassab, 61, 100
Baḥrey, *abba*, 20, 25–26, 30, 34–35, 65, 140n46
Bahru Zewde, 43, 124–25
Bahta Ḥagos, 75, 83–84, 88
Bairu Tafla, 117, 121
Bakkäffa, Emperor, 22, 28, 30–32
Bäraqit Abbay, 68, 69, 168n9
Bäyen Bäraki, 74
Berhan Mäsqäl Dästa, 120
Berhanenna sälam (newspaper), 11, 43–48, 50, 51, 53, 83, 95, 98–99, 123, 129–30
Berhanenna Sälam (press), 44–46, 100, 102, 114
Berhanou Abebe, 117
Berhanu Denqé, 119–20

Berlin, University of, 56
Bétä Esra'él (Falaša), 20, 51–52, 75
Bethlehem, 99, 108
Boas, Franz, 132
Bollettino ufficiale del governo dell'eritrea, 71
Bose, Sugata, 109
Braudel, Fernand, 67
Britain, 96, 105, 114, 137, 147n27
British Military Administration (Eritrea), 74
Burke, Peter, 7

Cairo, 94, 98, 112–13, 147n24
Capuchins, 68–71, 90, 168n6. *See also* missionaries
Carrara, Camillo, 68–69, 80
Cerulli, Enrico, 81, 129–30, 137
Chakrabarty, Dipesh, 7, 63
Chattopadhyay, Bankimchandra, 6, 113
Chaube, Ram Gharib, 128–29, 132
China, 54, 60, 98, 116
Christianity: Catholic, 20, 39–40, 45, 64, 68–69, 72, 75, 80–81, 83, 88, 109–10; influence upon historical writing, 25–26, 63–64, 108–10, 112; inter-Christian sectarianism, 19, 34, 64; Orthodox, 1–2, 19, 39, 40, 56, 58, 64, 68–69, 71–72, 75, 78, 83, 108–10; Protestant, 39–41, 45, 72, 75, 109–10. *See also* missionaries
Cold War, 9, 115
colonialism, 38, 53, 67–73, 76, 78, 83, 86, 88–90, 92, 104
concubinage, 79
Conrad, Joseph, 146n18
Conti Rossini, Carlo, 91–92, 129, 176n168
Coptic (language and literature), 17, 23, 81, 97
Copts, 20, 109–10, 112
Crooke, William, 128–29, 132

Da Bergamo, Aquilino, 69
Da Cristofero, Colonel, 87
Da Desenzano, Apollonio, 69
Da Iseo, Ezechia, 69–70
Da Mezzana, Galdino, 70
Da Milano, Giandomenico, 69
Däbäb Araya, 87
Däḫané Wäldä Maryam, 43–44, 47
Dämessé Wäldä Gäbr'él, 44, 46, 48
Dér Śelṭan, 80–81, 109
Di Maggio, Major, 83
Dike, Kenneth Onwuka, 8
Dire Dawa, 132–33
Djibouti, 38, 94, 99, 100, 104, 111–12, 132
dynastic history. *See* historiography

East India Company, 128
Egypt, 5–6, 8, 11, 16, 34, 53, 57, 61, 78, 94, 99, 105, 107–09, 111–13, 116
Enbaqom, *eččägé*, 19, 152n42
England, 53, 99, 111, 129
Equba Enderyas, 82
Eriksson, Olle, 2, 42–44, 48, 54, 60
Eskender, Emperor, 18, 157n125
Ethiopian Revolution, 9, 11, 121–26
Ethiopian student movement, 121, 123–26
Ethiopian studies, academic field of, 116–19, 126–37
Ethiopian-Eritrean Federation, 74
ethnocentrism, 53, 125
eurocentism, 63, 138. *See also* historiography
Europe, 1, 7–8, 49, 54, 60, 62, 80, 94–95, 97–98, 100, 104, 110, 112, 116, 127, 135. *See also* Austria, Britain, France, Germany, Greece, Italy
Europeans, 6, 38–40, 42, 46, 53–54, 62, 71, 78, 79, 90–91, 96, 99, 100, 107–10, 136
Evangeliska Fosterlands-Stiftelsen (EFS), 39–42, 44, 46, 48–49, 51, 54, 56, 81, 131. *See also* missionaries
Ézana, Emperor, 15

fascism, 47
Febvre, Lucien, 100
Feśśeḥa Giyorgis, 2, 78–81, 83–84, 95, 97, 99

feudalism, 64, 122–23, 167n186
Fioretti, Maria, 82, 174n115
folklore, 14
France, 51, 111
Franchini, Vincenzo, 117
French Revolution, 60, 65, 114

gäbbar, 64–65, 123
Gäbrä Egzi'abḥér Elyas, 45
Gäbrä Egzi'abḥér Gilay, 76–77, 160n40
Gäbrä Ḥeywät Baykädañ, 41, 49–51, 53–56, 58–59, 65, 123
Gäbrä Iyasus Haylu, 82
Gäbrä Krestos Täklä Haymanot: life and career, 2, 11, 37–49, 139; writings, 2, 11, 37, 49, 59–66
Gäbrä Mäsqäl Wäldu, 74, 82, 170n46
Gäbrä Mika'él Besrät, 74
Gäbrä Mika'él Germu: life and career, 11, 67–72, 74–75, 93, 139; writings, 11, 67, 71–73, 75–76, 84–93
Gäbrä Yoḥannes Täsfämaryam, 75
gädl, 1, 151n37
Gälawdéwos, Emperor, 13, 19–20, 26, 30, 31, 34, 36, 55, 110
Gandhi, Mohandas, 6, 50, 146n15
Gärad Emar, 33
Gärima Taffärä, 120
Gebru Tareke, 125
Geoffrey of Monmouth, 18
geography, 2, 11, 24, 44, 48, 54, 70, 96, 97, 108, 110
Germany, 49, 56, 161n76
Germu Märḥun, 68
Getatchew Haile, 117
Gezäw Ḫaylä Maryam, 117
Ghurbāl, Muḥammad Shafīq, 8
Gila Mika'él, 81, 83
Giudici, Benedetto, 39–41
Giyorgis of Sägla, 150n18
Gobäna Dači, 24
Gobezé Gošu, 81
Goǧǧam, 24, 55, 58
Goḥ Ṣebah, 54, 161n57
Gondär, 21–22, 27–30, 32, 56–57, 99, 111, 120, 155n73, 177n9
"Grañ." *See* Aḥmad Ibrāhīm al-Ġāzī
Graziani, Rodolfo, 119
Greece, 34, 98–99, 104, 111, 115
Greek (language), 15, 16, 17, 81
Greeks, 20, 42, 60, 102, 108–9, 114, 116
Guha, Ranajit, 7–8, 65, 147n24, 147n27, 176n169
Guidi, Ignazio, 2, 56, 129

Ḥädgä Anbäsa, 83
hagiography, 1, 4, 14, 24, 35, 55
Haile Selassie University, 117, 136
Ḥamasén, 24, 39, 41, 81–83, 88
Harär, 19, 44, 77, 160n40
Hartog, François, 65–66, 167n193
Harvard University, 132, 134–37
Ḫaylä Śellasé, Emperor, 1, 11, 54, 94, 99, 110–12, 114–15, 119–20, 122, 182n20. *See also* Täfäri Mäkonnen
Häzzäga, 81, 83
Ḫeruy Wäldä Śellasé: life and career, 1–5, 45, 47–48, 54, 65, 94–96; writings, 1–5, 9, 11, 14–15, 18, 25, 44–45, 49, 56–59, 80, 87, 92, 94–6, 99–100, 102–13
Ḥimyarites, 16–17
historical consciousness: absence of, 6; origins of, 6–8, 14, 137–38
historicality, 7, 16, 9, 65
historicism, 63–65, 113, 115–24
historiography: dynastic history, 4, 18, 22–23, 25, 36–37, 54–55, 58, 75, 77, 78, 80, 113; Eurocentric, 6, 63–65, 124–26, 162n100; positivist, 7–8, 49–51, 129; royal biography, 18, 20, 22–23, 25, 36–37, 54–55, 80, 113; universal chronography, 22–23, 25, 28, 37, 54, 59, 80; vernacular, 5–9, 13–14, 49–59, 76–84, 96–102, 119–21, 137–39
Hooton, Earnest, 132, 137
Howard University, 123

Iberia, 20, 28, 168n6
Ibn Khaldūn, 8
Ifat, 18

imperialism, 38, 46, 53, 67, 84, 90, 122–23, 125, 127. *See also* colonialism
India, 5–8, 37, 54, 95, 98, 116, 128
Indian Ocean, 10, 38, 148n39
Indians, 42, 60–61, 64, 96, 128
indirect rule, 72
industrialization, 63–64, 114
Institute of Ethiopian Studies, 76, 117
Isenberg, Karl Wilhelm, 2, 54
Islam, 2, 5, 20, 53, 77, 116, 121. *See also* Muslims
Israel, ancient, 16, 19, 27, 34, 60, 94, 97, 102. *See also* Palestine; Holy Land; Jerusalem
Italian East Africa, 74, 130, 137
italianità, 68, 93
Italy, 37–38, 47, 51–52, 62, 67, 73, 75, 78, 80, 84, 86–88, 90–92, 95, 99, 111, 119, 161n108, 176n169; *See also* Rome (ancient); Rome (city)
Iwarson, Jonas, 39–40, 42, 59, 159n16
Iyyasu I, Emperor, 22, 28, 29
Iyyasu II, Emperor, 22–23, 26, 29, 73
Iyyasu V, *leǧ,* 49–50, 55–56, 60, 181n68
Iyyo'as, Emperor, 22, 29, 155n73

Japan, 37, 54, 60, 62, 122, 133; Ḫeruy's writings about, 94–95, 99, 102, 104, 111–12
Jerusalem, 27, 34, 49, 80, 95, 97, 98, 99, 104, 109, 111–13
Jesuits, 20, 168n6. *See also* missionaries
Jewish studies, academic field of, 52
Johnson, Samuel, 5
Journal of Ethiopian Studies, 117

Käbbädä Mika'él, 114–17, 120–21
Kagwa, Apolo, 6
Kaléb, Emperor, 15, 149n9
Kāmil, Muṣṭafa, 5
Kärän, 80
Kebrä nägäśt, 17–18, 28, 55–56, 94, 97–98, 113, 149n9
Keflä Egzi'e Yeḫdägu, 40
Keflä Giyorgis, 81
Kenya, 127
Kenyatta, Jomo, 12, 127–30
Kidänä Maryam Käśśä, 81

Lal, Vinay, 6
Lalibäla, Emperor, 18–19, 20, 29, 35, 57, 98
Lapiso Gétahun Delébo, 123
Lazarists, 88, 90, 168n6. *See also* missionaries
League of Nations, 46, 105, 107, 111
Lebnä Dengel, Emperor, 19–20, 33–34
Legesse Lemma, 123–24
Lindfors, Louise, 39
Littmann, Enno, 56, 73, 130–32, 136
Liturgy, 80–81
Lugard, Frederick, 105
Luxor, 94, 107–8

Mackenzie, Colin, 128–29
Macola, Giacomo, 8
Maḫbär Feqri Hagär, 74
Mahdi, Mahdists, 38, 57–58, 62, 79, 84, 87, 172n90
Maḫtämä Śellasé Wäldä Mäsqäl, 120, 155n80
Makedda, 17, 53, 56, 58, 61, 79, 94–97, 112. *See also Kebra nägäśt*
Mäkonnen Dästa, 132–37
Mäkonnen Wäldä Mika'él, 78
Mäläk Säggäd, Emperor, 27
Mänän Asfaw, 11, 94, 96, 104–8, 110–14, 119
Mäqällé, 62
Mäqdem, 25
Märäb Mellaš, 76, 93
Märḫa Ṭebäb, 43–44, 161n57, 183n30
Marse'é Ḫazan Wäldä Qirqos, 21, 46, 48, 58, 99, 111, 119, 120
Martin, Henri-Jean, 100
Martini, Ferdinando, 91
Marxism, 9, 11, 50, 121–22; influence on historiography, 122–24
Mäsqäl, Feast of, 71–72
Mätämma, 57, 64
Mboya, Paul, 6
Mediterranean, 10, 15, 98, 104, 135, 148n39

Meherkä Dengel, 22
Menilek I, 17, 97
Menilek II, Emperor, 21, 24, 37–38, 41, 43, 50, 53–58, 60, 62–63, 73, 75, 77–79, 81, 84, 86–86, 89–92, 95, 110, 120, 122–23
Mentewwab, Empress, 22, 33
Merid Wolde Aregay, 117
Messay Kebede, 124
Michelet, Jules, 60
Middle East, 1, 6, 38, 94–95, 98, 104, 108, 128, 138. *See also* Egypt; Holy Land; Israel; Palestine
Mika'él Seḥul, 28–29, 33
Minas, Emperor, 20
Ministry of Education (Ethiopian), 121
Ministry of the Pen (Ethiopian), 24. See also *ṣähafé te'ezaz*
missionaries: policies of, 40–42, 68–69; presses of, 41–42, 44, 49, 54, 68; schools of, 39–43, 49, 51, 54, 56, 63, 68–71, 98, 131. *See also* Capuchins; EFS; Jesuits; Lazarists; Waldensians
Moreno, Martino Mario, 130
Muslim League, 74
Muslims: 10, 17–19, 27, 30, 33, 35–36, 38, 57, 68, 74–75, 96, 109, 130–31; literary representations of, 20, 30, 34, 57, 157n118, 164n120; relations with Christians, 17, 19, 34–35. *See also* Islam
Mussolini, Benito, 47, 163n109

Na'od, Emperor, 18, 31–32
Näffa'e Wäd Etman, 130–32, 136
Naipaul, V. S., 6
Nandy, Ashis, 6
Naṣraddīn b. Aḥmad, 30
National Library (Ethiopian), 115, 117–18
nationalism: 5, 8; Eritrean, 92–93, 74–75; Ethiopian, 37, 43, 45, 50, 66. *See also* Maḥbär Feqri Hagär; reformist movements; šelleṭṭané
Nay értra sämunawi gazéṭa, 74–75, 82

Orientalism, 127–28
Oromo, 2, 19–20, 27, 31–32, 34, 36, 42, 53, 57–58, 73, 79, 157n135, 163n106
Oxford, University of, 1, 129
Özdemir Pasha, 19

Palestine, 11, 94, 99, 105, 108–9, 112, 180n63. *See also* Israel; Holy Land
Pan-Africanism, 125
Pankhurst, Richard, 76, 117
P̣awlos, *abba*, 27
P̣awlos Män Amäno, 99, 104
Peabody Museum, 134–35, 137
Peterson, Derek, 8
Pocock, J. G. A., 146n21
Pollera, Alberto, 82, 130
Pontifical Ethiopian College, 80, 98
Pontifical Gregorian University, 40
Prempeh II, Osei Ageyman, 6
Princeton Archaeological Expedition, 73, 130, 132
printing, 1–2, 40–41, 43–46, 60, 62, 101–2, 109
progress, idea of, 38, 50, 58–59, 61–66, 102–4, 106, 108, 110. See also šelleṭṭané
Puccioni, Nello, 129

Quotidiano Eritreo, Il, 71–72, 74–75, 82–83, 95, 99

racial identity, theories of, 52–53, 61, 135, 166n166
racism, 84, 133–35, 185n55
Raggi, Giuseppe Salvago, 68
Ranke, Leopold von, 7–9, 65, 80, 146n21, 147n26
Rao, Velcheru Narayana, 6
Red Sea, 2, 4, 10–11, 15–16, 19, 39, 43, 94, 97, 111
reform, idea of, 11, 38, 43–44, 50–51, 62, 100, 102, 105, 110, 123, 139; reformist movements, 5, 10–11, 38, 40, 43–44, 46, 50–51, 62, 100, 102, 105, 110, 123, 139
Rome (ancient), 34, 84
Rome (city), 40, 47, 78, 80, 97, 98

Rome, University of, 80
royal biography. *See* historiography
Royal Oriental Institute of Naples, 78, 99
Rubattino Shipping Company, 38, 90–91
Russia, 64, 125

Ṣä'azzäga, 83
sacred history, 25–26, 34, 61, 108. *See also* historiography
Sägänäyti, 69–70, 84, 87–88, 168n9
ṣäḥafé te'ezaz, 20–21, 24–25, 44, 47, 51, 54, 62, 65, 87, 120
Ṣäḥati, 82, 84, 86–87
Ṣāliḥ, *qadi*, 30
Samuel, Herbert, 112
Sänbätu Keflay, 68
Santo Stefano degli Abissini, 97
Ṣärayé, 87
Sarkar, Jadunath, 8
Śärṣä Dengel, Emperor, 20, 28, 30, 34–36, 73
Šäwa, 24, 27, 38, 52, 57, 87
School of Oriental and African Studies, 137
śelleṭṭané, 43, 62, 110, 114. *See also* development; progress
Semitic studies, academic field of, 52, 127, 130
Sennä Krestos, 19, 152n42
Sereke Berhan Gäbrä Egzi'abḥér, 117
Sergew Hable Selassie, 117
Shulman, David, 6
Solomon Aṣqu, 81
Somalia, 17, 38, 69, 130
Spengler, Oswald, 60, 65
Subrahmanyam, Sanjay, 60
Sudan, 6, 38, 57, 87. *See also* Mahdi
Susenyos, Emperor, 21–22, 51, 55
Syrians, 60, 109

Tä'ammrat Amanu'el, 47, 51–52, 54–55, 59, 113, 130, 136
Tädla Täklay, 82
Taddesse Tamrat, 117
Täfäri Mäkonnen Press, 1, 43–44, 99
Täfäri Mäkonnen, Crown Prince, 2, 42–47, 49, 54, 78, 94, 99, 105, 110–11, 122. *See also* Ḫaylä Śellasé
Täklä Haymanot, *azmač*, 35
Täklä Haymanot, *azzaž*, 22, 27–29
Täklä Haymanot, Emperor, 21
Täklä Haymanot, *ras*, 57
Täklä Iyäsus Wäqǧirä, 24, 55
Täklä Maryam Sämḫaray Sälim, 80–81, 83
Täklä Ṣadeq Mäkweriya, 120–21
Täklä Śellasé ("Ṭino"), 21–22
Täklä Täsfä Krestos, 40
tärikä nägäśt. *See* historiography
Täsfä Ṣeyon, 81
Täwäldäberhan Andu, 68
Täwälde Medhin Gäbru, 40
Tayyä Gäbrä Maryam, 2, 56, 58, 65, 121, 145n1, 166n167, 171n64, 172n91, 179n30
Tegray, 16, 28, 39, 33, 71, 73, 75, 77–79, 93, 172n92
Teshale Tibebu, 125
Téwodros II, Emperor, 21, 24, 53, 60, 62, 75, 78–79, 162n97
Third World, 117, 124
Tipografia Francescana, 68
traditionalism, 10, 14, 28, 36, 66, 108, 139
translocality, 10
travel writing: European, 96; Ethiopian and Eritrean, 11, 58, 95–102; non-Western, 96
Tron, Alessandro, 40–41

Unionist Party, 74–75, 92
United Nations, 74, 120
United States, 1, 37, 60, 95, 106–8, 114–15, 136, 185n55
Universal chronography. *See* historiography
University College of Addis Ababa, 117

Venice, 97–98

Wäldä'ab Wäldä Maryam, 74
Wäldebbä, 73

Waldensians, 40, 158n12. *See also* missionaries
Weččale, Treaty of, 78, 84, 87
White, Hayden, 7, 63

Yaréd Gäbrä Mika'él, 119–20
Yeḥa, 16, 73
Yekunno Amlak, Emperor, 17
Yoḥannes Gäbrä Egazi'abhér, 82
Yoḥannes Ṣeggai, 74
Yoḥannes IV, Emperor, 2, 24, 29, 53, 57, 62, 64, 73, 82, 84, 86, 87–88, 92, 172n92
Yoḥannes Wäldä Maryam, 121

Zagwe, 17–18, 22, 56, 58, 79, 151n24
zämänä mäsafent, 22, 61, 79
Zännäb, *däbtära*, 21
Zanzibar, Sultan of, 90
Zär'a Ṣeyon Musé, 41, 81
Zär'a Ya'eqob, Emperor, 18, 32
Zäré Germu, 68
Zäwditu, Empress, 21, 37, 46, 55, 56, 60, 155n80, 161n62, 164n31, 181n68
Zaydan, Jurji, 6, 113

Ethiopia and Eritrea are home to Africa's oldest written historical tradition, which began in the third century with the monuments and manuscripts of Aksum and has continued to the present day. This study explores the development of this rich tradition, focusing in particular on the dramatic lives and original thought of a group of early twentieth-century Ethiopian and Eritrean historians. James De Lorenzi examines how these scholars used historiography to not only record the past but also grapple with the changes of the modern era. Through their history writings, they made provocative political claims, explored the nature of their communal ties, assessed their inherited institutions and ideas, and critically evaluated the people and cultures of the wider world. Opposing the view that historiography is a uniquely Western intellectual pursuit, *Guardians of the Tradition* provides new evidence of an African historical consciousness and the vibrancy of history writing outside the West.

"James De Lorenzi provides an insightful historiographical taxonomy of centuries of Ethiopian and Eritrean scholarship, revealing the complex, often contested processes by which African intellectuals selectively meshed vernacular approaches to history with foreign concepts and methodologies. Interesting, smart, well organized, and effective, *Guardians of the Tradition* makes a major contribution to the nascent field of Ethiopian and Eritrean intellectual history."

—Tim Carmichael, College of Charleston

James De Lorenzi is associate professor of history at John Jay College, City University of New York.

www.ingramcontent.com/pod-product-compliance
Lightning Source LLC
Chambersburg PA
CBHW070802230426
43665CB00017B/2459
* 9 7 8 1 5 8 0 4 6 9 2 8 9 *